*Coca-Cola, Black Panthers,
and Phantom Jets*

Coca-Cola, Black Panthers, and Phantom Jets

ISRAEL IN THE AMERICAN ORBIT, 1967–1973

Oz Frankel

STANFORD UNIVERSITY PRESS
Stanford, California

Stanford University Press
Stanford, California
© 2024 by Oz Frankel. All rights reserved.
No part of this book may be reproduced or transmitted in any form or by any means, electronic or mechanical, including photocopying and recording, or in any information storage or retrieval system, without the prior written permission of Stanford University Press.
Printed in the United States of America on acid-free, archival-quality paper

Library of Congress Cataloging-in-Publication Data

Names: Frankel, Oz, 1958– author.
Title: Coca-Cola, Black Panthers, and Phantom Jets : Israel in the American orbit, 1967–1973 / Oz Frankel.
Description: Stanford, California : Stanford University Press, 2024. | Includes bibliographical references and index.
Identifiers: LCCN 2023057991 (print) | LCCN 2023057992 (ebook) | ISBN 9781503636262 (cloth) | ISBN 9781503639522 (paperback) | ISBN 9781503639539 (epub)
Subjects: LCSH: Israel—Civilization—American influences. | Israel—Relations—United States. | United States—Relations—Israel. | Israel—History—1967–1993.
Classification: LCC DS112 .F73 2024 (print) | LCC DS112 (ebook) | DDC 327.7305694009/04—dc23/eng/20240315
LC record available at https://lccn.loc.gov/2023057991
LC ebook record available at https://lccn.loc.gov/2023057992

Cover design and illustrations: Jason Anscomb

For Varda and Rafi

Contents

	Preface	ix
	Introduction	1
ONE	Consumer Modernity and the *Everyday*	21
TWO	Keeping Up with the Cohens	60
THREE	Electioneering and the Feedback Loop	89
FOUR	Technology Transfer: The Phantom Jet	112
FIVE	Panthers in Black and White	140
SIX	American Gangster in the Promised Land	169
SEVEN	Emissaries of Liberalism in Crisis	194
EIGHT	Back to Anatevka	220
NINE	America on Stage	250
TEN	The American Figure in the Israeli Mind	272
	Conclusion	293
	Bibliography	299
	Notes	341
	Index	361

Preface

As young children in the mid-1960s, playing in the streets of my hometown Holon, we used to challenge each other with questions such as "Which country do you admire the most?" "Which do you dislike?" Answering the second question was tricky, but when it came to the first, the answer in many cases—certainly mine—was clear, Israel's greatest ally at the time, France. France was rather easy to adore, a place of beauty, its language so musical, its music so melodious. At home, I leafed through geographer Dov Nir's lyrical *Landscapes of France: Essays and Travels* (1960). The castles of the Loire Valley occupied my imagination. The United States, by contrast, seemed grittier, too utilitarian, populated with objects of enormous size—rivers, mountains, skyscrapers, bridges, highways, and cars. There was an air of arrogance to such natural and man-made overachievements.

But then June 1967 happened. The Six-Day War abruptly terminated the Israeli-French bromance. President Charles de Gaulle was furious. The decade ended with remarkably popular revues based on the repertoires of the two quintessential *chansonniers*, Georges Brassens (1969) and Jacques Brel (1970), but acute Israeli Francophilia was largely over. The United States, which had always been on the Israeli mind, seemed now politically and culturally ever more present. Like many others, we had relatives in America. By the late 1960s they began visiting more frequently and traveling to Lod (now Ben-Gurion) Airport to welcome them became a recurrent and rather exciting ritual. My parents took a course to brush up their English as well as one of those fashionable Dale Carnegie–type seminars on human relations and self-improvement. I returned from my first trip to the United States with baseball gear, which was soon tucked away and never used. But the item I brought back which inspired the greatest surprise among my cohort was a pair of Bermuda shorts.

I invoke these childhood memories not because they served as the impetus for writing this book but as an example of how the Israeli-American encounter could become intimate and personal. Those years also taught me that embracing one American sensibility could collide with another. One incident comes to mind. In 1971, we hosted an American cousin, still in her early 20s. Showing her around, we stopped at the country's premier department store, Kol Bo Shalom. The store was well stocked. From the ceiling hung large twirling mobiles with the iconic image from the film *Love Story* of Ali MacGraw leaning back on Ryan O'Neal's shoulder, looking directly at the camera. We were proud of the store. Alas, the guest from Michigan shook her head in utter disapproval. "How pathetic," she muttered, by which she didn't mean to disparage the tragic couple.

American encounters transpired under diverse circumstances. On the eve of the 2008 US presidential elections my mother, who ordinarily did not opine about American politics, told me she hoped Barack Obama would win. She then recalled that when she first traveled to the United States in 1956, another passenger on the boat was a renowned Israeli dancer, Rachel Nadav—who would later perform with Martha Graham's troupe. When the ship anchored in Miami and most passengers embarked on northbound trains, the dark-complexioned Nadav, who was born in Yemen, was asked to take the car designated for "colored" travelers. It came as a shock to everybody.

My interest in the topics explored in *Coca-Cola, Black Panthers, and Phantom Jets: Israel in the American Orbit* began with studying the Israeli Black Panthers. My initial impression was that missing from the existing literature about the movement whose story—well known in Israel, but which never ceases to elicit surprise from American audiences—was a full account of the American context. The perceived collapse of the alliance between Jews and

African Americans was a major subject in the Israeli press back then. It was the moniker appropriated by the young poor politicos from Jerusalem that scandalized mainstream Israel, convinced that the American Black Panther Party was rabidly antisemitic.

Writing in English about Israel at the turn of the 1970s has been admittedly a tad odd, even after three decades of living in the United States. But English also allows me to keep a modicum of necessary distance. From time to time, I added background material for the benefit of readers who are not entirely familiar with Israeli life and history but, nevertheless, I sought to avoid the ambassadorial tone that is characteristic of some of the attempts to present Israel to the rest of the world.

Many individuals and several institutions supported me through a lengthy research process. I am grateful for the assistance I received from archivists and librarians at the Israeli Center for the Documentation of the Performing Arts and the Anda Zimand Film Archive—both at Tel Aviv University, Beit Ariela Library in Tel Aviv, the National Library of Israel, the IDF and Defense Establishment Archives, and the *Ma'ariv* Archive. The thirty-two individuals who generously agreed to interrupt their daily affairs in order to be interviewed for this book are owed deep gratitude. My thank-you list also includes research assistants, especially Yoav Fromer, Anat Livshits, Yoav Mehozai, and Efrat Waxman. The entire team at Stanford University Press, especially my editor Margo Irwin, was tremendously supportive. Rafi Mann read an early version of the manuscript and offered invaluable advice. Many hours of conversation with Uri Ram were a consistent source of inspiration.

I am indebted to my dear colleagues at the New School for Social Research and Lang College, especially in the History Department, as well as to the participants in the 2019–20 resident fellowship at the University's Graduate Institute for Design, Ethnography, and Social Theory (GIDEST). The camaraderie and hospitality of colleagues, friends, and family in Israel made recurrent research trips so productive and so pleasurable: Yuval Avigdor, Gadi Becker, Carmela Haft, Shlomo and Raya Kashi, Nitzan Mann, Noga Mann, Yuval and Inbal Mann, Adi Nitzan Becker, Nava Schreiber, Zivya Seligman, Chemi and Nili Shalev, Shaul Stav, Vered Vinitzky-Seroussi, Ilana Vorobyov, and Michael Zakim.

This book would not be possible without the love, affection, and inexhaustible support of my Rock-of-Gibraltar partner and muse, Alyson Cole ("Big Al") and my sweet and gifted son, Tammuz Frankel. Research in Israel gave me numerous and memorable opportunities to spend precious time with my mother Sara Frankel, who sadly passed away in May of 2023 as the book neared its completion. My debt to her is indescribable.

    I am dedicating this book to my sister and brother-in-law, Varda and Rafi Mann. It is a token of my love and admiration. Knowing that I can rely, as I have always done, on their boundless generosity, warmth, and conviviality is a source of great comfort to me.[1]

*Coca-Cola, Black Panthers,
and Phantom Jets*

Introduction

By the conclusion of the 1960s, Israel's susceptibility to American influence became fodder for rich, habitually scornful commentary. Journalist Ruth Bondi, an astute observer of social trends, averred, "Any breeze above the American continent raises dust on Israeli roads, whether nude advertisement or ecological holocaust, smoking drugs or New Left, Black Panthers or faded jeans."[1] Another discerning commentator, Amnon Rubinstein, a law professor and future member of cabinet, critically reflected on the seemingly rapid absorption of American culture. Examples included the branding of products with English names, the integration of American idioms into Hebrew (*"running* for election," *"selling* Israel abroad"), and the immense popularity of American paperbacks such as Leon Uris's *Topaz* (20,000 copies), Arthur Hailey's *Airport* (20,000), and James Michener's *The Source* (35,000). *Time* sold more magazines in Israel—in per capita terms—than in any European country. Other newly arrived customs included tipping waiters and the transition in university classrooms from formal lectures to ostensibly more egalitarian "round-table" exchanges.[2]

For Hillel Halkin, a young immigrant to Israel who reflected on his experience in the pages of the American Jewish magazine *Commentary*, the country seemed profoundly altered from its earlier self and yet, it inspired a sense of déjà vu, of time travelling to early 1950s America: rooftops sprouting forests of television antennas, frozen food, superhighways, Muzak wafting out of office-building elevators. Friday-night gatherings often shifted from discussions of current affairs to new appliances, washing machines, dishwashers, their prices, their comparative merits, a couple mulling over moving to the suburbs, someone getting a divorce, another in therapy.[3] Even Prime Minister Golda Meir offered her contribution to the genre. "With what joy we swallow everything that comes from abroad," she sighed. "Heaven help whoever dares criticize any of that—whether light songs, theater, attire."[4] Meir was baffled by the miniskirt fad for women and long sideburns for men. But upon receiving an honorary doctorate from the Hebrew University she warned more gravely against the threat to national unity if Israeli students and intellectuals pitched battles against the "establishment" as their counterparts abroad had done so disruptively.[5]

These remarks indicated lingering apprehensions and prevalent ambivalence about Israel's growing exposure to the outside world, especially the United States. Despite their critical tone, such comments often underestimated the depth, complexity, and political ambiguity of the transformation Israeli society underwent because of its engagement with all things American—much beyond the imitative reflex and the casual embrace of fleeting fashions. How, for instance, its iteration of the Black Panthers, the advent of feminism, and antiestablishment expressions exposed, deepened, and politicized existing cleavages in Israeli society.

In the wake of the Six-Day War, Israel and the United States became more overt geopolitical allies. Rather than revisiting the making of that famous partnership—about which there is no dearth of literature—*Coca-Cola, Black Panthers, and Phantom Jets* interrogates a different sort of intimacy emerging during this period, with often unexpected results.[6] It documents the ripple effects that the rise of Black Power in the United States had on both extremes of local politics, the adoption of American technology that fed the budding Israeli military-industrial complex, and performances that revisited the Diaspora and recalibrated Jewish identities in Israel—among other exchanges. While contributing to the burgeoning literature on the American presence in the world, this book seeks to decipher the inner workings of a nation—its social divisions, market behavior, military choices, political campaigns, daily routines, and culture, both high and low—through the prism of its busy negotiation with the ostensible outside, namely ideas, artifacts, practices, and people that appeared under the sign *America*.

The expanding contact between the two societies reordered Israeli culture and consciousness, affected the swelling ranks of the Israeli middle classes, but also contributed to the politicization of lower classes and to widening the gap between Jews and Arabs. However, the *orbit* metaphor in the book's title does not cast Israel as an American satellite; it instead signifies emerging ties characterized by a sense of affinity and kinship as well as by persisting distance, resistance, and mistranslations. These relations were critical to the interlocking processes of nation building and world making in late twentieth-century Israel. American rendezvous and chance encounters refined both individual and collective Israeli self-perceptions, whether Israelis embraced American ideologies and habits or, conversely, viewed themselves and their country in contradistinction to the American Other. The book demonstrates that rather than growing profoundly Americanized, Israelis forged unique paths into the American sphere.

The two wars, the Six-Day War of June 1967 and the Yom Kippur War of October 1973, serve as this study's nominal bookends—although discussion occasionally veers, as necessary, outside the six-year span. Concentrating on a relatively short period of time allows for a synoptic analysis of a society at work at a particular moment of great transition. Obviously, Israeli engagement with American culture, knowledge, and practices began much earlier. Concerns about "Americanization" were voiced as early as the turn of the 1950s, most strongly triggered by cultural consumption, namely the popularity of Hollywood films and their effect on taste, fashion, and youth behavior.[7] But during the turn of the 1970s, the meeting points between the two societies grew exponentially and the relationship along social and cultural axes intensified. Moreover, the content of the transnational dialogue then differed significantly from the recent three decades when the nation's proximity to the United States propelled it on the road to privatization, deterioration of its social fabric, and other symptoms of severe neoliberalism afflicting Israeli society today.

The 1960s were the zenith of American post–Second World War liberalism with Great Society programs, civil rights legislation, the radicalism of the antiwar and New Left movements, and the dawn of the conservative backlash. Beyond liberalism, a range of ideologies, progressive and illiberal, beckoned to Israelis, whether the feminism of Member of Knesset Marcia Freedman or the extreme nationalism and racism of Rabbi Meir Kahane, leader of the Jewish Defense League (JDL)—both American émigrés. In a different register, seemingly unbridled consumption, which was still rather modest from the twenty-first-century vantage point, crossed the ocean in tandem with its repudiation, as expressed by Ralph Nader's consumer activism, Herbert Marcuse's critique, and the nascent environmental movement. A slew of techniques that sought to ameliorate the ills of modern society arrived as well, "self-actualization" workshops, T-Groups, Eastern religions, and WeightWatchers, among others, although their relationship to consumerism is akin to that between the two sides of a Möbius strip. Youth culture, rock music, longer hair, sexual promiscuity, and drugs—albeit less prevalent than elsewhere in the West—were also a sign of the time.

Consumerist-inflected concepts such as "quality of life," which was adopted as a mantra in Israel, organizations that sought to protect and beautify cityscapes, and popular human relations techniques were promoted as a basis for reform and renewal, aspiring for higher standards of public behavior and sociability alongside new expectations of personal comfort. By the late 1960s, such ideas found receptive audiences in a society that, beyond the cohesion born out of the perpetual state of war, was already stratified and fragmented, to a large extent "post-ideological," and rather confused about its core values, especially after the dispiriting economic recession of 1966–67.

The onset of a mature consumerist order was certainly an important phase in the long-term elaboration of Israeli capitalism—but the decade between 1968 and 1977 was also a turning point in the making of the Israeli welfare state and the only decade in the country's history that witnessed a substantial reduction of income disparity.[8] In part this was based on a different kind of inequality—the employment of unskilled Palestinian workers from the newly occupied territories. But the rise of the Israeli Black Panthers in 1971, among other factors, instigated new welfare policies. Many of these were shaped by ideas and concepts borrowed from American-led, policy-oriented social sciences, while the era that economists now label the "Great

Compression" in American wages was still in place.[9] A major late 1960s education reform in Israel that sought to facilitate "integration" along ethnic lines also took its cues from the American experience.

Both American and Israeli societies were under stress and in flux. The United States appeared on the Israeli horizon as a fractured entity, as a powerful superpower and a paragon of consumerist lifestyle, but, at the same time, as a society too spoiled or profoundly divided and crime infested, perhaps crumbling from within, a mighty giant that lost its way.

The heterogeneous, often contradictory character of the American presence links the turn of the 1970s with a more recent political turmoil in Israel. In the summer of 2023, as this book was being finalized, a judicial overhaul initiated by Prime Minister Benjamin Netanyahu's ultranationalist coalition threatened to tear Israeli society asunder. It was met with unprecedented public protests. The proposed legislation to curtail the power of the Supreme Court was largely framed by an American-funded conservative think tank, Kohelet Policy Forum, led by an American-born immigrant, Moshe Koppel, who casts his organization as "the brains of the Israeli right-wing."[10] At the same time, the resistance movement looked to American democratic and constitutional ideals and to the moral support it received from President Joe Biden and his administration. For some observers the controversy over the judicial overhaul appeared to reenact on Israeli soil a conflict between competing American judicial philosophies. This is only partially true. The underlying divisiveness is indigenous and far exceeds the controversy over judicial matters, but at times it indeed speaks in and is made legible through American ideas and idioms. In general, the American impact on Israel over decades has been much more variegated and ambiguous than is often understood.

America in Israel

Israel's slide more deeply into the American sphere was a complex, rhizomatic process with many actors, convoluted causal chains, and at times surprising entry points. For instance, that most Israeli institution, the Israel Defense Forces (IDF), became a conduit for adopting—beside technology—American organizational methods and standards of professionalism. A retired general, Shlomo (Chich) Lahat, launched the first "American-style" political campaign in Israel (1973) that won him the mayorship of Tel Aviv. Appointed ambassador to the United States (1968–73), former IDF chief of staff Yitzhak Rabin interjected himself into Washington affairs with great self-confidence and a strong sense of personal affinity.

The American presence encompassed a hectic flow of people: immigrants, tourists, university students, and kibbutz volunteers—all arriving in greater numbers—as well as Americanization entrepreneurs, often on the Israeli *receiving* end; for instance, impresario Giora Godik, who staged lavish productions of Broadway musicals, or lawyer and journalist Natan Brune, who managed Lahat's campaign after carefully studying American electioneering techniques. American immigrants assumed leading positions in Israeli government and culture. Prime Minister Golda Meir grew up in Milwaukee. The Supreme Court's president Shimon Agranat was born in Kentucky and educated in Chicago. Nevertheless, American ideas and forms did not require human agents for their promiscuous circulation. They spread through media, popular culture, and other instruments and venues of transmission, including the organizational infrastructure of academia. Knowledge and expertise—managerial, scientific, social scientific, self-help—even Dale Carnegie's method—were paramount in this exchange. Individuals demonstrating proficiency in the American way of doing things accrued social capital.

The United States also exported social and political transgression—Black Power, feminism, the initial steps of the gay liberation movement, or the violence-prone right-wing Jewish Defense League, in addition to its mainstream electoral tactics such as polling and the merchandizing of political candidates. It modeled lifestyles, from consumerism to flower power and the counterculture as well as circulated artifacts, from Coca-Cola (1968) to military Phantom jets (1969). There was little in this hectic movement that was imposed on Israel. American power's imprint on forms of local life was not intentional as much as gravitational.

Even close relations with European societies that presumably could offer alternatives to American paradigms brought Israelis closer to the United States. Postwar Europe was preoccupied with negotiating its own broadening relationship with American culture. It was a particularly fraught but famously generative process in France; think of the cinematic "New Wave" and its extensive dialogue with Hollywood. In the decade prior to 1967,

France was Israel's closest ally, which left deep marks on Israeli culture as well. I would term this phenomenon "secondary Americanization." One of its dialectical effects was a suspicion of American culture some members of the Israeli intellectual classes shared with their European counterparts even before the country experienced the strongest effects of the American incursion.

Otherwise, *Americanization*, with its judgmental undertones and teleological insinuation, is a concept this book employs hesitantly and sparingly, and only as a shorthand for rather complex dynamics. The term implies one-sided acculturation, leading toward a singular goal. It conceives of the United States as a fixed entity, frozen in time. In contrast, *Coca-Cola, Black Panthers, and Phantom Jets* establishes that the processes that appear under the rubric "Americanization" were nonlinear, historically textured, and subject to constant change. Moreover, whereas the social, cultural, and political bonds between the two countries only gained strength in the following fifty years, American and Israeli societies are still quite distinct, regardless of the numerous comparative categories employed by friends and foes to couple them together, whether "immigrant nation," "liberal democracy," or, conversely, "settler colonialism."

Indeed, the comparative imagination is a feature of orbital relations in Israel and in other countries as well. As American iconography, events, and characters came to constitute a global lingua franca, a strong urge arose to find domestic instantiations of American phenomena.[11] Examples abound. In the press, journalists looked for the local Watergate or organized crime, and asked whether the Pentagon Papers leak could happen *here*. Ultra-Orthodox lawmakers voiced alarm about a music festival billed the "Israeli Woodstock."[12] Emulating the Vietnam-era political cartography, the local political map was redrawn to distinguish between *hawks* and *doves*.[13]

Recent scholarship on transnational exchanges underscores hybridity and reciprocity with terms such as the portmanteau *glocalization*.[14] Pointing to the dialogical interplay between outside forces and local agency is of great analytical value. Nevertheless, untangling the local/global dyad in Jewish Israel—a cosmopolitan society of mostly immigrants—where the *local* is already and inherently globalized—is particularly vexing. What the *global* stands for in this context is also unclear. At times it was the particular and local circumstances of the American Jewish community—rather than any universal force—that affected Israeli society. Indeed, Americanization entailed that Israel became a tad more *Jewish* during the period, moving away from its historical commitment to the "negation of the Diaspora." In addition, the Jewish presence in American culture and academia affected the dissemination of non-Jewish content in Israel as well. These triangular relations involving the United States as a whole, the American Jewish community, and Israel would not come into view if the discussion were to evolve around the term *globalization*.

The Israeli case stands out among the many explorations of the American Century's impact on other nations and regions in at least four ways:[15] first, the effects of American race and ethnicity discourse on Jewish ethnicism in Israel; second, the role of the Jewish American Diaspora; third, in Israel the American influence could not be easily folded into a conventional modernization narrative since it did not confront ancient traditions, entrenched customs, and peasant society, as it often did elsewhere; and fourth, Israel was a society at war and the geopolitical and its attendant volatility was always present in social and cultural transformations.

Two aspects of this volatility are at the backdrop of the ensuing discussion. First, the June 1967 war was followed by what was known as the "War after the War," Palestinian militants' infiltration along the Jordan River and terror attacks in Israel and abroad, including the hijacking and bombing of airplanes. Skirmishes along the Suez Canal escalated into a "War of Attrition" with Egypt that concluded in the summer of 1970.[16] In the first three years of our time frame, Israel was largely preoccupied with its security challenges. The lull in hostilities between 1970 and '73 allowed for greater introspective deliberations about Israeli society and its domestic disparities.

The other turbulent field was the relationship with the United States itself. In hindsight, it grew only stronger, especially after the summer of 1970, when Israel proved itself useful to American interests by deterring Syria from invading neighboring Jordan.[17] But the ties between Washington and Jerusalem were plagued by uncertainty. The White House deployed the ongoing Middle East crisis as a pawn in its maneuvers to reach a global understanding with Moscow and occasionally reassessed its arms supply to Israel. Israelis were particularly nervous about the prospects of a Middle East settlement imposed by the two superpowers.

Consumption/Race/Ambivalence

Bringing a wide range of topics under a single interpretative umbrella exposes threads and affinities among divergent historical phenomena. Despite the seemingly kaleidoscopic quality of the book's subject matter, the discussion returns to three major themes. The first is consumerism. Consumer modernity constituted one of the quintessential exports of the American Century. Beyond a cornucopia of goods, it featured marketing techniques, shopping venues, types of publicity, civic organizations, and new conceptions of society and the self. The making of a consumer society is a cardinal subplot of Israeli history in the 1960s and early 1970s, often obscured by the geopolitical narrative arc, namely the 1967 war and the military and political events that followed in its aftermath. The book proposes that by the late 1960s a full consumerist order was already in place, before Israel completely embraced capitalism.

Consumerism colonized the daily lives of Israelis, dispatching a bounty of appliances, grooming products, and other commodities to invade their homes. Consumerist thinking infiltrated management and politics, whether in the commodification of political figures or in the growing proclivity of political parties, state officials, and commercial outfits to measure, manipulate, and act on the preferences of consumers, voters, and workers. Indeed, the book argues that the *feedback loop*, expansively conceived, was among the most significant American imports at the time.

American products arrived in the guise of market commodities and in the form of military hardware as well. My analysis draws parallels between these two categories of artifacts and their reception, the knowledge invested in purchasing an appliance or in handling state-of-the-art military jets, the personal and national attachments they inspired, as well as their contribution to entrenching trust in the "technological fix," especially in military strategy.

The second theme focuses on ethnicity, race, and racism. *Coca-Cola, Black Panthers, and Phantom Jets* argues that the surge of identity politics in the United States affected both Ashkenazi and Mizrahi identities. The early stages of the "roots movement" in America, exemplified by the immense success of *Fiddler on the Roof* (1964), assumed a significant role in a short-lived revival of east European Ashkenazi culture in Israel, introducing the shtetl and Hasidic folklore into local popular culture, a terrain they had previously rarely inhabited. In 1971, the Israeli Black Panthers burst onto the scene. Seeking to radicalize Mizrahi Jews along the color line, the Panthers inaugurated a new phase in ethnic relations among Israelis.

Critical commentary about race that originated in the United States also entered public consciousness through theater, literature, cinema, music, as well as the social sciences. One of the questions the book tarries with is how racial tensions in the United States and the ethnic fault lines among Jews in Israel were rendered commensurable or comparable. Race/ethnicity is a theme connecting many chapters, whether through the story of the Black Hebrew Israelites, a tiny African American sect whose members began settling in the southern town of Dimona, the recruitment of Black basketball players and Black performers (for example, for the local iteration of the musical *Hair*), or, in contrast, the immigration of the militant Rabbi Kahane who brought with him to Israel forms of racism more common in the United States, which he applied to the Arab-Jewish divide.

In the 1960s, Israeli, mostly Ashkenazi, elites gravitated toward the aspirational West for reasons that, beyond the Israeli/Arab conflict, encompassed the consumerist tilt and their reaction to the large immigration from North Africa and the Middle East during the previous decades. Urban blight and other "quality-of-life" concerns were often blamed on the lack of Western values and the "Levantinization" of the country. Israeli elites became *whiter* also in reaction to the racial struggle in the United States. They expressed strong sympathy toward the civil rights movement and deep admiration for Martin Luther King, Jr. But by the late 1960s, the public was inundated with reports about Black antisemitism. The Israeli Black Panthers' ability to rattle society emanated, in part, from the perceived dangers associated with the American Black Power movement and the New Left.

The third theme is ambivalence and resistance. With all the uncertainties mentioned above, the United States was turning into Israel's staunchest ally. Ties between the two countries rested, in addition, on ideological, religious, and personal foundations. Many Israelis had relatives in the United States and after June 1967 the American Jewish community enthusiastically rallied in support of Israel. And yet, the social and cultural interaction at times prompted hesitation, and even resentment and opposition. Israelis demonstrated themselves to be eager participants in the American empire. For some, nevertheless, America's gravitational power presented concrete threats or nourished persistent angst about dependency and loss of autonomy, diminished values, and being drawn too far, too quickly into the American orbit.

The attitude toward American Jews was similarly divided.[18] Their invigorated commitment to Israel was lauded but the resulting impression that Israel relied on handouts was met with apprehension. And then there was the old rivalry between Zion and America as the competing promised lands for the Jewish people. While flexing its political muscle in favor of Israel, American Jewry was portrayed in countless articles in the Israeli press as a beleaguered community facing a pincer attack by the forces of assimilation and antisemitism, feeding the fantasy of an impending mass immigration to Israel.

The Israeli leadership was prone to moral panics. The Black Panthers spurred deep fears but there were other opportunities for disquietude. The aging American gangster Meyer Lansky's wish to spend the rest of his life in Israel raised concerns that if he were allowed to stay, hundreds of Jewish gangsters would join him and make Israel the epicenter of global crime. The threat of an unwanted American invasion was also induced by the slow trickle of Black Hebrew Israelites and the prospect that countless Black Americans, escaping poverty and racial strife, would follow suit. The Jewish participation in the American New Left generated anxiety as well. The conservative justice Moshe Silberg decried Jewish New Left circles as "perverse" and claimed there were many "wicked" and "evil" individuals among them.[19]

The counterculture faced contending views, largely divided along generational lines. Sixties youth rebelliousness often evoked official derision, although it reminded some of the utopian idealism and the fire in the belly of the early Zionist pioneers that by then had become little more than a faint memory. Moreover, the counterculture served as a venue for Jewish revival in Rabbi Shlomo Carlebach's musical evangelism or in the immensely popular

1968 revue, *Ish hasid haya* (There was a Hasidic man), that coupled the 1960s spirit with Hasidic folklore. Couched as "Hasidism in jeans," it dressed diasporic Jewish heritage in a modern, albeit rather tame, countercultural garb.

Such an assemblage of disparate styles and ideas was typical of the efforts to domesticate the foreign. American thought, customs, even products constantly required adjustments. The book documents the intricate processes that helped accommodate, normalize, and even birth a supplementary Israeli identity to American ideas and things. They involved linguistic and ideological measures such as translation, renaming, and repositioning. Coca-Cola, for instance, was often marketed as the proper drink for Jewish holidays. But material alterations were also not uncommon. This was the case with both the Phantom jet that had to be continually reworked and the family-size Coca-Cola bottle that did not fit well into the small Israeli refrigerator.

As we shall see, satire, parody, and irony were also tools both to reject or embrace the foreign. Even sheer mimicry or seemingly mindless absorption required agency and occasionally generated strong national feelings. Two examples from the cultural field: the Tel Aviv staging of *My Fair Lady* in 1964 was heralded as a historic turning point in the annals of Israeli theater, although except for the Hebrew translation, the show faithfully followed the Broadway production. In 1977, when the Maccabi Tel Aviv basketball team won the European championship, a wave of national pride erupted even though most of the players were American.

Historiography and Methodology

This study is indebted to previous research conducted under the headings of the Americanization or globalization of Israel. At the beginning of the twenty-first century, scholarly attention was directed at how the globalizing process and neoliberalism affected the country. It largely focused on the period following the mid-1980s. Important monographs in this vein are Uri Ram's *The Globalization of Israel: McWorld in Tel Aviv, Jihad in Jerusalem* (2007), and Tom Segev's *Elvis in Jerusalem: Post-Zionism and the Americanization of Israel* (2002).[20] Additional work on Israel and the United States has addressed management, the social sciences, Israeli basketball, and rock-and-roll music, among other topics.

The recent discussion about globalization and Israel follows and extends a thread of public discourse that grappled with the country's departure from earlier commitments to socialism, equality, and the pioneering spirit (*halutziut*). Its origins stretch all the way back to the early years of the state. In 1963, the embourgeoisement of society under state auspices was the impetus behind one of the most famous jeremiads in Israeli political history, Yitzhak Ben Aharon's article calling for the unification of the three workers' parties under the declamatory title, "Courage for Change on the Verge of Calamity."²¹ By the end of the 1960s, concerns about abandoned values proliferated.

This book's analysis contributes to the rich literature on "America in the World" and transnational historiography in general. The exploration of the advent of the consumerist age enters dialogue with research that speaks to comparable developments elsewhere, especially Victoria de Grazia's *Irresistible Empire: America's Advance through Twentieth-Century Europe* (2006) and Kristin Ross's writing about consumption and colonialism in *Fast Cars, Clean Bodies: Decolonization and the Reordering of French Culture* (1996). The highly nuanced, ethnographically inclined literature that in recent decades has reevaluated the American presence in Latin America is equally pertinent.²²

The notion of "contact zone" constitutes an effective conceptual tool for studying cultural interactions. It was first elaborated in postcolonial studies to denote "social spaces where cultures meet, clash and grapple with each other. Often in contexts of highly asymmetrical relations of power."²³ The idea of the "encounter" is similarly potent. It interrogates the dynamics of concrete meeting points, acknowledging their temporality and historicity, and allowing for a multiplicity of outcomes without occluding the ultimate asymmetry between the two countries: that Israel became only a junior partner in the American ambit.²⁴

The book's ten topical chapters shuttle between, on the one hand, exploring specific events or encounters and, on the other hand, delineating routinized patterns of the quotidian, especially in the context of consumption, its seeping into the fields of politics and leisure, and its relationship to other forms of the Israeli *everyday*. The experience of individuals is underscored. A major question examined is how the transnational becomes personal. Moreover, transnational intimacy breeds thick layers of public and private emotions, attachments, and desires as well as frustrations and anxieties.

The exchange also involved reenactments and performances inside and outside the theater, the staging of America for public viewing and commentary. One quality the book seeks to capture is the fecundity of the transnational encounter in spawning myriad anecdotes and endless storytelling that could provoke surprise, hilarity, or scorn. Another facet is the politics of knowledge, not just the circulation of American-produced information and expertise but the question of how Israelis became acquainted over time with American life.

Gender is an essential theme here. Marketing commodities advanced specific notions about femininity and masculinity. The new institutions of consumer protection, largely helmed by women, also contributed to molding gender discourse. Gender was also a constitutive category in technology transfer and the story of the Black Panthers. The period under examination witnessed the first steps of Israeli feminism, which was understood as an American import. As significantly, both high and popular culture conceived of the Israeli-American encounter in gendered, sometimes sexual, *geolibidinal*, terms.

This study highlights identity-formation processes, ambiguities, and paradoxes. In one case, human relations experts teach kibbutzniks how to improve social interaction. In another, Israeli pilots teach their American instructors how to dogfight in the air. Other episodes blur the lines separating the local and authentic from the foreign and supposedly inauthentic, as in the story of the Black Panthers.

Research is based on archival work, interviews, as well as a deep dive into the Israeli printed press, reading it against the grain, taking into consideration its biases and blind spots. Analysis draws from theoretical discussions on the consumerist *everyday* (Henri Lefebvre), cultural capital (Pierre Bourdieu), knowledge as a form of governance and subject making (Michel Foucault) as well as other theoretical formulations that pertain to globalization, performance, analogical thinking, and racial masquerade. Ultimately, the book argues for the historicization of the transnational encounter, paying attention to its path dependency and temporality. Ironically, the appropriation of American ways sometimes placed local culture *out* of step with the state of things in the United States in what might be termed the "glocal delay."[25]

Chapter Structure

The first three chapters of *Coca-Cola, Black Panthers, and Phantom Jets* focus on consumerism. Chapter 1 demonstrates the emergence of a full-fledged consumerist regime and how it reshaped notions of time, space, and domestic boundaries. Also examined are the local histories of specific commodities such as Coca-Cola. Discussion then turns to the relationship between the ongoing state of war and occupation, on the one hand, and the daily cycles of consumption, on the other. The next chapter connects consumption with ideas about citizenship as it follows elites' and the government's ambitions to promote models of good consumer behavior. Israelis were subjected to multiple disciplining efforts that urged them to curb their spending habits, whether to accommodate urgent national priorities or in the name of good taste. New organizations such as the state-sponsored Israel Consumer Council (1966) promoted consumer-based models of participatory citizenship, largely drawn from the United States and Europe. Another state-initiated project focused on instructing poor immigrants, primarily from North Africa and the Middle East, on how to maintain, cultivate, and beautify their domestic spheres according to Western standards.

The third chapter examines first Shlomo Lahat's successful run for mayor of Tel Aviv (1973) during which the personality of the candidate superseded party affiliation or ideological differences. Lahat's campaign and his leadership style are then situated in a set of new techniques employed to measure and control the preferences of voters, citizens, consumers, and workers. The chapter concludes with another former general, Yitzhak Rabin, and his own Americanization during his stint as the Israeli ambassador in Washington, DC.

Discussion then shifts to military technology transfer. By the end of the 1960s, the Israeli Air Force experienced the geopolitical shift more rapidly than other branches of the Israeli military and government. Its almost exclusively French stock was supplemented with, or replaced by, American aircraft. The process accelerated when Israeli pilots began flying the F-4E Phantom II planes in the fall of 1969 during the War of Attrition. Taking a mostly bottom-up approach, chapter 4 examines the Israeli pilots' encounters with American aviation technology, American airmen, American know-how, and the American military-industrial complex.

The next chapter documents the rise of the Israeli Black Panthers, who emerged in the early months of 1971 with a jolt. Led by a small core of activists, the movement launched a series of unprecedented demonstrations and rallies, staged media stunts, and circulated belligerent proclamations. The Panthers linked the condition of poor Jews from the Middle East and North Africa with Blackness as perceived through the historical plight of African Americans and their struggle for liberation in the 1960s. Chapter 5 argues that the emergence of Black Power in the United States informed the radicalism of the extreme Right as well. In the same year that the Panthers emerged, Rabbi Meir Kahane moved his operation from Brooklyn to Jerusalem, bringing with him symbols, slogans, and methods of operation he appropriated from his archenemy, the Black Panther Party.

We revisit Kahane, together with other American expatriates considered by government to be public threats, in the next chapter. Chapter 6 begins with the gangster Meyer Lansky's sojourn in Israel. Lansky fled to Tel Aviv in July 1970 seeking Israeli citizenship based on the Law of Return. After two years, the Supreme Court approved the government's decision to reject his application. The chapter explores Lansky's hiatus in Israel to assess aspects of Israeli sovereignty and diasporic loyalties. Discussion then turns to Kahane and then the small community of African American Hebrew Israelites.

The seventh chapter continues to trace the experience of American immigrants and American-trained professionals who modeled new approaches to individual agency, either through social activism, volunteerism, or through the language of rights—representing both American liberalism and its 1960s crisis. The first part focuses on the reverberations of American ideas about welfare and race in corners of the Israeli social sciences. The second examines the early history of Israeli feminism through the short political career of Marcia Freedman. The third part shifts to basketball and to another immigrant, Tal Brody, as an agent of professionalization in the Maccabi Tel Aviv team.

The last three chapters pivot to culture. Chapter 8 investigates the growing popularity of Yiddish, Yiddishism, and Hasidism. Israeli culture began flirting with east European Ashkenazi lore that previously had been shunned. The interest in the diasporic past was cultivated in tandem with

1960s American culture, including the global success of *Fiddler on the Roof*, the rise of countercultural Jewish folklore, and the integration of Yiddish expressions into American parlance. By the conclusion of the 1960s, the Yiddishkeit revival contributed to a cultural hyperethnicism that often appeared under the banner of rediscovering roots or tradition. This trend paralleled the new allure of Jewish religiosity. The American involvement is evident in early efforts to bring secular Israelis back to the faith.

The next chapter begins with Giora Godik's lavish productions of musicals, spectacles that signaled a new phase in Israeli cultural consumerism. By the end of the decade, when the conventional Broadway musical lost some of its luster, the local rendition of the countercultural musical *Hair* (1970) became a sensation, due to its nudity, sexual liberation message, and antiwar position. Chapter 9 thus investigates opposing representations of American values, on and off the stage, as manifested, for instance, in Godik's personification of the American-style risk-taking entrepreneur or the reenactment by *Hair*'s cast of a hippie community outside the theater.

The final chapter explores fictional American characters in Israeli culture, beginning with Godik's musical, *I Like Mike* (1968); director Uri Zohar's 1968 film, *Kol mamzer melech* (*Every Bastard a King*); and Amos Kollek's 1971 novel, *Don't Ask If I Love*. These three works simultaneously exhibit attraction to and unease with the American presence. Chapter 10 concludes with sharp critiques of the American dream featured in two avant-garde plays: Nissim Aloni's *American Princess* (1963) and Hanoch Levin's *The Whore from Ohio* (1977).[26]

Where Is Israel?

Following the 1967 war a set of questions emerged concerning Israel's space and boundaries, issues that more than fifty years later are still haunting the country. The occupation of new territories only exacerbated the tension between the ideational *Land of Israel* embedded in the biblical promises of return and redemption and the actuality of settling on concrete Middle Eastern soil. Also pulled apart were the modern, ostensibly secular Israeli state, on the one hand, and the messianic fantasy of Greater Israel, on the other.[27]

America also appeared in the Israeli mind as both a figment of ideological imagination and a concrete, although almost incomprehensibly enormous space. One narrative recurs in the testimonies of Israelis who spent long stretches of time in the United States, often in some official capacity. Upon arrival, they purchased a car and spent much of their free time traveling around and often far away.[28] Coming from a tiny and isolated Israel, this was their idea of American boundless freedom.

Coca-Cola, Black Panthers, and Phantom Jets proposes that the emerging orbital relations between the two countries affected Israeli locational practice and spatial perception and should be considered alongside other forces that fed the Israeli perennial wrestling with indeterminate borders and place. Many of the episodes explored here delineate both literal and figurative boundary crossing and demonstrate the eroding power of the membranes, ideological and tactile, separating Israel from the United States and the rest of the world. The Jewish outside, the diasporic, was also encroaching, and Israel softened its hardline position against its own Diaspora of former Israelis now living abroad. The Panthers claimed to represent an internal Diaspora and their public defiance evoked deep concerns about shamefully airing the country's dirty laundry for the world to see. The Lansky affair and Kahane's arrival indicated that unsavory parts of the diasporic experience were coming to settle in modern Israel.

Where was Israel in the world? Different answers were recorded, some surprising. The Hebrew Israelites in socially and geographically marginalized Dimona maintained that Israel was in fact part of Africa. When in the aftermath of the Six-Day War an Israeli magazine invited two West Bank Palestinians for a tour of Tel Aviv, their response was, "Ya Allah: This is like America."[29]

While in the early 1950s, Israeli elites were strongly critical of McCarthyism, appalled by Julius and Ethel Rosenberg's execution,[30] and suspicious of global American hegemony, by the end of the 1960s they saw Israel more comfortably as part of the American-dominated West whose values and aspirations they embraced, or as a vanguard in a global struggle against the Soviet bloc and its Middle East proxies. Alongside its defensiveness and occasionally claustrophobic insistence on national unity, Israel was exceedingly attentive to the outside world. By the late 1960s, the press augmented its coverage of the United States on topics such as presidential elections, culture, education, politics, and technology. Israelis displayed great awareness of and concern about their image abroad. Public diplomacy, *hasbara*, became a national cause, and in 1974 a short-lived ministry was created for that purpose. Israel also presented and marketed itself through its export products, the tourist and souvenir industry, and the cultural performances it sent to Broadway and elsewhere. At the same time, and since its inception, the country was subjected to international curiosity and scrutiny that Israelis were keen to satisfy.

One such effort was journalist Amos Elon's book *The Israelis: Fathers and Sons* (1971), published first in English with American readers in mind. A major success in the United States, less so domestically, *The Israelis* constituted a bold effort to encapsulate the Israeli experience past and present on the eve of the state's twenty-fifth anniversary (1973). Elon delivered not the official but an occasionally critical view that, for example, acknowledged the suffering that Zionism inflicted on the Palestinians. His book thus offered a rejoinder to the idealized representations of Israel in Hollywood films and yet shared with them a conception of the monumental and the epic in Zionist history. One critic labeled it "An *Exodus* for Intelligent People."[31]

Most importantly, for our discussion, is that Elon thematized Israeli history along lines familiar to readers across the Atlantic. He alluded to events and characters in US history and organized his narrative around a supposed generational, father/son divide that juxtaposes younger Israelis (he was particularly interested in the 1948 generation, individuals who by then were in their 40s and early 50s) against an aging cohort of septuagenarian and octogenarian "founding fathers." Elon's book furnishes one example of how in the process of self-representation, the foreign point of view was internalized. Israelis were gazing at themselves from the outside, so to speak. This was another form of gnawing at boundaries and identity play, which undergird so many cultural, social, and political encounters we will explore in this book.

ONE

Consumer Modernity and the *Everyday*

In April 1968, Prime Minister Levi Eshkol received the first case of bottled Coca-Cola produced in a shiny new factory in Bnei Brak just outside of Tel Aviv. The daily *Davar* remarked wryly that there was no reason not to rejoice when Israel joins the "family" of 138 countries in which the (almost) national American drink was served. "Is there a chance that Coke would become our national drink?" the paper asked and answered in the affirmative with another question, "Is there a shortage of snobs in Israel?"[1] This tepid response typified a somewhat reserved attitude. But Israelis soon proved to be enthusiastic Coke drinkers, their craving made stronger by an inventive and aggressive advertisement campaign for the fizzy concoction.

The arrival of Coca-Cola—by then, a recognizable metaphor for America's global hegemony—would stand as a sign of a new age of consumerism in Israel. It was introduced during the same year that witnessed the advent of Israeli television broadcasts that brought American and British sitcoms and police dramas to transfixed viewers in darkened living rooms across the country. In effect, however, private consumption began rising sharply since the turn of the 1960s. In early 1966, with the country on the brink of a recession, premier Eshkol reminded citizens that during the previous five years, the standard of living had leaped to an "astonishing height" by 35 percent on average. "This phenomenon has no precedent elsewhere among nations," he declared in a special radio broadcast. Israelis are better clothed and better fed, he added, some moved to larger apartments, others purchased new furniture, or equipped their homes with electrical refrigerators, sophisticated stoves, and vacuum cleaners. Eshkol asked, "Despite complaints and protests over prices and taxes, are there many among us who would not admit that their material condition is improving from year to year?"[2]

The 1967 war brought the recession to an abrupt and unceremonious end. An economic boom ensued. In 1968 alone the GDP grew by a staggering 12 percent, instigating an additional surge in the standard of living. Beyond cars, services, appliances, and travel abroad, the period ushered in a significant rise in the acquisition of high-end goods, from foreign-made shoes to cars and amenities-rich luxury apartments. A new culinary connoisseurship emerged, as manifested in fine-dining restaurants or the popularity of two books: Amos Kenan's *The Book of Pleasures* (1971), which interweaves recipes for sophisticated (and nonkosher) food with recipes for how to live the good, hedonistic life, and Yoel Marcus's *The Wine Book* (1972), a primer on the world of exquisite wines.[3]

Consumption denotes the acquisition and use, either material or symbolic, of commodities, artifacts, services, and culture. Laden with knowledge and steeped in ideology, consumerism stands for a comprehensive institutional and cultural framework that undergirds the circulation of goods in society, their diverse employment, and assigned meanings.[4] Indeed, the period heralded the consolidation of a consumption-centered cultural order in Israel. Targeting the public was not only a rather mature advertisement industry but also new specialized magazines that catered to women and youth, and a burgeoning celebrity culture that singled out teen idols and other revered figures, whether entertainers, politicians, or military generals. New shopping venues confirmed a new sense of abundance.

In late August 1958, the first supermarket (funding and expertise came from the United States) opened in north Tel Aviv. Ed Sullivan's wife (the former Sylvia Weinstein) cut the ribbon, clearing the way for a stampede of 2,500 eager customers on the first day alone.[5] By the late 1960s, the supermarket and the department store were joined by upscale boutiques and exclusive leisure spaces such as country clubs.⁶ Israeli commercial life featured dedicated locales of fashionable consumption, most glamorous of which was Dizengoff Street in Tel Aviv, although shopping abroad—for those who could afford the privilege—offered the ultimate pleasure and choice. Invigorated consumption defined the rising middle class that made up a larger swath of Israeli society than the older coterie of bourgeois factory owners, merchants, and top-tier professionals.

Commercial ads at the turn of the 1970s often alluded to "American standards" or the merits of American products. Peddling the locally assembled

FIGURE 1.1 Fashion on Dizengoff Street. A photoshoot for modern jewelry by designers Rachel and Eli Gera, Tel Aviv, 1971. Dizengoff was Israel's primary venue for high-end shopping. (Dan Hadani Collection, The Pritzker Family National Photography Collection, The National Library of Israel)

Electra-Westinghouse television set, a newspaper ad bragged that Westinghouse's technology could also be found in the entrails of the Phantom jet. An image of the military craft appeared on top of the company's TV set next to the slogan, "American Knowledge," and the phrase, in English, "You Can Be <u>Sure</u> If It's Westinghouse."[7] A 1970 Omega watch ad declared that as the first chronometer ever to be authorized by NASA, the Speedmaster was the only watch to have visited—twice—a place no other watch would dare go, the surface of the moon.[8] One appliance, a washing machine, was marketed under the brand name "Sonovox America" although it was manufactured far away from American shores.[9]

One of the most innovative ads for an American product featured a long-haired girl sitting self-assuredly on the hood of a Dodge car, hands clasping an upright knee. Under the title "My Dad Has a Dodge Coronet (Good Car from a Good Home)" she is quoted:

> We are from the United States. Two years ago, we made *aliya*. At the beginning it was a bit difficult but now we are happy. We gave up many things to live in Israel—a large house with many rooms, a swimming pool in the backyard. But one thing my dad was not ready to give up—his Dodge. Last week we sold our old car and bought a new one. Dad says he will always be faithful to this car because it has never disappointed him.[10]

The ad smartly conjoins sacrifice and self-gratification, Zionism and a luxurious American car. No split loyalty here. Dad is devoted to both his new homeland and his old American vehicle.

The practices, ethos, and sensibilities of modern consumption-centered mass society did not require a recurrent recognition of their American provenance. Yes, yardsticks for and examples of modern consumerism also arrived from Europe. Israel imported more goods from the United States than from any other single country, but all in all purchased more from Europe. However, as Victoria de Grazia demonstrates in *Irresistible Empire* (2006), in the interwar period Europe served as the staging ground for the elaboration of American empire as an emporium of goods and services. Europe adopted American marketing institutions, service norms, publicity techniques, measuring tools, and the promise of a "decent standard of living." Securing the material well-being of citizens was embraced as a goal not only by liberal democracies but also by rising fascist and communist regimes. Service-oriented organizations such as Rotary clubs promoted American business ethos and sociability. American films and movie stars titillated the European masses.

The process intensified after World War II. Like much of Western Europe, although slightly later, Israel experienced the transition to consumer modernity at a more frantic pace than the United States itself. Kristin Ross's description of French life in the wake of the Marshall Plan as "cargo-cult-like, sudden descent of large appliances into . . . households and streets"[11] might have applied to late 1960s Israel as well.

Through a few case studies, this chapter explores first the population of Israeli homes with durable goods, this trend's effects on notions of time, space, and boundaries, and the emergence of a robust consumerist culture and a consumerist *everyday*. It follows the domestication of specific commodities such as Coca-Cola and frozen food as well as marketing techniques, especially the popularity of sweepstakes and promotional gifts in 1960s Israel. The discussion then turns to the tensions and, conversely, the affinity between patterns of consumption, on the one hand, and cycles of geopolitical violence or the occupation of Arab territories, on the other.

The current scholarly interest in delineating the historical path Israel took toward neoliberal capitalism focuses mostly on top-down transformations that originated in the state or in party politics and involved ideological skirmishes and shifts among decision-makers and economists. The emergence of consumer society, this constitutive aspect of modern capitalism as well as its participatory, ground-up dimension, are mostly taken for granted, as are the ideological constructs pertaining to individuality, family, and nation in which daily routines and material objects are embedded.[12]

Boundaries and the *Everyday*

One critical response to the rapid metamorphosis that befell postwar French society was Henri Lefebvre's and, later, the Situationists' notion of the "colonization of everyday life" by the commodity form.[13] The allusion to colonization refers first to the totalizing ambitions of late capitalism and its capacity to occupy aspects of life hitherto shielded from its reach, such as leisure.

Looking at Israeli consumerism through the lens of the modern *everyday*, it appears that the consumerist quotidian yielded contradictory—unifying and fracturing—effects. Forms and patterns of consumption pushed Israelis in similar paths—as in television viewing—and sometimes even toward a single product. By the late 1970s, for instance, the average Israeli would be nicknamed *Subaroid* for his penchant for the Japanese car Subaru.

Consumption had leveling, even democratic effects, but, nevertheless, and quite expectedly, it revealed and widened social fault lines, between the haves and have-nots, Mizrahi and Ashkenazi, newcomers and veterans, women and men, Arabs and Jews, and among members of different occupational groups. The relative abundance of durable goods and the elaboration of a new Israeli everyday also reordered notions of space and time. The torrent of home appliances and consumerism in general mitigated to some degree the distance—cultural, political, and spatial—between Israel and the West, the magical *abroad* that preoccupies the Israeli collective consciousness and is often conceived of as a thrilling profusion of sights, experiences, and things. Western-style consumption allowed Israelis a taste and more of *hevrat hashefa* (affluent society) and convinced them to recognize their own society as such, especially as many of the products purchased and dragged into their homes were foreign-made and inscribed with foreign names. The Israeli investment in the symbolic erasure of these boundaries went far beyond the process we came to know as *globalization*, as it evinced Israel's unique regional isolation as well as its self-perception as a Western outpost.

At the same time, consumption also reorganized family life and reestablished, in fact, augmented, the boundaries separating the home from the literal and figurative outside. So, while consumption is often linked to the process of individuation, symptoms of which are evident in the Israeli case as well, it most clearly reconstituted the Israeli family. Incrementally but consistently, the intercom and the telephone protected the family unit from external encroachment, electrical refrigerators chilled and safeguarded its food, air conditioners and vacuum cleaners cooled and rendered dust-free its domestic space, and cosmetics and myriad other grooming products pampered its members' bodies, keeping them less sweaty and more hygienic. The private efforts to keep bodies and homes unpolluted, a typical byproduct of modern capitalism, was supplemented by recurrent public campaigns to clean streets and neighborhoods and beautify cityscapes (see chapter 2).

This play with boundaries, the spatial or locational function of consumption, should be considered an aspect of their *use-value* that goes further than Karl Marx's notion of utility, Thorstein Veblen's ideas about the communication of social position, or, relatedly, Pierre Bourdieu's conception of cultural capital and distinction. In addition, consumerism afforded Israelis an everyday material stability juxtaposed to either the volatility of the regional conflict or the erratic nature of the Israeli economy itself. Operating in similarly opposing directions, improved standards of living equipped the state with an instrument to ingratiate itself to its citizens, but efforts to control consumption and manage the economy in general also induced public alienation and mistrust. Private consumption often grew beyond or even in defiance of state intentions.

Beyond the impression of being taken over by the imperial forces of modern capitalism, the invocation of *colonization* in the catchphrase "the colonization of the everyday" points to additional mechanisms of domination. In the 1950s and 1960s, France was receding from its empire inward, into its European homeland or its citizens' private spheres, ostensibly substituting one form of colonization for another. In Ross's employment of the expression, the privatized arena of consumption, its circular, repetitious routines, and self-proclaimed timelessness counterbalanced the rupture and violence of the wars in Algeria and Indochina. Modern consumerism enabled the French to erase the memory and disavow the historicity of the colonial experience as it also rearticulated racial hierarchies and exclusions within territorial France, in which a growing body of former colonial subjects now resided and worked.

Dynamics of domination that involve consumption and the everyday are also discernable in the Israeli case, some comparable to the French example, others distinct. In the 1960s, several government-sponsored campaigns were launched to instill in the Israeli public Western practices and norms of consumption; a few of these efforts, as we will see in the following chapter, targeted Mizrahi Jews, especially new immigrants from North Africa.

Moreover, standards of cleanliness and personal grooming alongside invigorated consumption established stronger hierarchies within and outside the Jewish population of Israel and, after 1967, the occupied territories.

Otherwise, Israel was arguably advancing in the opposite direction to that of France, becoming a regional superpower, a proxy in the Cold War conflict, taking over territories three times larger than its own, and overseeing a substantial Palestinian population. The Six-Day War thus reordered the Israeli time/space. As significantly, it coupled victory together with a new prosperity, and was experienced as liberation from both a military siege and a crippling, dispiriting economic recession. As the War of Attrition raged on, observers noticed, either by way of critique or celebration, that while the country was engaged in an armed conflict, its citizens were busy improving their personal level of comfort. The poet Haim Guri summarized this incongruity with the parallel, "Tel Aviv is glowing. The Suez Canal is burning."[14]

Increased consumption was sometimes justified by the desire for and through the rhetoric of *normalcy*—an ambiguous term—but for some it appeared to dangerously fray the affinity between the military front and the home front. Nevertheless, while seemingly at odds with the ideological and aesthetic inclinations of the old socialist vanguard, consumerism was more accommodating of the figure of the citizen-soldier that assumed center stage in post-'67 Israel and even more so with the norms of the new professional/managerial middle class. The coupling of a thriving consumerist culture and an intermittent state of war or an ongoing state of occupation remained a permanent fixture of Jewish life in Israel, where the regional conflict forges its own quotidian and can hardly be completely erased or escape notice. The geopolitical condition was, for example, paramount in the story of Coca-Cola, whose introduction to Israel was considered not a sign of an advanced consumer market as much as a symbolic victory over the Arab boycott. The late 1960s War of Attrition was the crucible of that duality, which despite its seemingly schizoid characteristics and occasional strains proved over the decades to be quite stable.

The occupation of new territories, including the West Bank and Gaza Strip, opened a market of about a million-strong population to Israeli merchandise and, at the same time, supplied the economy with a cheap labor force. Whereas old borders were seemingly gone, elevated levels of comfort accentuated Israeli society's distance from the newly occupied territories, further distinguishing Israelis from the figure of the poor Palestinian day laborer crossing the Green Line.

The National Pie

Whereas the economics of consumption is largely outside the purview of this discussion, which foregrounds the role of daily practices, cultural trajectories, and the density of *things* occupying private and public spaces, the following is a short sketch of the forces that steered Israel's political economy at the time. The state, rather than free-market dynamics, was deeply involved in setting postwar Europe on the route to modern consumerism in regimes labeled by Lefebvre and others as *neocapitalist*. Lefebvre famously spoke of the bureaucratic society of controlled consumption. Assuring citizens of Israel universal education, health care, and the protection of their savings, Prime Minister David Ben-Gurion stated in 1951, "We want to achieve economic security that assures each individual that his existence is based on solid ground, and that he maintains a high standard of living."[15] Through its wholesale and retail apparatus and adjacent consumer coop organizations—the powerful umbrella trade union, the Histadrut, also took part in determining consumer choices and habits.

The state shaped private consumption by deploying taxes, subsidies, exemptions, grants, and myriad other fiscal and monetary instruments, both positive and negative, including its own role as a consumer. Private solvency was to a large degree a byproduct of the foreign capital that was funneled into Israel in the 1950s and early 1960s through American loans, Holocaust reparations from Germany, and funds recruited from world Jewry. This was, if you will, a home-brewed Marshall Plan. The German reparations granted directly to survivors significantly elevated the economic circumstances of a specific segment of the population and eventuated the first round in the fierce Israeli competition over the standard of living.[16] The government catered to the material well-being of new immigrants and provided consumer-oriented services such as radio broadcast and telephone.

Despite efforts to restrain consumption, the state also modeled and vicariously encouraged upscale or even ostentatious consumption. It did so through the perks it granted to high-level officials, the privileges it accorded to newcomers from the West and the USSR, and the encouragement of high-end exports, which also impacted local tastes. It endeavored to showcase Israel, turning the country into a commodity for the purpose of self-representation, tourism, or export, as in the case of the luxury, art-filled transatlantic ocean liner SS Shalom launched in 1964.

As importantly, the state accepted neocapitalist norms as well as the measurement tools—statistical yardsticks and visual representations—that concretized the notion of "a decent standard of living," for instance, the practice of the Central Bureau of Statistics to enumerate household goods. Another semantic product was the metaphor of the "national pie," in Hebrew, *ha'uga haleumit*, or the national cake. Thus, in his 1966 radio address, Eshkol thundered: "Don't any one among us think: how can I take for myself a larger slice of the pie. Let us all work together to increase the entire pie."[17] Sounding Kennedyesque, he was in effect reiterating a macroeconomics cliché often attributed to the Chicago School, namely, that the principle of economic growth overrides—or bypasses—the question of equal distribution. A bigger pie would serve everyone.[18] The national pie trope was entrenched in the public mind. In 1970, an op-ed writer argued that in a time of war Israelis should tighten their belt and focus on the national mission, declaring, "We don't have two but only one national pie."[19] The following year the Israeli Black Panthers' leader Sa'adia Marciano threatened, "We want our share of the pie and if not, there will not be a pie."[20]

The Israeli economy stood at a crossroads and pulled into seemingly conflicting paths. Labeled a pluralistic economy, it was a pastiche of collectivist and capitalistic elements assembled haphazardly in the name of serving the national mission of absorbing immigrants, settling the land, and protecting the borders. Alongside the public and private sector, it featured a unique historical phenomenon, a powerful workers' sector, Hevrat Ha'ovdim (Society of Workers) comprised of the industrial plants, financial institutions, building and shipping conglomerates, and marketing organizations owned by the Histadrut.

In the mid-1960s, the completion of several major construction projects, including the Ashdod Port, the National Water Carrier, and the Dead Sea Works, as well as the end of German reparations and American aid, threatened to severely worsen the balance of payments and deplete foreign currency reserves. The government deviated from its corporatist commitment to guarantee full employment and initiated a deliberate recession by severely cutting its expenditures, a rare move in world economy at the time.

As political scientist Michael Shalev argues, the recession was also devised to administer a jolt to a somewhat restless and increasingly militant labor force, buoyed by almost universal employment, as well as to discipline and energize the private sector, for the program also featured increased exposure of local industry to foreign imports.[21] This was in effect a measure of shock therapy, which manifested the government's wish to retreat from its granular involvement in managing the economy and to wean different sectors from overreliance on its support, a pioneering neoliberal remedy before neoliberalism fully materialized on the world stage. The austerity policy indeed succeeded in saving the balance of payment, but it was a Pyrrhic victory. Unemployment soared to 12 percent and for the first time in the history of Israel, immigration completely halted. The recession had far-reaching political consequences, contributing to a rift between the weakest segments of society—new immigrants from the Middle East and North Africa—and Mapai, the ruling party, which together with other factions would constitute the modern Labor Party in 1968.

There were other signs in the 1950s and 1960s that the government was adopting policy patterns borrowed from Western capitalism. The socialist Mapai incubated the private sector. Courting entrepreneurs and foreign capital, Minister of Industry and Trade (and later the Minister of the Treasury) Pinchas Sapir invested public funds in private industry. By the conclusion of the 1950s, policymakers and economists embraced the cause of economic independence, an idea that privileged export and exporters. They advocated making the Israeli economy more efficient and competitive globally. The potential commercial ties with the European Common Market drove some of the efforts to adjust the local economy to its standards.

Despite the early successes of the young country's economy, its architects, including Eshkol, Sapir, and David Horowitz, the governor of the Bank of Israel, as well as a group of young economists led by the University of Chicago–trained Don Patinkin, harbored doubts about its actual strength. Eshkol emphasized that the standard of living increased not because of higher productivity but because of foreign capital. There were ongoing apprehensions regarding the Histadrut's economic arm, Hevrat Ha'ovdim, which encompassed some of the largest corporations in Israel, as a model of production for export. Decision-makers in Jerusalem had some preference for the perceived dexterity and nimbleness of the private sector.

The younger generation of Mapai leaders—and, more so, its short-lived offshoot, the Israel Workers List (or Rafi)—embraced modern management tools and a mainstream, albeit still largely Keynesian, positivist economic approach. Its members often advocated unshackling bureaucracies from party control, instead instituting professional criteria in making appointments. This transformation could be cast as a struggle between older ideologues and younger technocrats. The infusion of retired military top brass into industrial and management positions, especially after the 1967 war, was also welcomed as a positive step on the road to depoliticizing the economy.

Known as the Millionaires Conferences, large investment summits in the era following the Six-Day War offered a platform for the strongest articulation of the new market-oriented spirit. Beginning in 1968, these gatherings of hundreds of Jewish entrepreneurs from the United States and elsewhere were orchestrated to hammer out plans for joint ventures with foreign capital.[22] The new economic climate called for price stability, manpower mobility, reduction of foreign currency restrictions, higher quality standards, and the elimination of bureaucratic red tape. Asher Yadlin, head of Hevrat Ha'ovdim, promised that the Histadrut would not put obstacles to partnerships with private capital. "Economy that does not guarantee profits does not guarantee the worker anything."[23] Ze'ev Sherf, minister of industry and trade, said in the Knesset, "I don't see great virtue in too much government interference and excessive supervision in the economy. Not all wisdom is concentrated in government."[24]

On the eve of the first summit, Sapir explained that previously, Jewish donors who had assisted in arming Israel, building high-employment industries, and establishing settlements acted upon their Zionist or philanthropist commitments. Now, he expected to lure them to invest in Israel based on their self-interest. Fully endorsing this approach, the poet and essayist Nathan Alterman wrote, "'Profitability' is the Samson's locks of the force we wish to activate in this conference, and any idealistic Delilah wishing to shear it off, supposedly for better appearance, would take away his power."[25]

The rhetoric and a few policy measures of the late 1960s promised market liberalization.[26] Nevertheless, as the economy became once again flush with foreign money it turned more centralized for complex reasons, some derived from enormous defense expenses, and yet others grounded in politics. The power of the Histadrut and its companies only increased. Sapir perceived the Histadrut as a counterweight to the rising clout of the Ministry of Defense in determining economic policy. He also labored to further strengthen the old Mapai bloc within the Labor Party.[27]

What seem to us to be giant steps taken in the direction of rendering Israel a capitalistic society were not quite clear to contemporaries. From the vantage point of the late 1960s, the (Western) world seemed rather flat in terms of its economic practices. The United States embarked on its most far-reaching social welfare program, the Great Society, whose goal was no less than the elimination of poverty. In the summer of 1971, a Republican administration under Richard Nixon was about to attempt state control of wages and prices. Moshe Mandelbaum, the official in charge of price control at the Treasury, said in 1972 that a free market as conceived by the visionaries of modern capitalism did not really exist in practice and each country in the world sees as its duty to intervene and restrict the free market since the mechanism of supply and demand was not working according to textbook economics.[28]

Home Invasion: TV

From 1965 to 1972, Israel's population grew by a quarter, to 3.2 million, not counting the residents of the occupied territories. Adjusted for inflation, private consumption rose by 65 percent. In 1958, 9.1 percent of Israeli households possessed an electric washing machine, by 1970 the share tripled to 27.7 percent, two years later it was 50 percent, and by 1975 it would reach roughly 75 percent. By 1975, 30.4 percent of Israeli families owned a car. This was still a modest share of the country but growth in car ownership was tremendous. In 1962, only 4.6 percent of households owned a car.[29] In 1972, a quarter of families used a vacuum cleaner, while in 1965 only 14 percent owned the appliance.

One device that increased by a factor of thirty within seven years was television sets. In 1965, 2.4 percent of households owned the device; by 1972, 68 percent. TV viewing eclipsed listening to the radio.[30] After many years of deliberation, television transmission was inaugurated on Israeli Independence Day 1968. It was preceded two years earlier by instructional television intended for the benefit of schools. David Ben-Gurion had forcefully opposed television, largely on moral grounds and concerns over cultural degradation.[31] Throughout the early years of the decade there were lingering trepidations over the quality of prospective programming and the possible rise in consumption. The fear that television would be harnessed for the political ambitions of the ruling party constituted another strong concern.

The decisive argument, however, was that thousands of Israeli Arabs and non-Arabs had already purchased TV sets and were tuned to broadcasts from neighboring countries and therefore exposed to "enemy propaganda."[32] Only members of the ultrareligious Agudat Israel Party remained steadfastly hostile to the new medium on the premise that "whoever admits a TV set to his home allows in an armed bandit who would rob the senses and thoughts of children and turn them against their parents."[33] TV was planned to be noncommercial, part of the state-sponsored BBC-style broadcasting authority, and funded by annual tolls.

The home invasion metaphor to describe the descent of television sets upon Israeli domestic spaces might be an apt one. It was not enough that forests of unsightly metal antennas metastasized on rooftops overnight, the bulky set had to be placed somewhere in a space that had not been designed to contain it. An advice column in the *Ma'ariv* daily recommended buying a dedicated wheeled cart to assure maximum flexibility or employing existing shelves provided they would be properly reinforced. The column informed readers that Americans are mostly exempted from such expenditure as their sets come with integrated feet; alternatively, they purchase large and expensive consoles for their entire audio and video needs.[34]

The advent of the television era exemplified the range of arcane information and types of knowledge that were attached to new consumer products. Newspaper articles provided instructions about transmission technology, attributes of antennas and sets, or the ideal position of bodies for viewing. Advertisements bombarded the public with propriety technical terms, often in English and sometimes in a manner that seemed to unnecessarily mystify rather than explain features that were otherwise rather common. Acquiring and managing the new cumbersome set epitomized the thrill and the torture attached to participation in the Israeli version of the consumerist shift.

Customers complained that they had been sold older sets of low quality or that the service was abysmal. They grumbled about not getting the same good reception as their neighbors. Experts countered that viewers harbored unrealistic expectations about tuning in to remote stations from Cyprus, Egypt, Jordan, and Lebanon. Vendors reported that buyers sometimes required three or four home visits by a technician, which cost them a fortune.[35] Others disparaged customers for not conducting proper research prior to purchase.[36] Antennas presented a particular challenge. Most customers and even many technical crews understood little about their placement, cabling, precise installation and tuning, or that they needed to be insured for third-party liability.[37]

Israeli consumers paid three times as much for their television sets than their counterparts in Europe, largely because of high customs, taxes, and excessive profit margins.[38] Forty-five different products from twelve different countries competed for the attention of prospective buyers. To promote its product, the Amkor Company invited the public to tour its assembly line in Herzliya. It maintained that because of extensive use of transistors, its sets do not get terribly warm—an advantage in the Israeli climate, that their TV is the only one that comes equipped with a key that turns it off—an early form of parental control, and, finally, that the European company Normanda, whose technology Amkor utilized, was among the first companies to sell its sets in Israel while other manufacturers now vying for the local market surrendered to the threats of the Arab boycott. Again, the geopolitical was interjected into marketing and consumption.[39] Some experts, however, opined that television sets were largely interchangeable. One company advertised that its unit could receive Telstar satellite transmissions as well as color broadcasts and that it displayed a brilliant image on its video-optic screen. These promises were mostly humbug according to the Israel Consumer Council.[40]

Television reconfigured the Israeli living room and dictated new sitting arrangements. It also reorganized the Israeli evening, emptied the streets, and offered a shared experience that was in its initial stage richly social. During the early phase, intermittent broadcasts occupied only several evening hours spread over a few days. Pioneering television owners hosted large gatherings of neighbors and friends. Watching appeared to cement social ties but homemakers complained that they were forced to watch their television from afar as guests occupied the first rows or while endlessly preparing snacks in the kitchen. After a few weeks of intensive hosting an early adopter reportedly hung a sign on her door, "A TV set for sale—five recipes for light refreshments for neighbors and friends are for free."[41]

In Wadi Salib, a poor Haifa neighborhood, a social worker removed a family from the roster of eligible welfare recipients after she discovered that it had just purchased a TV set. She subsequently pontificated to a delegation of neighborhood women how shameful it was to abuse public assistance for such a luxury. The women, however, remained unconvinced. It was not a luxury, said one, you do not understand what television means to a poor family. Since receiving this box, we can keep the husband and the children at home. They don't eat and run out. Neighbors come over. We crack sunflower seeds (a favorite Israeli snack) and eat homemade cakes. We sing together. The husband does not get drunk in the street. You are taking our support, you are taking away our family life, the Sabbath happiness. The welfare allowance was duly restored.[42] A sociological study confirmed that Israelis regarded TV as a medium that brings family members together and deepens their relationship.[43]

As the popularity of watching other Middle Eastern stations diminished and until the advent of cable TV and commercial channels in the early 1990s, Israelis watched a single television station. The fragmentation of the family along different viewing options, familiar in other societies, did not afflict Israeli domestic life. Throughout the next twenty years or so, Israelis would share the uncanny experience of walking in the street during the evening hours amid the flicker of TV screens bouncing in eerie unison off walls, windowpanes, and terraces.

Domestic Space

Another appliance that in a course of a little more than a decade infiltrated almost every household was the electric refrigerator. In 1958, only 34 percent of Israeli families owned electric refrigerators, in 1965 the portion jumped to 77.6 percent, and in 1972 to 92.1 percent. Electric refrigerators became so ubiquitous that the Central Bureau of Statistics ceased to register the number of remaining iceboxes. To fend off criticism about the social gap, the Director General of the Treasury Arnon Gaffney revealed in 1972 that the Welfare Ministry was giving away refrigerators and washing machines to poor families to encourage women to leave their homes and join the workforce.[44]

Refrigerators, washing machines, air conditioners, vacuum cleaners, and similar appliances also incrementally rearranged and defined domestic spaces, separating them from the outside world. One rather extreme example was the way refrigerators appeared to threaten the balance between community and family in kibbutzim. Mini refrigerators, mostly from the brand name Siberia, began entering the humble abodes of kibbutz members in the early 1960s. The tiny Siberia triggered anxiety over the coming demise of collective life since most food was consumed in the kibbutz's communal dining hall. Hakibbutz Ha'artzi's (the most left-leaning among the three kibbutz movements) secretariat sanctioned the mini appliance somewhat reluctantly, warning, "the refrigerator in the comrade's apartment might increase the affinity with the family cell as a unit of consumption and become a centrifugal factor in communal consumption."[45] It therefore recommended taking measures to countervail the refrigerator's fragmenting power. Only a few years later, similar concerns would be voiced about the introduction of TV sets to kibbutzim.

For urban families, refrigeration minimized the distance between the farm field and the family table, requiring less frequent replenishments of perishable goods. Homemakers could go to work ostensibly because they had to spend less time acquiring produce or preparing food. A related technology that exemplified most extremely the capacity of modern refrigeration—and capitalism—to transform spatial and temporal relations was frozen food. The first products were introduced mid-decade. In 1970 a joint venture between Clal Industries and American investors, for which the English oxymoronic moniker "Sunfrost" was selected, brought frozen vegetables to the Israeli dining table under the (borrowed) slogan, "Fresher than Fresh."

An ad for frozen baby carrots underscored the technicity of the product. The seeds were imported by Sunfrost. The firm followed all the stages of the vegetable's growth and ripening. "As all other vegetables that Sunfrost serves you, [the baby carrot] is 'fresher than fresh' due to the innovative deep flash freeze that stops time and keeps the vegetable in the height of its freshness and flavor—until the moment it is served." The new technology allowed the customer to serve fresh vegetables during all days of the week and even out of season, or as another slogan promised, "Today, Tomorrow, and Always Now."[46]

Coke ads also promised to arrest time. In Israel, the company faced a new technical challenge. Its large, one-liter bottles were too tall for the local refrigerators and when laid horizontally they started to leak. Coca-Cola dispatched a team of engineers that designed a new screw-top cap.[47] The company even coined a new Hebrew term for the cap, *shasgor*, a neologism combining "valve" and "sealed/closed." An ad for the family-size bottle, marketed as the "economizing giant," prescribed, "Turn and close! And return the bottle to the refrigerator. The *shasgor* keeps the wonderful taste of the Coca-Cola until the last sip, exactly like the first glass."[48] Once again, time stops.

Refrigeration, the chilling of homes, and washing clothes in a machine rather than by hand (dryers enjoyed a more qualified success—it was hard to compete with the Middle Eastern sun) protected the home from the harsh Israeli climate. These appliances were increasingly deemed indispensable, not luxuries. Air conditioning was first installed in offices and commercial spaces, furthering the divide between manual labor performed outside or in large production spaces and office work. In fact, some employees were reported to have accepted lower wages for the privilege of spending their days in chilled environments.

While refrigeration erased distance, air conditioning separated domestic and commercial environments from the outside weather. While Israelis accepted the need to shed blood and tears, they were increasingly less convinced about sweat. A medico-technological discourse about the health benefits, in fact, the indispensability of cooling (and heating) devices further justified acquiring such appliances as a necessity.[49] A 1968 early summer ad for an Amkor air conditioner urged customers not to wait for the hot days but purchase the appliance immediately. It first features an image of a perspiring young man next to a large sun. Next, the previously sweaty individual crosses his legs, sitting leisurely on a comfortable chair reading a book next to a closed window, blissfully protected from the punishingly hot weather.[50]

Other ads emphasized their products' ability to remove unwanted cooking smells and cigarette smoke.[51] The term "American kitchen," which can be found in real estate ads as early as the late 1940s, gained popularity by the mid-1970s, standing for a well-equipped and spacious kitchen, which is often endowed with an additional counter space or even an "island." In another variant, the American kitchen—as against the Scandinavian kitchen—hides most of its ware in closed-off cupboards and drawers rather than leaving them exposed either hanging or in open shelves.[52]

The telephone was also a technology that worked space in contradictory fashion, obliterating distance but also protecting the family home from unwanted intruders. As long as phones were the privilege of the few, guests often just showed up without prewarning. The slow pace of telephone installation was a source of enormous frustration. State-run phone services prompted many fraught interactions between citizens and government. Numerous complaints were lodged about unfairness and cronyism in the allocations of new phones.

A point of comparison was the situation in the United States, where telephones were reportedly installed by private companies within days or even hours of customers' requests. This miracle of modern capitalism recurred in the testimonies of Israelis living in or visiting the United States. Americans everywhere say, "give me a buzz," an expression uttered by businessmen and youth, by everyone, *Yedioth Ahronoth* daily reported.[53] A record 50,000 phones were installed in 1968, although 30,000 individuals were still waiting for years for their turn. The Yellow Pages (in Hebrew, "Gold Pages") were introduced the following year with the iconic slogan, "Let Your Fingers Walk Instead of You."

Grooming

Keeping food and domestic space cooler, cleaner, dust-free, and more hygienic was accompanied by an avalanche of specialized soaps, antidandruff ointments, hair conditioners, toiletries, disposable diapers, and paper tissues. Hogla, a paperware manufacturer, declared that the "modern home has Hogla products in each room and for every purpose."[54] Ads for beauty products promised supple and spotless skin, often employing images of foreign models. An ad for the acne ointment Adora displays a young woman's face in three different close-up increments, denoting greater degrees of public scrutiny. "Look at Me from Close By," the ad proposes, "I don't have pimples or other blemishes at all."[55] Much like appliances, cosmetic ads featured proprietary, copyrighted terms reprinted in their original English. Thus, Helena Rubinstein's eyeliner ad celebrated the company's "new and exclusive invention: Illumination Automatic Minute Eye Liner," a refillable easy-to-apply product. "Allow your eyes to speak, make them beautiful, large, innocent and open as though in surprise—like men love."[56]

The consumerist shift worked not just to regiment bodies but to sexualize women as well. An ad for heating radiators, for instance, featured a woman holding a component of a baseboard convertor. The title reads, "Central Heating in the American Way." The ad then explains, "These pieces are capable of warming up a whole apartment," playing on the colloquial use of "piece" in Hebrew to signify a young attractive woman.[57] Sexual innuendoes were part of advertisements, especially of cigarettes, much before the 1960s, but now nudity was increasingly visible. A new class of ads offered information and advice about dating and sex. One ad, "Who is the man for you?" featured images of fourteen men and asked women to mark the ideal face, send the coupon in, and allow an IBM 360/50 computer to identify the most suitable partner. "The electronic computer will . . . save you tens of parties and hundreds of dates."[58]

Exemplifying the process of reification, Eros's ads promised no less than "Happiness for Life." The firm distributed sex-aid and hygiene products, peddling its merchandise as scientifically researched and tested to provide healthy sex, diversify marriage life, and overcome failures and weaknesses. "Eros products stabilize and make you a person whose problem has been solved."[59] A year later, "Women Prefer Men" and "Men Prefer Women" ads featured spray deodorants for each gender including a spray for "intimate moments."[60] By 1972, Eros ads turned somewhat more concrete, offering a new and revolutionary massaging device, presented in English simply as "Personal Vibrator."[61]

Advertisements for beauty products typified the new consumerist era. They drew critical attention in 1950s and 1960s France. Roland Barthes analyzed ads for soap powders and detergents in *Mythologies* (1957). In *The Consumer Society: Myths and Structures* (1970) Jean Baudrillard titled a chapter "The Finest Consumer Object: The Body." In this regard, Israel was no different from other rising affluent societies. What is worth noting, however, is the extent to which a subset of advertisements targeted men in a culture in which masculinity had been historically defined either through proximity to the land and physical labor—during the pioneering, Diaspora-rejecting generation—or by the courage, self-sacrifice, and smarts of the Israeli soldier—rather than by a highly groomed or well-shaped body.

One company that marketed toupees for men was known by its slogan, "If No Choice Then Uri Gross."[62] The isometric fitness device Bullworker arrived as well. The ad, largely translated from English, featured the familiar beach scene in which an emaciated man turns attractive after bulking up in practically no time.[63] As importantly, the Bullworker's marketing technique, a mail-in coupon that allows prospective customers to try the machine at home for fourteen days for free, was also imported. In an ad for Lahav shirts, "For the man who understands fashion, Lahav shirt is THE shirt," three young men stand next to a woman who is sitting or kneeling, taking notes from one of the "bosses." The labels of the shirts are in Latin letters, Hawaii, Vancouver, and Dos Carros.[64]

Conventionally, advertisements for food, kitchen appliances, fashion, hygienic and cosmetic products addressed women and so did consumer-affairs columns in the newspapers. Ads for cars, banking, or tools targeted men. Nevertheless, in public discussions the proverbial consumer was often described as male as against the homemaker who was invariably female—and in the press there were occasional references to "the consumer and the homemaker" as though they stood for distinct social archetypes.

Coke: The Meaning of Life

Even before the curvaceous bottle settled in the country, Israelis were cognizant of the association between the dark-colored drink and everything American, including the way Coca-Cola came to signify the soft and not-so-soft power of American imperialism. In the mid-1960s, Tempo Soft Drink Company, a large Israeli bottling concern, sought a Coca-Cola franchise. But the Atlanta-based giant rejected the application, maintaining that the Israeli market had not ripened enough to assure mutual profitability.[65]

Israeli ambassador Abraham Herman did not consider bringing Coke to Israel a priority. Others, however, argued that the unavailability of the global drink might impair attracting other businesses and investments.[66] The Israeli embassy stayed in the background as the effort to pressure Coca-Cola became a cause célèbre for B'nai B'rith's Anti-Defamation League (ADL). An ADL report maintained that an Israeli franchise would be more profitable than any other Middle East Coke outlet. It asserted that "while submitting to the Arab boycott, Coca-Cola assiduously attempted to camouflage its submission as pure nonpolitical, economic decision."[67] The William-Javits amendment to the US Export Control Act passed a year earlier voiced strong opposition to restrictive trade practices or boycotts by foreign countries against friendly nations.

The pressure from Jewish organizations quickly swelled, demonstrating—merely a year before the Six-Day War—their ability to muster support for Israel and the enthusiasm with which they were willing to do so. Earlier in the decade, soda fountains became a locus for civil rights struggles in the South and two years later, Martin Luther King, Jr. would urge followers to boycott Coca-Cola. New York City's Human Rights Commission requested Coca-Cola to explain its decision about Israel. Representative Seymour Halpern demanded to toughen antiboycott legislation in Congress.[68] The company's offices were inundated with hundreds of phone calls, telegrams, and letters from merchants and restaurant owners announcing their intention to stop selling the drink. In New York City the head of the Teamsters' Union ordered members to cease delivering Coca-Cola products to retailers. Jewish organizations asked the company to remove its vending machines from their premises. Nathan's Famous hot dog chain threatened to stop selling Coke entirely.

Coca-Cola staged a defense rejecting the accusations about its complicity with the Arab boycott as "unfair and unfounded."[69] It also attacked Tempo, alleging that three years earlier an Israeli court found it guilty of impinging on Coca-Cola's trademark for marketing its own cola drink in a Coke-like bottle.[70] In a personal note that seemed as yet another iteration of "some of my best friends are Jewish," the chairman of the company, James A. Farley, a former postmaster general and New Deal political strategist, wrote that he is deeply distressed by the allegations since he had spent most of his life in New York City, "a community of diverse nationalities, religions and cultures."[71]

The boycott threat furnished a fine example of consumer activism. *Ma'ariv* underscored that whereas elsewhere Coke is a symbol of the penetration of "American civilization," Israelis must see in Coca-Cola a political entity.[72] The company eventually succumbed but decided not to grant Tempo the franchise.[73] Instead, it revived a 1949 agreement that had never been implemented for marketing Coke in Israel with Abraham Feinberg, a banker, women's apparel industrialist, and a confidant of Democratic presidents, including Lyndon Johnson. Feinberg had been a lobbyist for Israel and, in addition, spearheaded a secret campaign to raise money for the Israeli nuclear project in Dimona. He would become head of the Israel bonds operation in the United States.[74]

Feinberg entered partnership with the president of Coca-Cola in Miami and the Israeli Central Company for Commerce and Investments. Their Bnei Brak plant was initially expected to produce only bottled Coke (no cans), reaching, with time, a volume of seventy-five million bottles a year. It was Coca-Cola's policy that all its plants would be identical to the layout, both external and internal, of the company's main factory. The bottling plant was fully automatic and included a water purifying system.[75] Time and again visitors would comment upon its spotless appearance. Every bottle, they were told, underwent a thorough washing, boiling, and chemical treatment, after which it was examined by an electronic eye. The tiniest speckle of dirt resulted in disqualification even if the offending particle resided on the outside of the bottle.[76]

How to market a famous yet new and foreign drink? One of the first ads presented a large Coke bottle next to a *tembel* hat, the round, rimless head covering that had become synonymous with Israel. "Coca-Cola in Israel," it declared, mixing three categories, "A beloved guest that recently made *aliya* and became a permanent resident."[77] Coke ads would also link the beverage with different Jewish holidays. In the following years, ads would feature a bottle of Coke next to the four species in a family meal taken in a Sukkah, side by side with a cheesecake and blintzes for Shavuot, and in the hand of a circus clown toasting Happy Purim.[78] At the same time, the slogan "Better with Coca-Cola" was employed to celebrate Coke as an international drink. Ads reiterated the slogan in French, Italian, and German.[79]

Coke was promoted in accordance with patriotic sensibilities. A month after the opening of the Bnei Brak plant, and as Independence Day was looming, the company cooperated with the Soldier Aid Association to distribute thousands of bottles to wounded soldiers in Hadassah Hospital in Jerusalem, as well as to soldiers participating in the Independence Day parade.[80] The firm continued to invest in sponsoring public drives, for instance, by donating thousands of colorful posters to decorate IDF barracks.[81] In collaboration with the newly established Council for a Beautiful Israel (chapter 2), it funded a traveling flower show visited by about 20,000 elementary school children.[82]

It was an Israeli beer, Maccabee, not Coke, that employed American symbols in an ad that featured the Statue of Liberty—with the New York City skyline in the background—holding a bottle of Maccabee and raising a glass of beer. It brazenly proposes that the beer is a gift of love from Israel to America and underscores that the beverage passed all the rigorous tests of "importation authorities in the United States." This ad campaign furnished another example of how export could fashion domestic consumption. It determined that Israeli beer connoisseurs would also be able to enjoy Maccabee, "The Israeli Beer for Representation and Export."[83]

Coca-Cola's strategy was admired as a paradigm of the primacy of advertisement in marketing. In 1970, the advertising company Dahaf came up with a new slogan for Coke, "Ta'am Hahaim," which could be translated to "the taste (or flavor) of life" but also to "the meaning of (or the reason for) life." Dahaf won an international prize for its Coke poster campaign.[84] After the initial excitement, one rival forecast that the demand for the American beverage would subside, but the new plant found that quenching the Israeli thirst for Coke is no small matter and immediately considered doubling its capacity.[85] The "cold war" over the fate of cold drinks in Israel turned out to benefit all warring parties. Tempo, in fact, seemed to capitalize on the newcomer. Since its introduction the demand for its own cola increased fivefold.[86] Other brands also entered the fray, marketing their own cola versions.

Spectacle

The early years of the 1960s constituted a watershed in the history of advertisement in Israel. A major turning point was the advent of the government's Voice of Israel Reshet Beit (Station B) radio station, often referred to as Hagal Hakal (the easy listening station), which for the first time featured commercial jingles. Radio jingles left an imprint on Israeli musical culture; something of the cadence, rhythm, and bounce of broadcast commercials reverberated in popular songs, if sometimes by way of parody. They participated in the making of a new Israeli pop.

In 1961, fifteen major advertising firms banded together to establish the Israeli Advertisers Association. Other developments included the gradual replacement of illustrations with photography and greater emphasis on electronic, cinematic, and signage media. The post-'67 period ushered in another leap in both the resources available and the professional disposition of the industry. Between 1968 and 1973 the annual expenditure for advertisement more than doubled, from sixteen to forty-one million dollars.[87] The number of ads in dailies rose by 50 percent and in weekly supplements or magazines it doubled. Between 1965 and 1972 ads for hygiene and cosmetics tripled. Ads for home appliances, television sets, and radios went up by a factor of 2.5.[88]

Beyond extolling the virtues of specific products, some campaigns, such as Coca-Cola's, vied to build an overall image for a company. Copywriters grew more attentive to the consumer, her needs and world view, increasingly focusing on individuals rather than the Israeli *we*. The example given was the transition from, "The people decide: Elite coffee!" to "I feel good drinking Elite coffee."[89] Commodities now connoted prestige: the new apartments were built in "exclusive areas," the watch was for an individual who is "someone," and the new restaurant served the "who's who."[90] Advertising was still largely print based. However, movie theaters screened commercials and billboards received more sophisticated treatment.

In addition to advertisements, a primary tactic employed to seduce the purchasing public was sweepstakes and the massive allocation of promotional gifts. Keychains are arguably the most trivial trinkets dispensed for publicity. It was a fad imported from Europe, especially France.[91] In mid-1960s Israel, they furnished the fulcrum for an entire subculture of collection and exchange. Businesses, including small outfits, law firms, accountants, workshops, and construction concerns, even public agencies, distributed dedicated keychains to their clientele. Some were elementary, others rather intricate, featuring miniaturized renditions of their ware: tires, detergents, toothpaste tubes, wheels of cheese, soft drinks—sometimes ensconced in a transparent blob of Perspex, like a fly caught in a drop of primordial amber.

Young collectors besieged stores and offices rumored to be circulating such gifts, amassing huge collections, sometimes hung proudly on the walls of their modest bedrooms. Lefebvre regarded the appetite for keychains an example of "sign-consumption," arguing that they were symbols of property, and further cast their abrupt popularity as an example of cyclical waves of consumerist craze.[92] Israeli youngsters, in general, developed a strong proclivity for collecting, whether stamps, marbles, bottle tops, and trading cards sold with chewing gum or in a dedicated pack. These were immensely popular and carried educational pretense, as their subject matter encompassed geography, science, and history. Another example of how the commercial imaginary colonized the Israeli mind was the weekly contest in the *Haaretz* newspaper challenging readers to link an assortment of abstract commercial logos with the domestic and global companies they represented.[93]

Lotteries and sweepstakes offered lavish prizes. In 1972, the Amkor Company promoted its television sets through a special half price ("half-for-free") campaign. Purchasers received back half of the appliance's cost if they happened to purchase it during two "lucky days" over a stretch of four months. The dates were selected in a lottery.[94] In the spring of 1968, Hashaked, the almond-growers marketing association, implanted fifty fourteen-karat almond-shaped gold nuggets in actual almond shells and dispersed them among almond packages sold in stores. It urged the public to buy almonds as a treat or a gift for the coming holiday and search for the precious gold almonds.⁹⁵ Luckily, there were no reports of customers cracking their teeth trying to bite into a gold nugget.

A third campaign, this time Coca-Cola's, promised more than 29,000 prizes, ranging from posters designed by Israeli artists to state-issued bonds. Participants had to look for specific words printed on the lead of the internal spiral of the new cap, *shasgor*, then send in three leads that together spelled, "Coca-Cola's Economizing Giant."⁹⁶ Tempo beverage company invited customers to scratch under the film of cork at the bottom of each cap to dis-

FIGURE 1.2 Marketed as "The Economizing Giant," the family-size Coca-Cola bottle was equipped with a new cap designed by the company's engineers. Previously, the large bottle leaked when it was laid on its side in the smaller Israeli refrigerators.

cover letters that could be assembled into two different promotional slogans. The first-prize winner was allotted three minutes to scoop out as many fifty penny coins (*agorot*) as she could from a large pile of coins. The ad for the campaign bluntly challenged, "Catch as Many as You Can!"[97]

Raffles and sweepstakes were not an Israeli invention, but by the end of the 1960s they seemed to dominate advertisement culture and drew criticism as well as government attention. One study cast doubt about their efficacy but they seemed unstoppable.[98] Even the bus cooperative Egged, which had a monopoly over public transportation for much of the country, announced a raffle, a prize-carrying quiz, and a championship for the most frequent traveler, all to increase the number of passengers on its Tel Aviv–Jerusalem line.[99] One margarine producer circulated with its merchandize a facsimile of half banknotes promising that when two halves are matched the fake note could be replaced with a real one. A report from one Tel Aviv neighborhood described an increased demand for margarine and hectic bartering among customers.[100] Alas, it was rather clear that the two halves were not equally circulated.

Promotional trinkets as well as sweepstake prizes are tantamount to commodities disguised as gifts whose function beyond sheer publicity is to elicit customer loyalty as a reward for material generosity. Sweepstakes infuse market exchanges with an element of play and excitement, linking one commodity to another in chains that form the dream life of the consumerist everyday. Margarine and chocolate and other daily products that can be obtained at the corner grocery store unlocked a portal to a much grander realm of luxurious commodities. The consumer did not know what she was buying, a soup powder or a pair of bicycles, a Tempo bottle or a pile of coins, margarine or a flight ticket to Europe, a chocolate bar, or a week in a hotel. One psychologist said at the time that the consumer buys *luck* rather than what he needs.[101] The Consumer Council, which fought against the sweepstakes mania, argued that they mushroomed because of the scarcity born of the recession. The allocation of prize apartments, bicycles, tape recorders, keychains, or even gold nuggets took place in a society in which monetary or exchange value was determined more by the arbitrariness of the bureaucracy than the whims of the free market.

These publicity techniques involved greater level of participation than mere purchase, even if in the simple form of performing a modest task and mailing in an entry. To circumvent the law that granted the state exclusivity over games of chance, sweepstakes were often disguised as quizzes, supposedly requiring customers to demonstrate knowledge or skill, by, for instance, completing a commercial slogan.[102] Major philanthropic associations like the Red Star of David (the Israeli version of the Red Cross) and the Soldier Aid Association ran their own raffles. Lotteries were already promoted by the state monopoly, Mifal Hapais. In 1967, the Sport Betting Board launched the immensely popular *Toto* soccer betting.

Humorist Yonatan Geffen lampooned the ubiquity of marketing antics, including the obsessive allocation of promotional gifts and the ever-multiplying beauty queen pageants whose winning contestants served as mascots for different commercial enterprises. Geffen describes an imaginary trip to a nondescript gas station wearing his best fineries just for the honor of meeting the "Water Queen" who was scheduled to distribute a personal gift to each customer. Spurting famous jingles and commercial slogans, the queen was the veteran of endless promotional campaigns. She had already given away Coca-Cola's "economizing giant" with the famous *shasgor*. That morning she had a photo shoot for some pantyhose and in the evening was scheduled for a nude with an ice cream pop. The queen's honor is not undermined by this naked commercialism. It's only a phase, she explains. In the future she plans to travel to America and give lectures on behalf of Israel Bonds.[103]

Having beauty queens selling bonds was not such a farfetched idea. Since the inception of the pageant—also known as Miss Israel—in 1950, Israeli beauty queens were often dispatched to represent Israel in the United States. In fact, several of them eventually settled in America. Many faux queens were crowned in late 1960s Israel. Women's magazines ran Queen for a Day competitions. For twenty-four hours the chosen royal was pampered, attired, wined and dined, and hobnobbed with important people. Coca-Cola, on the other hand, sponsored a competition for Israel's Prince and Princess. The young aristocrats visited the plant in Bnei Brak and their families received free Coke bottles for the entire year. One princess explained, "Until now I knew how to get Coca-Cola out of the bottle, now I know how they put it in."[104]

"Beautiful People"

Youth and women's magazines, the gossip industry, hit parades split between foreign and Hebrew popular music, as well as films and television broadcasts all served as infrastructure for an emerging celebrity culture. The mid-'60s success of the Hayarkon Bridge Trio inspired one critic to label the three singers as the first Israeli stars. Apparently, they were the first to have received heaps of letters from teenagers, the first to dodge throngs of fans, and, in his view, among the first truly professional performers.[105]

Launched in 1969, *Lahiton* was a weekly magazine devoted to popular culture. It soon eclipsed and later merged with the veteran *Olam Hakolno'a* (Cinema World), which featured reports from Hollywood since 1951.[106] Inspired by European magazines such as the British *Melody Maker*, the publication provided readers with streams of information and gossip about popular music and entertainment. It made news, staging beauty pageants for youth and bringing to Israel TV and other celebrities such as Arnold Schwarzenegger, David Saul, Paul Michael Glazer (of the TV show *Starsky and Hutch*), and Roger Moore. Moore toured the country, visited the Western Wall, met with Defense Minister Moshe Dayan, and declared himself an enthusiastic Zionist. *Lahiton* also printed and circulated posters of pop music idols, both local and foreign, and even devised an original technique to assemble enormously large posters made of four or six smaller tiles.[107]

The songwriter Naomi Shemer mocked the advent of celebrity culture in her song titled in English, "Beautiful People." It describes a parade of enormously successful individuals frequenting Shemer's living room on Friday night after the children are tucked in. Only high-class people arrive: a top-tier painter, a top singer, a top tailor, a top model, a top thief, a top director general, and a top philosopher. She even once hosted a top IDF chief of staff with all the generals. All the glamorous people comingle with great amity. The scene, an after-dinner Friday night social gathering, is familiar to Israelis. But despite describing herself offering refreshments, Shemer implies that this parade of personalities might be entering her salon through the television screen.

One testament to the newfound appetite for celebrating individual personalities was the growing popularity of interviews either in the media or as a form of public entertainment in evening events dedicated to long interviews, sometimes interspersed with music, skits, and other performances. Interviewers such as the provocative humorist and author Dahn Ben-Amotz and the radio personality Shmuel Shai were themselves celebrities. In 1968, the producer Ya'akov Agmon launched his hour-long single interview show Personal Questions on the IDF radio station Galei Tzahal. It would become a fixture of midday Saturday radio for decades.

Nathan Alterman contended that these shows thrived because of the demise of the political forums where the heady ideological battles of old were pitched. He complained that the major problems the country was facing had become enticing entertainment in air-conditioned spaces, squeezed between the intermission's concession stand and the music band segment. "The big questions . . . are now like lions perched on stools in the circus, or tigers jumping through hoops that the interviewers place in front of them."[108]

The trend culminated in a short-lived project titled "Kaleidoscope 1968," an initiative to move the interview-based format from the intimacy of small venues to the largest performance halls in the country. A combination variety show, newspaper weekend supplement, and broadcast news magazine, Kaleidoscope purported to introduce a new type of publicness and audience participation on a massive, Cecil B. DeMille scale.[109] It coincided with the advent of television, a few of its first iterations were televised, and TV personalities participated as hosts. It offered an ambitious current affairs programming and discussions about new books, new records, and new bands. At the heart of the show was a lengthy interview with an individual pronounced "Person of the Month."

The Great Dissonance

The economic boom coincided with a period of national self-confidence qualified by pressures emanating from ongoing military conflicts, whether the War of Attrition along the Suez Canal, the repeated skirmishes with guerrillas attempting to cross the Jordan River, and terror attacks in Israel and abroad. These were years of intense international exchanges, diplomatic initiatives, shifting alliances, including a French embargo on arms sales to Israel and a growing Soviet presence in the Middle East. The geopolitical took an unprecedented command of daily routines, manifested in the public's enormous attentiveness to the hourly news bulletins over the radio. The sound of the morse code–like beeping seconds before the news broadcast had the absolute power of imposing abrupt and complete silence on small social gatherings as well as large crowds. The news briefs as well as the morning, noon, and evening radio current affairs magazines and later the televised 9 p.m. nightly news mapped the Israeli day.

Israelis thus had to contend with a distinct everyday texture, the everyday of national and international events and the everyday of civilian life, increasingly dominated by consumer culture. One corner of the Israeli public arena in which the two occasionally collided was Hagal Hakal broadcasts. The station's commercial jingles exuded cheerfulness and portrayed a happy and homogenous people with a lust for shopping. However, occasionally, the mundane realities of life in Israel as expressed in news bulletins and in radio commercials were at odds.

A specific example involves the July 19, 1969, IDF raid on the Egyptian military radar and electronic installations on the tiny but heavily fortified Green Island (Al Jazeera al Khadraa) in the Gulf of Suez. The Green Island operation was declared a military success, but six Israeli soldiers were killed and others were wounded. The names of the fallen soldiers were announced during the noon news magazine, which ordinarily combined reports with popular music and commercials. The musical editor already decided to swap the lineup of pop music with more subdued Hebrew songs. For the listening public, this signaled that grim news were about to be broadcast. But the commercial jingles could not be altered. The result was a hybrid of joyous, laughter-field commercials and melancholic songs. As the public was quite anxious about the operation, this strange cocktail of contending moods had an unwelcome impact.[110]

How did Israelis accommodate consumer life and the state of armed conflict, each with its own capacity to determine value and forge identity? How were the two fused or stitched together? The foundation of the Israeli consumer society was laid before the Six-Day War, during a rather calm period in the history of the country. By June 1967, it already defined the *normal* and therefore also designated what had to be restored. Written in the immediate aftermath of the war, David Atid's song "Hayiti na'ar" (I was a youth; music,

Yair Rosenblum) depicts city life returning to its everyday routines in lines such as, "At night, once again, electricity shines brightly in the streets / The lit signs sell falafel and hopes / On pavements, between tables, in fairs, the mini [skirt] returns to overtake the uniforms." At the same time the song implies that the normal is no longer attainable as the young soldier returning from battle is profoundly transformed, his gait heavy and his face sealed, insinuating a post-traumatic crisis.

The 1967 war itself might have engendered a wish for a more self-satisfying way of life. Author Amos Kenan testified that after returning home from the war, he began contemplating what was exciting about life, a reflection that inspired his *Book of Pleasures*. His formulas, however, rejected petty consumerism—money making, social climbing, buying a car, mistaking the car for sex appeal, leaving for the suburbs so the car would have a space to park—in favor of a more refined "good life," comprised of sophisticated cooking and sexual adventures.[111]

For some commentators, the routines of civilian life had an intrinsic value in a time of war. The general secretary of the Histadrut Yitzhak Ben Aharon was roiled by the question of how labor strikes could take place while soldiers are killed on the Suez and pilots risk their lives. Ben Aharon was not known for mincing words. Separating the blood-saturated front from the parasitical home front, he averred, is a Nazi trope. "This is the foundation for the fascistization of life. . . . Pilots fight so we could live our full lives. This includes striking and going to a discotheque and taking a vacation abroad and making money. . . . This is part of proper life."[112] Another variant of the argument deemed indulgence permissible as a refuge from and consolation for the material risks and the emotional toll of ongoing warfare.

In contrast, Dahn Ben-Amotz's controversial protest novel *I Don't Give a Damn* (1973) proposes that war and military service *are* the escape Israeli men crave to circumvent the drudgery of daily life. The novel's protagonist Rafi Levine is a wounded paratrooper who remains paralyzed from the waist down. His brother Eli, a co-owner of a plastic plant, represents the Israeli bourgeoisie. In a time of peace, Eli is preoccupied with taxes, strikes, cost-of-living-raises, the dollar exchange rate; he does not stop whining from morning to evening. But war solves all his problems, the narrator (Rafi) determines.

Suddenly, he forgets the crazed running after money-money-money. Forgets his wife, the heartburn and all the petty problems and in his private car—which he washes and licks every Saturday—he shows up at his unit even before he was called for service. . . . He becomes part of the dream that is greater than his God-dammed Frigidaire with the automatic freezing chamber and two air directions. Suddenly because of war he finds meaning again in his lousy life. It's a fact. We are a great and wonderful people at war but at peace we are ass worth.[113]

Arguably, the book's most poignant criticism does not target consumerist materialism but how the bureaucratic, actuarial state contributes to the normalization of personal sacrifice by translating loss into an inventory of precisely measured benefits. Thus, upon leaving the hospital, a paraplegic war veteran is entitled to a car, an Israeli-made seven-and-a-half-cubic-feet electric refrigerator, an Israeli-made washing machine to be replaced every six years, an air conditioner, a thousand-lira (the Israeli pound, the country's currency before 1980) allowance for furniture, etc.[114] Ben-Amotz drew this information from an official government document.

Also bear in mind that the Israeli state had elaborated techniques to dissolve the boundaries between civilian and military life through, among other means, what sociologist Baruch Kimmerling labeled the "Military-Cultural complex."[115] One example was the immense success of military singing troupes, reaching the zenith of popularity after the 1967 war. In those years, military bands gravitated toward commercial, celebrity-soaked pop culture, serving as the launching pads for teen idols such as Sassi Keshet, Shula Chen, and Yigal Bashan. Military troupes also evidenced the outsized egos of generals who aggrandized themselves by cultivating singing groups adjacent to their command.

Minister Dayan epitomized the fusion of military prowess and celebrity fame. Subjected to intense hero worship, Dayan's figure propped up an entire souvenir cottage industry, posters, greeting cards, keychains, commemorative plates, dolls, and other gadgets.[116] The iconic eye patch helped perpetuate Dayan's likeness as a commoditized metonym for Israel at home and abroad. For the record cover of the late 1967 American comedy album, *The Yiddish Are Coming! The Yiddish Are Coming!* the American voice actors—men and women alike—all sport a patch on their left eye. More recently, viewers of the sixth season of the AMC drama *Madmen* (2013) were treated to a glimpse of a minor character's (Stan Rizzo) bedroom, where above the bed hangs an enormous poster of the grinning Dayan.[117]

The culture sutured militarism and consumerism. One ad for the public drive to fund the Phantom jet deal (see chapter 4) features in the far background a crude, crayon-like illustration of the Phantom jet with its recognizable wing structure, and a single line that stands for a tarmac. In the foreground is a large image of a smiling pilot wearing his full gear and walking toward the viewer. The ad demands, "Give Him a Phantom." The

FIGURE 1.3 "Give Him a Phantom." An ad for the public drive to fund the purchase of the military jet (1969). It states, "Your part [of the Phantom] is the determinant one."

lone pilot marching toward the reader is evocative of the iconic figure of the Marlboro Man, spelling resolution, individuality, and masculinity. The little airplane in the back substitutes for the horse.[118] The title is reminiscent of a famous slogan for the Israeli beer Goldstar, first launched in 1966, "Give the Man a Goldstar!"

At the turn of the 1970s, new constituencies of consumers came into being. In a series of reports under the title "The Soldier as a Consumer" journalist Nahum Barnea surveyed IDF services such as food, entertainment, newspapers, radio and television broadcasts, and clothing. The IDF had recently discovered the refrigerator, he writes. Cheese, milk, and buttermilk arrived at the front. Soldiers enjoyed drinking cold chocolate milk from newly designed polythene bags. They reportedly loved steaks, hamburgers, hummus, and pickles. The IDF therefore introduced Wimpy hamburgers, which were exceedingly popular. Servicemen could also buy a steak at the commissary. The IDF was then considering frozen food. The colonel in charge of logistics supply told the reporter that his officers surveyed what food soldiers prefer by, among other means, peeping into the trash bins next to military kitchens to find out what was discarded and thrown away.[119]

The emerging consumer society and the exigencies of the military conflict were rendered more compatible as the latter grew repetitious and routinized, another form of the everyday: military skirmishes, terror acts, and diplomatic maneuvers that led nowhere—all came in endless cycles, drew great awareness but constituted familiar patterns that to some degree served as blinders, arguably preventing Israelis from properly recognizing their geopolitical condition. It took the perspective of later decades to understand that the War of Attrition was indeed a war not just by name, rather than a long string of disparate operations.[120]

The Occupation and the Standard of Living

In the first years after the June 1967 war, the promise of a better standard of living for the inhabitants of the West Bank and Gaza Strip was highlighted to demonstrate the supposedly benign nature of the occupation. In a May 1969 interview for the French weekly *L'Express*, Dayan maintained that the

Israeli government treats the Palestinians in the occupied territories as any government treats its own citizens. "We are willing to share with them our standard of living and to treat them as equals. . . . We do not relate to them as occupation forces that are only entrusted with maintaining law and order, but the way government handles its citizens. In my view they are our citizens as the residents of Tel Aviv." If a Palestinian abides by the law and does not engage in terrorist activities, he should enjoy the services and high level of prosperity Israelis do.[121]

It was Dayan's decision to allow residents of the occupied territories to seek employment in Israel. It dovetailed with his policy to grant Palestinians a measure of autonomy in running their daily affairs, which included retaining municipal leadership, even local elections and civil society organizations, as well as maintaining commercial ties with Jordan. This approach is attributed to Dayan's visit to Vietnam in 1966, from which he returned strongly critical of the American presence in the Vietnamese hinterland. He considered the effort to Americanize Vietnamese life by imposing American culture and methods of organization on the indigenous population to be patronizing and ultimately futile.[122]

The "citizenship" that Dayan assigned to the Palestinians was solely based on participation in the market of services and goods. More than half a century later, this inferior kind of citizenship is what the Israeli Right is currently envisaging for the Palestinians in the West Bank. It is now often peddled under the rubric of "economic peace," promoted by Prime Minister Benjamin Netanyahu among others.[123] Dayan maintained that the 15,000 Palestinians working in Israel at the time—there would be 55,000 by 1973[124]—receive the same wages as Israelis but could purchase much more than Israelis with the money they earned. The standard of living in the occupied territories indeed rose significantly but the Palestinians were employed in menial labor positions and often earned much less than Israeli workers, especially when hired without formal documentation.[125]

Dayan decried as false the accusation that the motivation behind employing Palestinians was their exploitation. He argued that lifting Gaza residents from abject poverty—and allowing them to work in Israel so they would have enough money for food, clothing, health, education, and housing—was "a social deed" while Israel was taking a major security risk. Under Egyptian rule they were starving. Telling them to fend for themselves would only lead to hunger and atrophy.[126]

The employment of Palestinians from the occupied territories continued to be a point of contention within the ruling party. Minister Sapir had strong reservations about "economic integration."[127] Prime Minister Golda Meir found "shocking" the prospect of Arabs providing unskilled labor while Jews exclusively assume white collar positions.[128] Foreign Affairs Minister Abba Eban warned that having Arab laborers come to Israeli towns during daytime and then forced to return to their enclaves at night replicated apartheid conditions in South Africa. While Dayan repeatedly insisted that Israel should not behave as a colonial ruler, Eban would write in his memoirs that much like British colonial governors Dayan had a genuine affection for the ordinary peasant and farmer but aversion toward urban intellectuals and their aspiration for national freedom, believing that "if the Palestinians were given the prospect of minimal economic advancement, they would lose the taste for flags, honor, pride, and independence."[129]

The ties between consumer culture and systems of domination are manifold. In the 1960s different public organizations vied to inculcate norms of public cleanliness in Israel (chapter 2). Palestinians living in the occupied territories and ostensibly left to run their own municipal affairs were not subjected to such campaigns. In general, however, the Western discourse of hygiene and cleanliness is often predicated on mechanisms of exclusion that mold perceptions of class and race at home and colonial encounters abroad. The playwright Hanoch Levin captured this principle in his 1970 satirical revue, *Malkat ambatya* (*Bathtub Queen* or *Shampoo Queen*), a scathing assault on the increased militarism and stifling conformity of the era. A cabaret of skits and songs, the show was staged at the height of the War of Attrition and drew a torrent of hostile responses. It was shot down after only sixteen performances and remains to this day one of the most daring acts of artistic protest in the country's history. No other theatrical piece agitated Israeli society so much.[130]

In the *Bathtub Queen*'s eponymous skit, Levin equates Israel with a nuclear family that occupies a bathroom indefinitely so a cousin, Yekutieli (a stand-in for the Palestinians), would not be able to use the facility. First, the family refuses to leave hot water for him. Then they expel him. The mother (likely representing Golda Meir) excommunicates the cousin for a minor infraction—he did not wipe the floor with a rag after he was done with the shower. She states, "If we want to prevent Yekutieli's infiltration into the bathtub, we must shower in sequence and incessantly." The family proceeds to conquer the toilet. The son who becomes a plumber proudly declares, "The toilet is in our hands," echoing the iconic line, "the Temple Mount is in our hands," communicated by an ecstatic officer over the military wireless on June 7, 1967.

Levin is arguably working here along the grain of the epithet, "dirty Arab." The mother remarks, "It's a pleasure to see. We are all fresh and pink and only Yekutieli is dirty. What is the ambition of a clean person? To take a photo next to a dirty person, this is the foundation of the composition." The cousin threatens: "Wait until I will throw you to the gutter! You will flow to the sea but not with Helen Curtis." The wife is crowned a queen while she occupies the toilet seat close to eighteen hours a day from atop of which she preaches peace. She ultimately establishes the Greater Bathtub Kingdom, an obvious satire of the annexationist Greater Israel Movement.

Conclusion

This chapter documented the content and reach of the consumerist transformation in 1960s Israel, the occupation of homes and minds with consumer goods as well as the elaboration of an entire cultural edifice conducive to modern consumerism. Material objects and the standard of living discourse reshaped bodies, families, and the nation. The discussion then addressed the tension between the consumer everyday and the state of war and occupation. Alternatively, the two modalities of the quotidian were rendered coextensive, supporting and enhancing each other. One thread running throughout the new consumerist order was the effort made to research and manipulate patterns of consumption. Shoppers, spectators of cultural extravaganzas such as Kaleidoscope, or even soldiers were now studied and surveyed as consumers and potential providers of *feedback* that as we shall see (chapter 3) was in effect a vehicle for the cybernetization of life and control.

TWO

Keeping Up with the Cohens

"Every doll is a wish, a dream, and in Israel the dream is American," wrote commentator Ruth Bondi. The wish of the Israeli girl in 1972, especially upper-class urban girls, was to be gifted a Barbie doll with a complete wardrobe. Bondi noticed disparagingly that Barbie did not share the attributes of traditional dolls. It was not soft and pleasant to hold in one's arms as an object of consolation for moments of sadness or as a remedy for the loneliness of scary nights. Instead, fronting endless accessories, Barbie is "a true mirror of a woman in consumer society," a beauty icon the West thrusted upon the rest of the world.[1]

One indication that Israel was indeed becoming an affluent society was that forms, venues, and articles of consumption fueled endless discussions, debates, and criticism.[2] Bondi's commentary conveyed typical apprehensions about the onslaught of American and other foreign commodities, the ideas that undergirded them, and the ideological webs within which they are ensconced, in this case about gender, childhood, and acquisition of goods. Barbie was a thing that *owned* things. The great advance in the Israeli standard of living was a source of pride. It evidenced the ostensible progress the country achieved and its affinity with the Western world. Nevertheless, the rapid and unequal increase of private consumption outpaced government intentions and prompted official concerns, harsh condemnations, and, occasionally, ominous prophesies. Private expenditure was blamed for the mid-1960s recession. In a February 1966 address, Levi Eshkol inveighed against "a frenzy of grab and eat, grab and drink [in which] each social group large and small has tried to grab more in order to sprint faster in the standard of living race."[3]

The consumerist tidal wave in the wake of the Six-Day War provoked additional ire. Government officials and pundits warned about impending economic disaster, collapse of values, unbridled materialism, or even the imminent disintegration of Israeli society. Establishing chains of equivalences, commentators linked the selfishness of runaway accumulation of luxury goods with other behaviors labeled antisocial, especially wild strikes and scandalous cases of corruption that rattled Israeli society. A perception took hold that alongside the consumerist tilt—and the influx of Palestinian workers—labor ceased to be a cherished value and Israelis were in pursuit of "easy money." The discovery of the social gap and the rise of the Black Panthers fueled debates over inequality. One product of the critique of Israeli consumerism were the incessant attempts to distinguish and police the lines separating legitimate and excessive consumption.

At the crucible of the Israeli consumerist age, the Israeli-cum-consumer found himself in a crossfire. On the one hand, Israelis were hailed by an increasingly sophisticated advertising industry promising convenience, satisfaction, and pleasure, including sexual pleasure. On the other, they were subjected to disciplining efforts leveled at their spending habits, whether to inculcate good taste, to accommodate urgent national needs—the always-fragile balance of payments or the ever-depleting foreign currency reserves—or out of solidarity with the soldiers fighting on the Suez Canal. These were not merely words. The government unleashed the wrath of fiscal measures—taxes, customs, mandatory bonds, devaluations, and even threats of another recession—to curtail private expenditure or to mitigate its effects.

A parallel, ostensibly gentler and kinder endeavor was underway to promote models of good consumer behavior and entrench consumerism as a means to empower citizens and bring stability, rationality, and courtesy to everyday market exchanges. On the road to minting liberal subjects, this specific discourse was a conduit for thinking in terms of *rights* and, as importantly, it opened a new arena for social activism.⁴ In addition, the state launched a campaign to instruct new immigrants, especially from North Africa and the Middle East, now living in "development towns," in maintaining and beautifying their homes and immediate surroundings. It engaged in a civilizing mission, a project of interior colonization, if you will, instilling Western norms through domestic and community life.

This chapter underscores the diverse ways in which *positive* consumerism was conceived of as a mode of participatory citizenship—juxtaposed to intemperate consumption, deemed as a type of negative countercitizenship. It focuses first on public concerns about rampant private spending, contemporaneous efforts to explain what propelled the Israeli consumer, and the bleak, apocalyptic prophesies regarding unstoppable consumption and the future of Israeli society. Discussion then turns to a few organizations established to rationalize and refine consumer behavior, namely the Israel Consumer Council, the Association for Better Housing, and the Council for a Beautiful Israel. As American goods and forms of publicity entered and reworked Israeli life, so did American-born ideologies and techniques elaborated to contain and counterbalance market forces. Lastly, the chapter turns to criticism about "commercialism" targeting American and American-inspired popular culture, especially television and radio programming.

Many efforts to restrain and mold consumption were ultimately proven ineffective. Unlike the French case, where American imports faced strong resistance, Israeli consumerism did not have to contend with long-held traditions—with the exception of the egalitarian commitments retained by members of the aging leadership of the labor movement whose ideological clout was rapidly declining. While some critics shared the European highbrow disdain toward American imports, there were otherwise no powerfully entrenched elites determined to combat the Coca-Colonization of centuries-old sensibilities and customs, no rural society and ancient towns turned upside down by the convulsive forces of free market consumerism, except for Arab communities that were largely left behind in the clamor to consume, and no robust cadre of intellectuals envisioning the possibility of an anticapitalistic uprising. No 1968. Despite its religious, indeed, messianic underpinning, which has become more pronounced after 1967, Zionism always gravitated toward the *modern*, now epitomized by American culture.

While it is not the purpose of this chapter to sanction intemperate consumption or to rescue the Israeli consumer from his many detractors, hostility to mass consumption should also be critically examined. For instance, allegations about selfishness or excessive indulgence were sometimes hurled, as in the case of labor strikes, to dismiss ostensibly legitimate claims of structural inequalities. Other criticisms occasionally manifested social hierarchies, as in the case of elites' wish to assert their cultural priorities, for instance, the disparagement of the nouveau riche or the apprehension of Mizrahi Jews' penchant for spending money on lavish wedding celebrations.[5] The oft-expressed contempt for contractors who made fortunes building the line of fortification along the Suez Canal obscured from view the fact that the entire Jewish population of Israel profited economically from the war and the occupation.

Dire Prophesies

At the turn of the 1970s, pundits and public figures, academics and state officials purveyed harrowing predictions about the dangers lurking on the road to unchecked consumption. Many such prophecies moved beyond the confines of economics to depict a moral crisis or to tie the coming financial calamity to other ostensibly disintegrative forces. Professor of law and political science Benjamin Aktzin, a conservative, labeled Israeli society "a fool's paradise." He saw selfishness everywhere, from affluent north Tel Aviv to the poor Hatikva neighborhood, from company managers to the cleaning staff, from the fortresses of the private market to the Hashomer Hatzair kibbutzim, everybody was vying for a higher standard of living. This ambition propels the demand for more profits, higher wages, foreign goods, and pleasure trips abroad—which all, in their turn, drive prices higher and trigger the vicious cycle of additional demands. Nothing helps. They all know this might destroy the economy, the country, and its people, but they embrace their material comfort as the essence of their lives. As fools they race on the path assuredly leading straight to the abyss.[6]

Aktzin warned against social dissolution. It was not merely that he refused to differentiate between the haves and have-nots—bundling all together—he also associated the consumerist race with other non-normative behavior: a rise in criminality and violence, increased carnage on the roads aggravated by wild driving, mimicry of foreign culture that manifests in the surging use of drugs, *pantherism* (see chapter 5), and even the soaring fanaticism of the ultra-Orthodox. Ultimately, he found the moment opportune to blame social collapse on the political Left, those who during war and international struggle called for returning the territories occupied in June 1967 or for admitting masses of Arab refugees to Israel, thus questioning the right of the country to exist.[7]

On the Left, Aryeh "Lova" Eliav similarly cautioned that the frantic race for an elevated standard of living might become a "philosophy of life." Israel was reveling in the external signs of a society of plenty but concurrently suffered from its worst predicaments. "The new spirit that afflicted segments of Israeli society is of disavowal of and blunt disregard for the fundamental and original values of Zionism in general and of humanist-socialism in particular." Eliav tied the crude materialist trend with the Right's appetite for maintaining Israel's hold on the occupied territories to the very last square centimeter, rejecting any possibility of compromise and depriving Arabs of their rights. The result must be emptiness, cynicism, and turning away from the best Jewish and humanist values of Zionism. "Economic efficiency, technological development, consumption and even abundance, should first and foremost serve social purposes, first and foremost social justice."[8]

When the Labor Party discussed poverty and the "social gap," Esther Herlitz, former Israeli ambassador to Denmark, reminisced that the party used to be tough on excessive consumption and even expelled two members accused of such conduct. "Once we sang songs for labor and craft—today they sing for Coca-Cola and washing machines."[9]

Conspicuous Consumers

One discourse about excess targeted extravagant products and services, although the line separating perceived indulgence and fundamental necessity was porous and constantly shifting. Durable goods considered an extravagance just ten years earlier—washing machines, air conditioners, and even cosmetics, were no longer regarded that way. The Ministry of Transportation, for example, now claimed that cars were a means of production, not a luxury. It sought funds to improve infrastructure and objected to additional taxes on new cars, arguing that wider roads were a prerequisite for economic expansion and for implementing the Zionist credo of population dispersion. Increasing taxes would thwart growth and might result in higher expenses for fueling and maintaining old, inefficient vehicles.[10]

Several schemes were floated to completely prohibit the importation of luxury items, for instance, whiskey. But the economic rationale of such a measure—as against its potential psychological effect—was doubtful. It was likely motivated by the impression that the rich drink whiskey like water but perhaps, someone suggested, a soldier on a furlough would also crave a shot. Whiskey's importation accounted for a mere half a million dollars. If prohibited, the well-off would find ways to continue to drink but the government would not be able to capitalize on the high taxes it levied on the liquor. It was suggested that buying subsidized eggs might be more wasteful in terms of foreign currency than purchasing whiskey, as some chicken feed was imported.[11]

Another method of targeting immoderate consumption sought to identify and denounce social archetypes rather than specific products. Visiting a supermarket in an upscale neighborhood on the first day of 1973, a reporter encountered a man loading his cart with whisky and other alcoholic beverages. "We could not go out yesterday," he said, almost apologetically, "so we will celebrate tonight. After all, it's the New Year. We must do something." "We live well," he otherwise acknowledged. Over the summer the family traveled abroad. He arranged it so the trip would be considered a work expense. They own two cars, bought a plot of land in the north, perhaps for a weekend home or, one day, for profit. Price hikes do not concern him much. "Money has no value. I get out in the morning with a big pack of cash and return without it. I don't know how it flows away."[12] The report captured this individual's comments that were most likely to antagonize the paper's readers: the seemingly unlimited purchase of expensive alcohol, the careless admittance that personal pleasures were reported as work for tax purposes, and even the celebration of the civil New Year, which in the 1970s was still widely frowned upon.

One group that attracted great approbation and became a symbol of predatory accumulation of wealth and ostentatious lifestyle was construction and dirt contractors who benefitted from hefty military projects, especially for building the Bar Lev Line on the Suez Canal. Costing a substantial two billion liras, the string of fortifications was erected in great haste beginning in 1968. Customary open-bid procedures were jettisoned to expedite construction. The notion that some Israelis might profit *directly* from war was met with alarm. The Bar Lev Line profiteers not only violated a moral code, they also transgressed an aesthetic one and were often cast as low-brow parvenus, indulging in tasteless aggregation of ostentatious goods. A poignant satire by Yonatan Geffen addressed an imaginary fallen soldier named Ofer. "There, on the hill over which you fought; contractors squabble over each plot of land; on the trench where you fell; speculators will build new houses; the bunker they sold for a hundred thousand; no-man's-land cost thirty. . . . It's a pity they didn't tell us beforehand that we are fighting for a contractor."[13]

Other targets of public criticism were the nation's politicians, senior officials, and company directors who were accused of modeling unacceptable levels of indulgence. One writer unfavorably compared the military ethos of "follow me" with the duplicity of office holders who while advocating belt tightening continue to surround themselves with luxuries. The example given was that senior officials sometimes travel to a public event in a convoy of ten to fifteen separate government-owned cars. "The people watch those convoys and then read about lavish ceremonies, cocktail parties and all the who's who donning fancy attire."[14] At the end of the 1960s, about 60 percent of the cars in Israel were still owned by the public sector. Phones in officials' homes at government expense were also perceived as symbols of bureaucratic misconduct.

Histadrut officials did not escape criticism either. Shmuel Tamir, a member of Knesset (then with the Center/Right Gahal Party), sneered that whereas scaled salaries in a private factory are negatively labeled "a gap" (*pa'ar*), when the Histadrut's bosses receive higher wages, it is fancifully termed "differentiality" (*hefreshiut*).[15] One union activist warned, "The Histadrut has been afflicted with the defilement of affluence, luxuriance, and waste," underscoring travel abroad, high managerial salaries, and personal expenses. "This is the beginning of the foreign road to values, that in those idealistic days, we saw as a symptom of diasporic, degenerate life we wished to escape as far as we could."[16]

Privileges enjoyed by public officials were instituted to compensate for the restrictions imposed on their nominal salaries. Circumventing the wage structure by granting perks, especially expense accounts, linked to the actual job by flimsy, largely fictitious threads—became normative and contributed to the perception of irrationality and even corruption in the Israeli economy.[17]

Veblen Redux

While Israel underwent a consumerist transformation, the period also witnessed the maturation of consumer society critique abroad by John Kenneth Galbraith, Herbert Marcuse, and Jean Baudrillard, among others.[18] Thorstein Veblen's idea that the emulation instinct drives competitive consumption and the term "conspicuous consumption," sometimes in the original English, were often invoked to explain the clamor to acquire goods and pleasurable experiences.[19]

Premier Meir complained about loss of individuality, the ambition to be like others, like one's neighbor, one's boss, the person deemed "a success," and consequently the temptation to furnish one's apartment with the same couch and the same appliances seen elsewhere. The wedding is no longer about family joy but a torture with dinner for three hundred people, she mused. And the bar mitzvah boy, rather than entering the world of good deeds, of *mitzvot*, stands by the door and collects checks from guests. "The ugliness is not just about our narrow and unclean streets. It is in the way we live."[20] Israeli society did not pursue equality anymore. In the past, she reminded her listeners, secretary general of the Histadrut David Remez received a lower salary than the clerk at the front desk because the latter had a bigger family.

Was a sense of deprivation hardwired into consumer society? One commentator maintained, it would be impossible for the proverbial housewife to concede, "Our income surpasses our needs. We don't know what we could further spend on."[21] In wealthy Beverly Hills, middle-class Ramat Gan, or poorer Beit Shean, homemakers complain about rising prices and inadequate family budgets. Bondi similarly observed that a salary that is not enough had become a status symbol. The young, dynamic Israeli always runs ahead of his income.[22]

Looking at the somewhat chaotic labor scene, she opined that strikes, some of which were declared by university-trained professionals, were no longer motivated by material needs as much as by status or the urge to determine value in a society in which it was unclear whose work was more valuable, that of a dentist, a car painter, a school principal, or a heating technician. "The Israeli worker is willing to endure everything, wars and inflation, terrorist acts and devaluations just not the impression that he is screwed over.... The feeling that he is deprived eats him, does not allow him to sleep, takes away his satisfaction at work."[23] Bondi's insight suggests that what drove Israelis was not keeping up with their neighbors as much as the suspicion of being somehow denied or hoodwinked out of what was their due. The fear of being taken advantage of, of being a sucker, so fundamental to modern Israeli culture, arguably operated as a leveling mechanism in a society that was drifting away from a positive sense of social camaraderie.[24]

The relational essence of the standard of living yardstick was a subject of reflection in the debate over social inequality spurred by the Panthers' revolt. Minister Sapir argued that the standard of living of all echelons of Israeli society had risen significantly, by a factor of 2.5. Others, most notably Israel Katz, director of the National Insurance Institute (see chapter 7), emphasized growing inequality and pockets of endemic poverty. Statistics were mustered to defend both positions. Bank of Israel governor David Horowitz maintained somewhat philosophically that an absolute good standard of living is exceedingly hard to define. "What is the proper standard of living in the gap between an Indian coolie with sixty-dollar annual income and an American multimillionaire with an income that from the point of view of consumption is limitless?"[25]

Horowitz quoted Marx, "Social existence determines consciousness." However, with all the wisdom and grains of truth they contain, such ruminations served also to stifle claims about disparity. At the turn of the 1970s, Israelis became growingly cognizant of the reality that their society is stratified. About 105,000 children were living in debilitating density and 200,000 children subsisted on only 40 percent of the average per child expenditure. According to some assessments, a quarter of the next generation lived in poverty.[26]

Pleasure and Pain

In 1969, Horowitz drew a red line of 500 million dollars under which the Israeli foreign reserves should not decline, but a year later the reserves dipped to 380 million. The incredibly fast growth of the Israeli economy due in large part to defense expenditure (from 984 million liras in 1966 to 1.384 billion in 1967, and 4 billion by 1970; from 10.5 to 31 percent of the GDP) but also to increased investments by 44 percent just from 1967 to 1968, entailed a rapid increase in the availability of money and consequently in private consumption. Horowitz maintained that the country is in a state of war, which could not be waged based on surging private welfare.[27] Reminiscing about his own childhood in starvation-afflicted World War I Vienna, he claimed no country at war had ever experienced such a rise in private consumption.

The government and the Bank of Israel already took action, restricting credit, hiking indirect taxes on luxury items, and restraining wage increases. Initially, they seemed successful in curbing consumption. In May, 1969, the government increased taxation on consumer goods and travel abroad. The Histadrut supported the move and so did the manufacturers' sector. Even the Phantom bonds drive (see chapter 4) was in part devised to whittle away at the public's purchasing power. Two years later, the Israeli currency would be devaluated by 20 percent, from 3.5 to 4.2 to the dollar.

Like Bluebeard in his torture chamber stroking his beard and pondering his sadistic options, each economist and pundit came up with his own painful medicine: mandatory saving, mandatory bonds, reduction of credit for imports, tax hikes, abolishing subsidies, differential conversion rates for the dollar, and radical devaluation.[28] Aktzin said that another government-triggered recession might be the only remedy for preventing "collective suicide" from happening. "To cure a sick person, we have to rely not on the patient's rational behavior but on the straightjacket imposed on him."[29]

Others, in contrast, scoffed at the strange nostalgia for austerity and administrative restrictions.[30] Some initiatives were susceptible to the laws of unintended consequences. The 1971 devaluation, for instance, sparked a rush to purchase electronics, furniture, and other products in anticipation of an impending increase in prices. Moreover, individuals who had foreign currency savings cashed in and purchased real estate and durable goods.[31]

The Histadrut's general secretary Yitzhak Ben Aharon claimed that about 200,000 self-employed and 60,000 to 70,000 wage earners (about 10 percent of the workforce) were responsible for the high volume of imports. Recipients of Holocaust reparations, beneficiaries of defense contracts, physicians, lawyers, exporters, and bankers were practically immune to all fiscal measures. It was generally agreed that the economy could not be decoupled from social and cultural forces and that the rational *homo economicus* paradigm is insufficient at best.[32]

In 1970, the Histadrut, private employers, and the government reached a package deal to control wages, prices, and taxes. However, for the next fifteen years, high inflation rates haunted the economy and determined patterns of consumption. Inflation rendered purchasing durable goods ever more alluring since material objects were perceived as an element of stability while money ceased to be a dependable gauge of value. Inflation generated another layer of skepticism, mistrust, and focus on the here and now.

Nevertheless, the alarmist premonitions of coming doom never materialized. The Treasury recruited enough foreign capital and, after the turn of the decade, American aid to further fuel the economy and compensate for deficit spending. Moreover, with all the rhetoric about war and national emergency, government policy was determined to a large extent by politics: power struggles within the Labor Party along its factions, the rivalry between the Treasury and the Defense Ministry, the relationship between the government and the Histadrut, and the Histadrut's own ambition to unify and represent a splintered workforce that turned more belligerent and unwieldy after the conclusion of the War of Attrition in the summer of 1970. And while playing cat-and-mouse games with the headstrong consumer, the ruling party also heeded electoral calculations, refraining from further alienating Israeli voters and foreign investors.

Reimagining the Consumer

We now turn to the host of novel associations established to protect, educate, and reimagine the Israeli consumer. The term "consumerism" has often been employed normatively either to deride the way life under capitalism is immersed in products and services, or, more recently, to denote a process of subject making and community building that endows participants with agency. However, in the 1960s "consumerism" designated efforts to empower consumers in their dealings with producers and retailers. Indeed, by some measures, that decade represented the heyday of the international consumer movement. Consumer activism was couched as an instrument of economic justice addressing some of the graver consequences of mass production, including safety and the environment. Ralph Nader's book *Unsafe at Any Speed* (1965) and public advocacy became a model for knowledge-driven consumerism. The civil rights and other progressive movements demonstrated the power of the purse and principled consumption, for instance, during the strike and boycott of the Delano grape growers in California (1966). Among its different missions, the United Nations endeavored to instill the tenets of good consumerism among third world societies.[33]

In 1966, at the height of the recession, the Ministry of Commerce and Industry established the Israel Consumer Council (ICC) as an advisory board. Four years later, the organization was entrusted with greater authority as a statutory, nonprofit government-sponsored corporation. Its list of assignments was long. It was mandated to protect consumers, safeguard their rights, and advance their interests; improve marketing practices, including quality control and prevention of fraud; help initiate and mend protective laws; initiate quality tests of products; and raise consumers' consciousness through lectures, exhibitions, and publications.[34]

Two rather small organizations had previously occupied the consumer protection niche. The Israel Consumer Union was founded some ten years earlier (1955) by the Women's International Zionist Organization (WIZO) as a trans-party independent association with a few hundred members. In 1964, the Histadrut launched its own Organization for Consumer Protection, but it could muster only meager resources. Nevertheless, Israel had already acquired some standing in the international community of consumer protection advocates led by the International Organization of Consumer Unions (IOCU), especially for training officials in the developing world, a task that intersected with the Israeli presence in newly decolonized Africa.[35]

Prototypes for the ICC were taken from the United States and Europe, especially Britain and the Netherlands. An early ICC internal document described how in America the "consumer revolution" had already taken root and an unbridled advertising machine, capitalizing on human vulnerability, was offset by regulatory legislation and institutions that offset the economic power of producers.[36] In March 1962, President John F. Kennedy presented to Congress a Consumer Bill of Rights that the United Nations would later adopt and expand as an international charter. Two years later, President Lyndon Johnson appointed the first special presidential assistant for consumer affairs, and in 1966–68, Congress passed several key consumer protection statutes.[37] Equally impressive was the network of grassroots pro-consumer organizations that had been in place for decades, including popular publications such as *Consumer Reports*.

The ICC was first helmed by Shulamit Aloni. An outspoken advocate of civil rights, she would assume a pivotal role in shaping the Israeli Zionist Left. In the mid-1960s, Aloni was a young lawyer and a fresh member of the Knesset on behalf of Mapai. She had already made a name for herself as a cohost of the radio show *Outside Office Hours* that addressed listeners' grievances about mistreatment, indifference, and discrimination by government offices and public institutions. The show stepped on numerous toes, gained notoriety, and established Aloni's reputation as an antiestablishment rabble-rouser. With courage that was rather lacking in public broadcast, she pointed to inefficiencies and injustices and did not hesitate to side with ordinary citizens in their conflicts with the rusty and legendarily obtuse bureaucracy. The stage she offered for criticism of the status quo in religious and personal matters, divorce, for instance, instigated the most vigorous public responses.

When Aloni entered the Knesset in 1965, a consumer protection body as well as a national ombudsman were among her pet projects. She conceived of the vigilant citizen who insists on her right to receive well-tested products and efficient services for a fair price as a civic educator and the most effective foot soldier for policing the marketplace. The timing was propitious. The recession forced Israelis to think twice before making a purchase. The public, she further proposed, revolted against the offensive attitude of vendors, manufacturers, and service providers. Government therefore resolved to encourage fair trade and to cultivate "Western ethics" in the service sector. Attentive, informed, and conscious consumption was constitutive of good citizenship. For Aloni consumerism addressed an even more fundamental social flaw that was troubling the Israeli everyday. "Our people were blessed with a fertile talent to talk about morality and conscience, the redemption of man and nation, while in their daily lives, in the relationship between man and his fellow man we are missing the simple ethical foundation of decency and courtesy in commerce, trade, and services."[38]

Raising Consumer Consciousness

One of the first ICC campaigns targeted price gouging of milk. In the mid-1960s, milk was still delivered to homes in reusable glass bottles for thirty pennies (*agorot*) a bottle. Some milkmen charged a tad more, for instance, by adding a penny to each floor they had to climb in the typical pre-elevator Israeli walk-up.[39] Some thought it was petty to go after the milkman for a couple of pennies. But the ICC director Aharon Niri insisted that the council intended on raising consciousness by demonstrating to the consumer her full rights even when it comes to the most basic, unthinking daily purchase. Adding a single penny to each bottle meant appropriating 3.5 million liras annually from the public. "In order to educate the general public to be alert and exercise active citizenship even a single penny is important."[40]

In early January 1967, three hundred canvassers, more than 60 percent of them homemakers recruited through volunteer organizations, knocked on the doors of twenty thousand homes in the Tel Aviv metropolitan area to survey the price of milk.[41] Conducted in conjunction with the Israeli Dairy Board, the operation received wide coverage in the press. Aloni asked the Knesset to deliberate over the state of milk delivery. A conflict was afoot between wholesale suppliers and distributors over a new proposal to package milk in plastic bags sold exclusively in stores rather than the recyclable bottles delivered to homes. Customer response to the new milk bags was reportedly enthusiastic.

The deliverymen put up a fight that they would soon lose, becoming obsolete in the name of hygiene, technology, and efficiency.[42] In future decades, however, strong doubts would be raised about the hygienic quality of plastic milk bags that once delivered in crates were left on the pavement to bake in the Israeli sun for hours before grocers pulled them in. The ICC also campaigned to curb price hikes in oil for home heaters, to improve packaging in four food industries, and for a law to guarantee fairness in commerce—among a flurry of other initiatives.[43]

The insistence on fixed prices and on instilling Western practices and norms ostensibly juxtaposed the modern marketplace with the Eastern bazaar in which prices are open to negotiation. Indeed, consumers were advised time and again to avoid street vendors. In effect, the ICC was serving the purposes of the bureaucratic state that monitored prices rather than the capitalistic marketplace that allows flexibility and competition and in which the consumer ostensibly weighs her options rather than helping enforce state regulations.

The initial ICC presence in print was formidable. The first issue of *Consumer Guide* circulated in a quarter of a million copies as a supplement to the evening dailies. Youth movements helped disseminate an additional 100,000 postcards. A leaflet titled, "There Are Complaints," had a circulation of 10,000 copies. A Voice of Israel program, *The Consumer Corner* was broadcast daily.[44] One ICC tactic was to shame offenders. For instance, an ICC newspaper ad went after a Tel Aviv furniture store: "Many complaints were submitted against the owners of Ruth Furniture on Sheinkin 10, Tel Aviv: flawed merchandise, violations of contract, impoliteness, disregard for complaints. Owners refused to compensate consumers for damages."[45]

As a warning to prospective customers, Aloni similarly decided to give publicity to the numerous complaints filed against the agency Hadar that imported the German car N.S.U. This practice, she wrote, is current in all democratic countries with consumer organizations. When Aloni went further and asked the minister of transportation to investigate the company, *Ha'olam Hazeh* magazine compared her to Ralph Nader. Hadar hired private detectives to collect information about the ICC, suggesting a political interest might be motivating the council's campaign.[46]

A complimentary ICC tactic was to shame credulous consumers—again, harping on the fear of being a sucker. One ad featured a face of a middle-aged man craftily smiling into the camera. "I am looking for gullible people who agree to buy from a street vendor, won't pay attention to interest and repayment plans, will sign a contract without reading the small print, won't look for a pricelist or menu, and won't care about the weight or service." The ad sends the gullible to the ICC offices under the slogan, "Because you are paying. This is your right. The lira is yours."[47] The ICC thus did not hesitate to utilize advertising techniques that were as manipulative as the industry it critiqued.

The government viewed consumer vigilance as another tool for improving the quality of local products for the purpose of export, which was regarded to be a national cause. Since the late 1950s, it promoted raising the standards of Israeli industrial design. American know-how and support were paramount. The Israeli Institute for Product Design—now the Institute for Packaging and Design—was launched in 1955 with the aid of the US government and under the guidance of the Institute for Contemporary Art in Boston. The short-lived Israeli Product Design Office (IPOD) was established a year later as an American-style design outfit.[48] In early 1967, the ICC cosponsored a

FIGURES 2.1A AND 2.1B Shaming gullible consumers. The man in the left ad concedes that he signed a contract but has no clue what is written in it. The woman in the right ad is told that she needs to know how to purchase from vendors as smartly as they know how to sell her on their merchandise. Sponsored by consumer organizations led by the Israel Consumer Council, both ads conclude with, "Because you are paying—this is your right, the lira is yours" (1969).

"Design Week." In a symposium titled "Product Design as a Way of Life," Aloni charged, "The industry and its practitioners exhibited vulgar taste and inadequate design that has a negative influence on the shopping habits of the Israeli consumer."[49]

The ICC and the Histadrut consumer organization advocated for introducing consumer curricula in schools. Public education in New York State was presented as a model. In chemistry classes, American high school students reportedly received practical lectures on popular medicines, in economics they learned about production and marketing standards, especially of food, and in math, how to calculate the real interest in installment plans.[50] In addition, the ICC solicited information from consumer agencies in the United States and Europe, in one case communicating with officials in California about the regulation of television repair businesses there. Later in the year, the ICC issued a brochure, "Everything about TV," with practical advice on how to purchase and operate TV sets.[51] Local products, for instance, kitchen toasters, were subjected to rigorous tests. Only four out of thirty-two brands of toilet paper were up to standards. The ICC ran a kitchen to model the best use of food products and to measure their nutritional value.[52]

Aloni envisaged a consumerist future in which small associations would be embedded in each municipality, responding to complaints in partnership with the local city hall.[53] Nevertheless, friction with other organizations and government offices marred the activities of the ICC. Minister of Welfare Yosef Burg, among others, questioned the efficacy of a government-sponsored consumer organization. The value of such an association rested on its autonomy, he maintained.[54] Three years after its launch and despite the effort to buttress its status and sharpen its bite, a budget cut signaled the end of the ICC's initial phase. Aloni decided to resign.[55]

As the ICC became a statuary corporation, the Histadrut revamped and expanded its own consumer agency. Ben Aharon embraced consumer activism as one of its chief missions. Following the 1970 package deal, he reasoned, employees should not expect a significant raise soon. "What we can give the workingman is in the form of protecting him as a consumer."[56] The new Histadrut body was named, somewhat grandiosely, the Central Consumer Protection Authority. It was headed by Nuzhat Katzav. Women ran the pioneering consumer organizations and were often the authors of consumer columns in the daily newspapers.

In the afternoon of January 29, 1973, Katzav led the first consumer strike in the history of Israel. It was a three-hour affair organized to combat rising prices. About 550 volunteers were dispatched to report on price hikes and gouging.[57] They patrolled central commercial sites and asked passersby to refrain from shopping. The short strike slowed down commercial activity in the main urban centers. According to Ben Aharon this was only the first salvo in a larger battle. But despite claims of success, plans for more focused strikes were not realized.[58]

Civilizing Mission

The Association for Better Housing (ABH—the Hebrew title refers to housing or residential *culture*) is today a ninety-branch government-backed volunteer organization whose chief mission is to support one of the most quintessential Israeli institutions, the co-op homeowners committee, in matters pertaining to home improvement, tenants' rights, and other legal and architectural services. It was founded in 1964 by the Housing Ministry in collaboration with the Jewish Agency and Amidar, the state's public housing company. Its charge back then was to improve the maintenance of deteriorating tenements by educating Israelis, in particular development town and inner-city dwellers, in cultivating the aesthetics and functionality of their homes.

The ABH was not a consumer association per se, but an important aspect of its didactic assignment was to teach residents how to occupy modern spaces and keep their domestic and public environments clean.[59] In the 1960s, cleaning drives proliferated and the call for improving urban environment complimented the invigorated consumption of domestic and personal hygiene and grooming supplies. Nominally headed by Rachel Shazar, the president's wife, and receiving support from a plethora of civic organizations, the ABH was inspired by the concern that tenements built for newcomers, *olim*, were quickly turning into slums; the English term was often mentioned.

An internal Housing Ministry document complained that many of the occupants of government-built tenements do not know how to utilize their domestic space, how to divide it according to the differing functions of receiving guests, sleeping, and drying laundry, and how to maintain the staircase and the building's immediate surroundings. Large families, in particular, required guidance in storing equipment and clothing, designating space for schoolwork, and buying cheap and adequate furniture.[60] One task was to introduce homemakers in development towns to basic household fixtures. Some of the initial ABH printed material was circulated in French, indicating that the target audience was likely of North African origin, mainly from Morocco.

Early government memos proposed to encourage residents to retain the aesthetic legacy each Jewish ethnicity brought from its country of origin and its expressions in decorations, furniture, and carpets. Nevertheless, ABH rhetoric betrayed prejudice. Thus, Minister of Housing Yosef Almogy proposed in public two different explanations for the rapid decline of houses built less than a decade earlier. On the one hand, he put the onus of responsibility on government agencies that provided low-quality housing and infrastructure. On the other hand, he intimated that a family with advanced "cultural tradition" would have converted even a ramshackle abode into a pleasant home, insinuating that the inhabitants' cultural inferiority is the root cause behind the abysmal state of their neighborhoods.[61] One journalist identified the culprit more explicitly as new immigrants "who were not raised adequately on the knees of proper civilization."[62]

Two development towns, Kiryat Gat in the south and Migdal Ha'emek in the north, served as sites for ABH's first branches. In October 1964, a nine-day cleaning campaign was announced in Kiryat Gat. Resident mobilization encompassed local institutions, youth organizations, and 4,200 schoolchildren. Public programming included lectures, instructional films, contests for the cleanest shop, cleanest neighborhood, and cleanest and best-organized school.[63] Among the issues raised were unsightly "decorations" in the staircase area and laundry hung everywhere.

The press paid close attention to startling stories of neglect, ignorance, and backwardness. In one Kiryat Gat apartment, an Amidar supervisor claimed to have found a watermelon floating in a toilet bowl. It was a method of keeping the fruit cool, explained the homemaker, who divulged, according to this (unconfirmed) tale, that a neighbor was making use of her toilet to pickle cucumbers. *Ma'ariv* surmised, "These stories sound a bit fantastical, but they demonstrate to what absurd use modern apartments can be put when their residents are lacking essential residential culture."64 There were reports about goats kept in apartments, destroyed gardens turning into garbage heaps, and North African clay ovens among rusting wired fences in delipidated backyards.65

Nevertheless, the association's secretary was optimistic about the prospects of change. In one case, loitering youth who had previously destroyed the vegetation planted around their building, were now asking for assistance in improving the tenement. The ABH accepted that inculcating "residential culture" would not be achieved by planning from above but by energizing the residents themselves for civic activism.66 Employing methods honed by Israeli youth movements to lure the young, the association would issue insignia, armbands, membership cards, and activity logs. Volunteers were eligible for prizes and lotteries as well as for the honor of being invited to the president's residence in Jerusalem for a special annual ceremony. The association published a brochure urging youth to organize and even to reprimand

FIGURE 2.2 Equipped with banners, insignia, and *tembel* hats, young students volunteer for the Petah Tikva branch of the Association for Better Housing (1973). (Oded Yarkoni Historical Archives of Petah Tikva)

adults if they violate the housing rules or do not keep their environment unpolluted.[67]

The first general exhibition of the domestic and foreign housing industry took place in June of 1965 in the Yerid Hamizrah complex in Tel Aviv.[68] With the help of miniature models, the ABH demonstrated how a new, squeaky-clean tenement turns into squalor.[69] The association sponsored a popular roving exhibition that featured two model apartments. Together with the Israeli Institute of Design, it promoted the manufacturing of a standardized high-quality, "tasteful," and functional furniture.[70] By its invitation, Nagar Brothers carpentry introduced a new line of kitchen furniture, Aromit, which employed natural wood veneer protected by a special synthetic treatment (Duralek) praised for having the capacity to endure water, tea, coffee, and alcohol stains.[71] However, some protested that Israeli-made furniture corresponded to the taste of an Ashkenazi family and not enough thought was invested in furniture that reflects the non-Ashkenazi residents' lifestyle and culture.[72]

Beautiful Israel

By the late 1960s, the deterioration of both urban spaces and natural environments sparked alarm beyond the specific problems that troubled tenements and development towns. This concern emanated from the rise in the standard of living, the discourse of "urban renewal" coming from the United States and Europe, and the emergence of modern environmentalism. Architects, artists, public figures, and various arbiters of taste denounced ungainly laundry hanging off terraces, dirty streets, and garbage piling by the roadsides. Newspapers habitually printed pieces on environmental and aesthetic hazards such as TV antennas mushrooming on rooftops (the "fifth façade") or the polluted waterfront.[73] They condemned the littering Israeli who was in the habit of leaving his name carved into tree trunks, inscribed on abandoned buildings, and even archeological sites.

Trepidations about the destruction of landscape and natural resources and advocacy for an environmental protection agency and tougher legislation evidenced a departure from an era in which the cult of material development, immigration, and settlement eclipsed most other considerations.

Causes such as cleaner cityscape and preservation frequently invoked the consumerist-steeped term "quality of life," which became popular at the time. Advocates often blamed the Orient rather than modern overdevelopment. Thus, journalist Ya'akov Ha'elyon bemoaned the neglect in cities and roads:

> We live in the Levant, an undeniable geographical fact. But we pretend to be a Western country in terms of mentality and social behavior. For instance, we want our country to be clean and beautiful. . . . We want very much—but do little. Our Land of Israel is dirty, neglected, uncultivated. In this sense, pardon the expression, we are very Levantine. . . . It's very natural for us to throw out of the window the orange peel and the sandwich wrapping paper. No easier way to empty the ashtray than send the cigarette butts with the wind onto the road. How many of us have ignored the pleas of the National Parks Authority, of nature itself, and destroy every plot of wildflowers so they would live for a day or two in a vase on the table in the living room? . . . No man would like that his wife would go around neglected and unclean. But a few think of the land to which they are wedded.[74]

Ha'elyon idealized the situation elsewhere. In other countries, he mentioned the United States in particular, heavy fines are levied for leaving garbage by the road. Cosmetics companies abroad sponsor ads for public beautification and cleanliness, but Israeli firms would rather not be associated with garbage.

The Council for a Beautiful Israel (CBI) was founded in 1968 as a nonprofit organization. Once again, the initiative to mobilize the public for civic action came from government, this time the Interior Committee of the Knesset and its chair Yosef Sapir (Gahal) after the committee received a disconcerting report about the declining urban "quality of life." The CBI sponsored repainting and greening projects, education and consciousness raising, ecological advocacy, and the consolidation of junk yards, among other projects. The citizen's responsibility for his material surroundings was at the ideological core of the association.

The CBI sought to improve street fixtures such as bus stations, trash bins, and pavement tiles. It campaigned against the practice of abandoning old cars and for the institution of regulated junkyards for vehicles.[75] The council helped popularize window boxes. In one operation, more than ten thousand boxes and plants were sold for reduced prices, made possible by the assistance of students who prepared the hardware and prison inmates who helped grow the plants.[76]

At the turn of the 1970s, the CBI also entered key debates about urban development and preservation, for example, the controversy over the future of Jerusalem. No longer on the frontier, after the 1967 war the capital underwent major transformation in part to assert Israeli sovereignty over the annexed eastern neighborhoods of the city. Mayor Teddy Kollek invited leading architects and city planners from the United States and Europe. The debate turned quite contentious. A few participants described the capital's master plan as a catastrophe for generations to come.[77] In contrast, the rightwing caricaturist Kriel "Dosh" Gardosh accused the leftist intelligentsia of using extreme preservationist criteria and treating the pure, undiluted landscape as sacrosanct to halt the rapid growth of Jewish Jerusalem. He urged Kollek in strong words not to heed such considerations.[78]

Civil Society

The three government-supported organizations we have discussed represent the proclivity of the Israeli state to intrude upon a public terrain that otherwise falls under the category of civil society. Nevertheless, this encroachment could also be seen as complementing the government's ambition to nurture and rear the private sector, a symptom of bureaucratic capitalism. State efforts at rallying citizens for civic engagement also occasionally followed a range of recruitment techniques associated with youth movements, or alternatively, the way commercial concerns enticed consumers with prizes, raffles, and free gifts. All three associations emulated but also sought and received the support of nongovernmental, American-born service clubs, whether Rotary, Lions, B'nai B'rith, or the Junior Chamber (JC).

These organizations launched their own quality-of-life initiatives. For instance, the Junior Chamber, a leadership-training organization for young (twenty-one- to forty-year-old) men (until the 1980s it was exclusively male) initiated, "The Minor Nuisance" campaign in Hadera to improve the appearance of the town and eliminate small hazards that burdened citizens in their daily lives. Residents were asked to fill out thousands of postcards about problems that escaped city hall's attention: broken pavements, leaking pipes, piles of garbage, and overgrowth.[79] Five years later, the JC organized a demonstration to demand new measures to curb the escalating number of deadly car accidents in town.[80]

Another demonstration, this time in Yavne, was called to protest that despite endless promises nothing had been done to upgrade the safety and lighting of the main road, no youth clubs were built, and the sanitation and welfare services remained woefully lacking. A thousand residents, mostly youngsters, blocked the main road to the village.[81] Despite JC's nonpartisan commitment and the refrain that its members "run away from politics"[82] the Yavne branch ran candidates for the local council with the platform of improving infrastructure and community services.[83] In Rehovot, to give another example, the JC proposed a campaign to educate citizens in "aestheticism," encourage residents to repaint their houses' façade, and improve lighting and shop windows. It further suggested that opening a nightclub might also help revive the sleepy town.[84]

The JC launched its first branch in Israel in 1955. By 1965 there would be 1,500 members in nine different chapters. In addition to its Tel Aviv base, the JC was particularly active in peripheral, mostly older communities such as Rishon Letzion, Rehovot, and Pardes Hanna—where the ruling Mapai party was not particularly strong. One of the most notable Israeli JC figures was Abraham "Buma" Shavit, a young charismatic industrialist who would become a leader of the Israel Manufacturers Association, chairman of El Al, and a political figure. Shavit explained the attraction of young Israelis to the JC by the great void left after the end of the 1948 war when youngsters were looking for both substance and play.[85] He claimed that unlike other JCs, the Israeli chapter was not limited to middle- or upper-class recruits or those who are looking to escape affluence-born boredom.[86] Nevertheless, it was clear that professionals, government officials, and merchants were the backbone of the organization in Israel as well.[87] One aspect of JC activities was sociability and joviality. For instance, the Kiryat Tiv'on branch joined the organization with an elaborate mock wedding ceremony that was reported in the national press, featuring a veiled bride and a cylinder-donning groom.[88] As Victoria de Grazia maintained in the case of interwar Europe, the American "Market Empire" also exported its civil society, voluntary associations, and civic spirit—together with its commercial methods and marketing venues.[89]

Commercialism without Commerce

Critics, pundits, and other gatekeepers jostled over control of public taste for cultural goods, reserving some of their sharpest barbs for imported American TV shows. Terms and titles taken from these programs were absorbed in the vernacular, for instance, the expression, "such a family," the Hebrew title given to the CBS sitcom *Family Affair*, which also became a local theatrical production. Playwright Oriel Ofek explained that he decided to keep the original American characters because the show could not be fully "Israelized." Live-in servants were unheard of and the transition from a remote and rather backward town somewhere in the American hinterland to the big city did not represent the local reality.[90]

Singling out *Family Affair* and the NBC fantasy sitcom *I Dream of Jeannie*, one commentator accused television executives of condescending to the Israeli masses by acquiring "television garbage from US commercial television—there at least it makes money—and peddling it evening after evening to innocent people who were not asking for it." He mocked the canned laughter and the jingle-like musical note at the conclusion of each scene. "Jeannie's sex appeal is sterile and vitality-less despite her semi-see-through attire . . . no wonder the poor astronaut is trying to escape this barnacle by all means necessary including (how funny) sucking her up in a vacuum cleaner."[91]

Local production did not escape the critics' scorn either. When the Israeli television began broadcasting its first drama series, *Hedva veShlomik*, in 1971, it was truculently condemned by Hedda Boshes, the dean of television critics, as "anti-educational" and "insulting anti-culture."[92] Based on Aaron Meged's 1950 novel *Hedva and I*, the series followed the trials and tribulations of a young couple that leaves a kibbutz for the big city. Dialogue was written in plain, colloquial Hebrew.[93] Boshes scoffed at the "infantile quips" and seemed personally offended by the very popularity of the series.[94] Despite her and other critics' blistering criticism, and the charge of cheap commercialism, the ratings for *Hedva veShlomik* were exceedingly high, 71 percent, and surveys indicated that most of the viewing public liked it.⁹⁵

Since the program was broadcast on commercial-free public television, the accusation of commercialism could not possibly point to any financial interest but instead implied pandering to popular taste. Critic Doron Rosenblum railed against what he described as a mercantile attitude in the programming of Galei Tzahal, the IDF radio station, another noncommercial, government-sponsored venue. In the late 1960s, the station adopted a new broadcasting formula, which integrated diverse content, from contemporary rock and pop music, to talk shows, entertainment, and serious discussions about politics and art.⁹⁶

For Rosenblum, however, the station that enjoyed great popularity, especially among younger listeners, was trying to ingratiate itself to its audience. Its editors incessantly sought to keep in touch with listeners by phone, allowing them to express themselves on the air and "set the level of broadcast judging by [listeners'] plebian taste" rather than relying on their own judgment. The young station thus turned into a self-service department store. The rules of supply and demand came to determine value.⁹⁷

In the case of *Hedva veShlomik* the irony was that the series was designed to satirize crude consumerist life in Tel Aviv. Shlomik is a second-generation kibbutznik whose father is an important figure in Mapai. Hedva is a daughter of a factory owner from the posh Herzliya Pituah neighborhood. Shlomik decides to leave the kibbutz to pursue his musical aspirations. "I want more," he says in the first episode. But in addition to the juxtaposition of bourgeois and kibbutz life—a contrast that by the 1970s was already a cliché of Israeli culture—the couple discover in the big city a whole new subculture of naked hypocrisy, insincerity, and greed. Shlomik's brother-in-law Eli offers him a position in his advertising agency and the second episode features—as a parody—a series of mock commercials, under the slogan "Etti Loves Spaghetti." Eli instructs Shlomik how to appeal to consumers' status anxiety or shallow respect for science and high culture; one version employs *Hamlet* to sell pasta.

Later, we encounter Shlomik's role model, Mishka Chodorow, a former member of his kibbutz, now an immensely successful entertainment producer. Mishka is a sleazy self-promoter who surrounds himself with an entourage of poseurs and narcissistic bohemians, drops English expressions right and left and does not care much about the quality of the cultural trash he peddles. His wife Yona is obsessed with Dizengoff Street shopping. The Chodorows brag about having conjoined two penthouses in the new Neve Avivim neighborhood in the fashionable section of Tel Aviv north of the Yarkon River. And, of course, Mishka drives a Mustang convertible. At the conclusion of the twelve-episode series, Hedva and Shlomik return to the kibbutz, abandoning their little car outside its gate. If indeed, as critics alleged, *Hedva veShlomik* faithfully represents the commercial spirit within which it was cradled, then lampooning commercial life becomes itself fodder for commercial culture, perhaps another indication for the capacity of capitalism to absorb or even profit from ostensible dissent.[98]

Apprehensions about popular taste were not limited to television. In *Ma'ariv* Uri Keisari cast aspersions at the efforts to mint new cultural idols that he saw as a product of "Israeli apes" jumping on the American "mimicry tree" advanced through the graces of such institutions as "the silly hit parade."[99] However, cultural arbiters ultimately failed to curb the public taste for popular culture, foreign or domestic. By the 1960s the old pioneer close-to-the-land asceticism and insistence on the instructional value of cultural artifacts were in retreat. A mid-decade Ministry of Education decision not to permit a Beatles' tour of Israel for lack of "educational value" would be mourned by Israelis for decades to come.

Moreover, while David Ben-Gurion despised television and mass-produced culture in general, Menachem Begin, the head of the right-wing opposition who would become prime minister in 1977, was known as an aficionado of Hollywood Westerns. When the cast of prime-time soap *Dallas* visited Israel in March 1982, Begin hosted them, donned a Texan ten-gallon hat, inquired, "Who shot JR?," and even claimed that Miss Ellie (played by Barbara Bel Geddes) reminded him of his own mother.[100]

Sharp criticisms of specific products of the American or the local television industry would continue in later decades, although highbrow castigation of commercialism subsided. By the end of the 1970s, some art critics, most famously Adam Baruch, who spent years observing the art scene in Manhattan, embraced the 1960s convergence of popular media and art, the American respect for commercial success in general, and the American fascination with "cultural heroes." The tony magazine Baruch launched in 1978, *Monitin* (Reputation), emulated *New York* magazine and other glossies from across the Atlantic, serving as a major vehicle for the introduction of New Journalism to Israel.[101]

By the 1980s, this auto-ethnographic, highly stylized form of reportage would leave an indelible mark on the printed press, arguably much greater than it had on American journalism, producing smart, personal, and customarily witty or sardonic writerly style. Its masculinist accents and mixture of eyewitness reporting with emotional distance were attractive to upwardly mobile readers. Israeli New Journalism contributed to an irreverent journalistic flair that targeted the establishment, especially the ascendant Likud party, but also manifested elite alienation from the Israeli everyman and, in this respect as others, retained some of the conservative DNA of its American progenitor.

Conclusion

The arrival of both runaway consumption and, conversely, campaigns to temper and refine it—gesture toward convergence between the United States and Israel. However, if we turn our attention away from parallels and similarities, we discover that the interplay between these contending vectors in effect exposed the differences between the two societies, manifested in the divergent power and function of the state, the constraints of the economy and its specific embeddedness in society, and the rationale for consumption or its regulation. This also applied to the figure of the consumer.

The Israeli consumer who emerged in the 1960s from a vortex of contradictory pulls was a beleaguered character. He was denounced for his selfishness and excess, subjected to campaigns aimed at altering his behavior either through harsh rhetoric or punitive fiscal measures, as well as more subtle efforts of indoctrination with the aspiration of molding a modern consumerist subjectivity. Cutting a rather stubborn and resilient figure, the consumer had to rely on his own resources, to endure the erratic nature of the price system that rendered durable goods sometimes doubly or triply more expensive than they were abroad, the indifference of importers and vendors, as well as subpar service.

He was constantly suspected of illicit behavior, of smuggling jeans and cameras through customs upon returning from a trip abroad, of buying foreign currency in the black market (which was secretly regulated and supplied by the government), and of expanding his apartment illegally by closing off terraces without the required permits. Indeed, he was often guilty of all the above. Resourcefulness and agency—that were left unchained or even encouraged in the battlefield—were hard to control in the marketplace, where the invocation of the national interest seemed much less persuasive. There was admittedly little heroism in this type of resistance, but it participated in the larger historical process by which the state lost much of its grip on many aspects of Israeli life.

THREE

Electioneering and the Feedback Loop

Known informally by his childhood nickname, Chich, Shlomo Lahat's successful run for mayor of Tel Aviv (1973) was heralded, although sometimes ridiculed, as the first American-style political campaign in Israel. Photogenic, self-confident, gregarious, and recently retired as an IDF major general—Lahat had his image emblazoned on handbills, billboards, stickers, and buttons. He stood at busy intersections greeting thousands of potential supporters. Only in his mid-forties, he was running against an incumbent, Yehoshua Rabinowitz, fifteen years his elder, and in many ways his opposite, cerebral and profoundly shy, an introvert with crossed eyes and a grim facial expression to boot.

This chapter situates Lahat's campaign in the emerging consumerist order in Israel. Lahat was peddled as a product but, as importantly, his campaign cast voters as individual shoppers in the emporium of politics. It therefore constituted one among other projects—a few of which we visited in the previous chapter—that sought to refashion citizenship in Israel in accordance with consumerist ideologies and practices.

A substantial apparatus of knowledge was consequently elaborated to garner information about voters' behavior and frame of mind. Beyond consumers and voters, studying the preferences of ordinary Israelis also entered policymaking and labor relations. It became a tool of workforce management in an era that underscored the need to secure employees' loyalty and engagement. The heightened desire for knowledge, either political, commercial, or managerial, operated on different scales. Both quantitative and qualitative measures were marshaled to supply what were in effect feedback loop techniques honed to register and respond to the point of view of large or specific constituencies. This instrument of self-correction, its distinct parts, and the ideational structures that keep them in motion serve, alternatively, as a mechanism of democratic governance and as a tool of mobilization, manipulation, and discipline.

The gray area between the ideal of responsiveness to others' wishes and the desire for control and empowerment also undergirded several American-born, psychology-infused interpersonal strategies that found home in Israel, many of which appeared under the rubric of human relations (HR). They enjoyed popularity, first as tools of management training and later as venues for personal actualization. HR workshops were joined by other trendy methods for overhauling and improving the self, whether Esalen Institute's "encounters" or Dale Carnegie's recipes for personal success.

Lahat's American-style campaign finally raises the question of the military as a conduit for American methods and ideas and leads our discussion to the former IDF chief of staff and future prime minister Yitzhak Rabin's experience as the ambassador to the United States (1968–1973). Rabin's and Lahat's respective adventures in the American contact zone display, albeit in a somewhat different manner, the confluence of the personal and the political and the role of affective dispositions in the engagement with the American gravitational pull.

Pressing the Flesh

Natan Brune, who led Lahat's campaign for office, had closely studied American electioneering tactics. He visited political campaigns in the United States and carefully perused the road-to-the-White-House literature that sprouted up after each presidential contest. Election campaigns in Israel were ineffective, unprofessional, and frankly, boring, he opined.[1] A lawyer and a former journalist, a member of the right-wing Herut party, his chance came in early 1973, when the Liberal Party in Gahal (the Herut/Liberal amalgamation), which that year founded the modern Likud Party, recruited Lahat for the mayoral run.

Brune assured Lahat that each hand he shook would increase its owner's willingness to vote for him. This explains why American political candidates—he mentioned John F. Kennedy in particular—stand outside in minus four degrees to engage the masses. Establishing eye contact and "pressing the flesh," an expression he learned in the United States and associated with Lyndon Johnson, were essential psychological tools. That winter, the initiative for direct mayoral elections was put on hold, a victim of political skirmishes in the Knesset.[2] But Lahat's campaign wasn't waiting. Its chief slogan was "This time the choice is personal."

First, the campaign published an enormous newspaper ad in which Lahat introduced himself in word and image—no fewer than ten photos—seeking to forge symbolic intimacy and affective ties with prospective voters, by, among other means, specifying his age and family status. Lahat promised that in the months to come, citizens would get well acquainted with him. "I will try to get to know you personally in order to understand your problems as a resident of Tel Aviv–Jaffa. I would be delighted to invite you to meet me, or to tell you about me and my plans. Write me: Shlomo Lahat, PO Box 16273, Tel Aviv." This bold invitation concluded with a facsimile of Lahat's handwritten signature.[3]

Then came the handshaking drive. Brune wanted 100,000 hands squeezed. Lahat showed up at the central bus station, discotheques, and swimming pools. It is hard to imagine any other early 1970s political functionary in Israel going down to the beach, greeting barely clothed, unsuspecting bathers with, "Shalom. My name is Chich. I am a candidate for mayor. Please vote for me." Some Tel Avivians were reportedly startled when the overzealous candidate approached them, unannounced, with an extended arm. Brune proved to be a critical mentor, but with Chich the style and the man were in rare synchronicity. One journalist who endeavored to remove the publicity mask ultimately submitted that what shrewd public relations experts sold the public was in fact an authentic individual.[4]

Thousands of visiting cards with Lahat's picture and signature were

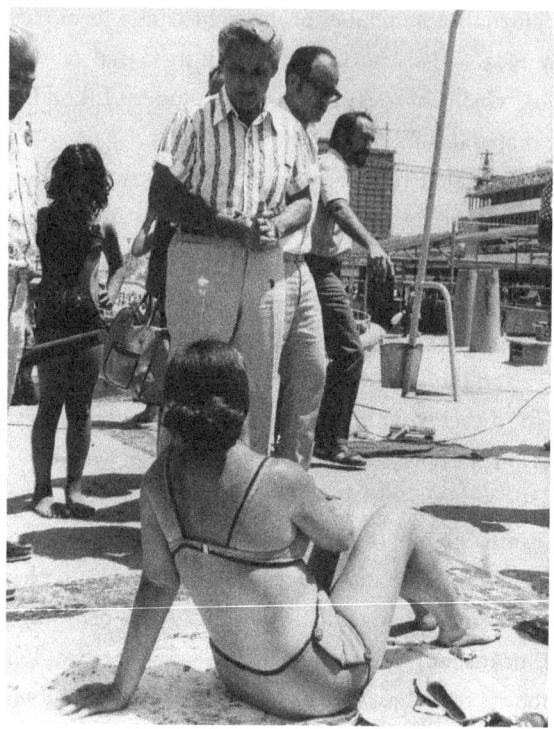

FIGURE 3.1 "Shalom, my name is Chich. Please vote for me." Campaigning in the American style, mayoral candidate Shlomo Lahat approaches unsuspecting sunbathers on the beach in Tel Aviv (1973). (Yossi Roth)

dispensed. Voters, claims Brune, kept the card and sometimes placed it on their TV sets. There were other tricks up his sleeve: Lahat's candidacy was launched with a press conference on the top of the tallest building in Israel, Migdal Shalom. A "Lahat and Flower" operation dispatched seventy female university students to distribute ten thousand flowers in city streets and cafés.[5] Presenting his plan to address traffic congestion, Lahat challenged Rabinowitz to a public debate. There was no precedent for such an exchange, and Rabinowitz declined, claiming that unlike his rival he had no wish to shape his campaign according to an American guidebook. The Histadrut daily *Davar* dismissed American-style political debates as wrestling in a circus arena.[6]

Meet-and-greet forums hosted in private homes (*hugei bayit*) also turned out to be incredibly popular. Replacing public rallies, which both camps now regarded as obsolete, they further blended the political with the personal, domestic, and social. This setting provided an opportunity to chat informally with a rather small group whose specific concerns and political inclinations were studied beforehand.[7] The candidate came prepared. Lahat participated in such events almost every night. Brune advised him to speak in short, accessible sentences.

Brune fashioned himself to be the first "campaign manager" in the country's political history. He gathered a company of professionals, including a pollster, a TV expert, a graphic designer, and a spokesperson. Most importantly, and again without precedent, he demanded that the party grant him a clearly defined budget, largely for advertisements, and assure him full discretion to make decisions without interference. Political parties don't know how to run campaigns, he concluded. Still in the opposition, the Likud was rather conducive to such experimentation.[8]

For Rabinowitz's Labor Alignment team, headed by the young Yossi Sarid, a future left-wing political leader, Lahat's electioneering stunts provided many occasions for sneering. The term, "American-style campaign" was hurled to deride a foreign import, supposedly unsuitable for Israel. The campaign dismissed Chich as a dandy, an inexperienced and superficial candidate, a "synthetic personality" sold as though he were a cosmetic product.[9] They said he was addicted to publicity. His sartorial style, especially fashionable vertically striped shirts, was mocked. Asked to confront the allegation that he became "a beauty king," working in the "American style," Lahat demurred, "I don't want to become a pamphlet or a clause in the platform. . . . I am flesh and blood, alive and breathing. And the citizen whose confidence I seek has a right to know me. So why are we talking about the 'American style'?"[10]

After the October 1973 war propaganda on both sides turned only more aggressive.[11] Rabinowitz's people continued to dismiss Lahat's supposed inauthenticity but complained that as a former general he was immune to criticism and that he was running a "crude and vulgar" campaign.[12] Despite Lahat's promise to separate national and municipal politics, his aides affixed the term *mehdal* (culpable inaction) used widely to denounce the grave blunders on the eve and during the first phase of the war—to Rabinowitz's mayorship.[13] One of Lahat's last-minute slogans was "something *must* change in the country; something *can* change in Tel Aviv."[14]

Rabinowitz's team was also populated with pollsters and professional public relations executives who were quite proficient in American electioneering literature, although with tougher merchandise to sell. Rabinowitz was reluctant to press the flesh but agreed to increase visits across town. A whole battery of Labor Alignment dignitaries reported for meet-and-greet events. In a last-ditch effort, a "Citizens for Rabinowitz" group was concocted, with another retired general at its helm.[15] In the aftermath of the election that was postponed because of the war and took place on the last day of 1973, some observed that both candidates behaved like marionettes whose strings are pulled by shrewd advertising experts.[16]

Ultimately, Lahat secured the mayoral position in the old-fashioned way—by establishing a coalition with two small factions in city council. There were truly no major differences between him and Rabinowitz concerning the future of Tel Aviv. Rabinowitz was already a modernizer committed to urban renewal projects. Lahat's campaign underscored that the new Hayarkon Park, Tel Aviv Museum, and a revamped beachfront did not address the daily drudgery that city dwellers had to contend with, struggling with traffic, filth, and a sluggish bureaucracy.[17]

Lahat spoke incessantly about "quality of life" and the citizens' level of comfort.[18] Only a few months before the war, he maintained that the existential questions facing Israel were a thing of the past, "our military situation was never better."[19] The country should focus not on how to survive but on how to live. His legendary passion for cleanliness—he would tell Tel Aviv sanitation workers "I am crazy about cleanliness"[20]—was often attributed to congenital pedantry or his German background. His family left Berlin when he was five years old. One of his first initiatives in city hall would be to place in every elevator a notice with his signature asking passengers to keep it clean.[21]

Human Relations

One day into his tenure, Lahat seemed hell-bent on campaigning forever. Ebullient as always, he popped into offices, extending his arm for a handshake, "Shalom, my name is Chich; I don't eat humans."[22] He removed the police officer who stood outside the mayor's office and insisted on taking the regular elevator with everybody else.[23] Lahat announced an open-door policy, proposing regular conferences with groups of municipal workers and promising to get to know in person each of the 11,000 city hall employees.[24] He also declared his intention to get together with constituents every week to hear their thoughts, problems, and aspirations, sort of perpetual meet-and-greet events. Against the old Mapai-era bossism, Lahat stated he would abolish nepotism (the dreaded *protektzia*) and manage Tel Aviv as a full partnership with voters and city employees.[25] "I hate barriers and love people, like that, direct contact, close, open. No mediation," he declared.[26]

Encouraging citizens and employees to articulate their opinions could indeed substantiate a more robust democratic process. Nevertheless, it was also characteristic of managerial tactics elaborated in the era of high Fordism to increase productivity, efficiency, and labor loyalty. Lahat's gestures toward employees should be considered in tandem with his sweeping rejection of strikes and advocacy of mandatory arbitration in all labor disputes under the pretext that in Israel every market is essential.[27] His enthusiasm for engaging with and listening to people might have been an aspect of his personality and, as we shall see, experience in the military, but it also dovetailed with the HR approach to labor that was in vogue at the time.

Sociologist Michal Frenkel points to the paradox that whereas HR evolved in the United States to bypass trade unions, in Israel it was first embraced by the Histadrut, epitomizing the organization's contradictory position as both a workers' union and a major employer. In America, HR was expected to facilitate solidarity between employers and employees. In mid-1950s Israel it stood more broadly for class and national cohesion.[28] By the turn of the 1960s, HR was popularized as a topic of managerial instruction, promoted by, among others, the Institute for Labor Productivity, which was established in 1951, and later, its offshoot, the Israeli Center for Management (1959).[29]

Labor unrest in the early 1960s invested the subject with greater urgency. Strikes were often explained away as a product of deficient leadership and wanting interpersonal communication rather than as a symptom of growing inequality in Israeli society.[30] Advanced training for state and Histadrut officials, summer courses, and weekend workshops that filled up the ascending Israeli managerial class's calendar customarily included an HR component. Expertise often arrived from the United States and American society and industry were invoked as illuminating examples.

In 1965, the Institute for Labor Productivity began organizing "labs" that offered lectures, role-play, and other group activities.[31] It would be followed by private outfits such as the Institute for Spiritual Hygiene. Comprised of a small assembly of ten to fifteen men and women, the lab, sometimes referred to as a T-Group, is dedicated to sensitivity training through problem solving, interpersonal encounters, and feedback. It aims at fostering introspection and self-confidence and coaching trainees to be empathetic to others.[32]

Participants in a week-long lab in Netanya, to give one example, described their experience as intense and even life-changing. One exercise involved spending a long time staring at each other from close proximity. In another, a blindfolded member crossed a room cluttered with obstacles and had to decide if and how to solicit his lab mates' help. A listening exercise had participants sit in a circle, where each shared an idea with the next person who was then expected to transmit it accurately to the entire group. "We teach people how to listen to others and accept the way they are without a critical attitude," explained the instructor.[33] These experiences, he insisted, encourage self-exposure and produce social cohesion, even love.

A growing number of individuals apparently fought for the privilege of participating in those workshops. In the name of dissolving boundaries, instructors encouraged nonverbal and even physical communication, feeling each other's hands, for instance, another iteration of the "pressing the flesh" motif. One instructor intimated that in the modern world physical contact was strongly repressed. "We want to cultivate it anew."[34] However, touching—which was reportedly more restrained than in American T-Groups—still sometimes turned overtly sexual. At least in one case it led a female participant to quit the lab.

HR labs became popular among the young generation of the kibbutz movement. It is somewhat ironic that Israelis, especially kibbutz members, turned to such techniques developed to augment qualities that were supposedly constitutive of Israeli culture, such as sociability and teamwork. Equally unexpected was the need for outside professional help in establishing candid exchanges in a society that prided itself on its direct and informal speech. One member from Kibbutz Mishmarot told a reporter that the workshop experience convinced him to turn down an offer to become the kibbutz's general secretary and focus instead on finishing his MA in social psychology. The kibbutz needs to allow members to reach their personal potential, he stated, "First it's me, then all other things."[35]

Indeed, American behavioral scientists discovered the kibbutz as a site of research and experimentation, establishing the American Council for the Behavioral Sciences in the Kibbutz.[36] The psychologist Robert Tannenbaum of UCLA, a proponent of organizational development (OD), launched a major research project.[37] Arguing that mutual reliance, openness, and full trust are crucial for sustaining an ethical community in the technological age, Tannenbaum warned that more than other communities, the kibbutz risks stagnation and decline unless it adopts intersubjective methods that guarantee candor and openness. Despite their commitment to collective life, kibbutz members are not open with their thoughts and emotions. All three kibbutz movements appeared quite receptive to these concerns and to Tannenbaum's "renewal project."[38] In collaboration with Israeli sociologists, he proceeded to conduct nine-month-long "intensive intervention" experiments in three kibbutzim: Gal'ed (focusing on intergenerational relations), Sa'ar (educators and parents), and Gadot (social interaction and education).[39]

The writings of the Adlerian psychiatrist Rudolf Dreikurs also left an imprint. Dreikurs worked on enhancing a sense of belonging as the key to collaborative group behavior and wrote extensively about parenthood, marriage, and classroom discipline. The Vienna-born American scholar visited Israel frequently, at one time by the invitation of the Defense Ministry, the Civil Service Authority, and the Society for Promoting Human Relations, an organization established by his local disciples.[40] One example of his impact was the management of the central district of the postal service. Heavily drawing on Dreikurs's methods, the district's entrepreneurial director sustained exemplary labor relations by, for instance, maintaining an open-door policy with his 750 employees. All workers received a copy of Dreikurs's *Social Equality: The Challenge of Today* (1971). *Ma'ariv* titled its report, "Human Relations Turn a Turtle into a Deer in the Postal Service's Center District."[41] Postal employees were subjected to other Taylorist projects as well, with a view of increasing productivity.

The Israel Aerospace Industries (IAI) provided yet another example. Under pressure from one of its American clients, it adopted the zero defects managerial system that was then all the rage in the American military-industrial complex. Encouraging employees to submit anonymous feedback for improving efficiency—by filling forms and depositing them in special boxes—it sought to stimulate workers' investment in the manufacturing process. Zero defects slogans hung everywhere at the IAI compound. After two years, during which it received 7,000 feedback forms, IAI management declared the experiment a success, resulting in a saving of 100,000 work hours and one million liras.[42] Workers received appreciation letters and were awarded a range of prizes from keychains to theater tickets.

The institution of the ombudsman also rested on a feedback mechanism. It proliferated in government offices and public institutions, mushrooming into an "ombudsmania," as one observer claimed.[43] In 1972, the IDF appointed its first ombudsman, former IDF chief of staff Lieutenant General Haim Laskov, who upon assuming his new role maintained that by insisting on his rights a serviceman is fulfilling his duty. For Laskov, the soldier who registers a complaint with the ombudsman's office contributes to rendering the military more disciplined and rule oriented. His input would help the IDF recognize which of its procedures and policies do not function well and thus require overhaul.[44]

Encounters

By the conclusion of the 1960s, HR-oriented training moved beyond managerial techniques or the challenges facing cooperative communities to the promise of personal growth. Unlike T-Groups that focused on social communication, "Encounter" sessions, associated with the Esalen Institute in California, offered individuals extreme experiences that violated social norms, ostensibly serving as a catalyst for self-realization. In one event in

Haifa, two hundred young and old participants ran around slapping each other's behinds, hugging, sharing secrets, sighing, screaming. After three hectic hours one woman uttered, "I feel that I stand on the abyss."[45]

The press turned ever more curious. In a northern kibbutz guest house, thirty people were observed checking each other's bone structure, sculpturing clay with eyes closed, and listening to a recording of a lute. At yet another event an instructor screamed at participants, "I hate you," demanding that each of them would echo the sentiment. He proceeded to castigate a young man for supposedly evading his feelings and asked whether he could hit him. The young person nodded in approval and was then treated to two slaps in the face. It was reported that a few Encounter alumni ended up requiring mental health assistance.[46]

In 1973, Dalia Ayalon, a daughter of former Israelis who grew up in New York, introduced the self-improvement methods of Dale Carnegie. She was the first woman in the Dale Carnegie organization to be entrusted with establishing a national branch. As in the United States, training focused on developing communication skills, increasing self-confidence, improving memory, and generating personal exuberance. Specific course topics included how not to worry, how to solve problems, how to get excited, the art of persuasion, positive self-perception, and of course, following Carnegie's ubiquitous slogan, "how to win friends and influence people." All instructors were trained in the United States. By the end of the decade, there would be 5,000 graduates of the Dale Carnegie courses in Israel.[47]

Personal growth was accompanied by efforts at bodily shrinkage— another dimension of affluent consumer society. Israel was the site of one of WeightWatchers' first branches outside the United States. It was established in 1967 and led by two newcomers, mother and daughter Regina Diker and Bat Sheva Silverman. WeightWatchers proved a success, offering, beyond recipes and strategies for losing weight, extensive social interactions and opportunities for public testimony. By 1973 the organization had a membership of 150,000 spread over eighty-four branches.[48]

Measuring Voters' Preferences

Lahat's successful bid for mayor of Tel Aviv was a watershed campaign, exposing an emerging confluence of politics and commerce in the country's political realm. One element was the tactics unleashed to market political candidates in an increasingly visual and televisual public sphere. But the nexus of politics and the marketplace ran even deeper. Alongside commodifying politicians, the voter was reimagined as an autonomous consumer, unshackled by previous party, social, and ideological loyalties, free to make her own choices in search of new options. Beyond the individuality of the candidate, therefore, the slogan "this time the choice is personal" underscored the individuality of the voter, interpellated in Lahat's campaign ads by the constant use of the singular "you," and the visceral bond forged, through real and imagined eye contact, or the tactility of charismatic touch.

The polity, however, was conceived in opposite terms. Individual voters were aggregated and serialized through statistical categories. While the supposedly autonomous voter exercises judgment and free will, voters' behavior en masse was deemed measurable and predictable. By the early twentieth century marketing research and political polling became inseparably intertwined in the United States.[49] In Israel, the 1965 elections saw the first employment of statistical research for political strategy. Mapai hired Dahaf, one of the largest publicity and polling outfits. Except for (then) Deputy Prime Minister Abba Eban all cabinet ministers doubted the innovation. It's good in America, not here, they scoffed.[50] Dahaf predicted 35.8 percent for Mapai/Ahdut Ha'avoda Labor alliance, but Mapai's headquarters decided to shelve the finding, deeming it too optimistic. It turned out that Dahaf was off by a meager 0.2 percent. In the following years, private firms that gauged consumer taste for soup and salami also began measuring political behavior. Research about politics and policy was at times tagged on to surveys that were funded by commercial concerns.

More precise market research techniques became available. For instance, the increasing number of private phones enabled pollsters to measure advertising effectiveness more accurately. The American-trained director of the firm Seker: Economic Services selected to inaugurate its operation with polls on political issues: the prospects of altercation with the Soviets, the

1970 "package deal" over wages, prices, and taxes, and the clash between the Histadrut and the Ports Authority.[51] Just a few years earlier, in 1965, a publicity firm promised 5,000 liras and other prizes for those who would guess the election results correctly. Contestants were asked to fill up a form and send in one lira to participate in the raffle. The survey had a clear marketing purpose, for it generated a database of newspaper readership according to region, sex, profession, and day of the week in which the ad was read. It also recorded the public's political mood, foreshadowing the coming convergence of politicking and marketing tools.[52]

The Israeli establishment whose cohorts continued to hold key positions in government into their seventies and eighties were suspicious or even contemptuous of public opinion polls. In their conception, opinion should be cultivated rather than measured; it should flow from and be couched in the language of ideology.[53] However, by 1973, both Labor Alignment (of which Mapai was the leading party) and Gahal/Likud utilized polling extensively to tailor their message and to figure out how to identify and recruit undecided voters.

In Tel Aviv, Rabinowitz's headquarters asked potential voters about social distress, pollution, and housing for young people, but Sarid suspected that such hot button *issues* do not truly affect how people vote. He preferred to study public views about the candidates' differing *images*.[54] The two campaigns dispatched spies to obtain their opponents' polls. It was not exactly a local version of the Watergate break-in but still, a symptom of the fierce competition and the psychological warfare evident on all fronts.

Another aspect of the colonization of politics by statistics was the advent of exit polls on election day. Again, the 1965 elections inaugurated the first broadcast of real-time forecasting. Using a sample of no more than six polling stations, statistician Hanoch Smith predicted the general outcome over the radio with great accuracy.[55] Smith studied at the University of Pittsburgh and Columbia before arriving in Israel in 1950, first to Kibbutz Gesher Haziv that just a couple of years earlier was cofounded by American immigrants. After three years as a dairy farmer, he joined the Central Bureau of Statistics and later the Bureau for Manpower Planning. In 1972, he would found a private business, Smith Consulting.

In the 1969 parliamentary elections, the sample comprised fifty-three stations. Data was fed to an IBM System/360 Model 50 computer. The medium was now television rather than radio. Alas, to Smith's great embarrassment, the forecast was significantly off. But in the 1977 elections Smith would be the first to announce the greatest political upset in the country's political history, the replacement of the Labor hegemony with a Center-Right coalition led by Likud's Menachem Begin. The genial Smith and his strong American accent became election night fixtures.[56]

The Permanent Survey

Louis Guttman assumed a decisive role in domesticating statistical research in Israel for the purpose of both policymaking and free enterprise. In 1947, he abandoned an unusually promising academic career at Cornell University to move to Palestine, where he established and led the Institute for Applied Social Research, now the Guttman Center for Public Opinion and Policy Research, in Jerusalem. He first made himself a name during World War II studying military morale and developing an innovative cumulative scaling model for statistical surveys, subsequently named the Guttman Scaling. In Jerusalem, he began by measuring public attitudes toward the radio broadcasts of the Jewish pre-state defense organization, the Haganah, and then, capitalizing on his war experience, studying the morale of the city's second-line defenders.

Guttman continued to manage the army's Psychological Research Unit, whose public opinion department was the first in the country to conduct social surveys on a national scale.[57] In 1955, his outfit was reconstituted as an independent nonprofit that, nevertheless, was officially designated as the body to which government offices should apply for assistance in their social research needs. By the conclusion of the century, the Institute would conduct 1,300 studies.[58]

Early surveys on morale were analyzed to dispense advice for the benefit of military commanders on how to establish a sense of pride and belonging among soldiers and the attendant importance of military rhetoric, symbols (such as insignia), and public propaganda.[59] Guttman translated to Hebrew the US military handbook on how to grapple with battle-generated fear.[60] He explored a plethora of topics emanating from the enormous wave of immigration and the consequent challenges of housing and social adjustment, attitudes toward austerity and rationing policy, juvenile delinquency, worker productivity, and more.

The number of interviewees in this initial phase was quite substantial. Knocking on doors, canvassers presented themselves as government emissaries and often received full and even enthusiastic cooperation.[61] Recurrent visits of officials and the representation of the nation through legible statistical charts are reminiscent of processes by which modern national sentiments are produced and sustained according to Benedict Anderson's "imagined communities" formulation.[62] Nevertheless, the 1950s were a time of struggle for the Institute and its leader. Guttman was one of the top experts in behavioral surveys in the world, but Israeli bureaucrats and politicians were indifferent to statistical research, unconvinced of its utility or desirability. The Institute was described in one document as an abandoned child. Some suspected it to be a political tool of Mapai.[63]

In response, Guttman contracted various branches of the American military and global businesses, offering Israel as a laboratory for social measurement. The Institute conducted research about husbands and wives for the US Department of Health, Education, and Welfare, on personality and social organization for the American Air Force, and on climate research for the Ford Foundation. Voice of America commissioned a study on how Israelis react to its broadcasts. UNESCO was interested in prejudice against immigrants. Volkswagen solicited information about client satisfaction, and Coca-Cola on consumer habits.[64]

In the 1960s, the pace of research accelerated. On the eve of the Six-Day War, the Institute conducted research on public morale.[65] In the war's aftermath, it launched the permanent survey (*seker shotef*) of social indicators and established itself as an essential arm of official decision-making. Every two weeks, five hundred Israelis were interviewed. Results were published every four months. Topics included government services, reliability of government information, the public mood, the peace process, Israel/US relations, the standard of living, political extremism, civil rights, and social cohesion.[66] That year one of Guttman's close collaborators, the sociologist and communication scholar Elihu Katz, who had moved to Israel from the United States just four years earlier, was entrusted with directing the task force that established Israeli TV. Katz attempted to apply the tools of the social survey to fulfill one of the nascent TV station's chief goals of communicating with the Arabic-speaking population. He sought to study the media consumption and other habits of potential viewers across the Green Line separating Israel from the occupied territories, for instance, when the average Palestinian goes to sleep.

Guttman saw in his brand of research a medium for democratic policymaking. In 1949, the Institute determined, "in a democratic country it is important and desirable from time to time to learn what the public thinks about specific issues."[67] Early on he suggested that the mere existence of the Institute was a tool for public diplomacy on Israeli democracy. Once again, soliciting and analyzing views and attitudes of ordinary citizens could buttress the democratic process but surveys are also vehicles of governance, making, rather than measuring opinion and, in addition, providing leaders with the means of shaping or manipulating perception. The contribution of statistical research to managerial rationality was ever more evident when, early on, the Institute entered the field of psychometric testing. In 1952, 15,000 state employees underwent a psychometric examination to evaluate the correlation between skills and placement with the purpose of increasing work efficiency.[68] Similarly, the emphasis on gauging morale bridged the gap between military affairs and modern management. It exemplified how knowledge could be aggregated and exploited to mobilize soldiers, workers, and immigrants.[69]

The theme of morale brings us back to Lahat's army career. At the end of the 1960s he served as the commander of an armored division in the Sinai Peninsula during the War of Attrition. As military commentator Ze'ev Shiff observed, morale and taking care of soldiers' and reservists' needs were then as important as fighting. Lahat's final appointment was as the head of the Personnel Directorate, which he jokingly labeled the Human Beings Department. He focused on improving the quality of military leadership, assuring a more equitable spread of reserve service, and ameliorating the difficulties emanating from recruiting underprivileged, at-risk youth.[70] Lahat certainly had "people skills." When fourteen Black Panther activists returned their military service cards declaring they did not want to serve a country that treated them like second-class citizens (see chapter 5), he was successful in persuading them to reclaim their military documents.[71]

A Sabra in the President's Court

Truth be told, contemporary observers sometimes found it hard to separate imported electioneering techniques from Lahat's personality or his generational and military background. His folksy mannerisms, chumminess (*hevremaniut*), and uninhibited directness also derived from the IDF habitus and the spirit of the '48 generation. Ultimately, Lahat's candidacy rested on the militarization as much the Americanization of Israeli society. At the turn of the 1970s, generals became much revered and sought-after celebrities. A few parachuted safely into politics or management. Compensating for its shaky position within Gahal/Likud, the Liberal Party recruited two generals, Lahat and future prime minister Ariel Sharon. Moreover, as we shall see in the next chapter, the IDF engaged American managerial knowledge, technological expertise, and professional ethos more intensely than other governmental bodies.

In the mid-1960s, when the IDF was still largely equipped with a French arsenal, the military leader with the most conspicuous American orientation was the then chief of staff Yitzhak Rabin. Upon his discharge in 1968 he served five years as an ambassador to the United States. In America he became involved in Washington politics and life without shedding any of his generation's native attributes, including a propensity to ignore conventions and decorum and to be direct and even blunt.

With no experience in diplomacy, aversion to small talk, and only a fair command of English, Rabin proposed to Prime Minister Eshkol to appoint him as the Israeli emissary to Washington. He would explain this unusual career move by his conviction that only strong American support could curb and balance the Soviet incursion into the Middle East. But there was also an autobiographical element that propelled his request. His father, Nehemia, left eastern Europe in 1905 for St. Louis, where he would stay for more than a decade. Rabin remembered that Nehemia had nothing but admiration for the American way of life. "Dad's stories about the United States and life there had a role in my desire to serve Israel there," he would admit.[72]

However, Rabin's first year in office produced major disappointments. He would claim to have found a country on its knees, broken apart internally, and humiliated and mocked internationally, a pushover. His portrayal of Washington, DC, in the wake of Martin Luther King Jr.'s April 1968 assassination is profoundly bleak. Just steps away from the White House, buildings were set on fire and stores looted. Night curfews reminded Rabin of the British occupation of Palestine. Slowly it dawned on him that America is becoming a second-rate superpower. Would Israel be the first victim of its demise? He seemed to be taking all of that to heart. "It was a very difficult year for the United States, it was a very difficult year for me," he would tell an interviewer, indicating that at the time he was quite depressed.[73]

In subsequent years, Rabin would emerge as one of the chief architects of the increasingly intimate "special relationship" between the two countries that despite ups and downs and lingering obstacles yielded substantially greater military, financial, and diplomatic support for Israel, culminating with the massive airlift of military supplies during the October 1973 war.[74] Rabin achieved direct access to the White House and eliminated the method of communicating with a sitting president through the graces of powerful American Jewish intermediaries.[75] With his wife Leah he plunged into Washington's social scene, fraternizing with officials, congressmen as well as journalists and pundits.

While Rabin was contemptuous of "court Jews," whom he blamed for blocking his access to the White House during Johnson's tenure, he turned into a rather shrewd player in Nixon's imperial court.[76] Confidently, he navigated his way through the thicket of the byzantine intrigue and conspiratorial atmosphere encouraged by the president who preferred that his administration would speak on foreign policy matters in multiple voices. Rabin's military background also proved a major asset. In Washington he dispensed advice on strategic policy, defense allocation, weapon development, the establishment of a base for the Sixth Fleet in Greece, and the war in Vietnam.[77] Violating diplomatic protocol in the other direction as well, he intervened in Israeli military decisions, at a certain point urging the cabinet to authorize deep penetration bombings in Egypt during the War of Attrition, insisting, with meager evidence, that the administration signaled its support for escalation.[78]

Rabin had another branch of the embassy making inroads into Congress. Amos Eran, the liaison to Capitol Hill, developed close relations with Senator Henry Jackson (D-Washington) and participated in framing the famous

Jackson-Vanik Amendment that linked American trade to the USSR with Soviet policy on Jewish immigration.[79] In another demonstration of boundary trespass, Eran, an embassy employee, drafted for Representative (and future President) Gerald Ford (R-Michigan) a speech in which the congressman made national headlines by publicly calling for the relocation of the American embassy from Tel Aviv to Jerusalem. Ford solicited the draft but advocating for moving the embassy was Eran's idea.[80]

The interests, events, and other factors contributing to the making of the geopolitical alliance are outside the scope of this discussion. International relations scholar Noam Kochavi argues that in addition to strategic considerations, the "conservative turn" initiated by Meir and Rabin, most importantly the public support Israel lent to Nixon's Vietnam policy, had a positive psychological and emotional effect on Nixon's attitude toward Israel.[81] However, there are indications that Rabin, too, was guided by personal dynamics that went beyond the cool, analytical acuity for which he was famous. He certainly adopted a Nixonian outlook on both global affairs and, to a large extent, American domestic upheaval as well.

Rabin's decidedly pro-Nixon diplomacy put him initially at odds with some officials in the Israeli Foreign Ministry, which he ultimately circumvented, working directly with premier Meir. With Nixon's blessing he was able to bypass the State Department as well, communicating with the president or Henry Kissinger. He distanced Israel from American Jewry's historic loyalty to the Democratic Party, advocacy of liberal causes, and opposition to the war in Vietnam. This arguably allowed Nixon, whose attitude toward American Jews was tinged with antisemitism and paranoia, to decouple Israel from the threat he perceived from liberal American Jews.[82] Rabin told his wife that Nixon had a mystical belief in the power of Jews.[83]

During his first year in office, Rabin developed a personal aversion toward President Johnson, which informed his dismissive attitude regarding Vice President Hubert Humphrey, who would become the Democratic nominee in 1968. Rabin confessed that he had harbored "an antipathy" toward Robert Kennedy as well. And while he conceded that his aspersions were based on instinct rather than reason, he wrote to an ally in Jerusalem, "I'd rather not have Israel's fate in his hands."[84]

Undiplomatic Diplomat

Nixon and Rabin met initially in 1966 when Nixon, back then at the very bottom of his political career, visited Israel. Rabin was the highest-ranking official who bothered to show up for a dinner thrown for Nixon by the American embassy. "What are your plans for tomorrow?" he asked Nixon and then suggested that he spend the day as an honored guest of the IDF. Nixon accepted and would never forget the gesture.[85] In a later meeting on the eve of the 1968 national conventions, Nixon told Rabin that while both Republicans and Democrats were intent on reaching an agreement with the Soviet Union, if elected he would negotiate with Moscow solely from "a position of power.... The only language they respect is the language of force."[86] Rabin was pleased. He saw an "almost uncanny" resemblance between Nixon's assertion and the Israeli approach to the Middle East conflict. The relationship between the two continued even after Nixon resigned in disgrace in 1974.

FIGURE 3.2 IDF Chief of Staff Major General Yitzhak Rabin hosts former Vice President Richard Nixon during his second visit to Israel shortly after the Six-Day War. Their friendship solidified before Rabin was appointed ambassador to the United States in 1968. (Photographer Ilan Bruner / Israel Government Press Office)

Rabin's aides recognized a few personal characteristics shared by the two socially withdrawn, reticent individuals.[87]

Much before Prime Minister Benjamin Netanyahu aligned himself with the Republican Party, Rabin signaled his preference for Nixon during the presidential elections. In June of 1972, he declared that no other American president had made such a far-reaching commitment to Israel as Nixon did in his address to Congress upon his return from Moscow. His remark to Israeli radio to the effect that "while we appreciate support in the form of words we are getting from one camp, we must prefer support in the form of deeds we are getting from the other camp" was understood as a rather conspicuous pro-Nixon wink.[88] Under the title "Israel's Undiplomatic Diplomat," a scathing editorial in the *Washington Post* inveighed against "an objectionable intent to intervene in American domestic politics."[89] Jerusalem firmly denied any intention of getting involved in American politics but some officials in the Israeli capitol were indeed concerned that the Democratic nominee George McGovern's insistence on an immediate withdrawal from Vietnam would foster isolationism and weaken America's global position.

Premier Meir also found common ground with Nixon that exceeded matters of policy and was likely rooted in a shared Manichean world view. Reflecting on her immense popularity in the United States, commentator Amnon Rubinstein speculated that in a world of rising question marks Meir represented for Nixon's "silent majority" their own old country, certain in its ability to distinguish between right and wrong as in the old days when mothers were always good and the Indians were always bad.[90]

Israel's stance on Vietnam and Rabin's support of Nixon entailed occasional tensions with liberal Jews, but ultimately they did not hinder the political backing and financial aid the Jewish community extended to Israel. Through Rabin's actions, Israel was asserting, in overt and subtle ways, its sovereignty and independence vis-à-vis American Jewry at a historic moment when it seemingly grew more dependent on this community's strength and support. The only places where Rabin was not entirely welcome were university campuses. The Students for a Democratic Society, Black Panther Party, and other radical factions adopted a pro-Palestinian stance and students demonstrated against his visits or interrupted his lectures. There were occasionally bomb threats as well. Rabin never hid his scorn toward the New Left.[91]

Rabin's spokesperson Dan Pattir, who at the time was also a graduate student at Howard University, tried to have him meet Black community leaders but Rabin preferred to focus on those in position of power.[92] He was the first Israeli ambassador to court Bible Belt evangelicals. Both he and Meir met on different occasions with Nixon's ally the reverend Billy Graham. Rabin would write that Graham's "unreserved support for Israel never failed to move me."[93]

Rabin's Washington stint was transformative for both Israel-US relations as well as for him. By the end of his tenure, Meir suspected that he was "going native," becoming too susceptible to the American policy approach.[94] Beyond experiential knowledge of American politics and life, love of tennis, and a penchant for wearing baseball hats, Rabin adopted an admiring view of the American entrepreneurial spirit and other aspects of its market economy. The son of two labor movement politicos (his mother was nicknamed "Red Rosa") he was now gravitating toward free market principles, harboring misgivings about trade unions and the centrality of the Histadrut in the Israeli economy. These new ideas became somewhat of a liability for him during the 1974 contest over Meir's replacement that he only barely won.[95] While this approach would have only minimal effect on his government's policies during his first term as a prime minister in the 1970s, it would certainly inform his second term as a prime minister and the privatization drive of the early 1990s.[96]

Conclusion

A few months after the 1973 elections the Israeli state TV broadcast a documentary titled "Chich vs. Rabinowitz." The two candidates had agreed to allow the cameras to follow their respective campaign trails. One critic regarded the consequent broadcast as an instantiation of the "making of the candidate" genre, maybe another sign of the Americanization of Israeli political life.[97] Lahat would serve for almost twenty years as an incredibly popular mayor. Under his leadership, the city that by the late 1960s was rather decrepit, losing residents to the suburbs, revitalized itself as a magnet for new generations of urbanites. He coined its slogan "city without a pause," an appropriation of New York's "city that never sleeps." As for Rabinowitz, soon after his electoral failure in Tel Aviv he was appointed minister of the treasury in Prime Minister Rabin's cabinet.

With the 1977 elections, the new, commercialized political culture matured and was no longer limited to municipal contests. Dahaf Company, headed by the publicity wizard Eliezer Zurabin, was put fully in charge of marketing the Likud.[98] In Lahat's first campaign, we have a glimpse even further into the neoliberal future of Israeli politics: highly professionalized electioneering, political parties coalescing around single personalities, politicians packaged as celebrities, and celebrities becoming politicians.

FOUR

Technology Transfer: The Phantom Jet

In Israeli Air Force lore there is a story about Uri Yarom, a helicopter pilot, who was dispatched one day to evacuate an injured sailor aboard a merchant ship somewhere in the Mediterranean. En route, Yarom realized he was short on fuel. To his great relief, he spotted an enormous American aircraft carrier sailing nearby and decided to land. The ship's crew was astounded by the audacity of the Israeli pilot who came on deck uninvited and, worse, had the nerve to ask for fuel. Yarom remained unfazed. "Sorry," he smiled, "I thought this carrier was one of ours." General Ezer Weizman delivered this anecdote to great effect as an icebreaker while meeting top American generals and admirals in Washington, DC, immediately after the 1967 war.[1] Although the veracity of some of the story's details remains unverified, its humor and public retelling betrayed a wish and a propensity to test boundaries with ease and a bit of chutzpah.

By the end of the 1960s, the Israeli Air Force (IAF), previously equipped almost exclusively with French aircraft, began a rapid process of switching to American-made gear. The direct supply of American weaponry began in 1963 with the sale of Hawk anti-aircraft missiles; continued, on the eve of the Six-Day War, with the A-4 Skyhawk jets deal; and turned a corner when Israeli pilots began flying the F-4E Phantom II planes in the fall of 1969. This rapid transition had far-reaching consequences. The Phantom constituted a powerful, versatile, and sophisticated piece of modern technology, a two-engine, two-seat fighter/bomber that featured hi-tech gadgets such as computerized navigation and weapon delivery systems.

This chapter examines the experience of the Israeli Air Force as it studied, adapted, and operated the new American technology. The American turn entailed a range of novel experiences for IAF personnel, from those of delegations of trainees traveling to the States, to the moment, in the early months of 1970, when Israeli pilots found themselves at the front seat of the global rivalry, flying American Phantoms against Soviet-made and Soviet-operated missiles and jets.[2]

While a sense of affinity and even intimacy began to emerge between the two forces—sentiments that would solidify by the 1980s and 1990s—the encounter also inspired resistance to aspects of the IAF's Americanization. The IAF often drew a line between the aviation technology it readily embraced and American tactics and doctrines it deemed alien to its own operational culture. Nevertheless, with the new hardware and exposure to American managerial culture, new types of authority, knowledge, and ethos infiltrated IAF life, sometimes unwittingly.

Beyond the cockpit, the new American imports affected both the design and output of the Israeli military industry, which grew exponentially at the end of the 1960s, and the strategic decision-making process that shaped the course of the War of Attrition, from the fall of 1969 to its conclusion in the summer of 1970. The fashion in which the Phantom was thrust into battle exemplified the growing Israeli trust in *and* dependence on sophisticated military machinery.

The following discussion places technology within social networks of air and ground crews, military commanders, cabinet ministers, news reporters, and the Israeli public in general. I examine how foreign technology became entangled with national loyalties and sentiments during a particularly fraught moment in the history of Israel. The domestication of the Phantom, renamed in Israel Kurnass (sledgehammer), involved both material and symbolic dimensions. There was strong pressure at the time to modify and improve the Phantom. Conversely, as a technological given, an ostensibly complete product of state-of-the-art design and production, the Phantom assumed an almost mythical status in the Israeli mind.

Object of Desire

In the late 1960s, Israelis developed great confidence in the ability of the Phantom jet to guarantee the survival of their country. *Davar* labeled the airplane "A Wonder Child of the Sky." A headline in *Yedioth Ahronoth* gushed, "Faster, Higher, Stronger: This Jet Can Dictate Battle Conditions."[3] The IDF weekly *Bamahane* explained that the Phantom's lengthy process of adaptations and upgrades rendered it a "soulful" aircraft whose virtues surprised even its most optimistic creators. It was "the airplane whose name is associated with more superlatives than any other flying war-machine."[4] The Phantom transactions would become both the currency and the ultimate gauge of the relationship between Israel and the United States. Washington occasionally reassessed its arms sales to Israel, in part to pressure Jerusalem or to open a space of negotiations with the Arabs and the Soviets.

President Nixon's Phantom deals maneuvering was curiously theatrical. In the spring of 1970, for instance, the White House publicly set for itself a deadline for finalizing a decision and then infringed on its own deadline. This staged equivocation only fueled the Israeli appetite for the jets. A *Time* magazine caricature depicts Golda Meir bidding farewell to Nixon after her 1972 visit to Washington while she is harnessed to a wingless Phantom fuselage. Nixon promises, "We'll send you the wings later!"[5] Suspension or threats of suspension of Phantom deals triggered great anxiety. Journalist Dan Margalit speculated that if the United States supplied Israel with the entire military arsenal it desired but withheld the "supersonic eagles," it still would instigate a public angst that would be impossible to allay.[6]

Satirist Amos Kenan lampooned the national obsession with the jet and the way it became a panacea for all the ills that afflicted Israeli society. Meir, he maintained, had a universal solution to all the country's urgent social problems: traveling to Washington and extracting more Phantoms from Nixon. She could thus offer "a small Phantom to cover the ethnic gap. Give the children a Phantom so they can continue to sleep on the floor."[7] The Phantom jet also surfaced in Israeli popular culture. It appeared, for example, in a children's book series authored by General Mordechai "Motta" Gur, future IDF chief of staff, dedicated to the outlandish exploits of a resourceful female paratrooper dog named Azit. In one volume, *Azit in the Palaces of Cairo* (1970), the brave dog thwarts Egyptian war schemes by spying in Nasser's presidential palace after being dropped from the air by an Israeli Phantom.[8]

In Cairo as well as other Arab capitals the Phantom also acquired legendary stature and stood as the most blatant proof that Israel was turning into an American proxy. Israeli POWs in Egypt would sense a special respect among their guards once they learned that their captives were Phantom pilots. The Egyptians attributed superhuman abilities to the Phantom crews.[9]

Epitomizing the public's deep investment in procuring the aircraft was a campaign launched in 1969 to solicit Israelis to buy special defense bonds. Under the slogan, "Your part in the Phantom," and the emblem of a tiny outline of the jet attached to a peace dove, the drive endeavored to collect 300 million liras (more than 90 million dollars) for a deal estimated at 350 million dollars.[10] One advertisement declared, "A wheel, a canon, armament, even a screw: Your part is the determinant one." In *Ma'ariv*, Ya'akov Ha'elyon described himself as besieged by children in every corner of his neighborhood, peddling trinkets or carrying donation boxes and imploring him to make a contribution.[11]

Youngsters washed cars or sacrificed their bar mitzvah parties for the national project. Thirty female workers at the sewing factory Epstein-Felheim in Jerusalem resolved to give up their annual trip, valued at a thousand liras.[12] The Israeli press relished in recounting such stories, and there were many to tell. One day, the office of the IAF commander received by mail a cardboard box filled with coins sent by two first graders from Kibbutz Giv'at Brenner. In hesitantly rendered angular letters they informed the general that "instead of the money we'd like to see the Phantoms in the air."[13]

The National Lottery announced two special raffles, "Phantom 1" and "Phantom 2."[14] One newspaper proposed to borrow an old Zionist fundraising technique from Jewish National Fund tree-planting drives and name individual Phantoms after the communities, corporations, or labor unions that assisted in their purchase.[15] In late 1960s Israel, the Phantom—rather

FIGURE 4.1 Children selling their toys and books in the street to raise money to support the Phantom purchase (1969). (Dan Hadani Collection, The Pritzker Family National Photography Collection, The National Library of Israel)

than any specific American consumer product—became the object of collective desire and the IAF cultivated the public's craving. Years before the jet was procured, doctored images of an "Israeli" Phantom hovering among clouds were already hung in the *IAF Magazine*'s newsroom. One reporter reminisced, "Stopping for the momentary cigarette break we would focus our gaze on those images and deeply inhale the smoke."[16]

Discovering America

In 1965, following a visit by President Lyndon Johnson's envoy Averell Harriman to Jerusalem, the IAF prepared a wish list of American aircraft. Facing Soviet arms supply to Egypt and Syria and seeking to enhance its presence in the region by selling jets to Jordan and Saudi Arabia, Washington agreed in May 1966 to provide Israel forty-eight Skyhawk jets. Another motive for the mid-1960s arms supply was Washington's bid to gain leverage over the burgeoning Israeli nuclear and missile programs.[17] However, requests to purchase the Phantom were initially rebuffed. In the aftermath of the Six-Day

War premier Levi Eshkol made another strong appeal while visiting Johnson at his Texas ranch in January 1968. It took almost a year but on December 22, the Pentagon announced a fifty Phantom deal, forty-four F-4E and six RF-4E aerial photography airplanes. This was then the largest arms deal in the history of Israel.[18] It was also the first time that any superpower was willing to share with Israel its most advanced airframe, though, initially, not in its most sophisticated iteration.

Four months later, in March 1969, a delegation dispatched to learn how to fly and maintain the Phantom jets arrived at George Air Force Base (AFB) in California's Mojave Desert: ten carefully selected aviators, the best of their generation, led by two young majors, Shmuel Hetz and Avihu Ben-Nun, future commanders of, respectively, the first (201 or, "The One," stationed in Hatzor) and the second (69 or, "Hammers," stationed in Ramat David) Phantom squadrons. IAF headquarters took a chance on relatively inexperienced, young, and impressionable leaders. About a hundred technicians accompanied the aviators. Participation was considered a great honor. A would-be Phantom aviator gave up on promotion at headquarters for a seat in the delegation. Another frequented the office of the IAF chief of staff day after day imploring him to send him to the United States.[19]

Before traveling to America, the delegation enrolled in a short preparatory course. The curriculum included essential manners—"How to eat with a knife and fork"—as one participant put it, ballroom dancing, and basic religious rituals in preparation for meeting Jewish communities, like putting on tefillin. Hanna Bavli, the foremost public expert on etiquette, supervised many of these workshops. She proffered a glimpse into American decorum, for example, cautioning her students that if someone greets, "How are you?" this should not be construed as an opportunity to launch into an account of what happened to you since childhood.[20]

For the technical crew, the first stop was a quick course in the Defense Language Institute English Language Center at Lackland AFB in San Antonio, Texas, where Israeli delegations studied side by side with a rather cosmopolitan group of Thai, Filipino, Iranian, and even Jordanian and Moroccan officers. Arriving in Texas, one delegation member was taken by the sprawling highways, enormous cars, large steaks, all-you-can-eat buffets, and free coffee. Coming from Israel, he found Texans to be very polite, accommodating, patient, and even soft-spoken.[21] These anecdotes are typical of the Israeli experience in the United States at a time in which traveling to America was an expensive venture reserved for the very few.

It took soldiers trained in the American South a while to understand the racial landscape and its fault lines. The IAF delegation that traveled to Huntsville, Alabama (Redstone Arsenal), in the mid-1960s to study the Hawk missiles arrived during a tumultuous moment in the history of the American civil rights struggle. The soldiers came across venomous flyers attacking Blacks and Jews but did not feel they addressed them directly. They were Israelis. A young Hawk technician, Nissan Limor, remembers one day taking his linen to a laundromat nearby, which happened to be in an African American neighborhood. The women looked at him funny. Back at the base he was chided for doing something "crazy."[22] Five years later, the IAF liaison in Washington advised the Phantom delegation to avoid raising the situation in Vietnam or the thorny issue of American race relations with their hosts.[23]

IAF delegates were expected to serve as emissaries of the State of Israel. In the late 1960s, senior Israeli pilots became much sought-after guests, paraded in front of American audiences, ranging from Jewish congregations to Hollywood moguls.[24] On Independence Day 1969, the Israeli delegation at George AFB staged a special celebration for the hosting squadron. The program included Israeli folk dancing, a film on Israeli landscapes, and a short lecture that encompassed, as Hetz reported home, tongue-in-cheek, "the history of the Jewish people from Moses and the Exodus to Moshe Dayan and the Phantom delegation." The guests were shown gun camera films documenting "kills" of enemy jets. Hummus and falafel were catered from Los Angeles.[25]

George was decidedly different from Israeli airbases where pilots and their families lived close to each other and the tarmacs. In nearby Hesperia, where most pilots resided, houses stood half a kilometer apart, amid the Southern Californian desert and Joshua trees. Green-colored gravel stood for a lawn.[26] Socialization happened largely among men, not families. Another difference was the informality, even chumminess, between the Israeli air and ground crews, which the Americans found unbecoming. An Israeli technician would not salute a pilot climbing into his cockpit. In Yuma, the Skyhawk team witnessed a poignant moment when during the weekly social

FIGURE 4.2 The "Americans." The Israeli Phantom delegation in George Air Force Base in California (1969). Left to right, Ehud Hankin, Yitzhak Peer, Rami Harpaz, Yoram Agmon, Menachem Eini, Shmuel Hetz, Avihu Ben-Nun, Shaul Levi, David Yair, and Eyal Ahikar. Over the next five years, four delegation members would die in battle, and another three would be prisoners of war in Egypt. (*Israel Air Force Magazine*'s Archive)

dance all the male officers stood together and the women whose husbands were stationed in Vietnam were given the privilege of selecting their dance partners first.[27]

Reversal of Roles

By May, Hetz reported to headquarters that the pilots were already confidently flying the jets and beginning to feel "at home."[28] The Israelis attained a special status among fifty other trainees at the 4452nd Combat Crew Training Squadron. America was stuck in the Vietnam quagmire, and morale at the base was low. In contrast, the guests from Israel basked in the glory of the June 1967 war. Their hosts were curious, admiring, and even envious, willing, in some cases, to infringe on military regulations to indulge their guests. The IAF Phantom aviators received more than what their government actually paid for — more training and more flight hours.[29]

Roles reversed, the Israelis often emerged as the reigning experts, sharing their operational tactics with their nominal instructors. The visitors were eager to impress. One story involved the exercise of shooting down a dragged target or DART (Deployable Aerial Reflective Target). Four jets participated. "What if one of us brings down the target in the first round?" asked the Israelis. "It never happens," their instructors assured them. The quartet took off. Hetz obliterated the target in his first trial. Ben-Nun did the same in the second sortie. Another anecdote involved Ehud Hankin, an IAF legend. His American instructor John Madden brought him one day to his office, shut the door behind, and demanded that Hankin not leave until he revealed how had managed to out-maneuver him in all aerial combats.[30]

Sharing battle-born knowledge took place alongside a hectic traffic of military intelligence—including captured Soviet weaponry—from Israel to the United States beginning with the Soviet MiG-21 jet, which Israel acquired in 1966 through the defection of an Iraqi pilot.[31] These ties would significantly strengthen by the mid-1970s. The IAF then provided General Robert Dixon, commander of the USAF Tactical Air Command, advice on the reorganization of his force, and he, in turn, invited a group of Israeli Phantom pilots to assess the performance of their American counterparts.[32]

The enormous scale and seemingly endless resources of the American military dazzled the visitors from Israel. The Skyhawk and the Phantom had undergone a lengthy period of gestation and revisions and were already "debugged."[33] French planes, which served as the backbone of the IAF prior to the Phantom's arrival, excelled aerodynamically but were notoriously prone to malfunction. They were not subjected to the same rigorous planning and testing. It was primarily the IAF that shepherded their process of maturation. Beyond the airframe and its systems, the American penchant for pedantry and order was best manifested in the exceedingly detailed and unfailingly precise instructional literature that accompanied their airplanes.[34]

However, for some IAF pilots, including those who later clamored to join the Phantom squadrons, the switch from the beloved Mirage jet produced mixed feelings. In memoir after memoir, top Israeli airmen describe the transition in strongly gendered—often unabashedly sexist—and national terms. The Mirage stands invariably for femininity, more specifically French femininity. It is portrayed as a coquettish, skirt-wearing, elegant, seductive woman. It "fits like a glove" around the pilot.[35] The Mirage's problems were also often joked about as symptoms of the capriciousness of French women.

Following a beauty-and-the-beast narrative line, the Phantom, deemed a "manly aircraft," proved harder to fall in love with.[36] There was something ungainly, unusual, and yet memorable about its droopy nose, upturned wing tips, and severely downturned tail fins. Large, noisy, ugly, a primordial reptile, it was slow to respond and somewhat harder to control as against the sporty and fun-to-maneuver French jet that fulfilled the age-old myth, so popular among aviators, about man-machine continuity. One pilot explained that the Phantom's qualities in air combat derived solely from its incredible power. It was essentially "a metal bar with two incredibly strong engines."[37] The jet was compared to other American products and symbols.

IAF's chief test pilot Danny Shapira writes, "The Phantom is an enormous airplane, its cockpit is wide, everything about it was larger-than-life in the American style, only a Texan cowboy hat is missing on the pilots' heads to complete the picture."[38] Brimming with switches, dials, and lights, the cockpit was often described as an "office." The Mirage continued to have its proponents and loyalists, and in its different iterations, including the two versions produced in Israel, the Nesher (vulture) and Kfir (lion cub), served as air-superiority aircraft throughout the 1970s.

"Square"

Israelis' assessment of their American colleagues was similarly mixed. A few strong and enduring friendships were struck between instructors and their trainees at George AFB. In 2009, marking the fortieth anniversary of the Phantom's arrival in Israel, they organized an emotional reunion. However, the IAF pilots were less than impressed with their interlocutors' performances in air combat. By the late 1950s, American military thinking focused on prospective nuclear warfare. Aerial dogfights were considered a relic of the past. The result was enormous difficulty achieving air superiority in Vietnam, evidenced in a disappointing downing ratio.

Pilot Rami Harpaz was typically dismissive: American aviators fly by the book, follow written instructions to a tee, in short, lack initiative and imagination. Every time before they took off for the firing range, his instructor would open the Phantom manual, look at the height of the range, compute figures on the chalkboard, and direct his students from which height they should bomb. He could not do it by instinct or by memorizing the manual. In dogfights they were told one thing—keep a benign five- to ten-unit attack angle to achieve zero g-force weight.[39] This level of caution and fidelity to formal instructions seemed intolerable to Israeli pilots who had been taught always to push toward the aircraft's actual rather than nominal limitations. For Harpaz and others, this was a culture incompatible with the daredevil improvisations on which they were weaned.

Archetypes were emerging. Americans excel at organization, methodical planning, and attention to detail. They are adept at participating in and managing large and complex systems but otherwise tend to be conformists, inflexible, or just woefully "square."[40] Perhaps counterintuitively, these observations contrast Israeli individualism with American groupthink or conformity. The Israeli pilot, by then a subject of cult-like admiration and a model for Israeli testosterone-rich masculinity, fashioned himself a resourceful, autonomous actor, with a proclivity for improvisation. This individuality was expressed in fierce competitiveness and an emphasis on personal achievement encouraged by postflight debriefings in which gun-camera results were meticulously compared and performance was critically analyzed. In contrast, the IAF was also conceived as a tightly knit family, more a branch of the kibbutz movement than a military order, as exemplified in on-base family housing and high level of sociability.[41]

One token of IAF-spawned individualism was the initial resistance to the idea of having a two-man crew for the Phantom. Some Israeli pilots preferred not to share the cockpit. IAF commander Major General Mordechai Hod instructed the delegation to find a way to integrate functions and abolish the weapon system officer (or the backseat "navigator") position. In California, however, the Israelis discovered that the navigator's contribution to handling the Phantom is indispensable. "After a month we communicated to [Hod], the Phantom is a two-seat airplane. Period."[42] IAF officers have entertained different explanations for the alleged American conventionality. Some were cultural, others structural, mostly attributed to the gargantuan scale of the American military. The exigencies born out of controlling a huge system push toward conformity and standardization and retard local initiative, so goes the argument.[43]

The real and perceived strengths of Israeli pilots assisted in accommodating the evident asymmetry in size and power and the growing dependence on American support. As journalist Uri Dan, an unfailing purveyor of Israeli chauvinism, wrote at the time, "The pairing of a dedicated, multitalented Israeli pilot and the advanced American fighter/bomber is incredibly powerful with scant competition in the world of flight. It won't be bragging," he continued, "to say that this combination surpasses an American pilot in a Phantom, Soviet pilot in a MiG, French pilot in a Mirage. I purposefully did not mention an Egyptian or a Syrian pilot. They are pitiful."[44]

Indeed, the reputation of the Israeli airman reached all the way to the White House. In May 1972, Richard Nixon, livid about a bombing hiatus the US Air Force took for three consecutive days in Vietnam on account of bad visibility, is heard on those infamous Oval Office tapes lashing at the joint chief of staff Admiral Thomas Moorer, "I've watched every day and the goddamn Air Force does not go back because they're afraid. The weather isn't good enough. They got to have five-thousand-foot ceilings. The goddamn Israelis fly a thousand-foot ceiling. Now tell them to get off their goddamn ass and do the job."[45]

Reworking the Phantom

The Israeli pilots' agency was also manifested in their intense involvement in the effort to modify and improve the Phantom's layout and capacity. The process began during the initial training when pilots pressured their instructors to explain or even justify elements of the airplane design and continued when they visited different factories that built and equipped the airplane. "We drove them a bit crazy," says navigator David Yair. The Israelis inquired why the plane could not take additional weight. Is it the tires, air ducts, engines, wings? No one could answer. The manufacturer, McDonnell, brought its chief test pilot to explain that the maximum takeoff weight was an arbitrary limitation imposed by the USAF. With modest alterations the Phantom was able to deliver a heavier load.[46] The pilots kept raising questions about all aspects of the airplane's design and performance. This cultivated inquisitiveness was an element of their ethos and identity. It was even proudly featured in newspaper reports about the trainees in California. *Ma'ariv* wrote, "The Israelis wanted to know, 'Where the legs sprout from?' In response to any explanation they received, they asked with typical sabra directedness, 'why?'"[47]

Pilots were alarmed to find that the airplane did not have a gun-sight aiming point camera, an instrument they considered essential for their ability to perfect their skills. (An IAF culture of debriefing was likely the product of its British heritage.)[48] Another example was that switching from missile operation to the cannon, and relatedly, from bombing to aerial combat mode required shutting off systems and several switches the pilots found too cumbersome and time-consuming. Pilots and technicians sent home sketches with proposed alterations ahead of their return.

Refashioning the Phantom accelerated once the jets arrived in Israel. Several changes were minute, with a view to adjusting the Phantom to the grueling rotational cycle to which Israeli squadrons subjected their airplanes, for instance, attaching metal fasteners to screws covering the maintenance compartments so technicians would use their thumbs for quick access to the entrails of the large jet.[49] A substantial upgrade involved subjecting loft-toss bombing (a maneuver during which the jet releases its bomb while climbing) to the aircraft's dedicated weapon release system that previously had been geared exclusively to control the dive-toss mode.[50]

So great was the urge to install some of the rudimentary alterations quickly and so wide was the discretion to perform those small revisions locally, that the Phantoms at Ramat David and Hatzor ended up being slightly different. Pilots sometimes did not know whether the jet they were flying had already undergone specific modifications.

There was, at the time, a great deal of technological entrepreneurialism, some wild and daring. In Hatzor, for instance, Hetz lent American Sidewinder missiles to a neighboring Mirage squadron without prior authorization or proper testing. They worked just fine.[51] This push to experiment and modify might be reminiscent of machinery tweaking in some kibbutz toolsheds but it was largely driven by the demands of ongoing war. Proverbial corners were constantly cut, for instance, the prohibition against fueling jets and filling up oxygen concurrently was occasionally violated.[52]

Modifications allowed Israelis to make the implicit claim that in effect they were redesigning the airplane—another aspect of the domestication of the Phantom. It was a source of national pride. In a 1972 radio interview General Hod revealed that Israel initiated a hundred alterations to the aircraft with an emphasis on self-developed upgrades.[53] Some of the French airplanes also received a facelift with American parts, engines, for instance, which were considered far more reliable.[54]

Arguably, the most important technological impact was felt outside the squadrons, and beyond the minutiae of switches and screws. The Israeli version of the military-industrial complex mushroomed after 1967 with the confluence of the French embargo, the exigencies of the War of Attrition, as well as the arrival of top-drawer American technology, including computer electronics and innovative precision ordnance.[55] Between 1968 and 1970, the Israel Aerospace Industries (IAI) doubled its ranks to close to 14,000 workers, becoming Israel's largest employer and chief exporter.

Ties were established with American military manufacturers, exposing Israeli industry to their research, design, development, and maintenance philosophy. As we saw in the previous chapter, the Israeli defense sector ushered in imported techniques for industrial management and quality control. Moreover, if in the 1960s it resembled the French model and was comprised largely of public firms, by the late 1970s it increasingly decentralized, featuring numerous small private firms and subcontractors.[56]

We tend to consider military history in isolated, national terms. However, by entering this specific American orbit Israel was joining an array of nations that were also busy developing relationships with the US military industry. The Phantom was one of the most produced military jets in the postwar era. Not only adopted by three branches of the US military, it was also purchased or leased by eleven countries. A few governments, Japan's for instance, were interested in obtaining the jet precisely because contracting with McDonnell opened a venue for interfacing with an American technological giant.[57] Tokyo signed a coproduction agreement and McDonnell engineers supervised the jet's assembly line on Japanese soil.

Under the American imperial umbrella, the Phantom became a multinational artifact. Participation in this global network allowed nations to compete in designing and producing parts locally. Israel was a beneficiary of that emerging arena and would become the most important modifier of the Phantom, extending its operational life significantly.[58] In the 1980s, the IAI would develop an upgrade package labeled Phantom 2000 and then the Super Phantom. Individual jets, either French or American in origin, were therefore organizational anchors around which the Israel military-industrial complex could coalesce.

Due to its size, larger crew, and double engines, the Phantom was particularly conducive to modifications. It stands in the annals of military aviation as an epitome of designing flux. Since its embryonic stages in the mid-1950, it underwent numerous and quite fundamental changes in a long and rather open-ended process. As the Phantom's biographer Glenn Bugos writes, "The Phantom was built by integrating parts into systems, then disaggregating these systems into smaller parts, and integrating them again in different ways."[59] This protracted cyclical process of assemblage and disassemblage manifested an organizational epistemology that rested on testing practices and rigorously followed procedures that helped navigate different paths and substantiated a culture of trust among a range of actors and constituencies.

There was an ongoing debate in Israel over the domestic production of airplanes versus the option of purchasing foreign technology. In the 1980s, this conundrum would pit the IAF against the IAI over the jet fighter Lavi (lion) project that ultimately never materialized. The fact that the military-industrial complex in Israel was still largely government owned did not guarantee harmony among its distinct components. The impetus to produce locally and the political clout wielded by the IAI and its workers' union had to contend with the IAF's desire to own the best jets possible regardless of their national origin.

The "Americans"

When Israeli airmen flew to Tehran in early 1970 to practice on the only Phantom flight simulators available in the Middle East, they discovered that the Iranian Phantom squadron looked exactly like the squadron they had trained with in George AFB, down to the smallest detail. In front of each office hung a Phantom-shaped shingle, a carbon copy of the squadron in California. The Israelis scorned such mindless mimicry. Their squadron back home was decidedly different.[60] Nevertheless, sometimes nicknamed the "Americans," the ten pilots and navigators, members of the Phantom delegation, brought back from California more than merely the skills of flying the awkward-looking fighter jet.

Several imports were trivial: small bits of Americana, like patches with personal names on flight overalls—no precedent for that in the IAF—or the inspirational, English-language slogans that Ben-Nun arranged to be hung on the walls of squadron 69—a custom he picked up in California—such as "The difficult we do immediately; the impossible takes a little longer." This happens to be an old USAF motto. Colleagues noticed English words and concepts creeping into Ben-Nun's speech in particular.[61] At the same time, IAF personnel began dropping previously common French terms such as *dégivrage*—for de-icing—and *jauge*—for the fuel gauge.[62] Technicians had to adjust to working in inches. Cutting-edge electronics and computers required the establishment of specialized laboratories.

Furthermore, the "Americans" returned from California with new perspectives, new personal ties, and new types of knowledge. They exuded great authority. A young aviator describes Ben-Nun and Hankin in Ramat David, "There were in our eyes important figures that spoke the words of God."[63] In the air the two would compete like rambunctious boys, violating all safety restrictions. However, "On the ground they exhibited enormous professionalism they acquired in the United States—of method and order, how to build a squadron and run it."[64] The Phantom squadrons were larger and more complex than those operating French jets. With the addition of the navigator aircrews doubled in size.

The two squadron leaders introduced a greater measure of organization, including periodic work plans, flight and practice charts, as well as written literature. Translating the hefty multivolume handbook began in California. Each aviator was put in charge of a different segment. It was sent handwritten to Israel, where it was typed.[65] Harpaz's English was improved by reading and translating the Phantom handbook. Later, as a POW in Cairo, he would keep himself and his fellow prisoners alert by translating Tolkein's *The Hobbit* to Hebrew sentence by sentence. The IAF soon followed the

American example when it produced professional literature for the Kfir.[66] The chief technical officers of the first two Phantom squadrons also imposed greater discipline, for instance, paying more attention to their crews' attire.[67]

Such instruments, some bureaucratic, others more habits of mind, were ultimately tools of governance and discipline. "Professionalism" became a common term in IAF parlance. Professionalism is a somewhat elastic, multivalent idea. Ben-Nun underscored that the more complex the airplane, the more computers and rockets it carries, the more it demands of its crew. Making split-second decisions—such as which of the Phantom's weapon systems to deploy—begs for greater knowledge and skills. Professionalism is not about what you do with your hands but how you think, your brainwork, he explained in a 1970 interview.[68]

Not everyone, however, embraced the imperative to professionalize. Some took it to denote achieving a high level of specialization in a narrowly defined field or to connote conventionality. Former IAF commander David Ivry sees in the professional ideal an unnecessary American import, foreign to the IAF's ethos of flexibility and pursuing knowledge beyond one's nominal assignment. Similarly, the Phantom's technical officers were surprised to notice that each ground crew member in George AFB had only a single role to perform from which he would never deviate for his entire career.

Pilots and engineers came to consider the Phantom not just another high-performing jet but an integrated, modern "weapon system." Harpaz, for instance, maintains that the Phantom eventuated a sea change in the performance of the Israeli aviator. In the French era the pilot was an omnipotent "knight in the sky," counted on to compensate for the "deficiencies" of the airplane. Success in missions was often predicated on his skills and experience. With the advent of the American period, he maintains, the pilot was no longer a sky-bound knight. Instead, he became a part of the total war machine comprised of all the aircraft's systems.[69]

Harpaz's conception rests on the evident complexity and interdependence of the airplane's navigational and firing gear. But it also draws on the rhetoric of *systems* that, by the early 1960s, pervaded the American military industrial landscape and at times served as an ideological tool to negotiate power relations within and among constituencies of managers and engineers.[70] In his formulation, the Phantom technology produced a new subjectivity and a somewhat less heroic role for the Israeli pilot.

There was another aspect of the American way of thinking and doing things that the technical crews encountered in the United States: the economical mindset. The USAF squadron's technical officer in George had a fixed budget. He sometimes had to barter equipment to keep within its constraints.[71] The Israeli logistical system, in contrast, was built on the "push" principle—keeping inventory levels steady.

A technician in another IAF delegation one day came across a malfunctioning part of a missile and told his American supervisor he would like to fix it himself. To his astonishment the supervisor took the entire module and threw it into a large trash bin across the room. To explain his behavior, he leafed through a pricing catalog pointing to the costs incurred by a technician's hourly labor, the work of the clerk who would order the part, shipping, and other expenses—as against the cost of the module. You see, he concluded, fixing it costs more than getting a new part.[72] A senior IAF pilot similarly recalls, "[In America] I discovered that war has dimensions other than a well-photographed cannon downing, or . . . placing a bomb directly on target. First, I discovered the economic dimension."[73]

Operations Research and the Matrix

Acquiring the Hawk, Skyhawk, Phantom, Hercules, and other specimens of American aviation technology did not provide the only schooling for organizational knowledge and modes of governmentality that began colonizing IAF thinking. The process unfolded through many portals. Since the early 1960s, for example, the IAF increasingly embraced the protocols of operations research, a discipline that emerged in the United Kingdom in the late 1930s but matured in 1950s America. One turning point was the design of Operation Moked, the IAF plan implemented in the first hours of the June 1967 war to destroy enemy air forces on the ground. Using computerized calculations—and fighting resistance from the operation's architects—a young officer, Adir Pridor, convinced the IAF top brass to attack a smaller number of airfields and to bomb enemy runways separately rather than targeting their intersections as originally planned. His proposal consumed more time and ordnance, but his calculations revealed that the intersections were too easy to miss.[74] Pridor did not find the operations research literature coming from the United States always helpful. Typically, one American training guide presented as a problem the scenario of attacking a bridge protected by two anti-aircraft missile batteries. The textbook solution called for the participation of no fewer than 280 aircraft.

Despite Moked's success, operations research did not become entrenched at the IAF until the turn of the 1970s. The venue for its general acceptance was the challenges presented by the myriad armament combinations that the new American jets could carry. Turning into a freestanding IAF department, Operations Research provided armament configuration choices for each type of combat. IAF experts also tackled the anti–air missile threat for which they developed a novel attack maneuver.[75]

Another episode further exemplifies the multiple entry points through which American know-how circulated. It involved Major (later Lieutenant Colonel) Ezrah Menashe Harel, who in the summer of 1970 arrived in Philadelphia as a recipient of a fellowship from Auerbach Corporation for Science and Technology. The company was a main beneficiary of the Nixon administration's funds for system analysis of social programs, for instance, urban renewal projects. In Philadelphia, Harel became acquainted with corporate matrix management. Each employee was affiliated with both a disciplinary department and specific project groups. This was also the principle that structured design at the Phantom manufacturer McDonnell and other US corporations. New recruits were encouraged to make themselves useful for project managers under the threat that if they did not achieve at least 70 percent billable hours in the first three months of their employment they would be terminated. For Harel this constituted a cruel, Darwinian system of natural selection and yet, he became convinced, it was an essential tool to reject mediocrity and guarantee excellence.

In the mid-1970s, Harel implemented a few of the management techniques he acquired in Philadelphia in his new position as the head of the IAF computer unit. There, he determined that the immediate solution for increasing productivity was tied to setting goals and deadlines.[76] He generated a list of tasks for his "workers," a detailed implementation schedule, and clear definitions of projects. As in the corporate world, their performance was assessed through self-reports that were fed into the computer and then served as the basis for face-to-face reviews with supervising officers. Strong emphasis was put on personal accountability.

The IAF leader who embodied the new scientific approaches to military organization was Major General Benny Peled, who, in 1972 replaced Hod as IAF commander. A self-fashioned military intellectual who would have fit quite comfortably in Robert McNamara's Pentagon, Peled was greatly influenced by the Rand Corporation's rational-choice literature on efficient bureaucratic processes.[77] The October 1973 war found the IAF under his command disorganized, with broken communications, precipitating an endemic confidence crisis between headquarters and individual wings and squadrons. It was this crisis, however, that allowed him to reorganize the force.[78]

A decade earlier, he had already contemplated a restructured IAF in which different functions would be separated and held accountable to their distinct and finely articulated tasks—and then reintegrated via the tools of modern, computerized information technology. Under his command, the IAF would establish "vertical" units that shouldered the responsibility for both planning and implementation alongside a "horizontal" structure of command and control that dealt with operations, personnel, and maintenance. This grid formation also had strong affinities with "matrix management" principles.

Attrition

The first four airplanes flown by McDonnell pilots arrived in Israel on September 5, 1969, to great fanfare in Hatzor. Hod was visibly giddy telling premier Meir that the IAF felt as if it had just given birth after a long pregnancy. (She quipped, "You probably don't know what a good feeling that is." Hod responded, "You don't know how the IAF feels.") Finance Minister Sapir reportedly cried like a child.[79] That day, the IAF insignia still drying on its fuselage, Hetz and navigator Menachem Eini took a Phantom for a victory lap over air bases throughout the country. Four additional Phantoms would arrive every month. The Israeli public was kept in the dark about the jets' arrival. The Phantom was shown publicly only many months later, on Independence Day 1970.

The introduction of the Phantom constituted a watershed in the IAF's operational capacity. The computerized navigational system replaced the map, compass, and stopwatch as the tools of navigation. The jet's radar would facilitate novel tactics such as "pull-up intercepts," capitalizing on the kinetic energy of the aircraft flying fast at low altitude for a rapid climb. New guided missiles, both electromagnetic radar-based and infrared heat-seeking versions, opened new possibilities for air-to-air combat. A weapon delivery computer provided greater bombing accuracy. A single Phantom could carry three metric tons of external stores—more than four French fighters combined.[80]

These and many other technological "marvels" were compounded by the reality that the Phantom squadrons were still in their infancy. Nevertheless, there was evidently a strong temptation to unleash the Phantom as the tie-breaker in an ongoing war. In early October, only a few weeks after the first quartet of Phantoms landed in Hatzor, the jets had their first patrol, still without loaded cannons, since their ammunition had not yet arrived from the United States. Soon after, they were thrown into battle. In November, a Phantom downed its first Egyptian MiG, which was kept a secret, in part to accommodate Washington's wish not to be seen as infringing on the balance of arms. "We are kings of the sky," enthused someone in the squadron's book following the first mission.[81]

Pressure was high. Airmen and ground crews were still learning on the job and, in addition, were expected to train new cadres of pilots, navigators, and technicians. Many pilots requested to switch to the new supersonic aircraft. In the morning Phantom crews took off for training sorties; in the afternoon they were busy with combat missions. This is not widely known but to compensate for the paucity of ground crews a few dozen American technicians had to be brought from the manufacturer McDonnell in Missouri to help maintain the Phantoms during this initial phase. When the first jets arrived, only two technical officers had returned from California, and neither of them had ever hung bombs on the airplane's hard points. The American presence in Hatzor and Ramat David was incomparable with the soon-to-unfold massive Soviet involvement in protecting Egypt's airspace and yet it was without precedent. It required, for instance, that basic records of the airplane's daily maintenance be kept in English.[82]

On March 8, 1969, President Nasser declared a new phase in the conflict, coining the term "blood-letting war" or War of Attrition. Egyptian artillery commenced heavy shelling of Israeli positions along the Suez Canal, accompanied by occasional commando raids. Israeli artillery forces—much smaller than the Egyptian—and tanks responded in kind. For eight days in July IAF jets hammered the northern part of the canal. Five hundred sorties were flown, destroying surface-to-air missile (SAM2) batteries, radar stations, artillery posts, and other defense installations. Previously, the air force played a secondary role in the skirmishes with neighboring countries, and mostly along the Jordanian front. Beyond functioning as "flying artillery," the IAF initiated missions to undermine the Egyptian air force directly by drawing its airplanes into battle.

Nevertheless, tactical achievements were qualified by a strategic stalemate to which Israel did not have an effective response. No wonder the Phantom was heralded as the silver bullet, ostensibly liberating Israel from constraints of borders and space. Operational needs and the aura surrounding the new jets gave the two young squadron commanders considerable clout in determining the character of aerial warfare. In early November, Hod dispatched a pair of Phantoms to generate sonic shockwaves above Cairo. Ben-Nun said, "We were looking for a substantial psychological effect that the entirety of Egypt would hear and find out about the Phantom's might."[83]

Phantoms were subsequently thrown into battle for strategic, "deep penetration" sorties, known by the codename Priha (blossom). Targeting training camps, storage facilities, and ammunition plants was expected to stunt the Egyptian preparation for outright war. But the underlying purpose was, again, psychological, to break the Egyptian resolve, bring the war close to their home front, and, moreover, undermine Nasser's prestige and preferably remove his regime altogether. It was also designed to reassure the increasingly nervous Israeli public.[84]

Meir's cabinet had been divided on the question of strategic bombing. Claiming to have received the administration's tacit blessing, Ambassador Rabin pushed for escalation. Others, especially Defense Minister Moshe Dayan, exhibited greater caution, voicing concerns over a potential collision with the Soviet Union. No one knew that Moscow had already committed itself to defend Egypt's skies.[85] There is little doubt that the arrival of the Phantom, with all of its technological promise, tilted the debate in favor of the operation.[86] On January 7, Priha was launched with an attack on military installations in Tel el-Kabir, fifty kilometers west of the canal, and two other targets in the vicinity of Cairo, a commando headquarters and a SAM operators' school.

The Phantoms achieved their nominal goals except for two grave bombing errors in which civilian lives were taken when a commercial plant and then a school were attacked. Israel attained and demonstrated air superiority over Egypt with scant opposition. Nevertheless, the campaign to undermine Egyptian public support of its leaders failed. Moreover, by the early months of 1970, Israel faced a transformed battlefield. That spring, east of Cairo, the Soviet 18th Air Defense Division began to piece together the densest and best-equipped antimissile complex built anywhere in the world. Several combat jet squadrons also joined what the Soviets labeled "Operation Caucasus." Equipped with improved SA-2s and the agile SA-3s, the latter being much more effective against low-flying jets, the Soviet batteries introduced new tactics such as missile ambushes, decoy operations, and electronic warfare.[87]

As with Priha operations, the IAF deployed Phantoms almost exclusively against the missile threat. Crews flying the French Mirages, Vautours, Super Mystères, and even the American Skyhawks watched on the sidelines with growing frustration. Fearing a direct conflict with the USSR, the Israeli cabinet phased out missions around Cairo. The Soviets, however, were already pushing toward the canal, taking a major leap on the night of June 29. On the following day, two Phantoms were shot out of the sky. One navigator (Yair) was evacuated, but three other crewmen (including Harpaz) were captured and held in captivity for the next three and half years. June 30 is still celebrated in Egypt as Air Defense Anniversary Day.

"Electronic Summer"[88]

Meir asked the White House for help. Hitting a dead end, the IAF rushed to adopt another American technology, electronic countermeasure (ECM) gear that had been used in Vietnam to disable Soviet SA-2 missiles. Housed in special pods carried under the airframe, their operation required that a rather large number of airplanes fly in tight formation, at a high altitude, and in horizontal lines toward their targets. Two electronic warfare experts were brought from the United States. The mission was hastily organized. No testing took place. In Vietnam, the USAF ran specialized Phantom units nicknamed Wild Weasels to operate the jamming equipment and used proper armament to disable radar, the Shrike missiles, which Israel had not received.

For the Israeli aviators who knew close to nothing about electronic warfare, everything about the mission seemed wrong, militating against their instincts and training, especially flying high and in a rigid pattern against missile batteries.[89] On July 18, a large armada of Israeli jets led by the Phantom's squadrons with Hetz and Ben-Nun in the front took off and turned toward the canal. The pods were effective in blocking SA-2 radar screens but could do little against the SA-3s, which, unbeknownst to the pilots, were already positioned on the ground closer to the Suez. The results were disastrous. One missile hit the Phantom flown by Hetz, killing the pilot. His navigator Eini parachuted into the hands of Egyptian farmers. Ben-Nun's airplane was severely damaged and barely made it back for an emergency landing at Refidim Air Base in Sinai. For a long half hour General Hod was convinced he lost both squadron commanders. He summarily called off the operation.

To this day many IAF veterans who participated in the attack remain bitterly critical of their leaders for being seduced by the promise of the "magical pods."[90] Eini claims, "We were sitting ducks."[91] Colonel Yosef Naor, who oversaw electronic warfare, argues that the Americans pushed Israelis to employ the pod formation because they wished to test it in the Middle East. "It was a political rather than a tactical decision."[92] Another officer maintains, "We stopped asking 'why' and received the American method without thinking twice."[93]

Only Hetz was killed, but as Ivry explains, his death traumatized the Phantom squadrons, profoundly affecting IAF headquarters.[94] Moreover, by then, five Phantoms were downed and two were badly damaged, representing a substantial portion of the rather small Phantom fleet. "The knight in shining armor failed," someone at IAF headquarters summarized.[95] Ben-Nun, who, two decades later, would become IAF commander, is rather alone in the opinion that the operation was in fact a success. After Hetz's and his plane were hit the missile batteries were essentially destroyed, he argues. Calling off the operation amounted to losing a golden opportunity to obliterate the Egyptian artillery on the Suez.[96]

In the absence of clear goals and a well-defined strategy, the War of Attrition between Israel and Egypt turned into a competition between American and Soviet technologies. Iftach Spector, an IAF gadfly, then a young Mirage squadron leader, has argued in recent years that worshiping the Phantom blinded IAF leadership from using other, tried-and-true airplanes and tactics against the SAMs. He proffers his own calculations of alternative scenarios for the deployment of the French squadrons—160 jets—against the Egyptian anti-air missile system.[97] Spector assigns at least partial responsibility for that eclipse to the Phantom squadrons' leaders and their apparent trust in all things American. Nevertheless, it is not entirely clear whether the pod formation incident represented a submissive acceptance of American technological supremacy, or, alternatively, another case of the Israeli penchant for on-the-fly improvisation and cutting corners.

Twelve days after the pod formation incident, on July 30, Israeli Mirages and Phantoms downed five Soviet-flown jets in a legendary aerial ambush. But the IAF was exhausted. Under American pressure, Meir's government decided to accept the ceasefire arrangement proposed by Secretary of State William Rogers. General Hod appeared to be in favor. The IAF needed time to fully absorb the American arsenal and to find a solution to the missile challenge. The initial ten Phantom trainees paid an enormous price in those years. By the mid-1970s, three of them would die in battle, four spent long years as prisoners of war, and two were injured. Only a single aviator remained unscathed. In the families' compound in Hatzor people began to whisper that the Phantom crews were being sacrificed.

Violating the agreement, the Egyptians and Soviets used the August 7 ceasefire to position their entire anti-aircraft system next to the canal. Israel balked. In Spector's view the introduction of the Phantom during the War of Attrition ultimately had a paralyzing effect on the IAF as the expectations had been too high and the pod formation debacle rendered Meir's cabinet and IAF leaders deeply reluctant to resume battle.[98] However, in the following years, the Israeli thirst for more Phantoms would continue unabated and Washington was willing to supply more sophisticated technology it previously withheld, including cluster bombs, electronic warfare equipment, and more.

Ideas borrowed from American air battle doctrines had a lingering impact on preparations for the next war. This was evident in the two master plans for destroying the Egyptian and the Syrian anti-aircraft missiles, known as Tagar and Dugman 5. Ben-Nun, who was put in charge of IAF planning, was one of their chief designers. These schemes prescribed large-scale waves of highly synchronized attacks that left little space for improvisation and maneuvering. Tagar and Dugman 5 were neither properly nor fully executed in the first few days of the Yom Kippur War.[99] Nevertheless, Spector, who by the war, became a commander of a new Phantom squadron, mocked them as aerobatic displays, American imports, alien to the spirit of the "Hebrew pilot." Ivry concurs. He also detects in these schemes traces of American influence—especially the massification of the attack ("saturation") that was foreign to the Israeli system of incrementally clearing up small areas in concentrated form. "Here the American approach was not the right approach for us," he concludes.[100]

Without adjudicating the wisdom or folly involved in embracing American tactics and weaponry, these controversies betray ongoing tensions over the balance between human agency and machines, as they also encapsulate the wish to preserve the sovereignty of what Spector calls the "Hebrew pilot," now challenged by sophisticated, computer-driven technology and rigid preplanning. A new disposition that was technologically inclined and knowledge oriented had to be forged for the Israeli aviator.

Conclusion

Three intersecting subplots converge in this account of replacing French with American arsenal that follows the purchase, modification, and deployment of the F-4E Phantom II jets. First is the appropriation or domestication of the Phantom/Kurnass. It began with the mobilization of Israelis to articulate their citizenship through participation in the collective purchase of the Phantom, by donating money or buying bonds to acquire some unknown part of the wondrous war machine. The Phantom, perhaps more than other tools of war, was shrouded in thick layers of emotion. It was an affective object, alternatively generating confidence, anxiety, mystery, jealousy, and disappointment, or used to induce fear. In 2004, after thirty-five years of service, the Israeli Air Force staged a retirement party for the Phantom, an unprecedented event.[101]

Another aspect of the Phantom's domestication was its alterations and upgrades, perceived as demonstrations of Israeli agency and independence. The question of national identity and technology would become even more acute in the 1980s with the controversial Lavi project, in which an ostensibly Israeli aircraft, an epitome of self-reliance, depended heavily on American technological know-how and American funding.

The second narrative zigzags between, on the one hand, opposition to the importation of American operational practices, and, on the other hand, the introduction of new American-inspired disciplining mechanisms and ideologies, modes of organization, and an ethos, "professionalism," that were ultimately even more intrusive. Knowledge constituted a major currency of exchange in the US-Israeli encounter after the June 1967 war. It flowed in both directions and included technical information, battle experiences, military intelligence, and equally important, research methods and managerial techniques.

Overlapping with the other two, the third narrative addresses the impact of the imported military artifacts on Israeli techno-military thinking. The trust in the state-of-the-art technology was shared by pilots, leaders, and, as we have seen, the public at large, and sometimes appeared to contribute to specific decisions, for instance, strategic bombing in the Egyptian hinterland, or the rushed adoption of the pod formation. Ezer Weizman, by then a member of Meir's cabinet, described in his memoirs Minister Yisrael Galili pacing up and down in the cabinet room after Hetz's plane was downed, stopping to ask, "Ezer, where's it all going to end? If we don't get that Shrike missile from the United States, what's going to happen?"[102]

The IAF would receive the antiradar AGM-45 "Shrike" shortly thereafter. But Weizman maintained that the psychological reliance on specific weapons became debilitating and that "technological limitation or the lack of some weapon or other" served as excuses for Israel's inability to win the War of Attrition. In the 1970s he would coin the expression, "the missile bent the jet's wing" to describe the competition between the two technologies. Still, in his view, strategic decisions rather than technology determined the course of the War of Attrition and the Yom Kippur War.

Nevertheless, following the 1967 war—and arguably ever since—the allure of technologism or the "technological fix" has persisted. It was often enmeshed with what might be termed the "vertical fix," the expectation that Israel's defense or security problems would be addressed and resolved from the air. As importantly, airpower is essential to what Eyal Weizman labeled "Israel's architecture of occupation," and it features, among other tactics, targeted assassinations from the air, which in recent decades became a tool of the American "War against Terror" as well.[103] The advent of American technology in the late 1960s also coincided with the emergence of the Israeli rendition of the military-industrial complex and constituted a significant turning point in the history of Israeli high technology in general. Many IAF personnel, whether senior pilots or engineers, would find second careers in either the design or the marketing of military equipment.

FIVE

Panthers in Black and White

In 1972, a gospel and soul musical revue, *Don't Call Me Black!*, premiered on a Tel Aviv stage. Written by Dan Almagor (music, Benny Nagari) the show dramatized the historical struggles of African Americans, featuring songs such as "Snow-White," "The Slave," and "Black and Beautiful." The second act offered a gospel version of the biblical narrative, casting major protagonists, Adam, Eve, the Snake, and Noah—as Black characters. Two foreign Black entertainers trained the cast in how to be "Black." Instead of blacking up with tar, the actors put on outlandish outfits, Afros, and heavy jewelry to signify racial difference. This aesthetic likely drew from the hugely successful musical *Hair* (see chapter 9) rather than any Black performance.[1]

Just a year before *Don't Call Me Black!* opened, a group of poor, young Israelis insisted on calling themselves Black, and "Black Panthers" no less, marking Jews who arrived from Arab countries as oppressed and exploited by an unfeeling, arrogant Ashkenazi elite. They emerged overnight with a series of raucous demonstrations and other public stunts. Their movement claimed to speak for and sought to radicalize poor Mizrahi (Eastern, Oriental, or Sephardic)[2] Jews who had immigrated from North Africa and the Middle East in the 1950s and still occupied the lowest echelons of Israeli society. Ostensibly committed to Jewish immigration, "absorption," and integration, the Israeli elite often considered the Mizrahi predicament in terms of a failure to modernize or an endemic resistance to change.

Embracing American racial militancy in the "Global Sixties"[3] afforded the Israeli Panthers a set of ready-made radical symbols and a defiant public style. Neither needed extensive explication. They took from the American Black Panther Party (BPP) icons such as the clenched fist and the image of the panther, as well as a few core tenets of their politics. Beyond any specific appropriation, assuming the Panthers' mantle rendered their complaint remarkably potent. The Panthers used their borrowed avatar inventively, at times deploying it as a threat of an impending upheaval, at other times dismissing it as merely an instrument for capturing attention; and enormous attention they indeed received, rattling the Israeli mainstream that was anxious about potential ties between poor Mizrahi Jews and the extreme Left either in Israel or abroad. Prime Minister Golda Meir claimed to have lost sleep over their protest. Despite their modest numbers and the movement's rapid demise, the Panthers did more than any previous group to politicize ethnic tensions within the Jewish population of Israel.

The BPP did not initiate the poor young Israelis' dissent. Still, the label "Black Panthers," which they initially stumbled upon, scandalized Israeli society not only for its evocation of armed insurrection but also because of its uncanny foreignness. Connecting themselves symbolically with a global conflict pitched over the color line, the Panthers threatened to expose Israel's interior life for the world to see. Their rise made mockery of the Israeli conviction that social cohesion and common purpose inoculated it from the convulsive social conflicts of the 1960s that it had observed from its Middle Eastern perch.

The Israeli iteration of the Black Panthers was only one among globally dispersed groups that borrowed liberally from the rhetoric and militant symbols of African American politics at the turn of the 1970s. Black Panther movements sprouted up in Britain, India, New Zealand, and elsewhere. Historian Nico Slate observes, "As Black Power moved abroad, the meaning of blackness within the movement changed. The transnational history of Black Power reveals the ability of racially based resistance to racism to cross not just national but also racial boundaries."[4]

However, the case of the Panthers of Israel featured especially complex transnational dynamics. They arrived on the Israeli scene at the very moment that the Jewish-Black alliance in the United States appeared to be falling apart. The rift concerned Israelis but also confirmed that, with all their confidence, their American kin were still members of a vulnerable Diaspora. The notion of Diaspora is particularly pertinent and multivalent here. At the time, American Jewry was spearheading the international fight for persecuted Jews in the Soviet Union. The Israeli Panthers sought to expose a domestic Diaspora, defined in terms of deprivation and disenfranchisement, challenging the pretense of Zionism to have ended the exile of Jews.

This chapter explores how poor Israelis came to embrace the label "Black Panthers" as well as the social and cultural circumstances that made such a seemingly improbable self-designation credible, and, more importantly, politically powerful, even if not universally accepted. The group's performances of *Pantherism* as vehicles for identity formation and masquerade are also integral to their narrative and bear examination. The Panthers phenomenon reveals an Israeli society, far beyond the Panthers themselves, grappling with the American experience of racial strife.

The emergence of Black Power in the United States generated rather surprising ripple effects on Israeli politics. It affected not only the Israeli Left but the radicalism of the extreme Right as well. In the same year that the Panthers rioted in Jerusalem, Meir Kahane, the fanatical rabbi from Brooklyn who had founded the Jewish Defense League (JDL), moved his operation to the Israeli capital, bringing with him symbols, slogans, and methods of operation he appropriated from his archenemies, the American Black Panther Party.

Protest Movement

The Black Panthers began as a street gang in the impoverished neighborhood of Musrara—just a fifteen-minute walk from downtown Jerusalem—where a quarter of families lived on welfare and 60 percent of the buildings were deemed unfit for habitation. Members of the rather small group were young, first- or second-generation immigrants from Morocco, with only partial elementary school education and numerous confrontations with the law, including stints in jails and reformatories for juvenile delinquents. Musrara had been an established Arab neighborhood, but, following the 1948 war, it deteriorated into a dilapidated slum on the frontier. After the Six-Day War, Musrara turned into a lively venue for illicit transactions, from drugs to prostitution, between Arab and Jewish Jerusalem.

By late 1970, the protracted War of Attrition with Egypt had ended. The Israeli economy was faring better, and the state offered new immigrants from the Soviet Union generous benefits, cheap housing, and tax-free cars. In contrast, most of the Musrara youngsters drifted in and out of low-paying jobs. That year, some joined a city-run club, the Cellar, where a new breed of community workers encouraged them to organize and to express their frustrations publicly (see chapter 7). A few of them, most notably Sa'adia Marciano and Charlie Biton, also cultivated friendships with Ashkenazi students and leftist politicos, chiefly members of a radical New Left group known as Matzpen (compass).[5] These much-storied meetings took place in downtown Bohemian hangouts. Selling and procuring hashish occasioned the initial contact, but these encounters soon bred mutual fascination and even imitation, in addition to long conversations about society and politics. When the kids from Musrara complained that the police were relentlessly harassing and humiliating them, their interlocutors explained that the policeman is a front for a larger edifice of power.[6]

In early January 1971, journalists covering the city beat reported that a group of street youth was planning to organize against the Ashkenazi government under the slogan, "We will not keep quiet! Violence will shake the establishment."[7] The young men declared, moreover, their intention to become the Black Panthers of the State of Israel. One of them informed a reporter he was seeking help to travel to America to learn the Panthers' methods firsthand.[8] The papers described fear of an impending crisis among city officials, but the mayor, Teddy Kollek, dismissed these reports, insisting, "Here, among us, no such thing could ever happen."[9]

Shortly thereafter, the Musrara youngsters applied for a permit to demonstrate in front of city hall. Titled "ENOUGH," their leaflet declared, "Enough of no work, Enough of sleeping ten to a room, Enough of looking at the apartments for new immigrants, Enough of prison and beatings every Monday and Thursday, Enough of unfulfilled government promises, Enough of deprivation, Enough of discrimination."[10] Meanwhile, the police received a report about a clandestine meeting in Musrara at which a Matzpen activist lectured the Panthers about their American namesakes and then instructed them to prepare black flags and spike their poles with nails to use against policemen during the demonstration.[11]

What followed was truly astonishing. This permit request from a few unknown youths was sent all the way to the prime minister's office, where Meir, meeting with the minister of police, the police commissioner, and the mayor, decided not to authorize the rally on the pretext that a few of the applicants were "hardened criminals" now operating under the tutelage of the extreme Left. In the name of public peace, police vans were dispatched throughout the city to round up and detain both the group's leaders and members of Matzpen.[12] The police even brought one of the neighborhood rabbis to persuade the detainees to abandon their scheme, but, instead, they began a hunger strike.

Even without the permit, the demonstration took place in early March 1971, attracting roughly five hundred people. The government's harsh measures prompted a public outcry, and most demonstrators, including writers Amos Kenan and Dahn Ben-Amotz, came mainly to protest the detentions and to defend the freedom of speech. At one point, the portly mayor, Teddy Kollek, peered from a window and thundered at the rather subdued demonstrators, "Don't step on the grass! Get off the grass!"[13] At subsequent events, the Panthers would wave a sign, "Teddy, we won't get off the grass." (In the water-thirsty Middle East, lush, manicured lawns signify both affluence and a distinctly European sensibility.)

This is how the Black Panthers of Israel came to be. In retrospect, it seems that Israeli society, more than half of whom had emigrated from Arab countries—had been waiting for their arrival. For almost two decades, the ruling Labor Party had toiled hard to identify and court "authentic" Mizrahi leadership. Now it was caught off guard. A senior police officer would explain that the youth did not initially present any specific demand but instead raised the ethnic issue expansively, couching it as "the problem of the oppressed Blacks."[14] The incongruity between the actual threat and official overreaction, which Tali Lev and Yehuda Shenhav labeled "moral panic,"[15] was derived from the prospects of a budding alliance between frustrated, economically marginal youth and the left-wing Matzpen, an axis whose disruptive potential was encapsulated in an exceedingly menacing moniker, "Black Panthers."

Maligned as serving the enemy's interests, the pro-Palestinian Matzpen was incredibly small, but the population of poor Mizrahi Jews was substantial, and memories of the last outburst of the so-called "ethnic genie"—the Wadi Salib (Haifa) riots of 1959—lingered. A press report from Beirut published only a few weeks before the Panthers' first demonstration featured a Fatah operative stating ominously that the Palestinians expect little of Matzpen but hang great hopes on "our Jewish Arab brothers."[16] Another spokesperson would later declare that the organization regards the Israeli Panthers an integral part in its war against the occupation.[17]

Official overreaction catapulted the Panthers to the center of public attention. The events of the weeks following the modest city hall demonstration were as remarkable as the initial campaign to suppress the protest. Attempts to intimidate and delegitimize the Panthers continued, but a new approach also emerged: to co-opt and disarm the disgruntled Panthers by personalizing their grievances and offering individual remedies such as jobs and work training. Leaders of all the major political parties, Right and Left, as well as a multitude of civic organizations, sought to meet with the Panthers, solicit their views, and find a way to placate them. The press could not get enough. Only three days after the first demonstration, the cabinet agreed on supplementary funds of 80 million liras to cover urgent social needs such as daycare programs. The headline in *Ma'ariv* read, "The 'Panthers' Helped the Cabinet 'Find' the Budget."[18]

The government's contradictory actions typified a rather claustrophobic insistence on national unity. The prime minister and others among the country's leadership were already preoccupied with emerging cracks in the national consensus. A year earlier, fifty-eight students from an elite high school in Jerusalem, led by a son of a cabinet member, ignited a public uproar by sending Meir an open letter questioning the government's commitment to making peace and raising doubts about their own participation in a purposeless war. It became a national pastime to listen to the younger generation and monitor its mood.[19] The Musrara gang, however, was not comprised of future soldiers but of social dropouts, many of whom the army had declared unfit for military service.

A delegation of five Panthers soon met with Meir. She offered them cigarettes from her own pack, but her gesture did little to ease the atmosphere. The tension reached a boiling point when Reuven Aberjil, who had joined the Panthers after the first demonstration and now claimed leadership, charged, "You're a liar" at Meir in response to her assertion that the government was doing its utmost to mitigate social inequality.[20] The Panthers presented her with a list of thirty-three demands, including the elimination of slums, free education from kindergarten through university, free housing for the needy, increased salaries for large families, and full representation of Mizrahim in all institutions. Her questions, however, focused on their life stories and personal distress, not on their social grievances.

On May 18, 1971, the group led a large demonstration known as the "Night of the Panthers" in downtown Jerusalem's Davidka Square. Clashes with the police broke out when demonstrators began marching toward another major site, Zion Square. A police water cannon sprayed rioters with jets of water dyed green, only increasing the panic on the street. More than a hundred people were arrested, many just onlookers, with several instances of police brutality recorded.[21] Arrests continued into the following day. Close to midnight, demonstrators threw three Molotov cocktails.

Railing against the "poison of disunity," Prime Minister Meir said of the Panthers, "They were good boys once. I hope some of them still will be, but some, I'm afraid, won't change. . . . How can a Jewish hand be raised in the State of Israel to throw Molotov cocktails at a Jew?"[22] These remarks were delivered in a public gathering only two days after the riot. When Shaul Ben Simhon, a leader of the mainstream Alliance of Moroccan Immigrants, sought to repair the rift, suggesting that all in all the Panthers were a bunch of nice youths, she shot back, "They are not nice!"[23]

In their first year of operation, the Panthers initiated roughly a dozen mostly small demonstrations in the capital and elsewhere. Sporadic Panther protests continued for several years. Activists and leaders came in and out of detention centers. The main event, in August 1971, had some 7,000 participants. Placards declared, "Golda—We are nice," "Away with spiritual oppression," and "Where half the people are kings and the other half exploited slaves." Marchers carried and then burned black coffins as well as a caricature of Golda Meir naked with a pair of wings on her back. The caption read,

"Golda fly away." The demonstration, one of the largest the city had ever witnessed, paralyzed downtown Jerusalem for several hours. Policemen used force to disperse the crowd, prompting demonstrators to hurl stones at them. Many were injured, including twenty-one policemen.[24]

The police first viewed the Panthers dismissively as a band of thieves, burglars, and pimps in need of an aggressive counterresponse. It did not hesitate to raid their premises, confiscate publications, rough up demonstrators, and engage in what amounted to political surveillance. The police infiltrated the movement early on, recruiting one of its leaders, Ya'akov Elbaz, as an informant. An older man, he had the reputation among the Panthers as a proponent of violent action. Now in the Israel State Archives, police records feature details about the group's meetings with members of the Knesset as well as their conversation with the prime minister. When protests continued, however, police headquarters proposed that officers sit down with their subordinates, most of whom were Mizrahi, and explain to them that poverty

FIGURE 5.1 Three coffins carried by Black Panther demonstrators through the streets of Jerusalem in August 1971. The middle one declares, "Discrimination." At the conclusion of the march the coffins were set ablaze. (Photographer Micha Bar Am)

in Israel was a social not an ethnic problem, and that the Panthers were far too volatile and unreliable to address this serious issue.[25]

Political Education

The Jerusalem Panthers emerged in a short and tumultuous period at the outset of which the small core group (never larger than a few dozen) received its initial political education and elaborated the content and form of its struggle. It was a work always in progress. The story of the Israeli Black Panthers is arguably an example of the forging of political subjectivities at the cauldron of multiple and often contradictory acts of hailing or interpellation—to borrow a critical term first proposed by Louis Althusser.[26] In other words, the Panthers were assigned differing roles and identities by competing authorities and interlocutors, among them the police that regarded the group as criminals, progressive social workers who encouraged them to express their discontent, left-wing politicos who imagined they would carry their radical politics to the disaffected Mizrahi masses, political parties that sought to maneuver them to serve their own aspirations, official Israel that sought to either crush them or disarm them, and foreign and domestic journalists who saw them as a titillating news-worthy story. They generated enormous curiosity and inspired efforts to make them legible. This is not to rob the Panthers of their agency. The opposite is true. Like their American counterparts, they assembled a pastiche of symbols and ideas with great creativity and to great effect.

Within their tiny leadership a range of questions emerged about both ideology and tactics. Should the Panthers, for example, establish their own party or remain nonpartisan, as they had initially pledged? Nonetheless, they all spoke of resistance and rebellion, social and economic injustice, and threatened to bring change "by any means necessary." The most ideological among the group veered leftward. Kokhavi Shemesh advocated a revolutionary transformation of Israeli society. Proclaiming that Mizrahim are fundamentally alienated from the state, he provocatively envisioned a strong collaboration between Jews and Arabs to fight the national establishment.[27]

Over time, Charlie Biton also came to perceive the conflict in neo-Marxist terms, identifying material exploitation as the foundation of the Mizrahi condition. Equally often, however, the Panthers capitalized on ideological ambiguity. They publicly belittled, and often directly denied their ties with Matzpen and the Left. For a long while they skirted the Israeli-Arab conflict. In one incident, Matzpen activists were kicked out of a Panthers' meeting. A few Panthers went further and asked the minister of the police to help them remove Matzpen members from their demonstrations. He refused.[28]

On many occasions they voiced loyalty to the state, which they otherwise castigated as the source of their oppression. The Panthers also demanded that juvenile delinquents be allowed to serve in the military. Seemingly odd coming from radical youth, this was a demand for basic social empowerment at a time when, in Israel, military service was a prerequisite to full participation in society. Sa'adia Marciano declared, "We want our share of the pie, and if not, there won't be a pie."[29] The message was belligerent, but their demands ultimately pointed toward integration.

Marciano cast the Panthers as a social movement that aimed to agitate and raise consciousness to eliminate the social gap. He said, "The important thing is that we woke them up. We showed them they have a right to speak out. Before, people used to say, it's all from heaven. Now—they know they have a right to speak out and shout."[30] Their concrete demands called for an enormous expansion of welfare policies, but the Panthers were also agitated over the low representation of Mizrahim in the Knesset and other state institutions, and among university students. And then there was the insult of day-to-day disrespect. Biton explained, "[In the US] the discrimination is between whites and Blacks and we felt almost like them. Everyplace we enter, every office we turn we are treated differently."[31]

In early 1973, the Black Panthers announced their decision to run for elections and joined with the Knesset member Shalom Cohen to form a new party, "The Black Panthers—Israeli Democrats." A rival Black Panther faction established the "Real Panthers" party. The Cohen-led list won three seats in the executive committee of the Histadrut. However, in the general election it received a paltry 11,700 votes (0.8 percent of the electorate), not enough to gain Knesset representation. The Real Panthers received half as many votes. The October war, it seems, had pushed the debate over social inequality to the bottom of the national agenda.

The fractious Panthers did not have the skills to mobilize a mass movement. Bitter, sometimes violent, infighting—as well as perennial confusion about organization and decision- making—further undermined their strength. Many Mizrahi Israelis, though sympathetic to the Panthers, had qualms about their reputation for violence—which in comparison to the American Panthers was exceptionally mild—and the group's association with the Left. Splinter groups under one title or another continued to be active throughout the mid-1970s.

In 1977, Biton joined the communist party Hadash, which he represented as a member of the Knesset for the next fifteen years. Marciano served as a lawmaker for about a year on behalf of a short-lived Zionist Left party, Sheli (Peace for Israel). Others found political homes elsewhere. The main political beneficiary of the Panthers' eruption was ultimately the Right, whose leader Menachem Begin became prime minister in 1977, due in part to the growing Mizrahi Jews' sense of alienation from the Ashkenazi elite associated with the Labor Party. By the 1980s, new political movements vied to represent the disaffected Mizrahim, most successfully the ultra-Orthodox religious party, Shas.[32] The Panthers' chief political effect was, therefore, the legitimacy they lent to "ethnic" Mizrahi politics.

The Panthers' protest, together with the publication in early 1971 of an alarming "Poverty Report,"[33] prompted an unprecedented public debate about social inequities, ushering in new government programs. This was a turning point in the history of the Israeli welfare state. Although the new policies were criticized as impulsive and piecemeal, hundreds of millions of Israeli liras were devoted to additional housing projects and remedial Head Start–style educational programs.[34]

The prime minister headed a committee to study the issue of "Children and Youth in Distress" whose professional work was led by the director of the Israeli social security administration Israel Katz (see chapter 7). The committee produced far-reaching recommendations. Even Defense Minister Moshe Dayan, who had argued that Israel could not afford investing both in its urgent security needs and in social reform, acknowledged the validity of the grievances raised by the Panthers.[35] In addition, police efforts to suppress Panthers' demonstrations was one impetus driving a group of academics and jurists to establish the Association for Civil Rights in Israel (1972). It took as its model the American Civil Liberties Union (ACLU).[36]

"Terrible Associations"

Accounts of how Marciano and his friends first came to adopt the brand "Black Panthers" form a Rashomon effect. Now, as then, the Panthers phenomenon is both enlivened by and mired in countless anecdotes and divergent reminiscences. In the beginning, they knew little about the Oakland-born movement. Avi Bardugo, then the owner of the bohemian Yellow Teahouse, takes credit for their initial education. "I told them about policemen roaming the street with hunting rifles shooting down Negroes. . . . They didn't understand what a bomb I deposited in their hands."[37] Meanwhile, the city hall–appointed youth counselors used the label "Black Panthers" to generate interest in the press, and were later faulted by the mayor for creating the Panthers.[38] The Musrara group considered other titles as well, toying for a while with "Tupamoroccanos," a neologism that blends Moroccan Jews and the Tupamaros, the urban guerrillas in Uruguay who had achieved notoriety in the late 1960s.

Soon after they captured public attention, the Panthers were bombarded with pleas to change their name. Meir was profoundly disturbed by the idea of Israeli Black Panthers. Meeting with the group, she repeatedly questioned them about the origin and meaning of their self-designation. They told her it was provocative and effective, nothing more. (Even Teddy Kollek conceded that Madison Avenue could not have selected a better name.)[39] Reuven Aberjil remarked defensively, "It could be the case that we have 40% of the ideology of the Black Panthers in the United States that have been also deprived and screwed over, and the fact is that they are violent, and we are not." That neither reassured nor satisfied the prime minister, who demanded to know whether the Panthers realized that their American counterparts were antisemitic.[40]

The BPP of course supported the Palestinian cause. Eldridge Cleaver was living at the time in Algeria, a hotbed of Arab radicalism. By the early 1970s, a debate raged over the question of the Panthers' attitude toward Jews as well as over the line distinguishing anti-Zionism from antisemitism.[41] The left-wing (Jewish) scholar Philip Foner dedicated a long passage in his introduction to the compilation *The Black Panthers Speak* (1970) to dispelling the allegation that the Panthers were anti-Jewish. Even the Israeli Panthers were split on the issue of the American Panthers' antisemitism. Meeting with Meir, Marciano conceded that the American Panthers were "against Jews," but Biton later argued defensively that the Panthers hated Jews only when they assume the role of exploiters.

The predominant Israeli perception of America was that of a violent and racially polarized nation. The hostility of the Israeli mainstream to the Mizrahi Panthers, by extension, was partly based on its bleak reading of American society, in general, and Black-Jewish relations in particular. Several weeks before the Panthers' first demonstration, the daily *Haaretz* translated and published a long *New York Times* piece on antisemitism and the American New Left in which Black Power leaders such as Cleaver and Stokely Carmichael (Kwame Ture) figured prominently.[42]

In the Israeli press, the appellation Black Panthers inspired both fascination and indignation. One commentator advised that if the Panthers were looking to influence public opinion they should jettison the improper and foreign "brand name," which summoned images of "hooliganism, car chases, and broken glass."[43] Others dismissed the name as "grating on the ear," "off-key," or stirring up "terrible associations."[44] Even the antiestablishment weekly *Ha'olam Hazeh* thought the name both pretentious and misleading, given the Israeli group's real aims, and poked fun at the establishment for mistaking the Israeli version for the "real Black Panthers, carrying submachine guns and hand grenades."[45] In a letter to the editor, one *Ma'ariv* reader denounced the American Panthers as "pathological Jew-haters. . . . Let's imagine that some group in Israel would have called itself, Nazis, S.S., or so."[46]

The moniker also forced comparisons—most often by way of contrast—between the racial situation in the United States and social friction at home. Under the title, "On Panthers and Hyenas," the conservative commentator Shalom Rosenfeld argued that there was no credible analogy between the original "Pantherism," nourished on extreme racial discrimination in the American "land of plenty," and the Jerusalem version, "which artificially assigns itself this distorted tag."[47] Rosenfeld further raged against "bohemian clowns" and "intellectual-snobs- scurrying-for-the-barricades" who callously incited the poor against their best interests.

When Minister of Welfare Michael Chasani visited New York City in June 1971, he was treated to a tour of its most notorious slums, reportedly to observe firsthand "the soil upon which the American Panthers grew." The Israeli journalist accompanying him remarked that the neglect, deprivation, and crime were tenfold more severe than in the most miserable parts of Jerusalem. "Here," said one of the minister's hosts, "you don't dare to walk in the street at night for fear of being attacked. I visited Jerusalem and I know from my own experience that in the worst poverty-stricken neighborhoods no one would be concerned taking a nocturnal walk."[48]

One commentator predicted that if the Israeli Panthers find their way to the United States, they would witness American policemen evicting families who cannot pay rent, while their colleagues brutally disperse American Panthers' demonstrations. They would end up singing the praises of Israeli police, he wrote.[49] Another observer took a somewhat different comparative tack, forecasting a coming "backlash" (the word was printed in English) against the Panthers like the way liberal America supposedly distanced itself from Black Power organizations once they resorted to violence.[50]

Thus, in their desire to undermine the implicit analogy the Panthers drew with the degradation of African Americans (one of their signs read "Musrara = Harlem"), Israeli journalists painted a grim portrait of American society, ignoring Great Society innovations for titillating, stock descriptions of merciless capitalism and wanton crime. In the process, they also seemed to adopt some of white America's prejudices.

During the civil rights era, Israeli commentators regularly expressed sympathy toward the Black fight for equality. When the play *Raisin in the Sun* was performed in 1959 one critic drew parallels between the racial problems in the United States and the lingering precarity of Jews even in the "civilized-liberal world." Some saw in *Raisin in the Sun* a symptom of "Negro-Zionism" that called for returning to origins and considered the possibility of establishing a homeland in Africa.[51] Martin Luther King Jr.'s "I Have a Dream" speech would inspire two Israeli popular songs. In 1969 Yehoram Gaon sang, "I Have a Dream" (lyrics, Yehiel Mohar; music, Moshe Vilensky). For *Don't Call Me Black!* Almagor wrote, "A Day Will Come."

However, the emergence of Black militancy in the 1960s and reports about anti-Jewish rage among African Americans altered Israelis' transnational sympathies. This could be gleaned, for example, from the critics' deep unease with the local production of James Baldwin's play *Blues for Mister*

Charlie (1965). Although Baldwin's previous plays were well received in Israel, reviewers maintained *Blues* was too angry, too noisy, too preachy, two dimensional, superficial, propagandist, banal, a "scream from a torrid throat."[52] Israeli commentators were seemingly offended by Baldwin's portrayal of whites. The rise of Black Power politics and rhetoric marked American as well as Israeli Jews whiter. As early as 1964, *Ha'olam Hazeh*, a magazine that often erred on the side of sensationalism, described American Jews as living between the white rock and the Black hard place. Its front cover screamed, "Pogroms of American Jews! Is a Holocaust Possible in the United States? Will the Jews Flee to Israel?"[53]

The specter of Black antisemitism became ever more menacing after 1967 with the rise of Black Power and in the aftermath of the Ocean Hill/Brownsville clashes in the fall of 1968.[54] Israeli responses reflected, and to a certain extent surpassed, the anxieties of American Jews. These concerns were characteristic of a society that, on the one hand, felt more isolated internationally, threatened by the rise of the New Left in Europe and the United States, and on the other hand, saw in the perceived rise of antisemitism confirmation of its Zionist ideology.[55] By the conclusion of the 1960s, the Israeli middle classes seemed ever closer to American and European elites. The June 1967 and later the October 1973 Middle East conflagrations further entrenched Israel's global position in this regard. In addition, these wars alienated African nations with whom Israel sought to develop special relations soon after their emancipation at the turn of the 1960s.

"Panthers in Yarmulka"

The initial Jewish American reaction to the Black Panthers of Israel was disbelief. Visiting the United States, political scientist Shlomo Avineri reported the shock and dismay of American Jews, which cut across political lines:

> Poverty and discrimination in Israel? Communal hatred among Jews? Social inequality in egalitarian, Histadrut-run Zion? Jewish police being stoned by Jewish demonstrators? Jewish police hitting Jewish demonstrators? Something must have gone wrong. . . . No parlor discussion of Israel could now be complete without the inevitable question, And

what about the Oriental Jews in Israel? There are many people around, in conventional living rooms and pot-reeking student dorms alike, who couldn't for the life of them name one Israeli political party but know all about the Black Panthers."[56]

Indeed, the *New York Times Magazine* reported on the "Panthers in Yarmulka" and put Marciano on its cover.[57] *Ma'ariv* journalist Philip Ben filed an anxious report from New York about the Panthers' visibility. American television viewers, he warned, could easily surmise that Jerusalem experienced the same mayhem as Harlem, Newark, and other Black ghettos, or even worse. Such distorted perceptions might erode the view of Israel as a "golden state" predicated on idealism and unified in its values. Moreover, the Panthers might sabotage the campaign on behalf of Russian Jews.[58] Apparently, when three hundred young protestors rallied in front of the Soviet embassy in Washington, DC, under the banner "Let My People Go," a Soviet diplomat approached and to the demonstrators' great amazement asked in perfect Hebrew, "Do you think that Israel is truly capable of absorbing Jews from the Soviet Union? Look what a reception they are getting from the 'Black Panthers.'"[59]

The Jewish Agency's immigration department reported that talk of the Panthers surfaced in almost every meeting with prospective immigrants. One potential immigrant worried that by moving to Israel he would increase the Panthers' bitterness and inspire even more violence. Another noted the irony that Israel seemed now to be experiencing the same social upheaval that he was seeking to escape. The only difference, as he saw it, was that in America the Panthers fight Jews and in Israel, they fight immigrants. Ya'akov Burstein, a yeshiva teacher in New York City, concluded, "Sadly enough, this proves that we [Jews] in fact are becoming a nation like any other nation."[60]

Key figures in the Jewish community, such as Rabbi Arthur Hertzberg, implored Israel to address the problems raised by the Panthers. Leading Jewish intellectuals published commentary comparing the ethnic history of the two countries. Seymour Martin Lipset, for example, labeled the challenge of integrating Sephardic Jews, as well as the disenfranchised Palestinian workforce, the "Israeli Dilemma," evoking Gunnar Myrdal's famous analysis of America's "Negro question."⁶¹ Such comparisons raised the thorny question of who were the genuine "Blacks" of Israel: Arabs or Sephardic Jews?

Lipset drew an analogy between the Mizrahim and ethnic whites and advised them to use their power as a voting bloc to improve their lot. Unlike many Israelis who dreaded the prospect of ethnic politics, he wrote, the Mizrahi Jews should organize politically to emulate the way Irish immigrants, for example, had made gains in America.⁶² For Judith Miller, writing in the *Progressive*, the Israeli Panthers seemed rather restrained, more like the civil rights activists of the early 1960s than the Black Power radicals of the latter part of the decade.⁶³

In Israel, some newcomers from the United States actively supported the Panthers. Young Jewish Americans were drawn to the loose and somewhat exotic, *Oriental* atmosphere of postwar Jerusalem. A recent account of this milieu credits Americans with acquainting the Musrara youth with the legacy of the American Panthers. "Steve," a boisterous frizzy-haired man from Borough Park, Brooklyn, was among the most flamboyant in this scene, earning the description, "the closest thing the city had to a Bob Dylan or an Abbie Hoffman."⁶⁴

But the most important American champion of the Panthers in Jerusalem was Dr. Naomi Kies, a political scientist who contacted the Panthers immediately after their first demonstration. She dispensed advice, communicated with foreign journalists, bailed out detainees, printed leaflets, and even provided chauffeuring. When the Panthers' headquarters in Aberjil's apartment burned down, the group moved for a while into her home. The police counted her among the Panthers' leaders. Raised in Yonkers and later educated at Swarthmore College and MIT, she had immigrated to Israel after the June 1967 war. Kies saw her work with the Panthers as an extension of her political activism in the United States. Hers was a model of political engagement increasingly common in America but largely foreign to Israeli academia.⁶⁵

One of the Panthers' most controversial schemes was to dispatch a delegation to the United States to tour Jewish communities and increase the pressure on the government to respond to their demands. They intended to ask their hosts, "Are you giving money to Jews in a state of Jews, or to Ashkenazim?"⁶⁶ The mere mention of the plan prompted an avalanche of condemnation, which depicted the prospective journey as a disloyal attempt to injure the country by washing its dirty linen in public. The sense of indignation at the Panthers for breaking taboos was augmented by fears of how their protest might influence foreign perceptions of Israel. One commentator warned that by visiting the United States, the Panthers would be walking into the "lion's den," where they were certain to alienate their Jewish interlocutors.[67] Following the "Night of the Panthers," Israelis noticed that the riots in Jerusalem, as well as their underlying social tensions, were widely reported in the Arab media, especially in Egypt.[68]

The Panthers' appeal to world Jewry exposed a double standard by contrasting apathy toward the Mizrahi condition with incredible empathy with Soviet Jews. The Panthers formed only weeks after two Russian Jews were sentenced to death in December 1970 for plotting to hijack a Soviet plane in Leningrad and fly it to Sweden. Later commuted, the sentences triggered global protests. In early January, Israelis stood for two minutes as air-raid sirens sounded throughout the country. In a radio address, her voice choked with emotion, Golda Meir charged the Soviets with continuing the tsarist tradition of murdering innocent Jews.[69] The Musrara youngsters complained that when "Black Jews" were hanged in Baghdad the year before the Ashkenazim kept quiet, but now when "white Jews" are about to be hanged there is a public outcry.[70]

The pressure on the Panthers not to travel to the United States was so intense that it occasioned a split within the group, with Eddi Malka leaving to form the patriotically named "White and Blue Panthers."[71] The Panthers ultimately did not send a delegation to America but developed some ties abroad, especially in Europe, where they capitalized on Matzpen's contacts and made strong links with the large Sephardic community in France. An international conference of radical groups in Florence, Italy, in November 1971, served as the backdrop for a meeting between Panthers from Israel and those from the United States. Biton sought their "moral support." The American Panthers reported that after the first arrests in Jerusalem, they held a press conference to announce their solidarity with the struggle of "Blacks" in Israel. However, the Israeli contingent rejected the American Panthers' proposals for joint anti-Zionist political action.[72]

Pantherism and Race

The Panthers' actions in the symbolic register had a lasting effect even after it became clear that they were unable to exercise conventional political power. These performances commenced with their recurrent invocation of Blackness. The Panthers' first bulletin announced that the "Black Panthers are the children of the Black workers of the State of Israel—who grew up in the jungle of discrimination and deprivation, the fruit of the labor of an ethnic establishment."[73] Another leaflet inveighed against "a government that sustains a Black and White state."[74]

They labeled the Iraqi-born minister of police Shlomo Hillel a "Black traitor." What right do you have, they asked, to deny members of your own ethnic community to demonstrate for rights that you already received because of your "Ashkenazicization"? Another printed circular colored Mizrahim "Children of the Black Diaspora."[75] Previously in Israel, "Black" had been applied (mostly in its Yiddish form) pejoratively to describe the Jews of the Orient, connoting cultural inferiority. By foregrounding Blackness, the Panthers in Jerusalem transvalued and reclaimed a term used largely against them.

The Panthers were not the first to suggest that Israeli society is a pigmentocracy or, more specifically, to point to the parallels between the Black-white divide and the Ashkenazi-Mizrahi split. In 1953, *Ha'olam Hazeh* published a series of articles on the prejudice directed at immigrants, comparing it to the situation in South Africa and the American South. Their author was Shalom Cohen, who would later join the Panthers in the short-lived attempt to form a radical party. His articles popularized the phrase "Blacks always get screwed over" (or "they always screw the Blacks").[76] But prior to 1971, comparisons with global battles over the color line were largely the material of occasional commentary, expressions such as "screwing over the Blacks," which were considered a tad too coarse for polite conversation, or academic discussions. The Panthers removed the scare quotes that previously surrounded the racially evocative "Black" and "white" in the Israeli conversation about disparities.

Moreover, by 1971, Blackness acquired a different resonance. The racial struggle in the United States was no longer the moderate, liberal campaign for inclusion, but a defiant, irreverent, and uncompromising challenge to the fundamental structure of American society. The radical analogy the Panthers declared with the American Panthers more intimately coupled Israeli and American social hierarchies, equating the armed and much larger BPP with its Jerusalem namesake.[77]

Nevertheless, in the Israeli lexicon of difference, Black was neither the most offensive nor the most frequently employed anti-Mizrahi epithet; instead (going back to the Bible), it was a complex designation that in modernity sometimes followed an Orientalist, exoticizing pattern. One anecdote that illustrates the different sensibilities attached to Blackness in the United States and Israel refers to a meeting between Kokhavi Shemesh and Angela Davis at the World Festival of Youth and Students in East Berlin (1973). In an otherwise friendly exchange, Davis became upset when Shemesh used the Israeli expression "Black labor" to describe the lowly forms of work assigned to Mizrahi Jews. She demanded he not refer to degrading labor that way.[78] It is also of interest that the Palestinians, who have been subjected to greater hostility and discrimination, were never designated "Black" in the Israeli vernacular. This suggests that a certain ambiguity was already ingrained in the initial use of the term to signify Mizrahim, arguably, a sign of domestic otherness as against the largely invisible—and differently marked—outsiders, the Arabs.

Racial terminology in the United States was itself in great flux at the time.[79] Also consider that the Panthers or Mizrahi Jews in general were not labeled *kushim*, the biblical term for Africans, which was also used for African Americans. By the late 1960s *kushi* became associated with the term "Negro" and incrementally excised from common language. The Panthers were in fact offended by the popular reference to military recruits enlisted in the month of May cycle—most of whom were poor and without a high school degree—as Mau Mau, the anti-British Kenyan resistance.

When the Panthers met with the opposition leader Menachem Begin, he proposed that they alter their name to "Black Jewish Lions."[80] His suggestion implied that it was the choice of feline, the panther—rather than Blackness—that was disquieting. The lion is a biblical animal that stands for Jerusalem, for Zion, and there are several Hebrew words for "lion." In contrast, the language has no word for "panther." The panther is foreign. It cannot be conveniently folded back into Jewish or Zionist iconography. Its adoption befitted the Panthers' refusal to pursue respectable discourse or to emulate the numerous organizations that already purported to represent Sephardic Jews. It is this irreducibility that rendered their revolt credible. In other words, the foreign-born "Black Panther," which the Israeli press derided as an irrelevant, improper, and woefully inauthentic import, paradoxically guaranteed the group's novelty and authenticity. The label also allowed a rebranding of the dividing line between Ashkenazim and a diverse, non-Ashkenazi communities, moving beyond the conventional modes of ethnic organization that typically were divided by country or region of origin.

The Panthers thus called into question the Israeli *we* and did so by violating cultural as well as political taboos. The walls protecting the Israeli sense of distinct national identity were sustained by, among other means, the decades-long insistence on Hebrew nomenclature in public life. By the 1970s, Israeli intellectuals voiced concern about the infiltration of the English language. The novelist Hanoch Bartov, for example, warned that while the "marginal youth" Panthers translated a decidedly foreign name for their own purpose, the Israeli mainstream was marginalizing itself or, in his words, "translating itself to the foreign," in a much more insidious way by increasingly accepting English. He pointed to two children of the famous: Yael Dayan (daughter of Moshe) and Amos Kollek (son of Teddy), who, to many Israelis' consternation, had published books they originally wrote in English (see chapter 10).[81]

For foes, "Pantherism" became a term of derision signifying lawlessness. A judge reportedly told a female defendant who spoke out of turn, I won't allow you to "pantherize" in this courtroom. In another instance, Pantherism was used in a Knesset debate to describe soccer riots in Tel Aviv that took place shortly after the "Night of the Panthers."[82] Pantherism also stood for masculinity. A strong feature of the Panthers' dissent was their conflict with the female prime minister, thus indexing gender and generational differences in addition to ethnicity and power. Her expression, "they are not nice," often taken out of context, came to epitomize her predilection for aloofness and has haunted the memory of her tenure in the prime minister's office to this day. She cut a self-righteous figure, grandmotherly at times but also overbearing and obtuse.

The Panthers' voice, rude and sometimes crude (they ran for the Knesset in 1973 under the Hebrew letter *zayn*, which in modern slang stands for the male organ), was that of emasculated Oriental immigrants who often conceived of themselves as the "screwed" or the "screwed over" (*dfukim*). For the Panthers, "screwed over" straddled the difference between class and ethnicity in a political landscape where the vocabulary of class was still monopolized by the ruling Labor Party, and in the absence of a strong conceptual apparatus (such as postcolonialism) to politicize ethnic differences.

"Black" and "screwed over" pointed simultaneously toward and away from strictly ethnoracial terminology. And being "screwed over" retained strong sexual undertones. In one event, the Panthers told the crowd, "The state is to blame that we are thieves and criminals and that our sisters are prostitutes. In Morocco we weren't thieves, and Jewish girls weren't whores."[83] Yet, with all its subaltern accents and resonance, the subject position of the screwed over is still ultimately that of the Israeli insider who has been wronged and now demands his due. Tellingly, it has rarely, if ever, been applied to or been appropriated by the Palestinians.

Assuming the name Black Panthers, the youth from Musrara therefore both confirmed the racial analogy and bypassed it, forging a political identity in which the intersection of ethnicity and class—conceived relationally in terms of the prosperous versus the oppressed who are perpetually "screwed over"—propped the figure of the defiant, socially awakened warrior, the Black Panther. Blackness was thus weaponized through the figure of the fierce feline. This identity radically departed from the sentimental, folklorist, and highly commercialized ethnicism that saturated Israeli popular culture at the time (see chapter 8). Also bear in mind that in the Panthers' rhetoric the Ashkenazim were obviously the oppressors but they were rarely designated "whites."

The process of becoming Black Panthers also provided an opportunity for playing with masks. There were ongoing doubts concerning the group's true identity. Were they insiders or outsiders, Zionists or anti-Zionists, "nice" or scary? The Panthers thrived on such ambiguities. They repeatedly maintained they were forced to call themselves Black Panthers; had they adopted a less provocative name, they insisted, no one would have noticed them.[84]

Even as they disavowed their affinity with the American Black Panthers or their links to the Left, the Panthers winked in both directions. At crucial points, it appeared that they had become Black Panthers so they would be recognized as Jews in a Zionist state, forgotten brothers rather than sworn enemies. Thus, when Aberjil said, "We are loyal to the state. We only demand of the state not to make us live like animals," he insinuated that it was the state that degraded them as beasts in the first place; by implication, they transformed themselves into Panthers so they would not be animals.[85] This remark is reminiscent of the performative logic underscoring the long tradition of American minstrelsy, by which putting on the black tar allowed blackface artists to mark themselves white.[86]

Street Theater

The screwed-overs' revolt erupted as a spectacle, and the Panthers continued to weave speech and action into political performances, which included, for instance, a clever employment of "Golda" and "Teddy" as both literal and discursive effigies to toy with and taunt. Their primary street medium was demonstrations that often metamorphosed into marches. Such events had hardly ever been staged in Israel. Demonstrations dramatized the Panthers' cause and generated an impression of action and of a large movement in the making. A few leaders emerged as gifted orators, each honing a distinct rhetorical style, sometimes featuring energetic dialogue with the audience. Aberjil now recalls the thrill and sense of empowerment when observing top police brass attentively listening while he was speaking to the crowd.[87] Young, frumpy, longhaired, perpetually angry and in your face, they also introduced new forms of visual presence and charisma to Israeli public life.

The public arena itself was rapidly reconfiguring in accordance with the new grammar of a televisual world. The Israeli TV station had a role in familiarizing Israeli society with itself in novel ways by, for example, introducing the realities of the slums to the screen. At times, the medium itself became a site of contestation. Early on, Jerusalem city hall accused a television reporter of choreographing a Panthers demonstration.[88] Later, when the nightly news claimed the Panthers suspected one of their own of setting the fire that consumed their Musrara headquarters, roughly one hundred youngsters set out to the main TV station, chanting, "They burned our house, we'll burn their house."[89]

The Black Panthers thus unleashed a range of 1960s radical tactics that, in the absence of substantial student or antiwar movements, fell under their sign. In addition, they borrowed from the protest arsenal of the anti-Soviet campaign, including hunger strikes at the Western Wall. A rally in support of Soviet Jews had featured the symbolic renaming of Zion Square, the "Silent Jewry Square." The Panthers renamed the site the "Real Silent Jewry Square."[90]

Adding drama to their arsenal of symbolic action, they released rodents in Minister Yitzhak Raphael's building after he had dismissed the Panthers as parasites who simply refused to work. And one night in March 1972, a few Panthers came to the affluent neighborhood of Rehavia, collected bottles of fresh milk left outside the front doors, and whisked them off to the Asbestonim—a slum of asbestos huts on the outskirts of Jerusalem—where they redistributed the milk to needy families. This would become their most famous stunt. It was not merely a Robin Hood operation, but a jab at the welfare state, which in their conception was not truly helping the poor but subsidizing milk so the rich would be able to feed their pets. Other schemes that never materialized included queuing up in front of the Jewish Agency to demand air tickets back to their countries of origin or traveling abroad to talk on Soviet radio and TV. They even toyed with the idea of kidnapping Minister of Housing Ze'ev Sherf.[91]

The Panthers circulated publications, including their own version of the Passover Haggadah, which replaced the traditional "four sons" (wise, simple, wicked, and too young to ask) with the rich, the poor, the Ashkenazi, and the Sephardic. Their revised narrative had the "poor" character lament, "I am not asking for any favors and I have not risen against the government, and as I don't speak Yiddish—I get kicked out."[92] With this and other texts, the Panthers typically stitched together ethnic and class categories with a somewhat greater emphasis on class.

However, their notion of ethnic identity should be understood in situ. It was not necessarily conceived in terms of cultural difference as much as power relations. What they at times referred to as "spiritual deprivation" constituted an affront to their sense of honor. They were certainly sensitive to their representation in popular culture. One anecdote has them contemplating destroying a movie theater that screened the Israeli film *Malkat hakvish* (*The Highway Queen*) in which actress Gila Almagor portrays a streetwalker because it "slanders the Moroccans in particular and represents the ethnic problem in a disgraceful manner."[93]

Eddi Malka observed that what is often labeled as Oriental culture had been already appropriated by the Ashkenazim who praised it as magnificent and often kept an Oriental corner in their plush homes where they put ancient samovars and trays. "They so admire Oriental culture that they prevent us from getting a modern education. They may even one day call for 'Sephardic autonomy' in Israel."[94] Elsewhere, he provoked that the banner, "Golda teach us Yiddish!" they raised in their demonstrations could be understood as an invitation, not just a sneer. Malka was ready, or so he claimed, to acquaint himself with Yiddish if it would guarantee social mobility.[95]

Culture as a marker of difference would become more pronounced by the second half of the 1970s, in the wake of the Panthers' campaign, with new genres of Mizrahi expression, poetry and prose, as well as a lively underground subculture of Oriental music initially disseminated through cheaply produced cassette tapes sold in storefronts and major bus stations. And with Shas, Mizrahi identity would be closely linked with religiosity and tradition.

The Other Panther

In 1971, another American radical export arrived in Jerusalem, Rabbi Meir Kahane, the founder of the JDL and later of the ultra-Right party Kach in Israel.[96] In the late 1960s, the JDL joined the campaign on behalf of Soviet Jews. Beginning with protests, these operations escalated to assaults on Aeroflot airline offices and Soviet cultural agencies, and even outright acts of terror. The JDL also played an incendiary role in the Black-Jewish rift during the Ocean Hill/Brownsville confrontation (1968).

Even as he denounced Black antisemitism, Kahane still borrowed aspects of Black Power, especially from the Black Panthers. He emulated their revolutionary fervor and militant style, acquiring weapons and adopting the Black Power symbol of the clenched fist (engulfed by a prominent Jewish star). He declared that Jews must defend themselves "by any means necessary." Kahane talked and wrote about the Black Panthers with a mixture of animosity and admiration, defining his aim to achieve for Jews what the Black Panthers had for African Americans.[97]

Members of his movement sometimes styled themselves "Jewish Panthers." The JDL named its action squads *haya*—animal. When a bomb accidentally went off in their Catskills youth camp, JDL activists claimed at their trial that the device was produced according to a BPP manual. The JDL also adopted the emerging language of African American identity politics, forging their own versions of familiar slogans, as in "Jewish is beautiful." A female member confessed, "I used to straighten [my hair] because it seemed animal-like, but now it's a question of Jewish identity not to. . . . That happened to Blacks when they got their movement."[98] Kahane said in a public event, "We have a reputation, spread by our enemies, that we are Jewish Panthers. Never deny it."[99]

In 1969, the FBI, for whom Kahane had been an informant, conspired to recruit him to taint the Black Panthers in the Jewish press. The files of its covert countersubversive operations (COINTELPRO) contain copies of fabricated letters, supposedly mailed to Kahane by African Americans, purporting to disclose the BPP's virulent anti-Jewish sentiments, including specific plans to extort money from Jewish storeowners. By the early 1970s, however, the FBI had come to regard the JDL as a terrorist organization and the White House, concerned about the future of détente with the USSR, was determined to restrain him.[100]

Another child of 1960s radical theatricality, Kahane was fond of publicity stunts. As we will explore in greater detail in the next chapter, in Israel, Kahane continued to provoke, campaigning against Christian missionaries and the Black Hebrew Israelites. He quickly focused his attention on Arabs, however, promoting a transfer plan for the removal of the Palestinians from Israel and the occupied territories either through monetary incentives or, if necessary, by force.

He claimed to have found poor Mizrahim bitter, frustrated, and ready for his kind of militancy.[101] Kahane mirrored the Israeli Black Panthers' rhetoric when he blamed the Ashkenazi elite for the plight of Sephardic Jews, asking Mizrahi audiences whether in their country of origin the jails were populated by Jewish robbers and murderers as were Israeli prisons where he had spent many months. Among them, he peddled the nefarious racism he brought from the United States, inciting fears of predatory sexual behavior by Arab men against Jewish women. He would advocate for segregated beaches for Jews and Arabs and prohibiting intermarriages. Prejudice against Arabs was not uncommon but this species of hatred was unprecedented in Israel. His party Kach would produce a flier for visiting female Jewish students, warning that for Arabs the best way "to screw" the Jewish state was "to screw a Jewish girl and broadcast the fact as widely as possible."[102]

When Kahane was elected to the Knesset in 1984, he proposed an antimiscegenation law "for the preservation of the sanctity of the people of Israel." He came to embrace violence as a force of redemption—a tool of God's wrath to avenge the historical humiliation of the Jewish people. Kahane's fertile, apocalyptic mind envisaged another momentous calamity for the Jews. He even established a Museum of the Future Holocaust in Jerusalem.

Both Kahane and the Black Panthers of Israel vied to represent the disaffected and soon clashed. In June 1972, retaliating against previous attempts to break up their meetings, the Black Panthers raided Kahane's offices in Jerusalem. Four activists were arrested and charged with intent to use Molotov cocktails against the rabbi from Brooklyn.[103]

Conclusion

Returning to the anecdote with which we began, the revue *Don't Call Me Black!*, a paean to the civil rights movement, was inspired by Martin Duberman's documentary play *In White America* (1964), which weaves a tapestry of songs and snippets of historical documents and testimonies on Black history and life. Almagor, who saw the play in New York, also used its formulas for his Hasidic lore revue, *Ish hasid haya* (see chapter 8). He indicated that when writing *Don't Call Me Black!* he was thinking about current affairs in Israel.[104] The song that began with, "Until when we will live among shaky walls? And ten children in a single room? The country is thriving, the money flows. Only here the Ghetto barely breathes" could be easily sung about the Jerusalem slums as well.[105]

The Me Nobody Knows, a documentary musical play about children in

FIGURE 5.2 Blackface without tar. The revue *Don't Call Me Black!* (1972) depicts the historic struggles of African Americans. Left to right, Erela Bar-Lev, Dudu Zer, Yael Stern, Ruthi Navon (emerging behind the large trash bin), Avraham Ferrera (partially hidden), and Rafi Ginay. (Courtesy of the Israeli Center for the Documentation of the Performing Arts, Tel Aviv University)

the American inner city, also received an Israeli makeover in 1972. Director Miri Magnus retained the skeleton of the original script and the music but spent four months in Musrara and other Jerusalem neighborhoods, where she taped testimonies about criminality, prostitution, violent teachers, and hopeless menial jobs. A Black Panther leader provided one of the most memorable accounts.[106] Lyricist Ehud Manor had one song warning, "I am the sum of your mistakes, I am the gunpowder on which you sit." One critic wrote, "It is curious how it is possible to pour the life of a deprived community from one vessel to another, from one country to another, from one culture to another."[107] A few theater critics dismissed *The Me That Nobody Knows* and *Don't Call Me Black!* as too polished, contrived, and inauthentic. However, their success evidenced that the African American / Mizrahi analogy was already taking root in the Israeli mind.

In recent decades, the Israeli Black Panthers have been the subject of celebratory commemorative work including symposia, gatherings, exhibits, documentary films, and features in the press. As importantly, networks of scholars, journalists, and activists, such as the Mizrahi Democratic Rainbow Coalition, have elaborated an identity politics that critiques the historical treatment of both Palestinians and Mizrahi Jews.[108] This is a sophisticated and diverse movement, steeped in the critical tools and language of postcolonialism. For the new generation of progressive Mizrahi intellectuals, the similarities between the racial struggle in the United States and the Ashkenazi-Mizrahi friction in Israel are taken for granted. However, fifty years ago the Jerusalem Panthers did not discover as much as establish as a political act the analogy between their predicament and that of African Americans.

Ultimately, the Ashkenazi-Mizrahi divide is invoked today more frequently from the political Right than the Left. The place of race and the politics of pigmentation have become more fraught with the 1990s immigration of Jews from Ethiopia (the Beta Israel community), that in Israel were racialized, labeled "Black," and subjected to prejudice. The Ethiopian second generation's identification with African Americans, evinced in a vibrant hip hop subculture among other manifestations, seems to run much deeper than of any other ethnic group in Israel. Meanwhile, the racial makeup of the country has become more diverse as Israel is now home to a substantial population of foreign workers, predominantly from Asia, especially in farming and the home-care industry (about 105,000 legal and 25,000 illegal workers), as well as a destination for asylum seekers and undocumented immigrants from Africa (numbering 26,000).

SIX

American Gangster in the Promised Land

Sensing that the FBI was determined to put him behind bars by any means, Meyer Lansky escaped to Israel in July of 1970, accompanied by his wife Thelma and their Shih Tzu lapdog Bruzzers. Meanwhile, the FBI kept busy. He was indicted in Las Vegas and Miami for indirect tax evasion and failure to appear in front of a grand jury investigating illegal gambling. Neither of these minor offenses qualified for extradition. Still, the federal government indicated that it would like to see Lansky back home. His American passport was revoked.

Surrounded by a colorful entourage of friends and schemers, Lansky received a stream of fantastic business proposals from Israeli entrepreneurs. He declined all.[1] He periodically extended his tourist visa and later applied for citizenship. However, by then the Israeli press was busy recounting in gory detail the exploits of American organized crime and Lansky's alleged role in its making. It informed its readers that the aging man who looked like a harmless American tourist, everybody's uncle from Miami on a Holy Land vacation, was in fact a calculating gangster, the Mafia's brain, friend of the likes of Bugsy Siegel, Lucky Luciano, and Frank Costello—now in our midst.

After prolonged deliberations, Minister of the Interior Yosef Burg rejected Lansky's petition, citing a provision in the Law of Return that permits him to refuse citizenship to Jews with a criminal past who are likely to endanger the public welfare. Lansky appealed to the High Court of Justice but the court, sitting in a special five-justice quorum, validated Burg's decision.

In a final gesture, the state offered Lansky travel documents, which he used in November 1972 to find refuge in Latin America. It was there that the FBI finally cornered him. Country after country forbade him to set foot on its soil, until his flight reached its ultimate destination, Miami, Florida, where he was promptly arrested.[2] In the film *The Godfather II* (1974), the Lansky-like figure Hyman Roth arrives from Israel at Miami International Airport to be gunned down in front of scores of journalists and TV crews. The historical Lansky, in contrast, succeeded in fending off all federal attempts to convict him and died in 1983 a free man. His iconic presence in American culture only increased in recent decades, although, as it now appears, his notoriety as the stunningly rich grandmaster of American organized crime was much inflated.[3]

For some, the Lansky affair demonstrated that Israel had become an American satellite, succumbing to American pressure or, even worse, abandoning a helpless, old Jew in a cynical quid pro quo to save, so went the rumor, a coming Phantom jets deal.[4] For others, it evidenced that the Law of Return could jeopardize the balance between the promise of haven Zionism had made to all Jews and the country's domestic interests. In addition, Lansky's two-year hiatus provided Israelis with a learning opportunity, expanding on the rough underbelly of American life and the Jewish contribution to American crime—about which they had known little—another form of "discovering America." It enhanced the perception that the United States is a dangerous and crime-ridden society, not a model to be followed.

This chapter groups Lansky's case together with two other contemporaneous episodes that involved friction between American newcomers and Israeli authorities: first, the arrival of Meir Kahane, another veteran of skirmishes with American law, and then the tiny African American sect known as the Black Hebrew Israelites whose members sought to settle in Israel beginning in 1969. All three cases forced government officials, judges, and the public at large to consider the lines distinguishing acceptable—indeed, warmly embraced—from unacceptable immigrants, and more broadly, those separating the Jewish homeland from the Diaspora.

The question of how to respond to Lansky and the Hebrew Israelites perplexed the Israeli government. And whereas the Hebrew Israelites epitomized radical alterity, Lansky and Kahane inspired profound unease not just with what was foreign and seemingly dangerous about them but also with what was familiar and yet too close for comfort. Kahane and the Black Israelites also introduced bits and pieces of the American racial experience into Israeli life. The former, as a purveyor of overt racism, the latter as a manifestation of Black Power and Black nationalism.

"Little Big Man"

In the United States Lansky was haunted by the Nixon administration and its law-and-order campaign as well as by the forces of mass culture, which once again became preoccupied with the figure of the gangster. In May 1970, the popular *Reader's Digest* magazine published an essay about Lansky under the title, "The Shocking Success of 'Public Enemy No 1,'" inviting readers to meet the "shrewd, unobtrusive, brutal mobster who for more than 40 years has reigned . . . as a prince of plunder."[5] Shortly after, the *Atlantic Monthly* featured an article titled "The Little Big Man Who Laughs at the Law," asserting, "Lansky is the main architect of the giant conglomerate that is organized crime in the United States."[6] In the 1930s, Lansky allegedly brought mafia families together with other criminal groups to form a tightly structured crime colossus that in a phrase attributed to him was "bigger than US Steel." In 1971, journalist Hank Messick completed a most damning biography of Lansky, making the fantastical claim that while other gangsters grabbed the headlines, this "mystery man nobody knew" amassed a 300-million-dollar fortune.

Lansky-inspired literature—especially Messick's book that was soon translated to Hebrew and serialized in *Haaretz*—crossed the Atlantic to capture the Israeli imagination together with Lansky the man. The *Reader's Digest* article was the only source of information Israeli police had at its disposal when it first became aware of Lansky's arrival. Lansky brought

FIGURE 6.1 Gangster Meyer Lansky on his way to the pool at the Acadia Hotel, Herzliya. *Ha'olam Hazeh*'s June 2, 1971, cover reads, "The Battle around Meyer Lansky. Will the Law of Return Apply to the King of the American Mafia [?]"

the article to introduce himself to his Israeli lawyer Yoram Alroy, so Alroy would know what he would have to contend with. Meanwhile, Mario Puzo's *The Godfather*, a novel published in 1969, had already acquainted readers worldwide with the characters and the lexicon of the Sicilian Mafia. *The Godfather*'s mob stood for a community governed by premodern familial codes of loyalty and honor. Lansky's alleged organization, in contrast, was often cast as a branch of corporate America: modern, efficient, and decidedly professionalized.

Lansky's stay in Israel, the global interest in organized crime, and the rise of domestic crime rates inspired yet another exercise in analogic thinking, measuring a domestic social phenomenon through the American lens. A series of articles by journalist Ran Kislev in *Haaretz* launched a long-term debate over the question of whether Israel incubated its own organized crime.[7] The press inundated the public with titillating stories about the annals of American crime—translated from the American press or reported by journalists sent to the United States for that purpose.[8] The Tel Aviv chief of police employed a *Godfather* term when he proposed, "You can't find the real Don Corleones in the newspapers headlines."[9]

When Solicitor General Gavriel Bach defended Burg's decision in the High Court, journalists noticed on his desk a pile of cheap American paperbacks about syndicated crime. For Bach, the Lansky affair furnished a unique opportunity for a transnational knowledge expedition. He traveled to Washington, DC, to gather information at the Justice Department. Upon his arrival, he was whisked to Attorney General John Mitchell's office.[10] Mitchell, who a few years later would be incarcerated for his involvement in the Watergate scandal, assured Bach that the United States did not plan to intervene in Israel's domestic affairs. Nevertheless, he expressed his confidence that Lansky's wealth would not purchase him shelter in Israel, thus conveying the administration's wish and, possibly, insinuating his own prejudice as well.

Mitchell suggested that many figures in the American underworld were waiting to find out whether Lansky's quest for Israeli citizenship succeeds, for they would like to follow suit. In Washington, Bach became acutely aware of rampant urban crime. As he recounted decades later, each night his hosts insisted on bringing him back to the hotel and he was instructed not to take a taxicab from any other place but there.[11]

Bach's access to Justice Department's files was so comprehensive, he could even see the names of the FBI agents dispatched to follow Lansky in Tel Aviv. In Washington, he would say, he learned the extent to which organized crime corrupted American justice and politics. Particularly shocking for him was that the FBI profoundly mistrusted local police forces and prosecutors, suspecting they were all susceptible to bribery. This otherwise temperate individual who had achieved a measure of fame as one of Adolf Eichmann's prosecutors argued in the High Court with uncharacteristic passion.

Lecturing on the history of syndicated crime, Bach peppered his speech with English expressions and mafiosi terms such as *omerta*, the vow of silence. Portraying the American crime world with vivid color, he dropped names of legendary mobsters and murderous gangs, asserting confidently that no one could be eliminated in New York without Lansky's approval. Bach quoted from the publications he brought from the United States and recommended passages for the justices to read by themselves.[12] What about Lansky's age and ill health, they asked. He would never be able to retire, Bach warned ominously, no one leaves the mob alive. But Lansky is in Israel now, remarked Chief Justice Shimon Agranat. Bach responded that in this age distance and borders lose their meaning.[13]

Bach appeared to adopt the federal government's point of view. Yet, something was lost in transit. He brought with him from the United States and introduced into the Israeli court's proceedings a suitcase worth of material no American court would ever dare considering, illegal FBI wiretaps, congressional reports, common knowledge incriminations, and sensationalist journalistic accounts. Lansky's lawyer underscored that this material was largely based on rumors and hearsay. The High Court decided that its task was not to define the meaning of "criminal past," an elusive category, made more complicated by the fact that Lansky was never convicted of any serious crime, but whether Burg acted reasonably and based on relevant information, even if the evidence mustered for that purpose was not admissible in court.[14]

Lansky had almost no prior convictions and spent only ninety days in jail for gambling-related minor offenses; Bach marshalled this fact as yet another proof of the power of organized crime. Even the justices seemed somewhat uncomfortable when he maintained that by invoking his constitutional rights and refusing to testify in front of the famous 1950s Estes Kefauver Commission on organized crime, Lansky missed an opportunity to clear his name. Again, this rationale would have been entirely foreign to any American jurist.

To fend off the avalanche of damaging publications, Lansky offered the Israeli public a counternarrative. For the first time, he sat down with a TV reporter and granted a series of exclusive interviews to Uri Dan of *Ma'ariv*.[15] In the 1940s, he told Dan, he helped the Haganah, the pre-state defense organization, and exploited his Mafia connections to dump into the New York City waterfront an arms shipment destined for an Arab country. He raised money for Israel soon after its inception and ever since. As we know today, these claims were rooted in historical truth. Attorney Alroy reports that he agreed to take Lansky as a client after a high-ranking official in the Israeli government asked him to do so.[16]

But Lansky went further, recasting his whole life in a manner commensurable with Zionist prescriptions about the proper use of Jewish force. He portrayed his immigrant childhood on the Lower East Side as a tale of diasporic misery, harassment, harsh antisemitism (especially from Irish gangs), and blocked upward mobility, which pushed young Jews like him to crime. The Bugs and Lansky mob, the notorious gang he led together with his childhood friend Benjamin "Bugsy" Siegel, was essentially a self-defense group. Young Meyer was determined never to bow down to Christian domination. "I was always proud as a Jew. . . . Ever since I came to my senses, I decided that I would rather die than suffer humiliation because I am a Jew."[17]

Lansky told Dan that the tag "gangster" was pinned on him in the 1930s when he and his Lower East Side buddies heeded pleas from Jewish leaders and cracked a few heads to disperse pro-Nazi German Bund gatherings. Jews who were keen on assimilating in American society did not approve of his methods.[18] Much of the law-and-order campaign against him was driven by prejudice. Journalists with antisemitic predispositions and federal, including FBI, officials were convinced that only a Jewish brain could be pulling the strings behind the criminal world. They sought to personify crime through him. He had been told by FBI agents, "The press can't let you go. It makes such a nice living out of you."[19] Lansky maintained that after World War II he engaged exclusively in running casinos and ever since Fidel Castro took over Cuba, he was no more than a pensioner with ulcer and heart problems. With Uri Dan and a photographer in tow, Lansky traveled to Mount of Olives in Jerusalem to say Kaddish over the graves of his grandparents who were buried there at the beginning of the century. He had his picture taken wearing a yarmulka standing by the Western Wall.

Granting these interviews, Lansky interjected himself into the newspaper wars in Israel. He got *Ma'ariv* on his side but sued *Yedioth Ahronoth* for libel. He was able to muster some public sympathy. One rabbi stipulated that the Halacha forbids surrendering any Jew to the gentiles.[20] Yoram Sheftel, then a law student and later a lawyer and a controversial right-wing pundit, organized a signature campaign in his support. A group of new immigrants from the Soviet Union set up a desk in downtown Jerusalem asking passersby to sign a petition to grant Lansky Israeli citizenship.[21]

Asked about Lansky, Kahane, another proponent of Jewish pride and self-defense and opponent of assimilating Jews, whom he dismissed as "Scarsdale Jews," responded emphatically that no Jew, even a murderer, should be deported.[22] Still, the *Ma'ariv* interviews left many cold. The Israeli elite, from top police brass to Uri Avnery, editor of *Ha'olam Hazeh*, wanted Lansky out. In *Yedioth*, Ziva Yariv spoofed Dan's piece, sneering at Lansky as Rabbi Meir Ba'al Haness, the greatest Zionist ever, who stood behind the Basel Congress, the Balfour Declaration, and smuggled whiskey only for the purposes of Kiddush and Havdala.[23]

Mobsters' Paradise

A chief concern at the time was that if the alleged Mafia boss remains, Israel would become a hub for the global underworld. The Nixon administration harped on those fears, leading officials in Jerusalem to imagine a tidal wave of hundreds of Jewish American mobsters descending upon Israel demanding citizenship. Indeed, a major turning point against Lansky took place in June 1971 when three of his American associates, Benjamin Siegelbaum, Eduard Marcus, and Bernard Ross, planned to visit him in Israel. Interpol warned Israeli police that an underworld summit was likely to convene and asked for surveillance. Israeli authorities preferred to deport all three the moment they landed.[24] Journalists speculated then that Lansky was just the most visible scout in a crime empire's attempt to find itself a new home.[25] With scant evidence, *Ha'olam Hazeh* determined that Israel is about to occupy the place hitherto assumed by Batista's Cuba and Papa Doc's Haiti (which it confused with Tahiti) as the "command center and sanctuary of the crime syndicate's leaders."[26]

Still, Minister Burg of the National Religious Party was sympathetic to Lansky, whom he ultimately viewed as a wandering Jew from Grodno, born Maier Suchowljansky. The Justice Ministry, however, was adamantly opposed to accommodating Lansky.[27] When Golda Meir heard from Burg about Lansky's mob connections, she responded, "Dr. Burg, Mafia? No Mafia in Israel."[28] Meir grew up in the United States. Chief Justice Shimon Agranat's acquaintance with the story of American gangland is evident in his ruling in this case.[29] Lansky was an embarrassment, a public relations disaster for a country immensely preoccupied with its image abroad. The Anti-Defamation League already protested that advertisements for Messick's biography carried a fake headline announcing that Jews control American crime.[30] But rather than an exotic Other, Lansky was a bit too familiar, an emblem of a still-too-immediate diasporic past that had to be suppressed.

Lansky's petition for the High Court included a letter from a Florida rabbi testifying that beyond assisting the local community and Jews in need Lansky donated funds to Israel in the aftermath of the Six-Day War.[31] However, some commentators began casting doubts about the motives driving foreign donations. Was fundraising abroad so successful at least in part because it afforded donors respectability, a kind of a certificate of good conduct? A photo with Levi Eshkol, a thank-you letter from Golda Meir, a birthday telegram from Pinchas Sapir—could all be an asset, opined one commentator.[32]

Journalist Yigal Laviv maintained that underworld figures used donations to Israel to disguise illegal operations.[33] *Ha'olam Hazeh* further claimed that powerful Jewish leaders close to Golda Meir, Lou Boyar and Sam Rothberg (the chair of the Israel Bonds), attempted to intervene on Lansky's behalf.[34] Both Sam and his brother Harry Rothberg were at one point invested in Las Vegas's Flamingo Hotel where Lansky had a share as well. The suspicion that American Jews' donations might be employed to launder the reputations of those with an unsavory past betrayed a deep ambivalence toward the United Jewish Appeal and similar organizations. Fundraising drives cemented Jewish solidarity across the ocean, but they also attested to the Israeli reliance on what was derisively labeled in Yiddish *schnorr*.[35] Some Israelis who participated in public fundraising events found their proceedings rather troubling.

The following episode provides a fine example. Only a month after the June 1967 war, four Israeli pilots who arrived in Florida for training were featured guests in a large Israel Emergency Fund event in Miami. The chief marquee attraction in the packed hall was the comedian Bob Hope, who was crowned an honorary colonel of the IAF.[36] After opening jokes from Hope, the Israeli guests shared air battle stories before the evening turned to the labor of fundraising. The visiting pilots were initially bemused but were soon dismayed by the crudity of what transpired next. Members of the audience were prodded to increase their donations through an uninhibited ritual of shaming in which their personal income, the luxury cars in their front garage, and their neighbors' donations were all alluded to in public.[37]

Coming on the heels of the Benjamin Shalit, "who-is-a-Jew?" High Court ruling,[38] the Lansky episode raised the thorny question of who is a Jew good enough for the Law of Return. In the *Jerusalem Post*, the East Jerusalem Palestinian leader Anwar Nusseibeh expressed sympathy toward Lansky for being forced to prove he did not have a criminal past. But Nusseibeh's real aim was the Law of Return itself and the principle behind it, which was in his view responsible for the suffering of the Palestinian refugees.[39] During the debate over Lansky's fate Israelis were also reminded of the case of Robert Soblen, an American Jew who in 1963 was convicted as a Soviet spy and fled to Israel. Soblen was deported without a hearing and, on the way back to the United States, committed suicide by slashing his wrists.

Minister Burg explained that Israel was established for any Jew who was hounded as a Jew. "If anyone is hounded as a criminal and not because he shares my religion, nationality, history, and destiny, it's a different matter."[40] Minister of Justice Ya'akov Shimshon Shapira was blunter, "We will not be a safe haven for the scum of the Jewish people."[41] Paradoxically, this expression of Israeli sovereignty was suspected by some to be a capitulation to the American imperial node, a manifestation of impaired sovereignty. *Yedioth* journalist Yohanan Lahav seemed to confirm this suspicion by reasoning, "Deporting Lansky is a debt of honor that Israel owes its loyal friend."[42]

The concluding act of the Lansky affair demonstrated the capacity of Zion to reproduce the worst of the Diaspora. Lansky left in November 1972. A story circulated that he offered a million dollars to any country that would accept him. A caricature in *Miami News* featured Lansky landing in an Arab country bringing the locals an "offer they couldn't refuse," suitcases full of dollars.[43] Planning to settle in Paraguay, he traveled first to Zurich and then to Rio, Buenos Aires, Asunción, La Paz, Lima, and Panama City. Prodded by the American government, all destinations following Rio refused him, in effect handing him over to the FBI.

Israel then experienced pangs of guilt. Commentators remarked with poignancy that South American nations that granted asylum to Nazi war criminals closed their gates to the Jew Lansky. In a letter to the *New York Times*, two law professors protested what they saw as a repeat of the 1930s. "The spectacle ... of an old Jew being shunted across national borders, haunting the anterooms of consulates ... raises too many memories lying uneasily just below all our consciousnesses."[44]

Kahane Revisited

Another immigrant from the United States—with a criminal past, alliance with the mob boss Joe Colombo, a comprehensively demonstrated proclivity for violence, and a tremendous potential for imperiling the public welfare—arrived in Israel in mid-September 1971. In subsequent years, some would ask why Lansky was refused citizenship while Rabbi Meir Kahane—as well as some of his most extreme Jewish Defense League (JDL) disciples—were accepted without pause.[45]

On the eve of his emigration, Kahane and his followers faced multiple indictments for a staggering inventory of charges: rioting, assault, burglary, and other criminal transgressions, including explicit acts of terrorism. A major target were Soviet representatives—persistently followed and harassed—and Soviet interests, but JDL activists also pressured and even tried to intimidate American politicians and officials, mainstream Jewish organizations, and companies doing business with the USSR. A bomb exploded outside the Soviet cultural center in Washington, DC, another in the doorway of Aeroflot and Intourist offices in Manhattan. Later, in 1972 a smoke bomb would go off in the offices of the impresario Sol Hurok, who brought Russian performers to America. A secretary was killed. The JDL also continued its professed mission of defending poor, old, and other vulnerable Jews from crime and (especially Black) antisemitism and, in addition, attacked Arab delegations in New York. In September 1970, a young couple carrying forged passports and weapons was caught boarding a flight heading for Europe with the intention of hijacking an Egyptian plane there and landing it in Israel.[46]

One of Kahane's most memorable acts of antiestablishment defiance on the eve of his emigration took place in Brussels during an international conference of Jewish leaders convening to discuss the plight of Soviet Jews. Kahane was not invited but with his followers behind him he charged the podium demanding the right to speak. A melee ensued and soon after the Belgian authorities threw him out of the country.[47] In 1971, an American court sentenced him to a suspended five years in prison and a $5,000 fine for conspiring to manufacture explosives.

Resolved to curb Kahane's incessant troublemaking, perceived as a threat to the détente between the two superpowers, Washington asked Israel to help tame the JDL. Jerusalem responded that it did not have anything to do with the organization.[48] Nevertheless, Prime Minister Meir expressed strong opposition to its tactics, insinuating there was kinship between the JDL's and global terrorism. She averred, "It can only damage our just struggle and play into the hands of our enemies by enabling them to equate us with those being denounced in most parts of the world."[49] The American embassy in Tel Aviv requested that Israel not allow JDL members facing trials to avoid prosecution. Embassy "talking points" further stated, "We ... believe that there is a mutual American-Israeli interest in assuring that these individuals not be allowed, if admitted to Israel, to organize or otherwise promote acts of violence or other lawlessness in the United States."[50]

In the internal Israeli government discussion that followed, Minister of Justice Shapira opined that Israel could not treat American JDL activists as though they were suspected of belonging to a crime organization. However, if they commit extraditable crimes they certainly would be extradited, and Israel would not allow them to act against the American government.[51] Attorney General Meir Shamgar rejected a proposal to have JDL members sign upon entering the country a commitment to limit their activities. The issue, reasoned government legal experts, was fundamentally political, not legal. Since the JDL is a topic of intraparty disagreement in Israel, refusing entry to JDL activists would ignite public controversy.[52]

Kahane would become an important figure in the making of the Israeli radical Right. By the early 1980s, he developed a political program that championed turning Israel into a halachic state as well as the forced expulsion of much of the Arab population. Ehud Sprinzak labels Kahane's politics "quasi-fascist" based on its legitimation of violence and terrorism, inherent xenophobia and racism, the employment of propaganda and smear campaigns, and Kahane's authoritarianism or the "leader principle."[53] The rabbi's political agenda was cloaked in increasingly apocalyptic views of Jewish fate, identifying impending holocausts everywhere—in the USSR, the United States, and Israel, lest Jews repent.[54]

But much of this lay in the future. Relatively little was known in Israel about Kahane prior to his emigration. Despite official denunciations and Meir's annoyance at the claim that Israel was not doing enough for Soviet Jews, which Kahane compared to official Jewish inaction in the 1930s and 1940s, his exploits on behalf of beleaguered Jewish communities in either the United States or the Soviet Union earned him a measure of approval. In the United States he announced, "We're here to change the traditional Jewish image as a patsy."[55] This posture of muscular, fist-happy Jewish agency was popular on the Israeli political Right. Indeed, Meir suspected that the JDL received guidance and support from elements in the right-wing opposition.[56]

Kahane promised that in Israel he would stay out of party politics and only work for national unity.[57] However, upon arrival he hit the ground running into perpetual clashes with the police. The FBI kept an eye on Kahane in Israel as well. He established a new party, Kach (Thus) that was unsuccessful in the 1973 elections. Eleven years later, in 1984, he would be elected to the Israeli Knesset. In the following election (1988), Kach was disqualified because of a new law that prohibited parties with a racist platform from participating. Two years later, Kahane was assassinated in New York City by El Sayyid Nosair, an Egyptian-born member of a terrorist cell that would later become part of Al Qaeda.

Public Brawls

Kahane brought to Israel 1960s street theater, publicity stunts, and direct action—all appropriated from the New Left's tactical arsenal. A few schemes, however, crossed into terror. Together with Amichai Paglin, the former head of operation of the pre-state right-wing Irgun (National Military Organization) underground, Kahane hatched a bizarre plan to smuggle arms abroad with the intention of attacking the Libyan embassy in Rome as a reprisal for the 1972 Munich Olympics massacre. This scheme earned him a suspended two-year jail sentence.[58]

He continued to threaten the well-being of Russian diplomats, warning that Jewish militants will assassinate Soviet diplomats if harm befalls Jews serving prison terms in the Soviet Union.[59] In June 1973, he was indicted for sending his JDL comrades in the United States plans to disrupt the coming visit of the Soviet leader Leonid Brezhnev. He proposed the abduction and possible killing of a Soviet diplomat, bombing the offices of Occidental Petroleum, and firing shots at the Soviet embassy from a nearby location. Prosecutors determined that these acts "were designed to harm Israeli interests with regard to relations between Israel and the United States."[60] Kahane was sentenced to an additional two-year suspended jail term.[61]

But the theme of Jewish pride and self-defense that animated Kahane's mischief in America seemed out of place in a country in which the state took upon itself to provide both. In subsequent years, much of the JDL's public actions focused on harassing religious and ethnic minorities. Activists were arrested for setting fire to a Christian missionary institution, the Interna-

FIGURE 6.2 Rabbi Meir Kahane clenching his fist and clashing with the police during a demonstration. (Photographer Shmuel Rachmani)

tional Center for the Holy Scriptures on Mount of Olives, and attacking an employee.[62] In another publicity stunt that got him arrested, Kahane sought to affix a mezuza to the Damascus Gate, an entry point to the Muslim quarter of the Old City of Jerusalem.[63] He announced he was organizing a public trial for Sheikh Muhammad Ali Ja'abri, the Palestinian mayor of Hebron in the West Bank, for the 1929 massacre of Hebron Jews.

His most egregious initiative—foreshadowing his future plans—was to launch a campaign to encourage Arabs in Israel and the occupied territories to leave the country, offering financial aid to prospective emigrants.[64] Since Arabs do not have equal rights, he reasoned, they were likely to rebel once they become stronger, "like the Negroes in the United States."[65] Kahane anticipated a wave of 100,000 Arabs packing to leave. In early 1973, he claimed 450 people already agreed to participate. But, in effect, only very few families accepted his appeal. The project only succeeded in fanning anger among Arabs across the Green Line.

Official Israel was incensed and Kahane's scheme was widely denounced. Some commentators who might have been sympathetic to Kahane's antiestablishment stance abroad found his intervention in Israeli affairs intolerable and soon lost patience with his antics.[66] Member of Knesset Shmuel Tamir (then of the tiny Free Center Party), who previously protested the official anti-JDL stance, now accused the organization of outright racism.[67] Tamir speculated that Kahane might be a provocateur operating on behalf of foreign interests seeking to embarrass Israel by questioning its capability to protect the holy sites in Jerusalem.[68] The attorney general indicted Kahane for incitement under the Law of Sedition—a controversial legacy of the British Mandate.[69]

A few maintained that Kahane was bringing the Diaspora to Israel. A Labor Party publication railed against political violence imported from the most extreme margins of the American Right. "The League's activities are accompanied by tremendous noise, ostentatiousness and publicity in the spirt of the American mentality."[70] Member of Knesset Yitzhak Koren (Labor) warned against the rise of Jewish fascism.[71] Minister of Police Shlomo Hillel dismissed the plot to wage a private war against terror in Europe as infantile, "This is the psychology of Brooklyn that is scared of Harlem, but not of an organized state with a proper regime."[72] In a phone conversation, Minister of

Defense Dayan demanded, reportedly using an expletive, that Kahane cease interfering with Israeli policy toward Arabs.[73]

Nevertheless, and despite repeated arrests, indictments, and suspended jail time, at this stage it seemed that the authorities were still treating Kahane with kid gloves. Menachem Begin even considered including him in the Likud's candidate list for the 1973 elections. In the trial for smuggling guns judge Hadassah Ben-Itto stated that while they indeed violated the law, the co-conspirators did not venture to benefit themselves but labored for the public good and that JDL's mission to allow Soviet Jews the freedom of immigration and to find ways to combat Arab terrorism is legal and accepted by the public.[74]

Kahane's was a strange, uncanny presence in early 1970s Israel when religious parties were still associated with political moderation and Gush Emunim, the settler movement, was yet to emerge. His insatiable love for public brawls worked well for the dawning television age and yet did not comport to models of sabra masculinity. It convinced many then and ever since that Kahane was profoundly unhinged. But while obviously a product of a faraway land, his capacity to embarrass was rooted in part in the manner he exposed—by way of burlesque but without a smidgen of parody or irony—something uncomfortable about Zionism itself. His contention that Israel could not be both democratic and Jewish is still very much at issue today, although it is often raised from a radically different political corner.

Kahane railed against the hypocrisy of the Israeli establishment that blamed him for racism while denying its own. According to journalist Yair Kottler, his trial on incitement charges was suspended in 1975 and never resumed because Kahane's lawyer Aaron Papo intended to put Zionism on trial. He planned to introduce to the court a long history of similar population transfer schemes espoused over decades by mainstream Zionist leaders and even threatened to summon cabinet members as witnesses.[75]

From Liberia to Dimona

Soon after arriving in Israel, Kahane traveled to the desert town of Dimona to stir anger against the tiny Black Hebrew Israelite community. He told a crowd of seven hundred locals, "These people who are not Jews but racists and antisemites come here to bury Israel.... You must press the government to expel them and not to permit others to come."[76] Founded in Chicago by a former steel worker Ben Carter, members of the small millenarian community officially known today as the African Hebrew Israelite Nation of Jerusalem view themselves as descendants of the tribes of Israel returning to claim their ancestral land.[77]

They are among small and disparate communities of African Americans that have claimed direct descent from the ancient Hebrews—beyond the general sense of affinity of fate between Blacks and Jews derived from the centrality of the biblical narrative in African American culture. The Hebrew Israelites represent a unique amalgamation of Black religiosity, 1960s Black Power and Black nationalism, and ideas and aspirations derived from Marcus Garvey's 1920s Back to Africa movement. They reject American materialism and the integrationist civil rights politics of the mid-twentieth century in favor of self-sufficiency and separatism.

The charismatic Carter, who assumed the Hebrew name Ben Ammi Ben-Israel, informed his group that in 1966 he was instructed by the angel Gabriel that the time had come for the children of the Israelites to return to the Promised Land and establish the Kingdom of God. With 350 followers, he settled first in Liberia, but after encountering deprivation and hostility, they decided to move to Israel. In the footsteps of the biblical book of Numbers' spies, two individuals (including Ben Ammi) made their initial reconnaissance over the summer of 1968. First, a small group of eight adults and twelve children arrived in August 1969 and settled in the southern town of Arad. That December the second and much larger contingent (39) showed up at Lod Airport. The American press was notified beforehand and Israeli diplomatic delegations received phone calls and telegrams urging Israel to open the country's gates for the Israelites, threatening to launch a protest campaign if it failed to do so.

The newly arrived spent twenty-four hours at the airport before the minister of the interior (back then, Haim-Moshe Shapira) reached a seemingly schizophrenic decision that would shape the story of the Hebrew Israelites for decades to come. They were taken to the Negev development town of Dimona and given all the privileges of Jewish immigrants, *olim*, under the Law of Return: housing, jobs—mostly in textile—allowances, social services, and access to schooling. However, their passports were stamped only with three-month tourist visas—until their status as Jews could be clarified. At first glance, their customs seemed to fall within the purview of Jewish practice. They kept the Sabbath, circumcised their sons, and followed other biblical prescriptions. They even asked to register their children in publicly funded religious rather than secular schools and indicated they might be willing to undergo formal conversions to substantiate their status as Jews.[78]

The initial reception in Dimona was warm. One of the Israelite leaders was visibly emotional. Tears in his eyes, he said, "It is wonderful to be in a free country and among one's brothers who behave so kindly to you."[79] Cathrielah Baht Israel, who arrived at the age of fourteen, remembers attending intensive Hebrew-language instruction with students from Morocco, Romania, and India. At school students insisted on touching her "Afro"-style hair.[80] Another newcomer, Peninah Baht Israel, found Dimona welcoming and was relieved to have access to running water, which had not been the case in Liberia.[81] *Lamerhav* daily titled its report, "The 'Black Jews'—Return to Their Homeland."[82]

The third group of forty-nine individuals, including Ben Ammi, arrived in March 1970. Ben Ammi emphatically rejected any possibility of conversion, declaring that the Israelites are the true children of Abraham, Isaac, and Jacob, who were Black men, and had no intention of following the dictates of the Jewish Halacha. The honeymoon was over. A small contingent was sent to Mitzpeh Ramon, but a subsequent large group was refused entrance in October 1971. Those who were somehow able to run the security and immigration gauntlet at the airport did not have access to housing and social services.

In a couple of years, about three hundred people crammed into the initial ten apartments. The decline of the Israelites' material condition in Dimona was held against them and became part of their perceived identity. Friction with neighbors increased.[83] The mayor who initially welcomed them with open arms now turned into a foe. After a member of the community was killed in a violent altercation among the Israelites their public image further deteriorated.[84] The press that was initially enthralled by the exotic newcomers with their colorful West African attire seized upon reports about trouble in Dimona. It now underscored Ben Ammi's authoritarianism and alien practices such as polygamy. Under siege, the community closed ranks, adults left their work, children were homeschooled.

The Israelites engaged in public protest. At one point a group entered a supermarket, purchased goods worth 3,000 liras, and then refused to pay—all in front of American TV crews invited to witness the event. Ben Ammi escalated his rhetoric, declaring that Israel in its biblical boundaries—a country he regarded to be part of Africa—belongs to them.[85] He wrote to UN Secretary General Kurt Weldheim that the United Nations created the State of Israel but gave it to the wrong people. Modern Jews were nothing but imposters and usurpers.[86] After reading unconfirmed reports that Meir's government and King Hussein were considering a federation between Jordan and the West Bank, he protested that the Hebrew Israelites were not consulted first. The Israelites were not just a religious sect but a political movement that competed with and to a certain degree mirrored Zionism—as did the Garveyites in the 1920. One dimension of Zionist emulation was the claim for exclusive rights over the land.[87]

The following year the tension in Dimona appeared to subside, at least for a while. One group that helped bridge the divide was the Israelites' musical band, the Soul Messengers, which following the Yom Kippur War even performed for IDF soldiers.[88] Over the decades, Ben Ammi tempered his declarations about Jews and Israel. But despite the appearance of a truce, conflicts between the Black Israelites and the authorities would occasionally flare up.

Finally, in 1992 most of the community received temporary residency status and in 2003 permanent residency. Young members can now serve in the IDF and a musical group represented Israel in international competitions. President Shimon Peres visited the community in 2008 and declared, "You are beloved in Israel, you bring it joy, singing and longing for a better world."[89] Prior to his death in 2014, Ben Ammi was granted full Israeli citizenship. The chief rabbi of Dimona was among the eulogists at his funeral.[90] Together with the Southern Christian Leadership Conference, the group set up a conflict resolution center in Dimona to teach nonviolence and reconciliation. Still, most of the members of the community that is now about 5,000 strong (although assessment of its numbers vary) have yet to become full citizens and their outsider status continues to pose difficulties.[91]

The Looming Invasion

When the High Court heard a petition from the Black Hebrew Israelites their lawyer asked why Lansky was allowed to stay—this occurred before the aging gangster was denied citizenship—and his clients were refused.[92] Those two ostensibly unrelated cases intersected. In interviews and public appearances Minister Burg was often asked to address both.[93] One connecting thread was the double concern, first, regarding Israel's reputation abroad and, second, about impending invasions behind the horizon if the Hebrew Israelites and Lansky were permitted to stay. The Israelites contributed to this scenario. On Israeli TV Ben Ammi announced that there were two to fifteen million Black Jews in America, and one million were getting ready "to come home to Israel" very soon.[94]

Israeli diplomats suspected that other Black Jewish communities were mulling immigration to Israel, especially two small groups in New Jersey and Philadelphia, where the Association of Black and White Jews was campaigning for the Dimona Israelites.[95] Decentralized and tiny Black Jewish groups sprang up in inner cities between the two world wars. They had almost no connection with mainstream Judaism until the 1960s when Jewish organizations began reaching out. One association, Hatza'ad Harishon (The First Step) extended assistance to young African Americans interested in Judaism. Rabbi Wolfe Kelman, a leader of the Conservative Movement who had marched in Selma, Alabama, with Martin Luther King, Jr., opined that every person who declares himself a Jew should be recognized as such. One Jewish civil rights activist wrote, "The awareness of the presence in our midst of Jews with black skin color and 'Afro' hair-styles may also just temper the hysterical, racist backlash that has become respectable among American Jews, from the JDL to *Commentary*."[96]

Israeli diplomats were quite concerned about these views. They were encouraged by an opinion piece by Robert Coleman, an African American convert who was serving as the director of the Synagogue Council of America's Division of Social Justice. Coleman questioned the Jewish identity of those Black communities.[97] However, most mainstream Jewish organizations were disinclined to jump into the fray. Israeli consulates were instructed to do their best to keep the topic out of the news.[98]

FIGURE 6.3 Rashida (left) arrived with a group of Black Hebrew Israelites from Liberia in December 1969. In an otherwise positive report, *Ha'olam Hazeh* provokes, "Do you want another 200,000 like her?" (*Ha'olam Hazeh*, April 1, 1970)

Danger appeared to be lurking in both accepting or deporting the Israelites. By late 1969, the Foreign Ministry was nervously looking for more information in Monrovia, Chicago, Philadelphia, and New York. The head of the consular department, Mordechai Shalev, spent a couple of weeks in the United States composing a report on different Black Jewish communities.[99] Minister Burg speculated that the trickling in of the African Israelites might be an orchestrated conspiracy to bring Israel into disrepute in the eyes of the world.[100] Premier Meir also raised the specter of a conspiracy to embarrass

Israel, declaring that she would not be surprised to find out that behind the group there were those who wish "to paint Israel with the negative image of racism."[101] Hinting at the Lansky affair, she added that Israel is allowed to protect itself from lawlessness even when it comes to Jews.[102]

The Israeli consul in Philadelphia urged Jerusalem to offer the group quick conversions and the opportunity to remain in Israel, for otherwise, this would be construed not as a religious matter, but as racial discrimination. A new public relations front is not what Israel needed.[103] The Israelites understood the Israeli vulnerability in this regard. A group of eighteen Israelites who had to be removed from the airport by force declared upon their return to the United States that the Jews in Israel are white European racists.[104] In a press conference in front of Zion Gate in the Old City of Jerusalem, Ben Ammi, surrounded by eight robed men holding Bibles and incense, declared "We came here offering Shalom. . . . We have met with no jobs, no decent housing and Jim Crow policies like what we left behind."[105] The case of the Hebrew Israelites was used by Arab countries to condemn Israel.[106]

Israeli diplomats emphasized defensively that the country absorbed hundreds of thousands of people of color it accepted as Jews, including a community of Cochin Jews from India who were also sent to Dimona, and refused white people. This was the case of Oswald Rufeisen, known as Brother Daniel. Born in Poland to Jewish parents, he converted to Catholicism and became a friar of the Carmelite Order. After moving to Israel, he asked to be naturalized under the Law of Return, arguing that while a Catholic he was still ethnically a Jew. From the point of view of halachic law, a Jew who practices a different religion is still a Jew. However, the court adopted a more stringent but supposedly secular yardstick, the common public perception that a person who converted to Christianity is no longer a Jew.[107]

In 1970, in the wake of the Shalit affair, the Knesset amended the Law of Return to ascertain that a Jew is someone whose mother is Jewish or converted to Judaism and who has not changed his or her religion—incorporating the yardstick of the Rufeisen case. The new law moved in opposite directions. On the one hand, it occluded a more inclusive understanding of Jewish identity, following but then further restricting a religious prescription. On the other hand, it opened the door to Reform and Conservative conversions and, most importantly, it vastly expanded the category of those eligible for immigrant status to include the spouses, children, and grandchildren of Jews.[108]

None of this applied to the Black Hebrew Israelites. A year later the High Court rejected the petition of two Israelite families who had settled in the West Bank city of Jericho to rescind the deportation order against them. It determined that the minister of the interior has discretion concerning whom to admit to the country and that the Israelites do not qualify as Jews. The justices, however, recommended that the minister reconsider allowing those who were already in Israel to stay.[109] The Foreign Ministry continued to object to deporting the Israelites en masse and despite various plans for such an expulsion it never took place. Another obstacle the authorities faced was that some of the Israelites renounced their American citizenship, which complicated their return to the United States.[110]

The police were instructed to cast a gimlet eye on African Americans arriving at the airport and to make sure they were bona fide tourists who had return tickets and sufficient means to sustain their visit. Groups that aroused suspicion were sometimes followed in a cat-and-mouse game throughout the country. Ben Ammi explained that the Israelites resort to cunning and illegal means to infiltrate Israel, much like Zionists had done in the late 1940s. The occasional refusal to allow Black visitors entrance triggered additional bad publicity for Israel.[111]

It is debatable whether the Israelites could have been accepted under the Law of Return, especially following its 1970 overhaul. The law itself is controversial, to say the least, as it constitutes one foundational building block of what political geographer Oren Yiftachel characterized as the Israeli regime of ethnocracy.[112] But by profiling African Americans arriving at the airport, easily detected by the color of their skin, Israel was engaging in an American racial practice.[113]

Lod (now Ben-Gurion) Airport constituted concurrently a gateway for Israelis' increasingly affordable and much cherished vacations abroad and a frontier post that defended the country from the imagined dangers of the outside world—whether gangsters, Black Israelites, or Western tourists and volunteers who arrived in greater numbers and were associated with drug use and other behavior considered antisocial.[114] And then there were real dangers made ever more painfully palpable in May 1972 when three members of the Japanese Red Army, operating on behalf of Palestinian Popular Front, raided the airport, killing twenty-six people and injuring eighty others.

Conclusion

Decades later, Yehudith Huebner, the deputy general director of the Ministry of the Interior, who was the point person for both Ben Ammi and Meyer Lansky, would recall that back at the turn of the 1970s Israel did not know how to accommodate the world. The Law of Return ostensibly opened the country to the outside. Israelis were not ready. "We should not be afraid of everything that is different," she said. She also conceded that the public reaction to Lansky bordered on hysteria.[115]

While it extended its de facto borders, Israel turned ever more nervous about guarding its boundaries, and looked defensively for a thicker epidermis. However, if the Black Panthers, the Israelites, and Lansky met unsubstantiated fears and moral panic, the initial reaction to Kahane and the JDL was arguably not panicked enough. And whereas Kahane brought to Israel strains of American racism, the Hebrew Israelites faced mostly homebrewed prejudice.[116]

The Lansky affair with which we began resurfaced from the recesses of historical memory first in the context of other Jewish immigrants with strong underworld ties, for instance, in the 1990s, when it appeared that the Russian Mafia was treating Israel as a staging ground of a new criminal empire.[117] In 1994, Lansky and Kahane were alluded to after an American immigrant, Baruch Goldstein—a member of Kach—massacred scores of Muslim worshippers in Hebron (see chapter 7). Minister of Immigration Yair Tzaban proposed then to prohibit the immigration of Jewish extremists. He said that Kach members "are a danger to the Jewish soul."[118] Kach was outlawed as a terrorist organization. Nevertheless, its remnants are now a stronger force in Israeli politics than Kach had ever been. Most visible is Itamar Ben-Gvir, the leader of the Far-Right Otzma Yehudit (Jewish Might) Party that as part of the Religious Zionist Party enjoyed substantial gains in the 2022 elections. In the 1990s Ben-Gvir was convicted of supporting a terrorist organization

(Kach) and for racist incitement against Arabs. Prime Minister Benjamin Netanyahu appointed Ben-Gvir minister of national security.

Meanwhile, Lansky or a Lansky-like figure have become a perennial motif in the endless representations of the Mafia in American popular culture, often featuring the attributes of the mythic Lansky: a brainy, calculating, omnipotent individual who dispatches others to do his dirty work. In recent decades, the figure of the gangster also assumed its place in Jewish American memory, fueling the fascination with tough "badass" Jews. The historical Lansky was famous for bridging ethnic boundaries by making alliances with Italian mobsters. The Israeli episode, in contrast, inscribed his perception as a lonely, tragic Jew. A recent Off Broadway one-man play recasts Lansky's life as an alternative to the conventional story of the Jew as a pariah. The play, starring Mike Burstyn (see chapter 8) has Lansky narrating his life of overcoming adversity while sojourning in Tel Aviv.[119] Nostalgia creeps in. Actor Richard Dreyfuss, who played Lansky in a David Mamet show on HBO said, "I know people like Lansky from my own family, my immigrant grandfather on the Lower East Side, who spoke like him and looked at the world through the same eyes."[120] Meyer Lansky's life, including expulsion from Israel, stands for the complexity of the Jewish American experience.

SEVEN

Emissaries of Liberalism in Crisis

The American presence in Israel at the turn of the 1970s had a palpable, in-the-flesh character. American visitors arrived in substantially greater numbers than ever before. From 1967 to 1972, tourism from the United States increased from roughly 90,000 to 290,000.[1] The aftermath of the Six-Day War also witnessed a significant rise in the number of immigrants from North America, reaching a peak of 7,364 in 1971.[2] Obviously, neither Meyer Lansky, Meir Kahane, nor Ben Ammi were the typical American figures moving to or visiting the country. The tourist with the large camera dangling off his shoulder, the long-haired backpacking hippie, the kibbutz volunteer, the United Jewish Appeal (UJA) mission participant, the Women's International Zionist Organization (WIZO) volunteer, and the exchange student were all much more recognizable social types. Israel beckoned to American entertainers and politicians, the latter frequenting the country especially during election seasons.[3] In 1972, to give one example, visitors included Senators Edmund Muskie, Birch Evans Bayh, Jr., Henry Jackson, Frank Church, all Democrats, and New York governor Nelson Rockefeller, a Republican.

A few newcomers assumed visible roles in Israeli culture. Sociologist Elihu Katz ran Israeli television at its inception. Tal Brody revolutionized basketball and heralded an influx of American players in the top Israeli league. Director Nola Chilton introduced socially conscious documentary theater.[4] John Bale headed the newly constituted art department at the Bezalel Academy of Arts and Design. Settling in bucolic Ein Karem, painter Ivan Schwebel would place on his canvas biblical figures in modern attire roaming downtown Jerusalem. Mel Keller composed music for films and led a well-known jazz quartet. Making *aliya* three weeks after the conclusion of the Six-Day War, Marcia Freedman would be elected a member of Knesset, representing the quite miniscule—and yet already fractured—feminist movement.

Josie Katz, who arrived in 1959, was a decade later a popular singer and sex symbol. Danny Sanderson, leader of the popular rock band Kaveret (beehive) that epitomized the Israeliness of a younger generation, spent his youth in New York City. His lyrics carry the indelible mark of American pun-dependent one-liners and the hilarities of *Mad* magazine. Sanderson recounts that upon returning to Israel he was still thinking in English ("I still talk from left to right")[5] and was struck by Hebrew idioms. He heard people remarking, "herein the dog is buried," meaning, this is the crux of the matter. The expression sounded weird and funny and years later (1973) would become the basis of a tremendously popular song.[6]

A few members of an older generation of American immigrants were already occupying key positions in Israeli society. Chief Justice Shimon Agranat secured political and civil liberties by relying heavily on American jurisprudence, most famously in the Kol Ha'am decision (1953) in which he incorporated a freedom of expression doctrine into Israeli law. As his biographer Pnina Lahav writes, due to his transformative rulings "the canvas of Israeli legal culture is liberally sprinkled with American motifs."[7] Another Chicago-trained scholar, Don Patinkin, was considered the dean of Israeli economists. Adolph "Al" Schwimmer, who smuggled airplanes from the United States in the 1948 war, managed the Israel Aerospace Industries (IAI). And then there was Prime Minister Golda Meir, who immigrated with her family from Pinsk to Milwaukee at the tender age of eleven. Meir's command of the English language, let alone her intimate knowledge of American Jewry, would fuel her rise in the leadership of the Zionist movement. Both would continue to be political assets during her tenure as prime minister. However, and despite a lingering touch of American accent in her voice, her public persona and deep emotionalism connoted for many the stereotype of the east European Ashkenazi matriarch rather than the modern American woman.

Far from an exhaustive survey of American-born or American-educated Israelis, this chapter follows a few notable individuals and the ideas, practices, and ethos they introduced. Their careers often exemplified core beliefs of American liberalism about social activism, volunteerism, and the language of rights. Nevertheless, the liberalism that reached Israel at the turn of the 1970s was already affected by the brokenness of American liberalism. It was a liberalism in crisis.

The global traffic of American knowledge did not require immigrants or visitors for its dispersion. But the unmediated encounter with American newcomers rather than popular culture, theater, academic publications, and other such conduits involved interpersonal dynamics that shaped the transfer—sometimes, as we shall see, by eliciting resistance. The following discussion ultimately demonstrates the limited capacity of new ideas and approaches coming from the United States to take root in the Israeli political and bureaucratic landscape. A secondary theme highlights, once again, the thread that connected the racial discord in the United States with Israeli social disparities.

The chapter first explores a few corners of the social sciences, focusing on the early career of Eliezer Jaffe of the Baerwald School of Social Work at the Hebrew University and Avner Amiel, an American-trained social worker who was involved with the Black Panthers in Jerusalem. We then turn to the nascent phase of Israeli feminism through the seemingly implausible political career of Marcia Freedman. The third part focuses on the Americanization of Israeli basketball, exemplified by Tal Brody, who brought to the game a professional spirit and a vision of the role of the athlete in society. By the mid-1970s Israeli basketball would eagerly recruit American players, including African Americans.

Liberals or Fanatics?

The turn of the 1970s saw the apex of American immigration to Israel. Seeking to further encourage newcomers from Western countries, the government instituted a new status, "potential immigrant," that conferred the rights and material benefits reserved for *olim* under the Law of Return but granted prospective immigrants a three-year waiting period before they decide whether to accept Israeli citizenship. By 1973, roughly 25,000 potential immigrants journeyed to Israel. Additional privileges that would fan the Black Panthers' resentment included lower tax rates on income and the purchase of vehicles and housing.

American immigration to Israel received substantial scholarly attention at the time. Asked about their motivation, immigrants often accentuated their Jewish identity rather than Zionism. A 1969–70 survey found that half of the participants had not been members of any Zionist organization prior to making *aliya*.[8] Some felt increasingly alienated from the United States, voicing concerns over crime, racial strife, assimilation, drugs, and antisemitism. Others found America too conformist and materialistic. Anthropologist Kevin Avruch observed that unlike other immigration movements, American Jews were not seeking modernity but instead wished to return to gemeinschaft and a sense of Jewish togetherness or home. In the United States they "had made intense investments in their ethnic identity, Jewishness, to the point where their social identity was primordialized."[9] Paradoxically, in Israel they would be categorized "Anglo-Saxons" and turn into agents of modernization, purveyors of efficiency, rationality, and business mentality.

Newcomers emphasized the positive attributes of American culture such as civility, tolerance, commitment to progress, and honesty, which they contrasted to the debilitating bureaucratic red tape and nepotism as well as to "Levantinism" they came across in their new homeland. In this regard their sensibilities cohered well with those of the Israeli elite. One immigrant described arriving in Israel through a mélange of mostly unappealing odors wafting from the open falafel and shawarma stands, the sweaty porters at the Haifa port, the polluted highways or, alternatively, the sea breezes. Seeing someone urinating in the street convinced him that he arrived in the Levant.[10]

The newly arrived, writes Avruch, "came to believe that in Israel only by being better Americans can they be good Jews."[11] Identities—American and Jewish—that in the United States appeared to be drifting apart fused well in Israel. An American émigré confessed, "I think if I went back to America now, I'd have some sort of identity crisis. Here I have none: I'm 100 percent an American."[12] The expectation that American/Jewish/Israeli identities could be mutually constitutive was evident in other sites of the American-Israeli encounter. In his memoirs, Yitzhak Rabin claimed that Israel normalized the Jews of America, freed them from the stigma of being "strange," and thus made them better Americans.[13] Some olim, however, complained that the evils that plagued America were coming to Israel: crime, delinquency, drugs, keeping up with the Joneses.[14]

Most (57 percent) identified as Democrats, the rest were independent, and only 2 percent Republican.[15] Nearly 40 percent claimed to have participated in peace or antiwar demonstrations. Nevertheless, in subsequent decades American immigrants would not be associated with moderate liberalism as much as sheer fanaticism. Typically, a 1980 piece in *Ma'ariv* singled out a few former Americans as practicing "aggressive citizenship" and occupying the "crazy margins" of Israeli society.[16] It pointed to Marcia Freedman and Naomi Kies on the Left, Meir Kahane on the Right, Moshe Hirsch, the self-fashioned foreign minister of the extreme *haredi* group Neturei Karta, and Simcha Perlmutter, an Orthodox rabbi who embraced Jesus and in 1967 established with two wives a tiny community, Ir Ovot, south of the Dead Sea.

By the end of the century, American immigrants would be linked with extreme right-wing politics and the settler movement in which they are evidently overrepresented. The most extreme case was that of Baruch Goldstein, the physician who in February 1994 perpetrated the Cave of the Patriarchs massacre that killed twenty-nine and wounded 125 Palestinians in the city of Hebron. Goldstein was born in Brooklyn and immigrated to Israel in 1983.

Much of the Jewish settlement in the occupied territories took place after the conclusion of the period explored in this book. But American Jews joined the fledgling settler projects in Hebron and Kfar Etzion prior to the October 1973 Yom Kippur War. In 1972, Gar'in Yamit, the group that would coestablish the short-lived city of Yamit in the Sinai Peninsula, was formed in Cincinnati.[17] American immigrants are now estimated to comprise about

15 percent of the West Bank settler population, more than 60,000 out of roughly 400,000.[18]

However, research conducted in the 1980s revealed that relative to other settlers Americans living in the territories upheld rather liberal opinions, mostly rejecting the views of Kahane and his movement and overwhelmingly condemning the actions of the early 1980s anti-Palestinian Jewish underground. Less than 40 percent pointed to ideological factors as paramount in their decision to move to the occupied territories.[19] Historian Sara Yael Hirschhorn recently sought to correct the focus on American immigrants' messianism and right-wing extremism, highlighting instead their progressive background and the paradoxical way it has continued to mold their identities and ideology. They brought to the settler project their suburban utopian aspirations, the tactics of direct action, and the rhetoric of rights, believing (or at least professing) that they were defending "their human and civil rights to fulfill their Jewish destinies."[20] Among other examples, Rabbi Solomon Riskin, one of the founders of the settlement Efrat, often mentions that he marched with Martin Luther King, Jr. "Now," he told the *New York Times*, "we, the settlers, have become the Blacks of Martin Luther King."[21]

Still, it is unclear what remains liberal under the hood of rights talk. Grassroots organizations, civil disobedience, and political arguments couched in the language of rights and of righting historical wrongs are not necessarily attributes of progressive or liberal politics in either the United States or Israel. New Deal rights discourse was appropriated in 1950s America by whites who were defending their neighborhoods' racial purity.[22] Grassroots forms of mobilization were central to the rise of the New Right in the 1970s. One example would be Phyllis Schlafly's anti-ERA campaign, another is the pro-life movement.[23]

American liberalism in the 1960s was already experiencing a crisis that affected political alignments and coalition building in addition to ideology. And among the immigrants, whereas many claimed to have participated in peace or antiwar activities, in surveys conducted in 1972 and 1975 a majority agreed with the statement, "Blacks in America have gone too far in their demands."[24] Kahane represents an extreme case of the 1960s crisis of liberalism but liberalism's fissures and fault lines are also visible in the case studies we follow in this chapter, for instance, between modes of scholarly and professional behavior that underscored neutrality and objectivity, and denied their own ideological slant, and emerging paradigms of politically engaged social science; between older forms of civil rights and newer types that jettison universalism in favor of the politics of identity.

Empire of Knowledge

Among other instruments that guaranteed its ascendancy, the American empire has been an empire of knowledge. In the wake of World War II, the United States substantiated its global leadership in producing and circulating scientific, managerial, industrial, and other forms of knowledge, transforming academia in Europe and worldwide.[25] If the Hebrew University was constituted as a German university (1925), Tel Aviv University was fully accredited in 1969 under the leadership of the American entrepreneur George Wise. It took American academia as its model. American orientations infiltrated specific disciplines as well. Sociologist Uri Ram demonstrates the momentous shift in the Hebrew University's Sociology Department when in 1951 Martin Buber was replaced as chair by Shmuel Noah Eisenstadt. This amounted to a transition from the humanistic, speculative, and philosophically rich German paradigm to Parsonian structuralism-functionalism and a policy-oriented approach; from a suspicion of modernity in the former to a celebration of modernization and positivism in the latter; from an emphasis on community to an emphasis on the state.[26]

Academic hegemony was maintained through international networks, scholarly associations, research grants, journals, the enticement of American PhD programs, and recurrent visits of foreign scholars to Israeli academic institutions. One observer noticed the growing number of researchers and experts sporting American accents heard over the radio.[27] By the late 1960s, American-born or American-educated scholars reshaped the Israeli knowledge apparatus, overhauled academic fields, established institutions, and helped forge policy in economics, education, public statistics, management, and social work, among other disciplines (see chapter 3). This transformation coincided with the zenith of social science authority in American public life that was akin to a civil religion and epitomized post–New Deal liberalism. The mid-1960s was the high point in the elaboration of the American welfare state, culminating in the Johnson administration's Great Society initiatives. Also keep in mind the significant postwar Jewish presence in the American academy in general and particularly in the social sciences.[28]

American social and behavioral sciences rested on a shared positivist epistemology that foregrounded field research and exhibited a slant toward measuring social problems and evaluating their prospective resolution through quantifiable and ostensibly objective, scientifically proven means. It exhibited great confidence in the possibility of knowledge-driven social change and injected into Israeli public life particular framing idioms and other constitutive terms for the consideration of the social terrain and whatever afflicts it. Moreover, the presumed scientificity of the social sciences was predicated on their universality and iterability across time and space, obscuring their origins in the concrete social and cultural circumstances in the United States and Europe.

By the early 1970s, however, policy-driven social science was subjected to growing criticism in the United States from both sides of the political arena. From the Left's point of view, it was accused of a proclivity to "blaming the victims" and for its complicity in substantiating systems of domination, ethnic and racial hierarchies, and oppressive state power.[29] Such criticism would grow more powerful in the decades to come, exposing the illiberal effects of modern liberalism and its blind spots. This was not just an outsiders' critique. Radicalism grew within a few academic disciplines that turned away from claims of professional neutrality toward embracing advocacy on behalf of the poor and the marginalized. Social work furnishes a good example of this transition.[30]

Is Israel a Welfare State?

Starting in the pre-state era, social work in Israel was cultivated by the American Jewish Joint Distribution Committee (JDC), known as the Joint. In the mid-1950s, the Joint convinced a reluctant Hebrew University to establish the Paul Baerwald School of Social Work and Social Welfare. Some leaders of the university did not consider social work to be a full-fledged academic discipline. Eileen Blackey, a non-Jewish social worker, was recruited as the school's first dean. She was a pioneer of emergency relief services that helped care for displaced Jewish children, survivors of the Holocaust. A tall, charismatic woman, Blackey traveled across the country in a chauffeured American car visiting transit camps that housed new immigrants.[31]

The school's international resources and location in proximity to some of the deepest pockets of poverty in Israel as well as to the corridors of state power allowed Baerwald a unique role in shaping social thought and policy. Faculty labored to publicize the scope of poverty in Israel and to proselytize for change. In 1964, two German-born, American-educated faculty members, Lotte Salzberger and Yona Rosenfeld, received a grant from the American government to design services for families in distress. Their research (with Yehuda Matras) concluded that social services in Israel had a limited reach and were not extended to all who required them. They documented alienation and distance between providers and their clients.[32]

The two then published a series of articles in the Histadrut's daily *Davar* under the title "Is Israel a Welfare State?," in which they exposed the dissonance between the country's self-image of equality and the reality of poverty, housing congestion, and social marginality, exacerbated by the absence of an encompassing social policy.[33] The authors maintained that the invisibility of Israeli poverty and apathy toward the poor rested on an approach that calcified into ideology. Insiders who are part of established institutions and movements, including kibbutzim and cooperatives, are exempt from concern about the well-being of outsiders who are ostensibly taken care of by anonymous state agencies about which the public knew very little and cared even less. Existing social security mechanisms predominantly served the already organized and powerful populations.[34]

Salzberger and Rosenfeld further alleged that the value of labor and productivity—so cardinal to Israeli society—served to shame welfare recipients, many of whom were unable to work. The emphasis on rehabilitation both ignored their actual needs and undermined their sense of dignity. Judging by the responses to these articles, some among the cohorts of the old Left still associated the idea of the welfare state with Western capitalism rather than labor-oriented socialism.[35]

Baerwald rejected the posture of the academic ivory tower and called for the university to become socially engaged and for social workers, practitioners of a discipline that historically focused on individual or family casework—to involve themselves in policymaking. Social workers' chief commitment was to represent the needs of their clients rather than the institutions that employ them. Israel Katz, who earned his PhD at Case Western Reserve University and was the first Israeli to lead Baerwald, spoke of the democratization of welfare. He would assume key roles in shaping national social policy. In 1968, Katz was appointed the director of social security administration (National Insurance Institute) and a decade later he became the minister of labor and welfare. Baerwald faculty were also central in establishing a union of academically trained social workers as against an existing union in the Histadrut. The school continued to generate a biting critique of the state's welfare system. Seven different ministries dealt with welfare issues at the time, each under the control of a different party in the governing coalition.

A newcomer from the States, Eliezer Jaffe (University of Cleveland PhD) joined in 1960 to head the research wing of the school. In 1970 he suggested that welfare recipients should unionize. "It is about time that those who are in need of welfare assistance organize and articulate what pains them, what their needs are."[36] Jaffe's prescription was likely inspired by pioneering initiatives in the United States, such as the National Welfare Rights Organization, largely comprised of African American women. Its inaugural event took place on June 30, 1966, when thousands of protesters participated in the Poor People's March in sixteen cities across the country.[37] One of the movement's key demands was for a guaranteed income for welfare recipients, an idea that was also raised by Baerwald faculty. The director general of the Welfare Ministry demurred, maintaining that giving the floor to the needy would only lead to confusion. "The weaker population has difficulty ascertaining its needs objectively," he said. "Obviously, it would not be able to determine priorities."[38]

Jaffe further maintained that the disadvantaged are ignorant of their rights and do not receive proper guidance. In Israel only those who apply for help receive it, and even then, it is not extended as a right but as the kind of favor that the strong give to the weak. Social workers operate in the office, not in the field as they should, because this is a convenient way for the authorities to dispense of their supposed benevolence.[39] Jaffe would institute one of the first affirmative action experiments in Israel. Beginning in 1978,

Baerwald reserved twenty among 120 slots for "opportunity need" students, including minorities. They scored below the required threshold but were accepted based on exhibited high motivation. The program was deemed a resounding success.[40]

The Panthers

To the surprise of many colleagues, in 1970 Jaffe took leave of his academic position and, at the invitation of Mayor Teddy Kollek, assumed the leadership of Jerusalem's welfare agency, renamed the Department of Family and Community Services. He regarded this administrative position as a laboratory for innovative ideas about social welfare and an opportunity to satisfy the "bug of social activism."[41] Jaffe set about tackling the cumbersome structure impeding the work of welfare services in the capitol. He decoupled financial aid from the work of assisting families in distress and decentralized social work to local neighborhoods. Budget and personnel increased, and criteria were set for the allocation of funds beyond basic welfare support. In early 1971, his department published a brochure detailing the rights of welfare recipients.

Jaffe became increasingly cognizant of the ethnic dynamics of aid dispensation. The person who extends the support is often of European descent and those who are in need mostly come from the Middle East and North Africa.[42] His immediate response to the initial reports on the Black Panthers from Musrara was that the government would pay a high price for not treating seriously the predicament of youth in distress. Describing the situation as explosive, he suggested that Kollek recognize the Panthers and open a dialogue with them. In a private letter Jaffe characterized the police decision to prohibit the first Panthers' demonstration as completely out of touch. "How scared and idiotic can you get?"[43]

The social worker most involved with the Panthers was Avner Amiel, a Mizrahi Jew of Moroccan descent who earned his MA in social work from Case Western Reserve University in 1964, where he studied group work and community organization. Amiel developed new services in the municipality, including street work, community centers, and senior clubs for the elderly.

He embodied the model of the social worker as an activist, occasionally seeking public confrontation to advance underprivileged communities. Kollek compared him to the famed American community activist Saul Alinsky.[44]

Even prior to the Panthers, Amiel employed radical tactics to mobilize the needy. In 1966, he began organizing the elderly poor. Hadassah terminated the medical services that provided care for those not insured through the Histadrut. Amiel urged the elderly to fight for their rights by shifting responsibility to government.[45] Through role-playing he trained them to talk to officials and the press. He then staged what amounted to a demonstration against his own employer. A convoy of buses paid for by the department's budget brought six hundred protesters carrying banners and placards in front of Kollek's office, demanding medical services as a right.[46] A warning was conveyed that the funeral procession of the next elderly citizen to perish for lack of treatment would depart from the homes of the minister of health and the mayor. It was quite effective and a solution was found.[47]

Amiel's unit ran the club where the would-be Panthers congregated and were urged to think more broadly about their predicament and to organize. When the Panthers group coalesced, Amiel and a few other coworkers assisted by collecting information from friendly sources in government agencies. They coached the Panthers before their meeting with Meir. Amiel helped phrase the Panthers' Poverty Haggadah. World and local press frequented his office to cover the Panthers' activities. In what was likely a retaliation, the municipality decided to move the community services Amiel built outside the social welfare department. He was marginalized.[48]

Israel Katz, who directed the Prime Minister's Committee on Youth and Children in Distress, which sought to address the problems publicized by the Panthers, also opened lines of communication with the Panthers. In one instance, he was horrified when it was brought to his attention that they considered kidnapping Minister of Housing Ze'ev Sherf. Katz begged them not to proceed with the scheme that could have ended in a national tragedy.[49]

Jaffe was fired from his position—only a few weeks before his own resignation went into effect—after he discovered and made public that state funds earmarked for his department were put in the general municipal budget.[50] City hall contended that he mishandled his budget. Apparently, he spent the annual allocation early on to force the municipality and the Ministry of Welfare to come up with additional money.[51] But his department's involvement with the Black Panthers was also a major impetus.

Meanwhile, press reports raised alarm about the Americanization and the consequent radicalization of social welfare services in the capital. In one welfare office journalist Nahum Barnea found that most of the workers were immigrants, especially from the United States. Shaul Harris had left Chicago only ten months earlier and still found it hard to adjust to people shouting all the time.[52] In America basic procedures are followed. Here, he was told, a public row is a sign that you really care. Harris said that consciousness about poverty is much stronger in the United States but that he noticed some resemblance between American racial conflict and ethnic tension in Israel. "There is not the same hatred, of course, but there is a sense of deprivation, and the constant contention is that if I were an Ashkenazi, I would have received everything."[53]

A year after the Panthers' eruption on the scene, another press report alleged that American immigrants, mostly university students in Jerusalem and Haifa, were seeking to radicalize the poor using Black organizations as a model. There was little evidence for such a drive but Jerusalem social workers did form an action committee headed by Yona Rosenfeld with a list of extensive demands for overhauling welfare policy.[54] They threatened to induce welfare claimants to besiege the offices of the Treasury and the Ministry of Welfare and demand that poor people receive adequate support. However, the Histadrut's social workers' union did not rush to support their action. Its leader stated, "There is a difference between social work and social revolution. . . . We take a longer route . . . and do not climb on verbal barricades."[55]

Jaffe returned to academia, shifting his agenda from government to volunteerism. He would cofound Zahavi, an organization that promotes the rights of large families as well as Ogen, the Israel Free Loan Association. Again, the paradigm was American.[56] Jaffe is credited with proposing the *twinning* concept for the late 1970s Project Renewal, the signature welfare program of Menachem Begin's Likud-led government that revitalized 160 poor areas and communities in Israel.[57] The underlying idea was to encourage Jewish community federations and private philanthropists worldwide to partner directly with disadvantaged neighborhoods in Israel. Amiel called

Project Renewal "an escape to philanthropy and an attempt to free the Israeli government from its responsibility for the welfare of its citizens."[58] However, by the 1980s the model of the state-employed social worker as a social activist largely disappeared.

Reforma and *Integratzia*

The American racial experience was fundamental to the restructuring of Israeli education in 1968. The new policy the Knesset authorized—known simply as the *reforma*—extended compulsory education to the age of sixteen and replaced the dual system of an eight-year elementary school and a four-year high school with a three-tier system at the center of which was a new institution, the middle school. A major motivation for the *reforma* was to adjust the school system to the challenges born out of the massive 1950s immigration, especially the disparities between the formal scholarly achievements of Ashkenazi and Mizrahi students. Since the mid-1960s, public discussion about education turned to the "ethnic gap" and the promise of national cohesion through integration, or in common parlance, *integratzia*. An American institution, the middle school, was designated as the site of social coalescence.

As sociologist Julia Resnik argues, education reform in the name of democratization in Israel and elsewhere involved global scholarly networks propped up by international organizations anchored in American and European academia. Language that arrived from the policy-oriented American social sciences rendered commensurable the ethnic situation in Israeli education and the racial predicament in American schools. Furthermore, the integration of American education along racial lines assumed a paradigmatic status. Professional Israeli educational discourse appropriated idioms such as "inequality of opportunities," "social failure," "dropouts," and other such categories and diagnostic terms.[59]

Essential in this regard was the famous and famously controversial "Coleman Report" (1966). Social psychologist James Coleman's research was mandated by Title IV of the American Civil Rights Act (1964). His report supplied the rationale behind the mass race-integration busing policy in American public schools. It determined that the variable that best accounts for African American students' achievements was the composition of the classroom. The larger the proportion of white students, the better the educational performances of their Black classmates. Coleman tied his findings to the promise of upward mobility, which then migrated into Israeli reform. Throughout the next two decades, he followed and even reflected publicly on integration efforts in Israel. Coleman maintained that the gap between children of Ashkenazi and Mizrahi descent resembles the Black-white divide in the United States, although in Israel it shrank radically in the second generation while in the United States there was no such improvement.[60]

"My Body Belongs to Me"

In early 1974, Marcia Freedman entered the eighth Knesset by chance or serendipity—she would say, "I fell into the Knesset," as part of Ratz, the Citizens Rights Movement.[61] She was reportedly the first radical feminist to be elected to a national legislature anywhere in the world.[62] Freedman often employed survey research to expose the low status of women in Israel, underscoring, for instance, that a quarter of Israeli physicians were women but that there were almost no female department heads. Whereas the American military had opened 135,000 positions to women, in the IDF there were only twenty-five positions available to them. In a study she coresearched on gender stereotypes in primary school textbooks, she found that men appeared in two-thirds of the texts, women in only a third, only 4 percent of whom were adult women. Women did not seem to exist unless they were portrayed as teachers, mothers, or grandmothers.[63]

One of the numerous barriers that feminism had to scale was the myth that Israeli society genuinely practiced gender equality. Betty Friedan fell for that Zionist mystique when in 1961 she pointed to Israel as the one country where men and women were equal.[64] The perception was based on the rhetoric and social experimentation of the early pioneering era, the kibbutz movement, and later the widely circulated images of female soldiers carrying an Uzi. By the late 1960s, the global visibility of Prime Minister Meir fortified Israel's reputation in this regard. The National Organization for Women in the United States circulated Meir's portrait with the caption, "But Can She Type?"[65] But Meir lashed out at modern feminism. Interviewed by Oriana

Fallaci for *Ms.* magazine, she said, "Do you mean those crazy women who burn their bras and go around all disheveled and hate man? They are crazy. Crazy. But how can one accept such crazy women who think that it's a misfortune to get pregnant and a disaster to bring children to the world?"[66]

The turn of the 1970s witnessed the pinnacle of the cult of masculinity in Israel and one of Freedman's sharpest commentaries was to couch the October 1973 war as a gendered crisis when the mass mobilization of men brought Israeli society to a standstill. The war, she contended, entailed a situation like the one described in Shulamit Firestone's *Dialectic of Sex* (1970). One day, women wake up and discover they live in a world without men. Since modern technology is operated by men, society returns to its primitive state. The emotional turmoil experienced by men was an opportune time to make progress in terms of gender equality, she proposed.[67]

Freedman and her then husband arrived in Israel a few weeks after the Six-Day War as part of a group of young American academics whose destination was the new University of Haifa. In high school in Newark, New Jersey, she had been a cheerleader. She was now a doctoral student and a lecturer in the philosophy department. During a visit to the United States a year later she acquired a few early books of second wave feminism. Freedman came to recognize in this literature an insight into her own life as a mother and a wife who also sought to carve out a professional career for herself. An invitation by a Beit Hillel rabbi, Bernie Hock, also an American immigrant, to direct an extracurricular seminar led her to initiate a women's only faculty and students' discussion forum on women's liberation. By the end of the first year, there were eight groups in Haifa that convened weekly for consciousness raising. Beginning in January 1973, they distributed a publication, *Women for a Renewed Society*.

Students and faculty at the university asked for a daycare center. Hundreds of women and children participated in a sit in.[68] A daycare center was duly opened. Other American faculty such as Marilyn Safir, who arrived in Israel in 1972, also launched similar conversations.[69] They supported a wildcat strike of female factory workers for equal pay, collected signatures for a petition for reproductive rights reform, and protested at the rabbinical court against existing marriage and divorce law. "Tranquil Haifa, and the rest of the country were shocked," Freedman would reminisce in her memoirs.[70]

This was the birth of the Haifa branch of the still embryonic feminist movement. A Jerusalem group emerged concurrently. It was largely an outgrowth of the New Left Matzpen and Shasi (Israel Socialist Left) factions and developed more of a French orientation.[71] Jerusalem feminists joined the Panthers' demonstration in Davidka Square, railing "against the repression of women and their discrimination in Israel and abroad and in solidarity with all the groups that are exploited and repressed."[72] In the first years the two factions coexisted with some tension. The Tel Aviv branch consolidated slightly later and for the rest of the 1970s was the most conservative of the three groups, embracing an apolitical posture.

In the summer of 1973, on the eve of the election, the feisty civil rights advocate Shulamit Aloni left the Labor Party in haste. Seeking the support of the feminist movement, she offered them a third place in her new party's candidate list, which was considered by all unlikely to enter the Knesset. The first choice for the slot, Ruth Resnik, could not accept the offer for personal reasons. She asked Freedman, a rather new immigrant with only partial command of Hebrew, who, to everybody's surprise, found herself in the legislature.

Local feminism followed the foundational texts and the publicity tools of the American movement, including rallies, street theater, and public opinion campaigns—all on a rather small scale. Another import was the comparison of women and African Americans. One manifesto declared, "The myth of the superiority of men is as false as the myth of the superiority of the white man."[73] Freedman's approach to the question of reproductive rights was largely inspired by the Roe v. Wade Supreme Court ruling as the foundation for the right of women to make decisions over their bodies. She introduced a bill to end all restrictions on choice during the first trimester of pregnancy.[74]

Her most radical public demonstration took place in July 1976 during the annual meeting of the Association of Obstetricians and Gynecologists at the Tel Aviv Hilton. Weeks earlier the association rejected the proposed pro-choice legislation under the pretext that gynecologists were not consulted and because it allowed unrestricted abortions. They warned that if passed, they would not cooperate with the law's implementation.[75] Eleven women, including Freedman, burst into the conference carrying banners, "End to the Black Market," "My Body Belongs to Me," and "Legalize Abortion."

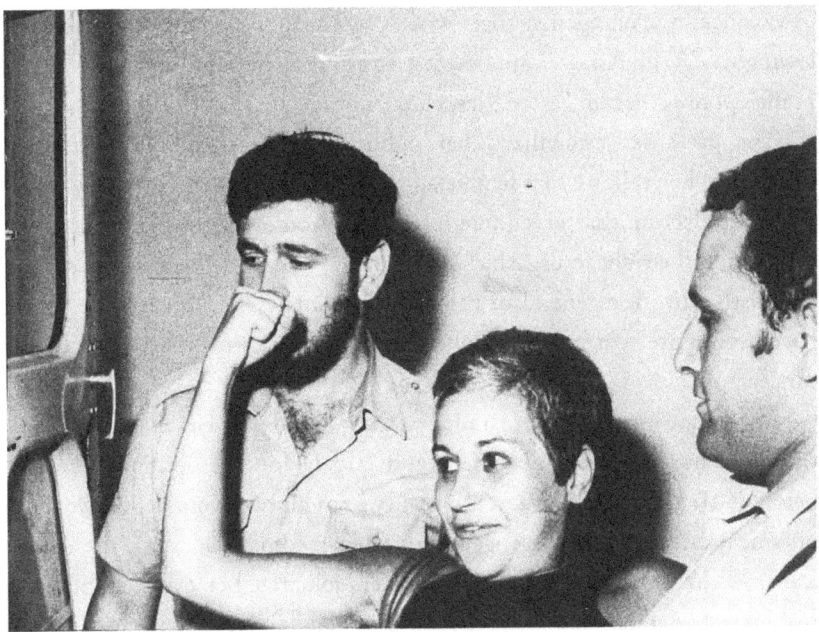

FIGURE 7.1 The newspaper *Al Hamishmar* described this image on its front page (June 24, 1976) as Marcia Freedman raising "a small and cute fist" during a "noisy" feminist demonstration. She was arrested for interrupting the annual meeting of the Association of Obstetricians and Gynecologists. (Photographer Hanoch Guthmann)

A doctor threw a water pitcher at Freedman's head. Refusing to leave, the women were arrested. The press reported that "eleven wild-haired, sloppily dressed women caused a wild riot."[76]

"The American, the Crazy Feminist"

Freedman was the first politician to raise a taboo topic, domestic abuse. Based on WIZO research in 123 municipalities, she claimed that in the Tel Aviv area 40 percent of women were exposed to spousal violence but in the south of the country abuse rose to 85 percent.[77] During the Knesset debate her colleagues across the political aisle kept joking about men abused by their wives. Minister of Police Shlomo Hillel stated that he did not understand how this issue is relevant to the police. "I can't say there is a specific problem of violence by men against their wives."[78] *Ma'ariv* began its report the following day, "The Knesset amused itself yesterday with an unusual topic."[79] Haifa's police chief suggested, "Jews do not beat their wives, only Arabs do."[80]

The press sensationalized her public pronouncements. A journalist who heard her talking to a female audience about women's sexuality wrote upon her election that Freedman intends to promote legislation guaranteeing women the right to orgasm.[81] Freedman appalled the Knesset by stating that if the director general of the Health Ministry had breasts, he would have been more sensitive about the paucity of clinics for diagnosing breast cancer.[82]

Feminism was another instance of the *glocal* delay. Israelis knew about the women's liberation movement and largely formed opinions about it before it arrived. It encountered hostility even among women and women's organizations.[83] A bus passenger identified Freedman aloud as "the American . . . the crazy feminist."[84] Lawmakers joked at her expense. She was nicknamed Marsha Hamarsha (Permissive Marcia). Isolated in the Knesset, she proposed to establish a women caucus, but the response was "What for? We don't belong to the same party."[85] Freedman also faced criticism from fellow feminists apprehensive of her support of legalizing drugs, her embrace of the cause of a Palestinian state, or scandalized, as was the rest of the country, when she proposed that a Ministry of Justice committee on prostitution would also include sex workers' representation.

Some feminists claimed that she does not represent them.[86] The foreign origins of feminist pioneers rendered feminism easily dismissible as an unwanted "American import." The tactics were American, much of the literature was American, some consciousness-raising meetings were conducted in English. It strained relations among feminists. One early participant, Dorit Ortal, would say, "The elitism bit and the knowledge of English annoyed me greatly. I understood that it does not allow me to stand in opposition and say, thank you Kate Millett, but we also have things to say that are perhaps more relevant to our lives here."[87]

Despite her radicalism, Freedman presented the American experience in the brightest of lights. In a programmatic piece for the *Jerusalem Post*, she reported that Israelis she had met when she first visited in 1959 espoused a one-sided view of the "ugly American." But times have changed. Now she found among young sabras a growing discontent with conformism, political apathy, and an arid and unsatisfying cultural life. "Young Israelis look across the ocean for a model . . . America is a highly pluralist society, it has a genuinely and vigorously free press, it has a fine history of social and political rebellions, and it is a country in which protection of individual rights is guaranteed by one of the finest constitutions ever written."[88]

She suggested that American newcomers could serve as the carriers of that legacy. There could be a natural alliance between young Israelis and American *olim* for the purpose of social and political reform and a new "pioneering period" in building a genuinely democratic society. "My hope is that we will play that role actively and without apologies."[89] Asked whether legalizing abortion addressed a major Israeli problem or was just a fashionable import, she retorted that the kibbutz and Zionism were also imports.[90]

Freedman's relationship with Aloni, who had no prior knowledge of her, turned rancorous.[91] Ratz joined another Labor Party refugee, Member of Knesset Aryeh "Lova" Eliav, to form Ya'ad-Civil Rights Movement. Later, Freedman and Eliav left to establish the Independent Socialist Faction. After four tumultuous years in the Knesset, Freedman decided not to run for another term. She felt much safer as an activist and organizer than a politician. A women's party she cofounded received a paltry 6,000 votes in the 1977 elections. That year she helped establish the feminist press, Hamin Hasheni (The Second Sex) and a domestic violence shelter in Haifa and then a rape victims' shelter in Tel Aviv (1978). She also cofounded the first lesbian association. By the turn of the 1980s, after coming out as a lesbian, she left the country and returned to the United States.

Basketball as a Way of Life

The reporter caught up with Tal Brody washing dishes in his kitchen. "He is 188 centimeters tall and looks like an ordinary tourist from 'Uncle Sam's' country. In his long and smiling face there are a few Jewish features. His English is an American singsong. He is modest and shy with an MA in education."[92] The basketball star from Trenton, New Jersey, arrived in Israel a year earlier to play in the Seventh Maccabiah (1965), an international gathering of Jewish athletes billed as the Jewish Olympics. His father Max Chernobroda had spent some time in Israel before immigrating to the United States and renaming himself Max Brody.

In the 1965 NBA draft Brody was picked twelfth by the Baltimore Bullets—now the Washington Wizards—after playing college basketball for Illinois, but Maccabi managers persuaded him to return to Israel and play for their team in the coming season.[93] Brody soon emerged as one of the most celebrated athletes in Israel, shaking an erstwhile rather sleepy sport and inaugurating the American era in Israeli basketball. Early on he struck enthusiastic spectators as possessing inexhaustible energy. He became a teen idol.[94] Selected as the Israeli Athlete for 1967 he helped Maccabi with its greatest achievement to date: victory over the European champion Real Madrid. He then left to serve in the US military, playing for the Army basketball team. In the summer of 1970, he finally settled in Israel.[95]

Brody was described by a player in an opposing team to be "precise like an IBM computer."[96] Maccabi's coach had to adjust his team's playing style to accommodate his capacities, adopting a quicker pace, a rapid-motion game based on "fast breaks." Another coach, Ralph Klein, said, "Tal showed us that basketball is more than a game—it's a way of life."[97] Brody stood for a new kind of dedication and professionalism. One of his teammates would recall that on Brody's first day on the team management told the players they brought a star. They were in the dressing room when someone entered with a side bag from which he began removing pants, a shirt, knee protectors, gauze, ointments, and creams. "I thought perhaps it was a mistake and the new guy is a masseuse. Only later we learned about his seriousness in preparing for training as though it were the actual game."[98]

The American turn involved coaches and managers as well. Klein spent a few months training in the United States, where beyond defensive and offensive tactics he learned how to connect with and energize players and how to build a cohesive team.[99] An ambitious and aggressive management was led, since 1969, by Shimon Mizrahi, a lawyer who modernized ticket sales and had the team's European games broadcast on Israeli TV.

Brody was not the only American recruit. Hapo'el Tel Aviv brought Bill Wold, a physical educator, for the 1966/67 season. He would be the first American to play for the Israeli national team as a new immigrant. In the 1966/67 season there were two foreign players, eight in 1968/69, ten in

1972/73, and by 1974/75 twenty-four American players; 40 percent of the starting "fives" in the top league were American born. By the mid-1980s Israeli basketball teams had about forty Americans on their rosters.[100]

The initial impetus came from the European basketball federation, which, facing lavishly supported east European teams, decided to allow American players. The first recruits were American Jews. Bob Podhurst arrived in Israel as a volunteer in the last days of the June 1967 war and was sent to Kibbutz Yiftah in the north, where for two months he worked in the irrigation canals. He then decided to call Maccabi.[101] The following year, team managers traveled to the United States in search of players. Efforts to limit the number of foreign players were scuttled by having Jewish players seek immediate citizenship. Non-Jewish players hired once the pool of Jewish athletes was exhausted—it happened quickly—could convert to Judaism. Barry Leibowitz, Lou Silver, Erik Menkin, Steve Chubin, Bob Griffin became household names. Coach instructions were given mostly in English.

When the league was organized in the mid-1950s there was a strong commitment to the amateur ethos. By the late 1960s a hidden semiprofessionalism had already taken hold, as was the case with Israeli soccer even without foreign players. Market conditions determined compensation.[102] By the 1980s foreigners would earn five or six times as much as locals. Beginning in 1975, the food concern Elite sponsored Maccabi, and its team members would wear the company's logo on their jerseys—another sign of the commodification of sports (and the everyday) in Israel.

By the 1972/73 season teams turned to African American players, beginning with Ron Dunlap in Maccabi Tel Aviv. Black players were first brought for the sole purpose of participating in the European championship games but later were integrated into the domestic league as well: Lawrence McCray, Bill Pells, Aulcie Perry, and later Earl Williams in Maccabi Tel Aviv and Larry "Butterfly" Cheatham (previously of the Harlem Wizards) in Maccabi Ramat Gan.[103] Perry was recruited in late 1976 and later converted to Judaism and was given the name Elisha Ben Avraham.

Americanization was not without its discontents. *Ma'ariv* called them basketball mercenaries and accused managers of building basketball empires at the public's expense.[104] Jewish players often settled in Israel, but others, Jews and non-Jews, came and left. Some claimed that the imports stunt the careers of local players. Danny Bracha, an Israeli-born player, felt he was second-rate, a plug.[105] Others were alarmed by rumors about lightening quick conversions to Judaism and fictive marriages—two methods employed to grant basketball players Israeli citizenship almost instantly.[106] The counterargument was that the foreigners made Israeli and European basketball stronger and that immigrants were Israelis regardless of when or from where they arrived.

"In the Map"

Maccabi Tel Aviv excelled at recruiting and retaining foreigners and capitalizing on their strengths, as manifested in its performance in European tournaments. A string of successes culminated with the European Champions Cup of 1977.[107] The final win over the Italian team Mobilgirgi Varese in April clinched the championship for the team. But the event that instigated an outburst of national sentiment and has been remembered ever since as a latter-day incarnation of a David and Goliath story, was the earlier victory over the Soviet CSKA Moskva, the Red Army team.

In 1967, the USSR broke off diplomatic relations with Israel. The Soviet team refused to come to Israel and therefore lost a game to Maccabi on a technicality. As Maccabi athletes were barred from entering the Soviet Union, the next game between the two teams took place in a tiny basketball courtyard (high school gym size) in the Belgian town of Virtun on February 17, 1977. Coach Klein framed the game in national terms, telling his team members, "We are fighting for our country as well as for thousands of Jews who cannot immigrate to Israel because of Soviet policy. Let's beat the Soviet bear."[108] But Lou Silver told *Ma'ariv*, "They are Russians—and we are Americans but in addition also Jews and therefore we will fight them as Americans and as Jews know how to do."[109] When the game concluded—the radio announcer burst into tears—jubilant Brody, the team's captain, told a nation, "We are on the map and we are staying on the map, not just in sport but in everything." Brody in fact blurted out in Hebrew, "We are *in* the map," a mistranslation that, nevertheless, became idiomatic in Israel.

Regardless of the massive foreign presence—the starting five featured four American-born players—Maccabi was lionized as though it were Israel's national team. Prime Minister Rabin said, "As usual Israel is always successful with the Israeli spirit and a bit of American aid." Fans were not bothered by the fact that these achievements were secured with the help of foreign players.[110] Maccabi's games in the European cup endowed basketball with great popularity. The club operated with the informal patronage of Moshe Dayan, who was known as the "friend of the club." Basketball became a middle-class sport.[111]

With his nice-guy aura and blend of Hebrew and English, Brody also brought to Israel ideas about the social value of sports that nevertheless were not quick to take root. He initially worked in sports education and later re-

FIGURE 7.2 Tal Brody shakes hands with Minister of Defense Moshe Dayan minutes before a game between Maccabi Tel Aviv and Real Madrid basketball teams in the European championship (February 22, 1968). The tall bespectacled player in the back is another American newcomer, Bob Podhurst. Dayan would become the team's patron. (Photographer Arieh Lova Knepper / Courtesy of the Yoash Alroey Collection)

membered that Israeli parents dismissed athletic training as a waste of time. In contrast, he had been brought up where athletic practice was considered essential for the personal and civic development of youth.

A journalist noticed that in public, Brody did not use the word "I" as much as "we," "we won," "we achieved," "we have arrived." She wrote, "The code that reduced egocentric reference and originates from a 'man in society' perspective could exude foreignness to those who operate within the ambit of the Israeli domestic culture."[112] Once again a dissonance between Israeli individualism and American teamwork came to view. Brody practiced civic engagement, for instance, bringing Golden Gloves clubs to Israel and participating in a project titled "Let's Play Basketball," dedicated to educating young Israelis—especially from the periphery—through sports.[113] He reminisced that when he began playing basketball in Trenton his team received and helped rehabilitate street kids that the police had picked up.[114]

Conclusion

One thread that runs through the episodes visited in this chapter pertains to American race discourse, evident in the ideas that guided social work, education, and sociology, in Brody's conviction about how sports serve social mobility, or even in West Bank settlers' fantastical claim that, somehow, they are following in the footsteps of American civil rights activists. Other recurrent themes include professional ethos, trust in numbers, and the modalities of social participation exercised through volunteerism, social activism, and forms of direct action and extraparliamentary politicking intended to capture media attention and public opinion. Indeed, the elaboration of civil society in the last decades of the century would, to a large extent, follow the American model. Since the 1970s, environmental, peace, and social justice organizations embraced two prototypes that originated in the United States, the issue-oriented "identity movement" and the resource-generating "empowerment movement."[115]

Like Jaffe in Jerusalem's city hall, Elihu Katz also survived only two years as a director of Israeli TV. He resigned because of a crisis of confidence with the managing board.[116] But there was also friction between Katz and his subordinates. Decades later, Shlomo Aronson, who was pushed out as the head of the news department, would blame Katz's alleged naiveté and 1960s American liberalism for shaping the station as "an organized mess" in the name of openness and creativity. He further proposed that Katz mistakenly conceived of the Middle East conflict in terms of the reconciliation between Blacks and whites in the United States and had unrealistic expectations about its possible resolution through Arabic-language broadcasts.[117]

The discord that characterized Katz's and Jaffe's short administrative careers could be attributed to lack of experience and the typically difficult transition from academic life to managerial positions. Hostility to Freedman's ideas exposed inherent sexism in Israeli society. But all three individuals had also to contend with the charges that they were bringing to Israel ideas that were too liberal, or too radical, or too American.

EIGHT

Back to Anatevka

Soon after the Six-Day War, lyricist/composer Naomi Shemer added a couple of stanzas to her iconic song "Jerusalem of Gold." It was first performed only a few weeks earlier, on the eve of the war, and already rivaled the national anthem in conveying patriotic sentiments. Initially, the lyrics portrayed the Old City of Jerusalem to be devoid of human presence, literally abandoned. Shemer now writes, "We have returned to the cistern, to the market, and the square." Another postwar song, "Shuv lo nelech" (We shall not leave again; lyrics, Shmulik Rosen; music, Effi Netzer) addresses the biblical figure Rachel as Israeli troops enter the West Bank town of Bethlehem, the site of Rachel's Tomb. "Look Rachel, look, look for heaven's sake, look Rachel look, they [the warriors] returned to their bounds."

In a later homage to Jerusalem, "Hineni kan" (Here I am; lyrics, Haim Heffer; music, Dov Seltzer) the city is summoned as a captured lover waiting to be rescued while her savior vows, "I am the man who always returns, returns." The messianic verve of the *return* motif touched the absurd with a tribute to the small hamlet Sharm a-Sheikh at the southern tip of the Sinai Peninsula, which except for a short occupation during the Suez Operation (1956) was bereft of any Israeli or Jewish history. "Oh, Sharm a-Sheikh, we returned to you once again, you have always been in our heart" (lyrics, Amos Ettinger; music, Rafi Gabai).

These popular songs were symptomatic of the euphoric state that commandeered the Israeli psyche in the wake of the military victory, the prevailing sense that the nation was not merely rescued from calamity but also reunited with its ancestral land—perceived by some as divine intervention, and the ultimate confirmation of Zionism, previously largely conceived in secular terms. However, as we shall see, throughout the second half of the 1960s, even before the war, Israelis were lured into returning to other sites and eras, outside their national boundaries, however defined, the biblical past, or the short history of modern Zionism.

Evoking a Chagall-like landscape of klezmers, beggars, and tailors, the title song of the film *Tevye and His Seven Daughters* (1968), "Tevye's Song" (lyrics, Haim Heffer; music, Dov Seltzer) rhapsodizes about the long road, the wagon, and the horse that unfailingly pulls the protagonist back to his shtetl. Two years earlier, in the remarkably successful musical *Kazablan* (see chapter 9) the eponymous character played by singer/actor Yehoram Gaon (who also sang "Hineni kan" and "Tevye's Song") longingly remembers his father's home in faraway Morocco, "The heart is there, beyond the sea / I hear a prayer from an empty house / There is a place that remains afar / To any place where I will escape, there will be a place I won't forget / I will always carry it in my heart, there is a place that I love." ("Yesh makom," There is a place; lyrics, Amos Ettinger; music, Dov Seltzer).

In this and other songs, Heffer, Ettinger, and other lyricists transport Israelis back to eastern Europe or North Africa. Indeed, in the middle years of the 1960s, Israeli popular culture began flirting with a subject matter previously deemed diasporic and as such pushed aside, at times aggressively repressed. Landmark moments included the 1965 Yiddish performance of Itzik Manger's *Di Megile*, starring the Burstein family of *shpielers*, for predominantly Israeli-born nonspeakers of the language; Giora Godik's lavish staging of the fictional town Anatevka in the musical *Fiddler on the Roof* in the same year; and the 1966 film *Shnei kuni lemel* (Two kuni lemel, renamed in English *The Flying Matchmaker*) based on a late nineteenth-century play by Abraham Goldfaden for which an entire shtetl was erected in Givatayim, just east of Tel Aviv. The later years of the decade witnessed an increased appetite for Hasidic folklore, with the 1968 show, *Ish hasid haya* (Once there was a hasid) and the popularity of Hasidic pop music.

The resurgence of Yiddish, Yiddishism, and Hasidic lore in 1960s Israel was carried by different cultural flows and eddies with discrete histories and paths. Interest in Yiddish, for instance, rested on the curiosity of the Israeli-born young who were not weaned on Yiddish and the nostalgia and growing self-confidence of post-Holocaust immigrants, a group less committed to the Zionist anti-Yiddish stance. At the prime minister's office, Yiddish's chief adversary David Ben-Gurion was replaced with Levi Eshkol, who famously peppered his speech with Yiddish expressions.[1] Hebrew was entrenched enough and no longer required state protection. In a different register, Adolf Eichmann's trial (1961) forced Israelis to grapple with the memory of the Holocaust and catalyzed efforts to commemorate a bygone Jewish culture.

One connecting tissue linking the three revivals is that the engagement with Ashkenazi language and folklore was shaped in conversation with American popular culture. *Fiddler* was a Broadway phenomenon. The Burstein family arrived from New York and their young scion Mike launched a career as a crossover artist performing in Yiddish, Hebrew, and English. Often referred to as "Hasids in jeans" *Ish hasid haya* resonated with American counterculture, and the Hasidic pop fad was fueled by Shlomo Carlebach, known in Israel as the "dancing rabbi," who at the time was also the spiritual leader of a hippie community, House of Love and Prayer, in San Francisco's Haight-Ashbury district.

These performances contributed to reworking and accentuating ethnic sentiments among Israeli Jews, certainly Ashkenazi, but—vicariously and dialectically—Mizrahi identities as well. For instance, capitalizing on *Ish hasid haya*'s phenomenal success, producer Ya'akov Agmon's Bimot Theater staged an equally popular revue titled *Bustan Sepharadi* (Sephardic orchard). And by the end of the 1960s, the Yiddishkeit revival intermingled with the predominance of the Mizrahi motif in the enormously popular comedies known derisively as *bourekas* films, after the savory pastries of the Balkans. The hyperethnicism that seemingly engulfed Israeli popular culture, at least for a short while, was often couched as a search for roots.[2]

Moreover, the new legitimacy bestowed upon Yiddish—Yiddish also provided an important link with the persecuted Soviet Jewry—was invoked and attacked by the Israeli Black Panthers when they arrived on the scene in 1971. For them it was Eshkol's replacement Golda Meir who epitomized the Ashkenazi Yiddish-speaking old guard that still dominated Israeli politics. A statement wrongfully attributed to her by which one can't be a true Jew without speaking Yiddish only made matters worse.

The return of Yiddishkeit and the reinvigorated interest in the Hasidic cultural legacy paralleled—and through a few vibrant threads interlinked with—the new allure of Jewish religiosity. The roots and causes of the return to the faith (*hazara bitshuva*) movement are also complex, but the American presence is evident in various efforts to promote Jewish revival, through Carlebach's music, the Diaspora Yeshiva in Jerusalem, and other forms of proselytizing among Jews. A growing fascination with the Lubavitcher Hasidic sect and its leader would render his home in Crown Heights, Brooklyn, a site of pilgrimage for Israeli leaders. Alternatively, countercultural spirituality brought and left traces of non-Jewish practices, whether Eastern religions, meditation and transcendentalism, or the occult influences on, for instance, the filmmaker and artist Jacques Katmor's group, The Third Eye. Jews for Jesus also sought to establish a bridgehead in Israel.

This chapter hopscotches through a few episodes in this trajectory. It employs as its ballast two theatrical productions, *Fiddler on the Roof* and *Ish hasid haya*. They represent contrasting dynamics of cultural appropriation and a dialogue with different facets of 1960s American culture.

Kanar al Hagag

Loosely based on a string of Sholom Aleichem stories, "Tevye and His Daughters" (or "Tevye the Dairyman"), *Fiddler on the Roof* debuted on September 22, 1964, to become a record-breaking commercial success. For the first time in the history of Broadway, a musical surpassed 3,000 performances. *Fiddler* would leave a lasting mark on American Jewish life, furnishing it with an affective space populated by iconic figures and symbols and accompanied by a widely familiar soundtrack. As the musical's biographer Alisa Solomon observes, "*Fiddler* eventually cemented the image of the shtetl as a metonym for all of east European Jewish culture and fixed Tevye permanently within it."[3] The musical foreshadowed and arguably helped clear the way for the early steps of multiculturalism and the ethnic roots movement. It would become an unlikely global phenomenon performed in more than two dozen countries.

Jerry Bock composed the music, Sheldon Harnick wrote the lyrics, and Joseph Stein the book. But it was the show's director and choreographer, Jerome Robbins, who dominated the process of fashioning the musical and endowing the plot with its thematic coherence: the struggle over customs and conventions (Tradition!) encroached upon both from within and from outside the community by the forces of modernity and antisemitism. Robbins was also primarily responsible for calibrating the delicate balance that resonated so well with audiences worldwide between the specificity of the troubled Jewish past and universal concerns, intergenerational conflict and familial loyalties, the pining for a lost world and optimism about what could hopefully replace it.

The story takes place around 1905 in a Pale of Settlement townlet and evolves around the struggles of Tevye, memorably first played by Zero Mostel, who struggles with the spousal choices of his older three daughters, each making a more daring leap from rigid customs in their selection of partner—picking, respectively, a poor tailor (over a rich butcher), a revolutionary, and, finally and most alarmingly, a gentile. Ultimately, antisemitism intrudes in the form of a pogrom and forces the Jews of Anatevka to flee to America. The show takes its aesthetic cues and atmosphere—as well as its evocative title—from Marc Chagall's artistry.

Fulfilling the musical's Jewish creators' wish, the first staging of *Fiddler* outside the United States took place in Jaffa in late spring 1965. Upon signing the contract with producer Hal Prince in New York, Giora Godik declared, "This is the first time that Jews are unashamed in presenting what is beautiful about the east European town. This raises Jewish heads."[4] There was an earlier Israeli intervention with *Fiddler*. Lyricist Dan Almagor, who had recently translated *My Fair Lady* to Hebrew, was scouting for Godik in the United States when he stumbled upon an early tryout in Washington, DC. Almagor introduced himself to Robbins and his team and later claimed credit for advice that inspired two new elements in the second act: Yente's decision to immigrate to Palestine and the farewell song to Anatevka.[5] Almagor would provide the translation for the Israeli production, a witty, clear

Hebrew version that avoids Yiddish idioms and yet occasionally employs original Sholom Aleichem expressions lost in the English text, such as "If I were a Rothchild" rather than "a rich man."

The show soon proved to be a smash hit. It ran for fifteen months. Tevye was first played by the affable, round-faced comedian Yosef "Bomba" Tzur. According to one source, a quarter of Israel's population of two and half million people saw *Fiddler*, in Hebrew, *Kanar al hagag*.[6] The *New York Times* reported that throughout the three-hour performance, the show was stopped by applause on several occasions, notably the wedding and the dream scenes.[7] The critical reception, however, was at best mixed and often outright dismissive. Reviewers generally praised Robbins's choreographic genius and occasionally offered a few good words about the set or the show's entertainment value. Otherwise, *Fiddler* was mercilessly savaged for its sentimentality, excessive optimism, and for sweetening the troubles of diasporic life. The dean of Israeli critics Haim Gamzu inveighed, "The heart of Judaism is drowned in schmaltz."[8] Another critic labeled the musical, "rose petals made of cellophane dipped in saccharine water . . . [with an] almost infantile text."[9]

Beyond such barbs, which were not radically different from American highbrow critiques, the Israeli response betrayed disquiet over the question of which community, Jewish American or Israeli, had the authority to retell the story of the Jewish people—and about historical narratives that do not easily adhere to the conventional tenets of Zionism. After all, Anatevka Jews, Yente notwithstanding, move to the promised land of America. Commentators who were quite enthusiastic about the local production of *My Fair Lady* a year earlier (see chapter 9) were now wary of American culture's incursion in general. The show's popularity and the claim that it makes Jews proud only turned their commentary more stinging.

Critic Boaz Evron maintained that *Fiddler* represents American technology in all its might. It exotifies and sugarcoats the Jewish shtetel like the South Sea islands or Harun al-Rashid's Baghdad to appeal to American audiences. "Even the refrain that emphasizes the word 'tradition' has a special meaning for the American public looking for some lost paradise with clear meaning and without problems." The pogrom on stage seems harmless, conducted by order from above, half-apologetically. (Evron is arguably correct in identifying the show's creators' reluctance to depict gentiles' hatred of Jews.)

Ultimately, love conquers all. "Allowing the God of love center stage—this is perhaps the real American religion."[10]

Critic Dov Bar-Nir urged the musical's spectators to uphold the distinction between "nostalgic musicalness" and the imperatives of their spiritual citizenship in Israel.

> The revival of the "shtetl" in the State of Israel more than it serves to shape modern Judaism . . . grafts and even plants in us petit bourgeois customs that "wondrously" correspond with the new Israeli self-satiated bourgeoisie [ba'al beitiut], the lack of social and personal ideals that characterizes it, and its desire to warm up by the bonfires of the past rather than to ignite its own new flame on fresh soil. . . . This invasion of musicalness among us requires introspection. It is an outcome of a society of plenty "without problems." It is a byproduct of the Americanization of brains and taste that increasingly characterizes us. Now "Judaism" is also marketed to us in an orderly and attractive American package.[11]

Other critics questioned the authenticity of the music and quibbled with Almagor's Modern Hebrew translation. It is ironic that cultural gatekeepers in a society that dismissed Yiddishkeit and *galutiut* ("diasporism" or exilic customs) positioned themselves as the arbiters of the proper representation of east European Jewish life or the authentic performance of Sholom Aleichem's texts—from which *Fiddler* certainly deviated, especially in its acceptance of Chava's decision to marry the *goy* Fyedka.

The most hostile response came from the aging Isaac Dov Berkowitz, Sholom Aleichem's son-in-law and original translator of his work to Hebrew. "It's a scandal! It's not Sholom Aleichem! We had an incomparably precious character, Tevye the dairyman, a good and simple Jew, and these scoundrels made him into a source of great wealth."[12] Berkowitz refused to see *Fiddler* for fear he would not be able to restrain himself and erupt mid-show. He sent his daughter to watch the musical but couldn't really escape the songs that were repeatedly broadcast over the radio. Joseph Stein, who came to Israel, wanted to meet him, but Berkowitz vowed he would throw him down the stairs if he would dare. (Berkowitz was eighty years old at that point.) He was livid.

In the United States, *Fiddler* signified a generational shift—children and grandchildren of the shtetl paying homage to their forefathers. Yet, it universalized the Jewish past. The new proliferation of Jewish themes on Broadway and later in Hollywood attested to the growing visibility and legitimacy of Jewish cultural identity. *Fiddler's* success also signified the Kennedy and Johnson era's progressive spirit, commitment to cultural pluralism, and the perception of the United States as a nation of immigrants.[13] The year 1965 witnessed the abolition of the highly restrictive immigration quotas that in the 1930s had blocked Jews escaping Nazi Germany. Very little of these aspects of 1960s American liberalism registered in the Israeli response to *Fiddler*.

Tevye the Ambassador

Critics would continue to lambast *Fiddler* and its cultural derivatives as emblems of dripping schmaltz, but toward the end of the decade the Israeli public embraced *Fiddler* more eagerly due in part to its stunning global success, which nevertheless baffled them a little. A critic wrote, "*Fiddler on the Roof* as a phenomenon that confronts millions of *goyim* in the entire world with the east European Jewish world that was eviscerated and disappeared a long time ago move beyond the boundaries of what could be explained rationally."[14] A story circulated that the show's Japanese director claimed he knew why the Japanese feel such a strong connection with the Tevye character but he couldn't comprehend what affinity English speakers find with him.[15]

Israelis also became aware of the currency east European Jewish culture was rapidly gaining across the ocean. By the late 1960s, the Israeli press reported that Yiddishisms had seeped deep into the American argot and even became bon ton. Examples included a senior Pentagon official talking about the "bagel strategy" to describe a bombing tactic during the war in Vietnam and graffiti scribbled on a university wall, "Marcel Proust is a yenta."[16]

As importantly, Israeli actors developed illustrious careers playing Tevye abroad. The character, in fact, emerged as an Israeli export commodity: Chaim Topol in London, Shmuel Rodensky in Hamburg, and Yossi Yadin in Vienna. The press regaled its readers with their success stories, especially Topol's celebrity status in Britain. Fawning articles gushed about his invitation to a garden party with Queen Elizabeth—albeit with thousands of other guests. Cab drivers recognized him, waiters were proud to serve him and his guests, and passersby pointed at him admiringly in the street. Dignitaries from all over Europe came to the Majesty Theater, including the king of Norway and even the Saudi prince Faisal.[17] Topol was praised as a model for the successful Israeli abroad and a symbol for Israel, "like the pretty kibbutz female soldier armed with an Uzi."[18] Fame did not spoil him, gossip columns assured their readers back home, he remained the quintessential Israeli who eats sardines straight from the can and peels an orange with his teeth.[19]

Topol's stint as Tevye coincided with the June 1967 war. In May, British Foreign Secretary George Brown was seen watching *Fiddler* teary-eyed. Visiting the actor in his dressing room, he said the show "makes palpable the problems of Israel."[20] Topol spoke at a 12,000-person rally in support of Israel and shortly after left his position in the hottest show in London to catch the first airplane back home.[21] A *Fiddler* performance in Utrecht, Holland, commenced with an announcement about Israel's victory. After the show, the actors, none of them Israeli, collected donations from the audience.[22]

Whereas in the past Sholom Aleichem tales could serve Zionism by emphasizing the misery of the Diaspora, Israeli performers were now claiming greater masculine agency and a Zionist élan for Tevye himself, in the process bypassing the modern American Diaspora altogether. After starring in the film version, Topol would maintain that he had worked to convince audiences that Tevye carried within him the chromosomes of contemporary Israelis. Fully expressing the Israeli prejudice against diasporic life, he added, "I avoided making him a cute, inoffensive yid [*yehudun*], who bent a little to stay alive and all the rest."[23]

Along with his thundering bass, the portly Rodensky traveled to Hamburg to play Tevye in the German-language rendition titled *Anatevka*. Unlike the other Israeli Tevyes, he was born in eastern Europe and his age and accent were more compatible with the role. His decision to perform in Germany sparked a dispute. Commentators asked whether German audiences should be shown a light musical about Russian pogroms. And what would happen if the Germans perceived pogrom scenes as entertainment?[24] A different concern was that Tevye's apprehensions about his daughter's marrying a gentile might encourage Germans to think that they were not the only ones to demand racial purity.²⁵ Rodensky countered that the Israeli ambassador to Bonn, Asher Ben-Natan, had written him a letter encouraging him to accept the role. He therefore reasoned, "If national institutions stand behind me—who am I to object?"²⁶

Rodensky's success in Hamburg, Munich, and Dusseldorf was also quite phenomenal. The star-studded Hamburg premier featured no fewer than thirty-two curtain calls and numerous celebrities were observed in the audience. The Israeli embassy invited the West German cabinet, including Chancellor Willie Brandt, for a gala performance. Coal miners in Essen named a small bridge after Rodensky. He received 30,000 fan letters and not a single hate mail letter.²⁷ Attending a performance, President Gustav Heinemann went on stage, lifted Rodensky's arm as though he were a triumphant pugilist and exclaimed, "Großartig! Großartig!" (Great! Great!).²⁸

Rodensky maintained that Tevye was his political success. "I am compared to Israel. . . . [The Germans I met] associate Tevye with the Six-Day

FIGURE 8.1 Tevye in the circus. Israeli actor Shmuel Rodensky achieved celebrity status playing Tevye the Dairyman in the German production of *Fiddler on the Roof* (renamed *Anatevka*). Here he is performing on New Year's Eve 1968 for a televised variety show held in Circus Krone, Munich. (Sueddeutsche Zeitung Photo / Alamy)

War. I have been told, 'We now understand how you fought one against forty'... [I told them] some of our generals are the sons of Tevye the dairyman. They loved what they heard."[29] Not only Israelis associated *Fiddler* with Israel. An Arab diplomat in Ankara protested the performance of *Fiddler* in Turkey, describing it as undiluted Zionist propaganda.[30]

Official Israel embraced *Fiddler*. Golda Meir and other ministers participated in benefit events during the film version's premiers in major Israeli cities. In a Knesset discussion about education and culture, one parliamentarian, David Koren (Labor) proposed to support performances such as *Fiddler on the Roof* and *Sephardic Orchard* that attested to the yearning for the nation's past cultural troves.[31]

In 1970, El Al Airlines announced that its "jumbo jet" Boeing 747's maiden flight would screen *Fiddler*. It was reportedly the first time the film would be shown aboard an airplane and Topol was expected to participate in that flight. To attract travelers in an increasingly competitive market, the company decided to foreground Jewish and Israeli themes. Sasha Dafna, director of customer services and design, explained, "We are a different and distinct company, we are a Jewish company, and we'll do our utmost to be identified with Judaism."[32]

This idea originated with Doyle Dane Bernbach, the Madison Avenue company that only a few years earlier launched its famed campaign, "You don't have to be Jewish to love Levy's real Jewish rye." The firm advised El Al to peddle Israeliness the moment passengers enter the plane. But the professed Israeli ambience seemed specifically tailored to the sensibilities of American Jews. Programmatic features included Laurence Olivier reading chapters from the Bible, Theodore Bikel leading a program of Israeli and Jewish songs, Edward J. Robinson with a presentation about Jerusalem, and Danny Kaye telling Jewish jokes about Israel.[33]

The Last of the *Shpielers*

Fiddler precipitated the proliferation of other Yiddish literary characters and productions in late 1960s Israel. A shtetl sprang up in the Upper Galilee next to Kibbutz Hagoshrim for the 1968 Israeli/German production of *Tevye and His Seven Daughters* starring Rodensky as Tevye. Director Menachem

Golan, whose prolific work was fundamental to introducing ethnicism to 1960s popular culture, explained that his intention was to direct a film with "Israeli eyes."[34] Golan also produced *Nes ba'ayara* (*A Miracle in Town*) or *Topelle Tuturito*, a musical movie also based on Sholom Aleichem stories. He then directed *Lupu* (1970), the seventh most watched film in the history of Israel. *Lupu* is often classified as a *bourekas* film although its eponymous protagonist is an old Ashkenazi man. Like Tevye, Lupu Abramowitz—played by the young Yehuda Barkan—who rides a horse-drawn wagon, is an indefatigable purveyor of shtetl-born wisdom. A central theme in the movie is Lupu's relationship with his only child, a daughter, whose love object is of a radically different class, a Ford Mustang convertible–driving son of a rich banker.[35]

Film scholar Rami Kimchi argues that the characters and plots of the *bourekas* genre, ostensibly telling the story of impoverished Mizrahi communities in Israel—and in recent decades criticized for stereotypical, indeed denigrating, portrayal of those communities—followed, in fact, the themes and motifs of Yiddish literature. They were almost exclusively fashioned by Ashkenazi directors, screenwriters, and producers. However, we should recognize that beyond the affinity of structure and plots lies a historical path: shtetl-oriented storytelling became popular in the mid-1960s at least in part because of *Fiddler*'s incredible commercial success.

As early as 1965, theater critics noticed the rising popularity of plays originally written in Yiddish. Performing Sholom Aleichem on the Israeli stage was certainly not a novelty. But in the wake of *Fiddler* and possibly capitalizing on the success of ethnic-themed international films such as *Zorba the Greek* (1964), it required a different framing. The director of *It's Hard to Be a Jew*, Avraham Ninio—not an Ashkenazi—insisted that the performance retain its Yiddishkeit and that actors adopt Yiddish intonation. Actors initially resisted, but then, he reported, they discovered that the characters "live inside their soul, like a pit covered with all kinds of layers. You wash the layers away and you arrive at your roots."[36]

Fiddler's popularity helped muster resources for the film *Shnei kuni lemel* (1966), based on an Abraham Goldfaden play (1880). Directed by the renowned Habima Theater actor/director Israel Becker, it was to be the first CinemaScope color film made in Israel, and color of all kinds it had in abundance. Like *Fiddler* it centered on shtetl life, featuring Hasidic dances and songs, intergenerational conflicts, fathers and daughters, and the matchmaker as a prominent social institution. Becker likened his film to lighting a candle in memory of the Pale of Settlement shtetl.[37] As many Hebrew-speaking 1960s films, *Kuni lemel* was a major box-office success (number 5 in the history of Israeli films). Ironically, Goldfaden's original play was strongly anti-Hasidic, ridiculing superstitions, irrationality, and backwardness.

In the shtetl Kabtsansk (Pauperville) Rabbi Kalman is a matchmaker summoned to the house of the town's rich man (*gvir*) Penscheschl to arrange for a *shidduch*. Penscheschl's daughter, however, is secretly in love with her French teacher, the local physician's son Max, who is ideologically and sartorially profoundly modern. Kalman finds an ostensibly better match, Kuni Lemel, the Hasidic son of Shalom-Muni, who presides over a nearby community. Only a few know that Penscheschl and Shalom-Muni are brothers and that their sons are dead ringers. Donning full Hasidic garb, Kuni Lemel limps, stutters, and is blind in one eye. Cool and calculating Max is determined, and meanwhile Leibele, the matchmaker's daughter, falls in love with Kuni Lemel, preparing the grounds for a future resolution. The New York–born twenty-one-year-old Mike Burstyn performed three roles in the film: Kuni Lemel, Max, and Max pretending to be Kuni Lemel—a twist which of course yields great confusion and numerous comic situations before the plot veers toward its inevitable happy conclusion.

Son of the Yiddish actors Pesach Burstein and Lilian Lux, and always told he was "born on stage," Mike was indeed on stage in utero, later as a toddler and then, from the age of seven, with actual speaking lines. The family's path epitomized the diminishing prospects of the Yiddish theater. The parents, Mike, and his twin sister Susan shuttled between New York, Buenos Aires, and Western Europe in search of audiences. They arrived in Israel in 1954 to encounter the young nation's hostility toward Yiddish. Between 1949 and 1951 performances were prohibited and then Yiddish was subjected to a special levy as a foreign language. Burstyn (he spells his name differently from his parents) remembers broken windows in the middle of a show. They were asked to leave.[38]

The Bursteins would return to Israel in 1962 to find a far more congenial atmosphere. Their first play was *Tate hov chatona* (Dad is getting married) and in the next three years they would act in a dozen different Yiddish shows. They had tiny roles in Ephraim Kishon's film *Sallah Shabati* (1964) that begins with two radically different groups emerging side by side through the gaping door of a Boeing 707 at Lod Airport: old Shabati (played by Topol) and his traditionally attired poor Middle Eastern family blessed with countless children—and a group of rich American visitors (the Bursteins) blessed with countless suitcases. It turns out that the Bursteins are important donors honored with having a grove of trees named after them in a public ceremony. However, the moment they leave the scene, the large sign carrying their name is removed to accommodate another group of foreign donors. (Golda Meir, then foreign minister, asked Kishon to cut the satire for fear it would alienate prospective donors and objected to screening the film abroad until it won awards, including the Golden Globes.)[39]

The Bursteins were invited to participate in an experimental Yiddish production of the poet Itzik Manger's 1930s reworking of the book of Esther. Director Shmuel Bunim and producer Ya'akov Agmon already began working on Manger's *Di Megile* with Israeli performers, but the results were unsatisfactory.[40] There were plenty of actors whose mother tongue was Yiddish, but they did not perform in the authentic tradition of the Yiddish theater. Mike recognized that *Di Megile* would be his bridge for crossing over to the Hebrew stage. His father hesitated. This was not the material they were used to perform. The previews in the Hamam Theater in Jaffa were abysmal. The elderly Yiddish audience remained cold. But after remarkably positive press reviews the Hamam filled up with audiences that did not speak Yiddish, relying on connecting passages written in Hebrew by Haim Heffer. To this day *Di Megile* is remembered as a magical moment in the legitimization of Yiddish in Israel.

Di Megile introduced Mike to non-Yiddish speaking audiences. *Shnei Kuni Lemel* made him an overnight star. The triple identity play paralleled Burstyn's own efforts at juggling three different identities as a Yiddishist, an American, and an Israeli. The Yiddish audience knew him as Motele. In Israel he became the American Mike. With a wide grin and spaced front teeth, Kuni Lemel limps, one of his eyes is permanently shot, and he is an unreconstructed stutterer, a ludicrous, pitiful character, the butt of many jokes. Traditionally, audiences laughed at his shortcomings and even his disabilities. Indeed, the film was challenged for supposedly perpetuating a negative depiction of Orthodox Jews.

Quiet ingeniously, Burstyn created a figure that beyond ridicule, generated compassion and empathy. He convinced Becker to allow him to play Kuni Lemel as a rather smart guy who pretends to be a fool, naïve but not stupid. Stuttering afforded him an escape hatch from subjects he'd rather not address.[41] The audience ultimately falls for Kuni Lemel, feels for him, especially in the moment when he staggers alone in the forest, abandoned, profoundly puzzled by his double, asking in a song, "If I am not who I am, who am I?" Despite the differences between the cousins, the shrewd Max and the burbling Kuni Lemel represent aspects of popular youth culture in Israel that somewhat crudely celebrated pranks, impersonations, and juvenile mischievousness.[42] Kuni Lemel appears at times as a transgressive character who speaks his mind and frustrates adults' schemes and intentions.

For Burstyn, scion of the Yiddish theater, the character of the grotesque clown seemed to come easily. But his performance, especially the decision to have him assume all three roles, underscored the character's artifice. He could thus become a young Israeli who impersonates diasporic archetypes, similar to the sabras Topol, who was only thirty-two years old when he launched his *Fiddler* run in London, and Barkan, who was twenty-five when he starred as old Lupu. Israeli culture in the 1960s was enamored with identity play and doppelgängers, as, for instance, in the case of the king/shoemaker in the musical play *King Solomon and Shalmai the Cobbler* (1964). At the time, Burstyn was also acting in the Yiddish version of Kishon's play *The Ketuba* with a double role of a kibbutznik and an uptight Hungarian statistician.[43]

Following the film's success, Burstyn could not walk in the street without children shouting "Kuni Lemel, Kuni Lemel."[44] He told his disheartened parents that he had to move on from the Yiddish theater. He wanted to be "mainstream like everybody else."[45] The following year he won first place in the annual Israeli Song Festival and continued to perform in Hebrew, English, and Yiddish for domestic audiences and tourists.[46] His was an Israeli career unlikely to thrive before the mid-1960s or, arguably, after the mid-1970s.

Ultimately, *Kuni Lemel* freed Burstyn from the Yiddish stage but then typecast him in a role that he would reprise in two sequels, *Kuni Lemel in Tel*

Aviv (1976) and *Kuni Lemel in Cairo* (1983).⁴⁷ Mizrahi Kuni Lemel characters would cropped up in a few *bourekas* films as well. In a segment for his 1971 Israeli TV special, aptly titled "Who Are You Mike Burstyn?" Burstyn appears in his Kuni Lemel Hasidic outfit singing in English, "Good Morning Starshine" from the musical *Hair*. Midway through the song he turns into a hippie.⁴⁸ A decade later he would return to New York to play the title role in *Barnum* on Broadway.

Hasids in Jeans

Ish hasid haya was conceived as the ultimate anti-*Fiddler*, representing a different variant of postwar secular Jewish fascination with the Hasidic world. Its director Yossi Yizraeli boasted that his show was stripped of the excessive sentimentality and corny props characteristic of shallow shtetl reenactments, no *kapottes*, *peies*, and *shtreimlach*, no looking back nostalgically to the past. Instead, six young men and women in simple street wear, one participant (Danny Litani) donning dark sunglasses, delivered Hasidic tales through song, movement, and gesture, accompanied by three guitars and a piano on a barren stage with only a few black stools. The wooden wall in the backdrop was covered with Dani Karavan's colorful acrylic ornaments in the curlicued style of the ancient synagogues of Poland, carrying symbols such as a tiger, a peacock, a whale, and Jerusalem interwoven around the Talmudic phrase, "The gates are locked except for the gates of tears."

In the playbill five of the six actors declared they don't believe in God. Two were members of the League against Religious Coercion. Only Shlomo Nitzan came from a Hasidic background: "I knew I was a Gur Hasid before I knew I was a Jew," he says. A grandson of Rabbi Binyamin Mintz, who was a cabinet minister, he spent his early years in *heders* and yeshivas but was no longer part of that world.⁴⁹

Delivery was subtle. One story involving a young man who followed his father's goat to Jerusalem had him blindfolded to stand for the night journey. The goat was represented by a guitar case held by its neck. American commentators would associate the show with Paul Sills's fairy-tale-based *Story Theater* that debuted in Chicago, also in 1968.⁵⁰ The short, incisive narratives exhibited the wit of village rabbis, the innocence and wherewithal of

FIGURE 8.2 With only three guitars, a few stools, and Dani Karavan's intricate illustrations as a backdrop, the cast of *Ish hasid haya* presents Hasidic lore in modern, 1960s garb (1968). From left to right, Hanna Rott, Batia Barak, Dvora Dotan, Lolik, Shlomo Nitzan, and Danny Litani. (Photographer Ya'akov Agor / Courtesy of the Israeli Center for the Documentation of the Performing Arts, Tel Aviv University)

ordinary people, and the humanity, soulfulness, and sheer joy of *Hasidut*, a rather romantic and secular view of the movement that became more popular after World War II.[51] In one tale, a Hasid is invited to Saturday supper with the rabbi and then, while stepping out, he is kidnapped to serve in the military. After forty years he stumbles back into the same home to find out that the rabbi is still waiting for him.

Ish hasid haya sought to negotiate the relationship between modern Israel and a reimagined Jewish past.[52] Its montage of stories and songs was couched in the aesthetic vocabulary and political grammar of the 1960s. The show's author Dan Almagor, who also happened to be *Fiddler*'s translator, claims to have been influenced by Martin Duberman's *In White America* (1964), which through similar means, interlaced songs, historical documents, and testimonies on the African American experience. Duberman's play also inspired Almagor's *Don't Call Me Black!* (see chapter 5).[53] Both he and Yizraeli had just returned from years of graduate studies in the United States. Producer Ya'akov Agmon had spent two years in New York, where he became involved with civil rights events, at one point marching together with Medgar Evers.[54] Most cast members joined from a theatrical production of *Spoon River Hill*, based on Edgar Lee Masters's macabre *Spoon River Anthology* (1915), a collection of short free-verse poems that narrate the tombstone epitaphs of a fictional town, Spoon River. Masters's was a work of social critique visiting disappointments, losses, bigotry, corruption, and greed. It demystified the often-idealized life in a small midwestern town.[55] Delivered with guitars and plain clothes, it led Nitzan to propose a similarly formatted show based on Hasidic material.

Yizraeli wanted to make *Hasidut* immediate and relevant again without the diasporic accruements: retain the content, jettison the form. In later years he would describe his work on the revue as the seed of a lifelong effort to build a "secular synagogue" and compared his *Ish hasid haya* experience to paving a road while driving.[56] Then in his late twenties, a wunderkind of the Israeli theater, he argued that theater should connect with the cultural DNA of its audience. He told critic Hedda Boshes, "This is not about dwelling on the past, but we have truly revolutionary things, hippies really, whose center of belief was not nihilism but God; a tolerant, honest, lively, and humane nonconformism."[57] Elsewhere he compared *Hasidut* to Oriental mysticism and anticapitalism. "Do you think it is only coincidence that [Martin] Buber's books sit in student bookstores in America next to the Zen Buddhism books?"[58]

The show, accordingly, assumed the aura of a protest play, emphasizing agency and defiance against poverty, suffering, authority, as well as against antisemitism, in a manner that satisfied the sensibilities of both the progressive 1960s and conventional Zionism. Such was the legend of Gedalia the tar-worker who becomes the Ba'al Shem Tov's (father of the Hasidic movement) neighbor in the afterworld even though he never followed Jewish prescriptions. Instead, Gedalia ate voraciously and incessantly so when the Cossacks would burn him alive, as they had done to his father, the flames would reach higher and higher. In the show, Litani raised his guitar high to his chest to symbolize the flames consuming a Goliath of a Jew. Coming at the end of the first act, this segment sparked the most enthusiastic audience response.

Almagor added a Holocaust segment. When the Nazis occupied Lublin, they assembled some of the town's Jews, ordered them to crawl to their execution on their knees and sing a happy Hasidic song. The Jews instead asked God to avenge their deaths. Almagor explained to Golda Meir, who found the scene "grating," that the Jews were saying, we will outlive you. "It was sort of like singing 'We Shall Overcome' today."[59]

The rendition of Hasidic tunes resonated with modern soul, blues, and jazz. Commentators accepted that these and other specimens of American popular music represented the taste and preferences of Israeli youth.[60] Although the cast wore corduroy slacks, critics loved labeling the show "Hasidim in jeans." With its preview in Kibbutz Ha'ogen it was recognized to be a major hit. Yizraeli said, "When you see a young kibbutznik getting excited by a story about rabbis that his rebellious fathers used to boycott—you feel that the theater returned to be what it must be—a place for the transference of emotions."[61] *Al Hamishmar* daily maintained that the Marxist Zionist pioneers were the children of *Hasidut* by the campfire.[62] President Zalman Shazar, who attended one of the shows, responded enthusiastically, congratulating the cast, "You extracted the eternal from the ephemeral and have made the worldly ecstatic."[63]

Some observers did not wholeheartedly approve of what they regarded a rather cool, alienated atmosphere devoid of the risqué, mystic quality of historical *Hasidut*, "turning it into a clever and shining show without the devil dancing on a grave. A church without God."[64] But ultimately it fared much better with critics who otherwise frowned upon theatrical projects that revived east European folklore. Gamzu, however, could not avoid his sarcasm about the shtetl's capacity to produce digestible Judaism, concluding, "All in all it was worth watching the sabras being 'Jewified.'"[65] Ruth Bondi concurred, "Slowly but surely the Diaspora is returning from its Diaspora to the lap of Zion dwellers."[66]

Ish hasid haya ran for 650 shows and was watched by a quarter of a million Israelis. The Public Council for Culture and Art selected it for the best original play award of 1969, citing its ability to connect with younger generations.⁶⁷ The show also launched a European tour encompassing Antwerp, Brussels, and Rome.⁶⁸ In 1971, it traveled to Broadway under the title *Only Fools Are Sad*, with the blessing and the patronage of Golda Meir. The Israeli consulate helped with publicity. A letter about the revue bearing Foreign Minister Abba Eban's signature circulated among metropolitan-area Jewish communities.⁶⁹

Almagor proposed tongue-in-cheek to rename the show *HaBa'al Shem Tov Superstar*, an allusion to *Jesus Christ Superstar* that was playing across the street from the Edison Theater. Two items were removed from the script in order not to "overburden" the American viewer: the story of Rebbe Nahman of Bratslav that is permeated with yearning for the Land of Israel and the murder of the Jews of Lublin.⁷⁰ Toward the end of the show, "Oh Fear Thou Not, O My Slave Jacob," was performed to a new tune reminiscent of *Hair*'s "Let the Sunshine In."⁷¹ In the local press the line, "You don't need to be Jewish to enjoy *Only Fools Are Sad*" appeared time and again.⁷² The critical response was mostly favorable.⁷³ However, whereas the show's creators emphasized their secular, modernist aspirations, the American press associated the show with religious revival and with *Fiddler*.⁷⁴ The enthusiasm the show generated in Israel was compared to Jesus Freaks, the countercultural Evangelical movement that spread in California in the late 1960s. *Only Fools Are Sad* had a run of only 144 performances. By early 1970s, Broadway was oversaturated with Israeli content, including *Shalom 72*, *To Live Another Summer, to Pass Another Winter*, and a solo performance of Yehoram Gaon in Carnegie Hall.⁷⁵

"Holy Hippielech"

An August 1970 performance of the musical *Hair* in Tel Aviv was interrupted when Shlomo Carlebach and dozens of his boisterous entourage climbed on stage, breaking into a string of Hasidic songs and dance before, fifteen minutes later, Tzvika Pick (playing Claude) retrieved the microphone.⁷⁶ The following month Carlebach teamed up with Arik Einstein and the trailblazing Israeli rock band the Churchills, in an evening titled "Ish Hasid and Ish Pop" (The Hasid and the popstar).⁷⁷ Carlebach hoped that those who came to listen to Israel's teen idols would be allured by the "song of the soul." We need to speak to youth in a language they understand, he explained, something most rabbis do not comprehend.[78]

The rabbi's figure, heavyset, bearded, long haired, with red silk kippa, love beads, and the mandatory guitar, singing with intense devotion, his eyes half closed, stomping, dancing—he was by then at the turn of his 40s—popped up in different corners of Israeli culture. He sang in schools, yeshivot, synagogues, kibbutzim, municipal halls, student discotheques, as well as demonstrations for Soviet Jews, for whom he wrote his most recognizable song, "Am Israel hai" (The Jewish people lives).[79] With infectious energy, his concerts often spilled into the night and outside their nominal venues. Typically, a performance for high school students in Netanya moved unplanned to enraptured dancing in the street, pulling into the human vortex passersby as well as some drivers out of their car seats.[80]

Carlebach was a Jewish revivalist, a pioneer of the *ba'al tshuva* drives, an inspiration for the neo-Hasid movement that combines New Age spirituality and countercultural sensibilities with conservative Orthodox Judaism and settler ideology.[81] He was the most prolific and influential writer of religious-themed Jewish songs in the twentieth century. Carlebach recorded twenty-seven albums, performed in roughly four thousand concerts worldwide, and is said to have composed five thousand songs, many with catchy tunes that color the Jewish *nigun* with themes from American folk and gospel, Viennese waltz, and even Spanish flamenco, coupled with simple-to-memorize phrases from the Torah and liturgy.[82] Several of Carlebach's songs have become staples of synagogue life regardless of denomination.

In 1949, the sixth Lubavitcher rebbe Yosef Yitzhak Schneersohn dispatched Carlebach and another would-be leader of the 1960s Jewish renewal movement, Zalman Schachter-Shalomi, as emissaries to Jewish youth in a campaign to fight the forces of assimilation and to save lost Jewish souls, a unique task that Chabad took upon itself after World War II.[83] The Berlin-born Carlebach had fled Europe in 1939 with his family. Carlebach's official mission lasted for six years. Conservative forces opposed his unconventional practices, especially bringing young men and women to sing together in public. He would continue by himself, now with the help of a burgeoning musical career.

Armed with a guitar, a decidedly non-Hasidic instrument, Carlebach made inroads into Greenwich Village's folk scene. Early on he had a particular appreciation of gospel. In St. Louis he visited Black churches and sang with them in Hebrew. He then brought twenty Black singers to appear with him in the local synagogue.[84] In Atlantic City, he met Nina Simone. Their acquaintance would serve as the basis of the musical *Soul Doctor: Journey of a Rockstar Rabbi* (2008).[85] Carlebach integrated spirituals into his repertoire, among them (Simone's) "Sinner Man," "I'm on My Way to Canaan Land," and "Kumbaya." He also sang spirituals in his early performances in Israel. One reviewer wrote that in Carlebach's voice the spirituals sounded so Jewish, "it makes you wonder why non-Jews are singing them."[86]

By the late 1960s, the center of his activities shifted to the West Coast. In July 1965, he performed in Berkeley between Jefferson Airplane and Alice Stuart. San Francisco was then the hub of Eastern spirituality with movements such as Zen Buddhism, Hare Krishna, and Meher Baba as well as Christian Evangelical groups like the Children of God and Jews for Jesus. Among the hippies Carlebach found a thirst for spiritual guidance. He called them "Holly Hippielech" and identified "sparks of holiness" in their quest, saying, "the hippies are my rebbes."[87] In the tradition of Jewish mysticism he came to regard the 1967 war that returned Jews to the biblical terrain of the West Bank and the immense spiritual energy that emanated from the cultural experimentations on the West Coast to be two interlinked messianic signs.[88]

In 1968, he became the spiritual leader of the Jewish semicommune, House of Love and Prayer. He told his followers that the six million who died in the Holocaust have come back to life as spirituality-seeking youth in the United States and we should not lose them again.[89] Timothy Leary dropped by and shared that he used to listen to the rabbi's songs while dropping acid. Carlebach admitted of experimenting with a *tripp'ele* that inspired him to write five songs.[90] He also wrote, "Lord Get Me High." The main halachic innovation, though, was not drugs but the absence of a divide between women and men. Carlebach would later secretly ordain women as rabbis and object to having the dividing *mehitza* by the Western Wall.[91]

At the conclusion of the 1960s, Carlebach was able to revive eighteenth-century *Hasidut*'s transgressive energy, whereas contemporaneous Hasidic communities were conservative as much as the rest of the *haredi* world. He encouraged a sense of a new Jewish piety that militated against walls and boundaries, including between Jews and non-Jews.[92] The message was optimistic, good triumphs over evil, the supernatural would become a mundane reality, people are about to transform and live at one with nature. Constant joy is a means of getting closer to God.[93]

Carlebach entered a dialogue with leaders of Eastern religions, appreciated and even admired the spirituality of Indian gurus, but also understood that many of their followers in the United States were Jewish. He maintained that the Lord sent teachers from the Far East, who had not been tainted by the Holocaust, to instruct how to connect to God with joy and love. The young Jews do not come first to Judaism because they are still angry at what happened in the 1940s. The ashrams may be their way station on the road back.[94]

There was something relentless, even compulsive, in Carlebach's desire to touch people, either figuratively or literally. In concerts he would get off stage to hug and kiss both men and women. (In recent years several sexual misconduct allegations have surfaced.)[95] Some of his disciples followed him to Israel, establishing a House of Love and Prayer in Jerusalem and then settling in moshav Mevo Modi'im. In July 1971, he led a weeklong Woodstock Religious and Mystical Festival. He consistently integrated his performances into the Zionist consensus, often performing in army camps and for hospitalized soldiers.[96]

Carlebach could be considered Rabbi Meir Kahane's twin and opposite. Both were occupied with Jewish survival in the aftermath of the Holocaust, and both reacted to the convulsions of the 1960s, although in profoundly different manners. Kahane upheld an apocalyptic view that summoned violence and spawned racism. Carlebach saw in the counterculture rebellion the foundation of the coming redemption. He spoke incessantly of love, which he extended to non-Jews. After the war, he reportedly walked into the Old City of Jerusalem and kissed each Arab he met saying, "You are my cousin." He proposed to the government to fly five thousand hippies from California and send them bearing flowers to each Arab home with a message of love.[97]

These sentiments never translated into a political program. Moreover, Carlebach became an early supporter of the settlers' Gush Emunim movement. He visited the Jewish prisoners detained after the Baruch Goldstein massacre in Hebron and spoke of Kahane and the radical settlers as Jewish heroes.[98] By the 1980s he moderated many of his more radical views and began a long process of reproachment with the ultra-Orthodox world, from which he never considered departing.

Hasidic Wave

Both Carlebach's music and *Ish hasid haya*'s folklore served as yeast for a cultural dough that was rapidly rising outside the reach of their creators' intentions. Hasidism and the Hasidic tune—by then it became difficult to define its contours and what it stands for—were in vogue. Signs included the popularity of the IDF Rabbinical Choir,[99] the emergence of electric guitar-based Hasidic pop with bands such as Avnei Hakotel (The Wailing Wall's stones) comprised of four young British Jews and two Israelis,[100] and special events featuring the Hasidic motif. One example was the annual Hasidic Week in the northern town of Safed, dedicated to singing, storytelling, and Hasidic music with the full support of the Israeli Ministry of Tourism.[101] The trend culminated in a Hasidic-themed competitive annual song festival, in the format of the national song festival that since the early 1960s was broadcast on Independence Day. It was an imitation of European song competitions, especially the Italian Sanremo Music Festival.

In 1969, producer Micky Peled (Solan Production) launched the first Hasidic Song Festival event at the Heichal Hatarbut venue in Tel Aviv.[102] There were doubts about the financial viability of the project but the two songs that won the second and third place, "Ya'ase shalom" ([The Lord] will make peace; music, Nurit Hirsch; singer, Yigal Bashan) and Shlomo Carlebach's "Veha'er einenu" (Bring light to our eyes) sung by the Shlosharim trio (The three'ngers) shot up on the hit parades and became among the most popular "Hasidic songs" of all time. None of the main performers was an observant Jew and not all were Ashkenazi. Nineteen-year-old Bashan was a descendent of Yemenite immigrants. The song festival traveled abroad. It was, for example, scheduled for forty-three concert tour stops in North America during Israel's twenty-fifth-anniversary celebration.[103]

The festival's success inspired similarly formatted annual events dedicated to ethnic communities and their cultural heritage: the Mizrahi Song

Festival, Yiddish Song Festival, Arabic Song Festival, and Children's Song Festival, in addition to other events labeled *festivals* celebrating Jerusalem, for example, or biblical-themed songs. The Hasidic theme was adopted by mainstream performers. The leading military troupe Lahakat Hanahal, a major cultural force in the 1950 and 1960s, made its own contribution, "Haben yakir li Ephraim" (The son dear to me Ephraim), based on Jeremiah 31:19. Arguably the best of the genre, it was an adaptation of the American cantor Shmuel Malavsky's tune, originally performed by his family choir.

Yair Rosenblum, the troupe's musical director, added rock tempo and a psychedelic tinge. A video clip filmed in an old winery with atmospheric arched ceilings features the soloist Miri Aloni and other uniformed singers—female soldiers in miniskirts—hand clapping, finger snapping, and swinging in a Hasidic dance.[104] The navy's troupe came up with a spoof of the Hasidic fad titled, "Yiddishe piraten" (Jewish pirates; lyrics, Yoram Teharlev and Danny Litai; music, Drora Havkin) about Old World Jewish pirates who after many adventures traveling from eastern Europe on a ship equipped with barrels of kreplach, cholent, borscht, and gefilte fish—land in Jaffa to be forced into the IDF Rabbinical Choir.

Director Yizraeli professed utter contempt at the "commercialized and shiny" Hasidic wave following the success of *Ish hasid haya*.[105] In *Davar*, Doron Rosenblum, a decidedly nonobservant Jew, lambasted:

> "Shma Israel" [written and sung by Tzvika Pick] was the prayer our ancestors uttered before they burned on the stake or entered the gas chambers. Is it possible that in Israel we would see in the state television repulsive and grating commercialization of the most sacred values of the Jewish people? Could it be that Shma Israel would be song number 4 or 5 in a pop contest intended for fourteen-year-old girls?[106]

Israel was now exporting *Hasidut* to the United States. Jewish radio stations reportedly broadcast the Hasidic festival record day and night. In parties, weddings, and bar mitzvahs Hasidic chants replaced older standards such as "Shalom haverim" and "Jerusalem of Gold." "Shma Israel" was the protest song performed in front of the United Nations building when Yasser Arafat spoke inside.[107]

Back to the Fold

Hasidic music constituted an important instrument in the campaigns to popularize religion and to bring secular Israelis closer to the world of mitzvot. They provided material for the weekend religious-themed shows on the nascent Israeli TV. One example was the program "Gilgulu shel nigun" (Reincarnation of a tune), dedicated to a dialogue between religious and nonobservant artists and an exploration of the Jewish musical tradition. It was led by Rabbi Shmuel Avidor Hacohen, who had participated in selecting material for *Ish hasid haya*.[108]

One commentator labeled the televisual mixture of tefillin campaigns, *Ish hasid haya*-style song, holiday quizzes, and other efforts to make Judaism more palatable, a kind of "Israeli paganism," turning religion into folklore.[109] "Jewish awareness" campaigns such as those initiated by the IDF chief rabbi Shlomo Goren proliferated. Conducting wedding ceremonies, some rabbis began departing from the traditional ritual to offer a short sermon in an accessible and often humor-filled contemporary language. The Histadrut installed mezuzas in two hundred rooms of its executive headquarters in Tel Aviv and so did one of the major kibbutz movements.[110]

Some kibbutzim began marking the entry of the Sabbath with candle lighting and hosted workshops and symposia on aspects of Jewish traditions and belief. More of their boys were now having a bar mitzvah ceremony. Orthodox rabbis visited. Chabad was particularly keen on dispatching its emissaries. These ultimately rather modest efforts received different explanations, from the demise of socialism as a hegemonic ideology to the curiosity of a new generation and Sixties-inspired search for meaning. The kibbutzim's gravitation toward Jewish heritage began before June 1967 but turned more pronounced by the end of the decade.[111]

At its outset the *ba'alei tshuva* movement in Israel was largely American. It was an American immigrant, Rabbi Mordechai Goldstein, who in 1966 established the Diaspora Yeshiva in Jerusalem, dedicated to drawing young secular Jews to the *haredi* word. Goldstein is described walking in the back alleys of the Old City in Jerusalem striking up conversations with long-haired young American visitors often carrying backpacks and guitars. He offered them a new experience. Many of the individuals who followed him back to Mount Zion came from the same countercultural milieu that surrounded Carlebach, young American Jews with meager knowledge of Judaism who might have been already flirting with communal life, Eastern religions, and drugs—hippies looking for meaning. They would first join out of curiosity.[112] Twice as many American-born youths than Israelis were among *ba'alei tshuva* in Jerusalem at the time.[113]

There was no institution like it in Israel or elsewhere beforehand, a yeshiva that is open to, moreover, courts Jewish men returning to the fold and a twin institution for women. By the end of the 1970s there would be another two. Goldstein's yeshiva is today one of the bastions of neo-Hasidism in Israel. It was recently portrayed in Shifra Kornfeld's autobiographical novel, *The Other Half of the Night* (2012) about former hippies led by a charismatic rabbi on a mountain in Jerusalem and the lingering culture of drugs and sexual permissiveness among students and leaders.

Chabad also invigorated its proselytizing campaigns. The seventh Lubavitcher rebbe Menachem Mendel Schneerson's home in Brooklyn became a site for visiting dignitaries from Israel; among the first was President Zalman Shazar, a labor movement intellectual who was born into a family of Chabad Hasids. In March 1971, he met with the rebbe in Crown Heights for four hours. They prayed together and exchanged gifts. There was a campaign in Brooklyn, probably instigated by the staunch anti-Zionist Satmar Hasids, against the summit. Someone phoned in a bomb threat during the meeting.[114] Two years later, Shazar visited once again, angering some in Israel who maintained those pilgrimages were undermining the presidency. The Lubavitcher rebbe had yet to formally recognize the State of Israel although he intervened in its internal affairs by, for instance, voicing his vigorous opposition to any territorial compromise.[115]

Meanwhile, the popularity of Eastern religions and New Age groups soared, which occasioned an opportunity for another moral panic. This would lead to the establishment, in the early 1980s, of a governmental committee chaired by Deputy Education Minister Miriam Glazer-Ta'asa to investigate the activities of Hare Krishna, Osho (Bagoin) Transcendental Meditation, Scientology, Iman, and EST (The Forum/Landmark).[116] After reports on the Israeli followers of the teenage spiritual leader Shri Guru Maharaj Ji, one commentator linked the yearning for mysticism and values to the war experience. He compared post–Yom Kippur War Israelis to American youth during the height of the Vietnam War, but ultimately blamed the Eastern philosophy "epidemic" on mimicry of American consumer society.[117]

Yiddish also maintained its visibility in late 1960s popular culture. Singer Chava Alberstein recorded an album in Yiddish—first of eight Yiddish albums in her career. The show *The Legend of Mordechai Gebirtig* celebrated the working-class Yiddish song writer who died in the Holocaust.[118] In April 1972, a Yiddish song festival was launched, featuring both traditional music and a contest for new songs.[119] Haim Heffer, who translated another Manger piece, *The Humash Songs*, waxed lyrical, "Yiddish is a juicy, idiomatic language. One expression in Yiddish equals in its sharpness to ten sentences in Hebrew."[120] Nevertheless, outside ultra-Orthodox circles Yiddish came to serve largely what Jeffery Shandler termed "postvernacular" purposes.[121] It was no longer a vehicle for the mundane communication of information as much as a tool for generating symbolic meaning.

The struggle for Soviet Jewry bestowed greater legitimacy on Yiddish. Even the Voice of America expanded its Yiddish broadcasts after seventy members of Congress demanded daily Yiddish programming for the benefit of Soviet Jews.[122] One of the participants in the first Yiddish festival was the Lithuanian-born singer Nechama Lifschitz, who immigrated to Israel in 1969 after many years of being refused a permit to leave. A symbol for the "Silent Jewry," Lifschitz would continue to perform in Yiddish both domestically and abroad. Golda Meir, who spoke Yiddish to different Jewish communities abroad, sponsored her concert tour.[123]

The Yiddish revival prompted an effort to celebrate Ladino, the language of the Jews of Spain that was still spoken predominantly among Balkan Jews. *Romansero Sephardi* was a show dedicated to both sacred and secular Ladino songs collected by Yitzhak Levi. It commemorated "the glory of the Sephardic heritage" and was led by Yehoram Gaon, whose father was a scholar of Ladino culture.[124] Yitzhak Navon, a Labor politician and future president of Israel, wrote the interludes. Gaon sought to represent Sephardic Jews in a new light. Too much of their image, he contended, was tied to misery, ineloquence, and incredibly spicy food.

Navon would also pen *Bustan Sephardi*, a Bimot Theater production that capitalized on the popularity of *Ish hasid haya* to offer another folklore-heavy evening. *Bustan* depicts the daily life of an old Sephardic neighborhood in Jerusalem. Narrated from the point of view of a former resident, the show visits colorful characters like the lamplighter Ben Zion who is yearning to meet the prophet Elijah, Victoria, who brandishes a stained linen to demonstrate her virginity, the *bourekas* monger, superstitions, familial drama, and the sound of Ladino.[125]

Conclusion

We think about the American gravitational power as beguiling worldwide populations with spectacles of consumerist modernity, but the American pull in turn-of-the-1970s Israel was also manifested in eliciting and shaping an approach to and a particular thirst for east European Jewish traditionalism—itself the subject of commercial enterprise and consumption.

Indeed, by the mid-1960s a new, commercially organized, performance-based popular culture took center stage. It was independent of the state, political parties, or the Histadrut. Impresarios such as Giora Godik, Ya'akov Agmon, and Avraham Deshe (Pashanel) upheld visions of artistic innovation and utilized new venues for entertaining and yet enlightening and markedly middlebrow productions. Together with writers such as Dahn Ben-Amotz and Haim Heffer they led a new generation of cultural entrepreneurs. In the 1940s and 1950s these two authors spearheaded the cultural labor of constructing the figure of the sabra. By the 1960s, they ventured into a more broadly defined, urban, worldly, and decidedly commercial popular culture.

The return of Yiddish, Yiddishkeit, and Hasidic lore and its attendant hyperethnicism provided early signs of the politics of recognition in Israel. Nitzan found in *Ish hasid haya* an affirmation of a culture that previously had not received respectful treatment. Gaon and Navon sought to address the misrepresentation of Sephardic culture. Even *Fiddler*'s creators were determined to depart from Jewish stereotypes, the vaudevillian "stage Jew." Robbins had contempt for the representation of Jews as dopes or "loveable schnooks."[126] Otherwise, those performances were ultimately lax in terms of their fidelity to criteria of authenticity. Mizrahi artists sang Yiddish and Ashkenazi musicians wrote Mizrahi songs. This would not be the case in future decades.

When Zionism seemed no longer unmoored from the diasporic past, seeking instead continuity and connection, this movement met many forks in the road and led in divergent paths. Folklorist hyperethnicism was mapped on and had to contend with existing social and economic disparities. With the Black Panthers, Yiddish's biggest enemies were no longer the zealots of the old Hebrew Battalion but the politicos of the new Mizrahi movement, for whom Ladino, a language they did not speak, was not very attractive either. Yiddish or gefilte fish became signifiers of Ashkenazi hegemony.

An alternative perspective highlights the contributions of ethnic motifs to a new Israeli national culture that incorporated more readily bits and pieces of Jewish tradition long after the short-lived Hasidic fad tapered off. This kind of national ambience departed from a secular, modernist style that characterized official culture beforehand. Both the SS Shalom (1964) and El Al's jumbo jet (1970) were designed to offer their passengers Israeli and Jewish aesthetic themes, but the luxury ship constituted a floating modern art museum whereas the oversized jet peddled Yiddishkeit. Yiddishkeit was now both explicitly and vicariously supported by the state. Jewish sentimentality was arguably best represented in the figure of Golda Meir. She was once asked at the National Press Club in Washington, DC, to share her recipe for gefilte fish, for her seven-year-old grandson claimed it was the best in the world.[127]

Contending directions could also be discerned in the trend toward religiosity. One thread links *ba'alei tshuva* with the late twentieth-century rise of Jewish fundamentalism that affected Modern Orthodoxy as well, or the messianism of the settlement movement. Another resembles the way morsels of Yiddishkeit and Ladino were embedded in the culture. Rather than a sign of messianism it indicated the rise of new traditionalist and inherently bourgeois national culture that matured when Menachem Begin entered the prime minister's office in 1977.[128]

In the fall of 1972, *Yedioth Ahronoth* noticed that Yom Kippur that year was characterized by religious awakening. The precarity of life—terrorism or the carnage of road accidents—could have been the impetus, but ultimately, the author determined, it became fashionable to be a little religious, not to take it too far. It was now cute to dress the kids properly and to attend synagogue occasionally, which served as a meeting place with other members of the Israeli middle class.[129]

NINE

America on Stage

Someone is playing the piano by plucking its strings directly, releasing harp-like long and odd tones. Voices emerge slowly from inside the theater, rhythmic wailing, knocking, blood-curdling cries. In an almost undetectable movement, strange, long-haired hippies rise among the audience. They proceed between the rows and crawl onto the stage. To the beat of a long electronic sound, they surround two women clad in priestess-like attire carrying pottery from which flames flicker. One actor produces a lock of hair and then throws it into the fire.[1]

Something strange, riveting, and foreboding was taking place inside the Oasis movie theater in Ramat Gan, a Tel Aviv suburb. True, by the spring of 1970 the musical *Hair* seemed to lose some of its radical edge. History moved fast in those years. New and even more daring shows were already attracting young audiences abroad. *Hair*'s marvelous soundtrack was appropriated by mainstream pop groups like the Fifth Dimension. It turned into a money-making machine. Nevertheless, the musical landed in Israel as a sensation, inspiring curiosity about its politics, the subject position of the hippie, and the identity, hair, and other body parts of its performers. Its candor about sex and drugs, antiwar stance, and, especially, display of naked bodies shocked and thrilled spectators and spawned endless comments in the press.

By the mid-1960s, the Broadway musical colonized the Israeli stage, largely through impresario Giora Godik's lavish productions. In 1961, he mounted an English-language version of *West Side Story*, and then, beginning with *My Fair Lady* (1964), continued to present a string of Broadway hits in Hebrew. A third turning point was the production of the first Israeli Broadway-inspired musical, *Kazablan* (1966). These spectacles bridged the gap between theater and popular entertainment and constituted a new phase in Israeli cultural consumerism. Moreover, Godik embodied the spirit of the risk-happy American-style entrepreneur.

The following discussion explores the staging of and the reactions to the American musical in both its mainstream and then radical incarnations. Godik's *My Fair Lady* was perceived as demonstrating that Israel could mount a complicated, Broadway-quality artistic production. *Hair* generated different responses, both artistically and politically, but ultimately it was mostly regarded as evidence that Israel did *not* share in the American experience. It provided Israelis with the voyeuristic double pleasures of staring at naked bodies on stage as well as, ostensibly, at another country's troubles. This chapter begins with a sketch of Godik's career, then focuses on two productions that engaged ethnicity and race, *West Side Story* and five years later, *Kazablan*, before we finally turn to *Hair* and the Israeli Sixties.

Giora Godik Presents . . .

Partly a P. T. Barnum, larger-than-life showman, partly a pedantic former artillery officer, Giora Godik singlehandedly introduced the Broadway musical spectacle to Israel. Godik's was a family of actors and producers in his native Poland. In the mid-1950s, after a seven-year stint in the IDF, and previously in Poland's Anders Army, he turned to show business, specializing in bringing foreign entertainers to Israel. The list is quite impressive: Marlene Dietrich, Louis Armstrong, Harry Belafonte, the Platters, Frank Sinatra, Pete Seeger, the British teen idol Cliff Richards (whose popularity in Israel rivaled that of Elvis Presley), the Portuguese "Queen of Fado" Amália Rodrigues, and the Golden Gate Quartet, among others. Israel became a station on artists' and entertainers' globe-crossing tours. Godik was uninhibited. When the Peruvian singer Yma Sumac—whose main claim to musical fame was her vocal range of over four and half octaves—cancelled her tour in the last moment under the pretext she was sick, he flew to Paris, threatened suicide, and brought her with him back to Israel.[2]

With no previous experience, Godik then entered the field of theater production. He first convinced the producers of *West Side Story* to allow him to organize a grand tour of the show in Israel and Europe and three years later staged *My Fair Lady* in Hebrew with an Israeli cast. Godik invested 580,000 liras in the show that featured 120 artists and, in addition, brought to Tel Aviv director Samuel "Biff" Liff, the stage manager of the original Broadway run (1956), and Hanya Holm, a modern dance pioneer and the musical's choreographer. Curbing their lingering doubts about the artistic value of the musical genre, reviewers were quite enthusiastic.

Following the premiere, the *Jerusalem Post*'s critic effused, "The opening of *My Fair Lady* was the most exciting evening that I can remember in my years of observing the theatrical scene of Israel."[3] Another reviewer concurred, "Let's not follow anti-American clichés: *My Fair Lady* is a good show, pleasant, entertaining, and it belongs to a genre that has a place, weight and purpose in our lives, the musical."[4] In *Yedioth*, Immanuel Bar-Kadma compared the relationship between *My Fair Lady* and previous theatrical productions to the gulf separating Ford Corporation in Detroit from a humble Tel Aviv garage.[5]

Lyricist Dan Almagor, who, with actor Shraga Friedman, was responsible for the Hebrew translation, remembers that there was a historic feeling at the time that Israelis were finally able to mount a no-compromise production with all the musical, visual, and dance trimmings, just like on Broadway.[6] Uri Keisari proposed that historians should write down that in February 1964 a revolution took place in the history of Israeli theater. It was not the quality of the musical that inspired his grand statement, but the emergence of the powerful private producer who was no longer hamstrung by the collectivist, seniority-oriented culture that allegedly stifled older theatrical companies.[7]

Godik was responsible for Broadway trophies such as *Fiddler on the Roof* (1965), *How to Succeed in Business without Trying* (1965), *The King and I* (1966), *Man of La Mancha* (1966), and *Hello Dolly* (1968), in addition to a potpourri of other performances, from Goldfaden's *The Witch* (1970) to *Barefoot in the Park* (1965), *Butterflies Are Free* (1970), or, on a different scale, from Miami

Beach's *Aqua Spectacular* (1964) to the experimental drama *Slow Dance on the Killing Fields* (1966). His early success inspired the staid Habima Theater to stage *Irma La Douce*, *Oliver*, *The Flat*, and *Sunday in New York*, a turn toward the commercial that some critics derided.[8]

Godik took over the Alhambra Hall in Jaffa's Jerusalem Boulevard, a 1,100-seat, initially Arab-owned art deco movie palace (1936) that he overhauled for his major productions. His initials in large letters were installed on the roof. Alhambra would draw theater spectators to this central but erstwhile run-down part of Jaffa, away from the traditional cultural venues of Tel Aviv to the north.[9]

Godik's impact on Israeli culture was not exhausted by ostentatiously curated large-scale musicals. He introduced the independent producer as a cultural hero, a *pioneer*, although his brand of relentless entrepreneurialism and courting of peril was diametrically opposed to the pioneering spirit of early twentieth-century Zionism.[10] In this respect, Godik had no predecessor and only few followers in the annals of Israeli theater and public entertainment. In the consumerist tilt of 1960s Israel, when capitalism was still largely a state-sponsored work-in-progress, Godik stood out as a most visible

FIGURE 9.1 Impresario Giora Godik sitting poised by his desk. Above his right shoulder is a large photo of Yehoram Gaon in the title role of the musical *Kazablan*. (Photographer Avraham Vered / *Waiting for Godik* documentary)

tightrope-walking businessman—as we shall see, with rather tragic results.

The self-aggrandizing biographical sketch in *My Fair Lady*'s playbill contends, "There is no other explanation to such an operational and financial audacity, but a professional and creative ambition that is in this man's 'blood.'"[11] Perhaps the boldest part of this blurb is that Godik brags about failures that would have obliterated any other impresario's career but rendered him, in this narrative, ever thirstier for riskier and grander projects. His chief aspiration was to stage a musical in the "American scale," with no improvisation, no Israeli-style *haltura* (moonlighting, shoddy work; from the Russian).

One of his associates, novelist Yoram Kaniuk, said in a recent documentary, "Giora loved America. He loved the American way of doing things, the American system."[12] The emphasis was on discipline and utmost professionalism. Actors were fined for being a few minutes late or any other minute infraction, including small deviations from script. The Israeli iteration of a Broadway hit followed religiously the original performance: an arm swung upward on 42nd Street would be raised in Tel Aviv at the same moment, in the same manner. One anecdote has Godik forcing an entire cast to stay put after an evening show and perform the play in its entirety just for him, an audience of one, because the public performance concluded a few minutes too early.

Godik's persona as a risktaker was complemented by his insistence on strong corporate practices required for putting a musical together, orchestrating numerous artists and performers in different fields: precision, supreme coordination, teamwork, an assembly-line creative process, in addition to, as he wrote, "money, money, and money, both in the general risk and in the expenses of production and maintenance."[13] Surrounding himself with a "brain trust" of cultural experts and advisors, Godik nevertheless insisted he was making decisions alone based on his intuition. His famous superstitions, written down by admiring journalists, also contributed to his aura, as did his reputation as a gambling man. One press profile argued that what motivates him is not money but doing things that have never been done before, speculating that he is driven by "a constructive inferiority complex" that pushes him to prove himself to himself.[14]

But the entertainment tycoon who prided himself on his intuition also made colossal mistakes, beginning with *How to Succeed in Business without Trying*—despite a major investment and an imported Broadway director. One critic labeled it "an infantile American success story."¹⁵ ("Infantile" was a term majorly favored by Israeli critics.) Moreover, while the local audience was able, somehow, to identify with the world of class privilege and strict etiquette inhabited by Professor Higgins and Liza Doolittle in late nineteenth-century London, it still could not find much interest in a satire on the rituals and caprice of the modern corporate world, for example, the institution of "management bathroom." *Man of La Mancha* also proved to be a flop. By the turn of the 1970s the novelty of musicals had diminished, the popularity of TV took a severe toll, and the golden age of the Broadway musical was fading even on Broadway. Godik was entangled in other failing projects as well. In 1972, he fled his many creditors to Frankfurt, Germany, where for a while he had to make a living selling hotdogs at the central railway station. Five years later he would die in Germany, never able to repay his debts or return to Israel.

From *West Side Story* to *Kazablan*

West Side Story and *Kazablan* occupy an important place in Godik's repertoire. Strongly interlinked, both musicals address ethnic or racial conflict. And *Kazablan* contributed to forging the Israeli folklorist ethnicism of the 1960s. Visiting New York City in 1959, Godik ended up spending each night attending a *West Side Story* performance. He intimated that he wanted to bring the show to Israel because the prejudice and conflict it grapples with were relatable to Israelis. "Sixty-nine countries are represented in Israel and the problem is similar."¹⁶

In January 1961, shortly after the closing of the Broadway run, a cast cobbled together from the American and London performances arrived in Tel Aviv. Godik orchestrated a publicity blitz maintaining that the visit set an Israeli precedent and probably an international one as well because such a large project—the cast numbered fifty-five—ordinarily relied on state support. Washington was apparently hesitant about having *West Side Story* and its portrayal of ethnic tension represent the United States abroad. The cast instantly became a Tel Aviv attraction. Curiosity seekers congregated outside the rehearsal hall. At the premiere, future prime ministers Levi Eshkol and Golda Meir as well as other dignitaries joined the musical's American producers Hal Prince and Robert Griffith.[17] Godik made the request that was then unusual in Israel that the audience show up in formal evening attire.[18]

The title *West Side Story* was not readily understood by Israelis who knew little about Manhattan's social cartography. It was translated to *Sipur haparvarim* (The suburb story), alluding to poor neighborhoods at the margins of large cities. The press noticed the Jewish background of the show's creators and that the original idea for this modern rendition of the Romeo and Juliet tale was a love story between a Jewish woman and a Catholic man. The Broadway–Tel Aviv axis in the 1960s relied in part on the Jewish presence in New York cultural life. Leonard Bernstein, Jerome Robbins, and other Broadway icons visited, a few frequently so, and even contributed to the local artistic scene.

One commentator identified the Israeli resonance of the narrative, "Despite the thousands of miles difference between Tel Aviv and New York, this topic is so familiar to us, to the residents of north Tel Aviv, Kerem Hateimanim and Shchunat Hatikva." (The latter two are poor neighborhoods of Tel Aviv.)[19] In contrast, Haim Gamzu in *Haaretz* saw a different analogy: "I have to admit, of the two camps the Jets frightened me more than the Puerto Ricans; for a moment they were the reflection of the youth that went blindly after its villainous leaders who brought a holocaust on us and the entire world."[20] But these were rather rare reflections. The press did not dwell much on the potential local relevance of the musical's political message. It was one of the show's American actors, Albert Ottenheimer, who privately noticed the similarities of conditions between "dark-skinned" Moroccan Jews and New York's Puerto Ricans.[21]

Godik never staged *West Side Story* in Hebrew, but in 1966 he assembled a team to overhaul Yigal Mossinson's 1954 play *Kazablan*, about a veteran soldier of Moroccan descent who is wrongfully accused of a crime, into a musical about Jewish ethnic relations in a poor Jaffa neighborhood. Choreographer Crandall Diehl and musician Arthur Harris, who would be responsible for orchestration, flew in from New York. It was Minister of Education Zalman Aranne who encouraged Godik to embark on the project. Aranne sought to bring new audiences to the theater and improve the perception and self-image of Mizrahi Jews with a "hero they can identify with."[22]

Kaza

The story revolves around a young Morocco-born man, Yosef Siman-Tov, who is known as Kazablan, or just Kaza, after his town of birth, Casablanca. Kazablan lives in a dilapidated house in Jaffa occupied by squatters from all corners of the Jewish Diaspora. He had been a brave soldier who saved his commander's life during the 1948 war, but with the war's end he lost his way. Shunned by other residents he is worshipped by an entourage of the neighborhood's hoodlums, nicknamed the Brilliantines, who live off protection money. Quick to erupt into song and dance, the Brilliantines are a latter-day incarnation of the Sharks and the Jets. Kazablan is fiercely proud, with a deep sense of honor coupled with immense sensitivity to any perceived slight. A tough guy with a heart of gold, he falls in love with Rachel, the daughter of a Polish Jew, Feldman. Her father, however, does not approve, to say the least. Another neighbor, Janos, a shoemaker from Hungary, derisively nicknamed Goulash, also falls for Rachel.

Meanwhile, having found his house on the verge of collapse, the municipality condemns the building. Residents come together to protect their home and collect funds out of their meager savings. But the money disappears and Kazablan is the major suspect. (In the original play he was accused of murder.) In the police station he realizes that the officer in charge is his former army commander. Kazablan feels betrayed by him since following the war neither he nor other Ashkenazi comrades ever showed any interest in him. The officer denies any prejudice or ill will. People drift apart. He urges Kazablan to take matters into his hands, to draw in his civilian life on the same resolve he exhibited in battle. He lets Kazablan go and Kazablan soon succeeds in finding the real thief, Janos the slimy Hungarian, and recovers the money. Leading the struggle to save the building, he gains the self-respect he was searching for. The musical concludes with Kazablan in a godfather role, holding a baby just born to a mixed-ethnicity Jewish couple during the ceremonial circumcision. The baby is named after him.

Kazablan is cluttered with quips, ethnic slang, and home-spun aphorisms. Its plot takes place in a formerly Arab Jaffa neighborhood now lying half in ruins and known for its demimonde atmosphere, just a scratching distance from the Alhambra. By then this part of town inspired rich cultural commentary and fantasy in popular songs, films (*Eldorado* and *Nini* both in 1963), and literature, and became a site for urban renewal planning.

The Brilliantines echo *West Side Story*'s "Gee Officer Krupke" when they sing shamelessly about their petty crimes, "We wanted to insert, a beautiful bracelet in our pocket, but the merchant, shouted: police. . . . What an egoist." Another song titled, "There Is a Place" seemingly points in the direction of "Somewhere" in its opening line, "There is a place for us," but instead of an imagined idyllic future Kazablan sings nostalgically about his father's home in Morocco (see chapter 8).

The musical attenuated the ethnic tension of the original play and made the chief character more palatable. Godik declined to incorporate a stronger social protest.[23] Nevertheless, some of the lyrics are defiant, even subversive. The song "Demokratia" (Democracy) declares, "The Sephardim are the majority but those who are well positioned are the Ashkenazim and this is not a laughing matter because they wrote the law. . . . Democracy is an office a nice clerk occupies, whoever comes he always says, perhaps buddy come back tomorrow." In another number, "Get Off My Back, Kazablan," the protagonist laments, "Everyone says there is no one like you, Kazablan, but they spit in my face, Kazablan, from the day you came to this world, they say you are not a human being, always goes for the knife, curses, blows, and blood, Kazablan." At the same time the play radically departs from the Romeo and Juliet plot line with a sentimental happy ending. The neighbors who bicker bitterly at the outset, often along ethnic fault lines, come together at the conclusion.

Critic Moshe Nathan confessed that some of his acquaintances told him *Kazablan* is nothing more than American schmaltz, an eclectic brew forged according to a Broadway recipe. "I don't give a damn," he declared. "If Godik found a chemical formula to turn schmaltz and sugar into a delicious concoction I will not be the martyr who would spit into the barrel from which I drank with great satisfaction and enthusiasm. . . . As someone who is stuck in the Brechtian desert, I felt like a silly kid loving Disneyland."[24] As other critics, Nathan observed that *Kazablan* is a pastiche borrowing a lot from *West Side Story* and then a little from *Fiddler on the Roof*, *Porgy and Bess*, Vittorio De Sica's *The Roof*, and more. He in fact praises Diehl for stealing from Robbins and Michael Kidd—of *Guys and Dolls* fame—and adding the hora dance, Middle Eastern dabke, along with buck buck jumps, and other such physical shenanigans, for taking "Broadway clichés" and adding the pseudo-folklore he found locally. His sharpest jab at Godik and his team was for their clear efforts to draw the attention of "cross-eyed" American producers hoping, "they will look at Alhambra and think Broadway."[25]

Kazablan was immensely popular and ran for 606 shows. It launched Yehoram Gaon, who had just returned from a year of studying acting with Uta Hagen at the HB Studio in New York, on a spectacular career. Some critics were harsh on Dov Seltzer's music, but the radio stations kept playing *Kazablan*'s songs. The film adaptation (1973) purported to update the politics of the play by inserting casual allusions to the Black Panthers. Feldman shouts at Kaza, "Go to your Black Panthers." But director Menachem Golan sends Kaza and Rachel not to Musrara, the Panthers' hub, but on a postcard sight-seeing tour of Jerusalem's major tourist attractions, because he made *Kazablan* as an export commodity.

With Haim Heffer's help, Golan updated the script, situated the story in the aftermath of the Six-Day War and amplified its sentimentality and folklorism. In *Davar* Yossi Beilin proposed tongue-in-cheek that the film proved to the world that Israel is a Greek dominion.[26] Golan added new ethnicities such as Georgian immigrants as well as brief (male) nudity and two American tourists looking for antiques in the open market. Shot in Panavision and recorded in stereo, the film cost 2.8 million liras to produce. Production involved sixty technicians, a cast of 130 actors, forty dancers, and 3,000 extras. It would be the second most viewed film in the history of Israel, with 1,222,5000 tickets sold. And Golan got his wish. MGM bought his film for international circulation.[27]

Kazablan's depiction of the Ashkenazi-Mizrahi divide has been critiqued as inauthentic or too "Ashkenazi." In recent decades, together with films in the *bourekas* genre, it has served as a prism through which a postcolonial-inspired debate about cultural dominance and the racialization of Mizrahi Israelis is waged. Nevertheless, the film was popular with both Ashkenazi and Mizrahi audiences. It was the first major theatrical show built around a Moroccan Jew who has the upper hand and gets the girl. Actor Shlomo

Bar Shavit, who played "Goulash" would tell, decades later, that in some performances the hostility of the audience toward him was so palpable that he had to be taken home in a police car.[28] Moreover, the animosity toward some Ashkenazi customs could be understood in generational rather than ethnic terms. In the movie version, Kaza's repulsion for the gefilte fish he is served—he tries to feed it to a cat under the table—is a joke many second- and third-generation Ashkenazi Israelis could easily identify with.

Kazablan and other popular *bourekas* films seemingly expose and foment Jewish ethnic hostility only to snuff it out as a matter of easily remedied misrecognition.[29] For the purpose of reconciliation they enlist humor and a heavy broth of nationalist sentimentality—as in *Kazablan*'s song, "We Are All Jews." It begins with insults and ends with camaraderie, "We are all Jews and so nice, A hundred percent Jews, the *schwartze* as we well the *vouzvouz* [epithets for Mizrahi and Ashkenazi Jews], We all have the same father, from Romania, Algiers or Kfar Saba, and if there are troubles and suffering, then we all speak the same language, and all of Israel, and all of Israel—are friends." One anecdote about the making of the 1973 film version, shot on location in Jaffa, was that the extras for the "We Are All Jews" scene were mostly local Arab youth.

Hair and the Israeli Tribe

The musical *Hair* premiered in Israel in June 1970 and would run for three hundred performances until February of the following year. British director Patrick Garland, choreographer Oliver Tobias, the original West End's Berger, and musical director Steve Gillette, who had participated in seven different *Hair* productions, were recruited for the show.[30] Godik had planned to import the London production in English—the musical was seemingly too shocking to be performed in Hebrew—but he could not close the deal.[31] Finally, a young impresario, Orgad Vardimon, in collaboration with European investors, produced the musical. They had sophisticated technical lighting and sound equipment flown in. Lyricist Ehud Manor was selected to write the Hebrew version, in part because of his previous contribution to the repertoire of bereavement, the 1969 song he wrote about his sibling who was killed during the War of Attrition ("My Young Brother Yehuda").[32] The venue, Oasis, a movie theater in Ramat Gan, away from the heart of Tel Aviv, was also unusual, although *Hair* would eventually migrate to Godik's castle, Jaffa's Alhambra.

A cardinal aspect of the *Hair* phenomenon was the curation of the cast as an organic social unit. Garland explained that *Hair* should be performed by those who are the show's protagonists—not professionals. "People who feel in their own body the experience of the show."[33] He insisted on recruiting inexperienced actors. In a more colorful manner, Tobias explained that the new wave of rebellious youth crests under the sign of water that no one has control over. "Theater of the Aquarius undermines the distinction between stage and audience."[34]

But it proved challenging to form an authentic tribe in Israel where hippies did not seem to freely roam. The recipe prescribed that half the cast would consist of English-speaking foreigners, of whom half would be Black. Many of the foreigners were veterans of various European productions. They were instructed to mentor the local participants. The Israeli-born were expected to carry much of the burden of delivering text and lyrics. Black participants were tasked, according to a press account, with providing "rhythm" and the parts that require their "special voice," and the imported hippies were supposed to generate the musical color. But with time, the Israelis were reportedly also thoroughly and authentically hippiefied.[35]

The cast and its lifestyle drew enormous public curiosity. The press noticed that the foreign contingent included Chris Jagger, Mick's younger brother, who was described as a spacey youngster, floating in "a sky of diamonds." Another budding celebrity was Alice Ormsby-Gore, daughter of the Fifth Baron Harlech, a former British ambassador to the United States who had been Jackie Kennedy's suitor. Alice was engaged to Eric Clapton at the time. Anita Hertz, born in England to a Jewish mother and a medical student from Ghana, spent most of her youth in Israel. She now declared, "I feel that my African blood runs deep."[36] Sporting carrot-orange hair, another participant, Darrel, had lived in Los Angeles, where he led an all-American lifestyle until he began walking around barefoot wearing bells because he liked their sound. "It also helped my mother find me."[37] Harassed by the police, Darrel flew to Europe and then found himself in an Israeli kibbutz. Originally from the Caribbean, George Harris, a young Black man arriving from Sweden, had studied theology and performed in churches.

The Israeli crew was no less colorful. For the main roles the producers enlisted three members of the pop/rock group Shokolad (Chocolate), Tzvika Pick (as Claude), Gabby Shoshan (as Berger), and Shuki Levi. With no stage experience, they seemed unlikely stars of a musical. The twenty-year-old Pick, whose role as Claude would launch him into a prominent and longstanding career, looked like an outsider even in a society of immigrants. Tall, emaciated, long-haired, he cut an enigmatic figure, observed by a journalist as having "a Copernicus hairdo, an ascetic face like Savonarola and a tortured expression."[38] Pick was born in Wrocław, Poland, Shoshan in Casablanca; neither seemed to be the typical sabra. Other would-be famous artists included Oshik Levi, Margalit Tzan'ani, Margalit Ankory, and future director, and one of the few professional actors recruited, Tzadi Tzarfati.

Hair's multinational cast was presented as a single community that lives together off and on stage. On Independence Day they stopped traffic in Tel Aviv and distributed flowers. On another occasion, they staged a happening, stepping into the circular pool in Dizengoff Square, where they played music.[39] They wore beads and grew their hair long—and as they testified many years later—experimented with LSD, other drugs, and group sex.[40]

On occasion, the cast would indeed reveal a modicum of independence that recreated on stage a sense of rebellion akin to the original spirit of the play. A few weeks into the show's run, the actors protested when nude pictures of them were made public; first were photos taken clandestinely and published in the weekly tabloid *Ha'olam Hazeh*.[41] For a short while they refused to take off their clothes. The cast declared, "Our nudity is part of the message of the play. We don't want anyone to make money out of it in any way. We don't want anyone to look at our naked bodies as their breakfast."[42] The audience was unhappy but there was no clause in the actors' contract that obliged them to disrobe against their will. Another revolt was sparked by Oasis's practice of screening commercial slides during intermission, as was the custom in other movie theaters. Actors regarded it as another form of exploitation. During the intermission they remained on stage with placards protesting the ads screened behind their backs. Many commentators would point to the dissonance between the anticapitalist message of *Hair* and the way it was used to generate revenue.

The playbill was filled with commercial ads. Shemen Company announced a special lottery among the customers of its Taltal (curl) shampoo and spray—five pairs of tickets to *Hair*.[43] Tickets for the show were expensive, between eight and fifteen liras. Polling among *Hair* attendees—about a quarter of a million tickets were sold—indicated that the audience was mostly comprised of well-educated, middle-class patrons and tended to be somewhat older than the performers on stage.[44]

Several Israeli participants confessed to undergoing personal transformation. Tzarfati reported that when he first saw the musical's choreographer weaving his long hair into two braids, he thought he arrived at a lunatic asylum. He considered foreign actors donning bandanas ludicrous. But one day he decided to sport this look himself. On Dizengoff Street everyone came out to see the guy with the headband. "Now I believe this is what the director wanted to get out of me: to be free, emancipated, not to give a damn."[45] Stage manager Amit Gazit concurred: "This show changes people." He had recently begun growing long hair and then happened to be called for his annual military reserve service. (Here, in abbreviated form, is the essence of the paradox of staging *Hair* in Israel.) The battalion commander said, "It's a shame, buddy, go and get yourself a haircut." Gazit didn't. It felt great. "I discovered something new about me and about the show. Fact: *Hair* is explosive."[46]

Shoshan said he had never seen himself being able to be nude in public. "When I auditioned, I had no intention to take off my clothes but at the end of the first act you lose your senses. When you get there . . . it comes naturally."[47] Like the character Berger, Shoshan's own parents did not understand his new way of life. Quarrels ensued. They wanted him to make something out of himself, to stop wearing those tight pants and get rid of the bracelets and rings, leave music, and become "a human being." "Now they got used to it. I do whatever I please and live in freedom. It's not that easy being a hippie in Israel."[48]

In the summer of 1970 long hair became a topic of public debate. Deputy Prime Minister and Minister of Education Yigal Alon said in response to a question raised during the inaugural conference of the National Student

Council that he would not mind if high school male students grow their hair long—provided they keep washing it often. Alarmed, the Barbershop Owners Association protested the minister's comment and asked him to rescind his public advice, voicing their concern about the future of their businesses if thousands of students would show up only once or twice a year.[49]

The musical's sexual content, especially the nude scene at the conclusion of the first act, drew enormous public attention. In another scene, four participants in a human pile simulated copulation while one of the Black actors put a long stick in front of his crotch, declaring in Hebrew, to the audience's delight, "This is too big even for a Negro." One improvisation implied sex between Golda Meir and Egypt's President Gamal Abdel Nasser.[50] Ultimately, the sexual liberty became one of the least controversial aspects of the musical—except for a *haredi* Neturei Karta's demonstration in Jerusalem.[51] One critic likened the nude scene to people taking off their clothes before they go to sleep. Actors look more like children saying good night than participating in an orgy.[52] The psychedelic lighting during the scene and its brevity further distracted the audience. It was noticed, however, that the first to remove their clothes were the foreign actors.

The picture of unity and hippie kumbaya was shattered by reports of tensions between the Israeli and the foreign actors, especially the Black participants, which sometimes amounted to physical blows. An explanation offered by one actor was that when Black cast members go out to Tel Aviv in their African attire, "the entire street runs after them, pokes fun at them, and asks them questions, so no wonder they are bitter and take their anger at us."[53] This was also apparently the experience of others as well. Long-haired cast members were heckled on the street, "Indians . . . hippies . . . degenerates . . . dirty people . . . phooey . . . or, just, *meshuggeners*."[54]

Unplanned events took place at Oasis. One night a naked man emerged from one of the entrances and charged the stage. The audience thought it was part of the show, but the ushers overtook him and called the police.[55] Cast members were encouraged to improvise. One actor said it is infectious, even the ushers sing, the cleaning crew sing, the cafeteria workers know the play by heart, and when during intermission the tea waiter comes into the dressing room with her tray, she chants Hare Krishna.[56] There were reports of repeat viewers who whispered to their neighbors what was about to unfold,

FIGURE 9.2 "Copulate, Don't Kill," prescribes the Hebrew banner in the middle. A mixed Israeli/foreign cast performs in the 1970 production of the musical *Hair*. (Photographer Ya'akov Agor / Courtesy of the Israeli Center for the Documentation of the Performing Arts, Tel Aviv University)

especially prior to the fleeting nude scene, and also that more audience members were willing to join the cast on stage.[57]

Critics found it challenging to classify the genre of *Hair*, a categorical confusion. What is it? They asked. A musical? Opera? Happening? Discotheque? A few selected to attend several times to better comprehend what they were witnessing. Most agreed, however, that *Hair* represented a watershed moment in the history of theater.[58] Otherwise, opinion of the musical's aesthetic value, its hirsute cast, rites, and music radically split. For the religious daily *Hatzofeh* the stage looked like a junkyard filled with profanities, crude and insulting movements—where the "riffraff" crawls like apes and sings about love but only means sex.[59] Novelist Yoram Kaniuk, who wrote three separate reviews of *Hair*, confessed that at first watching the strangely attired tribe "tearing the chewing gum off America's back side," he thought that they are crazy and he was sane. "After ten minutes I was not so sure. After an hour of *Hair*, it turns out I am crazy and they are sane." "In Jaffa," he alluded to Godik's theater, "they are still doing the 1940s musical but here we have the 1970s and the music is out of this world."[60]

But the most extreme personal response was critic Boaz Evron's in *Yedioth*. He seemed traumatized by what he observed, especially the erasure of boundaries between stage and theater, men and women, homosexuality and heterosexuality. He felt he witnessed a reincarnation of ancient bacchanalia, an orgiastic intoxication that could lead to hugs and even copulation or, as easily, to tearing someone to shreds. Forms of prerational consciousness, astrology, the occult merged with deafening loud music, bright lights and stroboscope pyrotechnics. "The scene on stage is perceived as though it literally takes place inside your skull, crumbling and destroying your brain and thought."[61]

"Salon Revolution"

Hair was not the only controversial American play performed in Israel at the time. Earlier in 1970, and facing obstacles from the country's Censorship Board, Ya'akov Agmon staged *The Boys in the Band*, with its trailblazing depiction of gay life.[62] But *Hair*'s politics seemed potentially more threatening. Indeed, the main question that haunted the mounting of the musical concerned its pertinence to the Israeli condition. *Hair* came to Ramat Gan in a particular fraught moment. For the first few months of the show's run, the War of Attrition was in full bloom. The public was subjected to a persistent trickle of grim announcements about casualties on the Suez or along the Jordan Valley. On the front pages of the morning papers readers faced the images of dead soldiers. Earlier in the year playwright Hanoch Levin's blunt and irreverent satirical revue *Malkat ambatya (Bathtub Queen)* mercilessly slaughtered some of the most revered sacred cows, including the cult of the war dead and the status bestowed upon bereaved families. It portrayed the ongoing war as a nation sacrificing its children.

A few months later, another eruption exposed widening fissures in the Israeli consensus. In April, Prime Minister Golda Meir decided not to allow the president of the World Jewish Congress Nahum Goldman to travel to Egypt for talks for which he had been invited by Nasser. Meir's decision provoked fifty-eight high school seniors in Jerusalem to send her a letter in which they cast doubt on the government's ultimate commitment to peace, "After the Cabinet rejected a chance for peace by denying Dr. Nahum Goldman's request, we do not know whether we will be able to fulfill our military duties properly under the slogan, 'There is no alternative.'"[63] The letter ignited a public storm. *Hair* therefore arrived in a rather volatile juncture, just before the ceasefire that terminated the War of Attrition in the summer of 1970.

In *Haaretz*, under the title "A Symbol of a Salon Revolution" Gamzu attacked *Hair* as a product of an affluent and spoiled society. "What is the meaning in refusing military service and burning conscription documents in a country such as Israel that is fighting for its physical existence? . . . We don't have leisure time for deviations of salon avant-gardism."[64] Others asked whether this was the right moment to stage a show in which draft cards are destroyed, the American flag is abused, Abraham Lincoln and other American symbols are ridiculed. "This is exactly when our physical existence, as simple as that, depends on the sympathy and friendship of that same nation whose inner sanctum is being violated."[65] A commentator suggested that what transpired on stage would be comparable to a call to evacuate the country and to identify with the Palestine Liberation Organization (PLO) when it was murdering Israeli citizens. The Vietcong does not pose a fundamental threat to the very being of the United States. There is an element of frivolity in this extreme protest.[66] Another claimed that the antiwar message of *Hair* is testimony to a lack of courage, "Dying for democracy is sublime but I am afraid."[67]

In contrast, Kaniuk argued that *Hair*'s destruction of conventions is essential for any society that wishes to renew itself. The musical confirmed America's democratic spirit. "It's a strong society and all our righteous compatriots should learn a lesson."[68] *Ha'olam Hazeh* adopted a sarcastic tone. "This week it was proven that there is a democracy in Israel. It's possible to stand on stage in the heart of Ramat Gan and curse the flag (the American one), to preach against military conscription (the American) and to ridicule social hypocrisy (in America)."[69] The magazine thought *Hair* to be much more radical than *Bathtub Queen*, a frontal attack on everything the American establishment holds dear. However, as *Yedioth Ahronoth* suggested, "The vast majority agrees that the topic is purely American, and we are just watching from the sidelines and need only to enjoy the music."[70]

In a film clip shot during cast rehearsals, director Garland is heard suggesting that the message of the show is "violence breeds only violence and war only breeds war . . . and you here in Israel really have to think [about it]. . . . Is war actually a solution?"[71] Still, members of the *Hair* tribe sought to distance the show from its clear antiwar message and local resonance. "*Hair* is not *Bathtub Queen*" was a common defensive refrain in cast interviews. Wishing to reassure the public, they highlighted the musical's optimistic, utopian, peace-loving, flower-power accents. The yearning for peace is innocent, said stage manager Gazit. He tells a story. The scene in which a cast member dispenses a pill to world leaders often changes. The character Berger is expected to give half a pill to Golda Meir and half to Nasser. One day he handed over Nasser's dosage to one of the Black actors who got up and thanked him with *salaam alaikum*. The audience went wild.[72]

Another actor, Moshe Goldstein or "Golly," maintained that in the show the actors "are playing Americans and not Israelis and the audience knows the difference."[73] Tzvika Pick said that military conscription or fear of being harmed and left disabled are pertinent issues all over the world, even in Israel.[74] But in another interview he rejected the idea of being a hippie. "Hippie is someone who does not give a damn about the rest of society. I am not like that.... I don't necessarily identify with what is going on stage. This is not *Bathtub Queen*."[75] Foreign actors also participated in the effort of exempting Israelis from the need to rethink participation in war. George Harris maintained that the Israeli mentality is based on specific reality and that Americans are fundamentally different from Israelis.[76]

Tzarfati presented a more nuanced view. The show is not against war but against war worship. He remembered how the Israeli cast was offended during rehearsals when the director said, "You Israelis are in love with war!" In the show, when his character bursts into the induction center and screams, "You must recruit me. I love to fight. I am dying to kill"—there is a deadening silence in the hall. When they perform in front of soldiers or kibbutzniks debates linger into the small hours of the night. The affinity of *Hair*'s tribe and the kibbutz appeared in other interviews as well. One actor said that when the tribe is looking for Claude and finds him dead—who would understand them if not kibbutz members. They are like the people of *Hair*—one tribe—and every tribe mourns its fallen soldiers.[77]

The Israeli Sixties

While *Hair* might have contributed to Israelis' self-proclaimed state of exception in the Global Sixties, it also helped domesticate political youth protests, at least by affecting aesthetic preferences and idiomatic choices. Even before it arrived in Ramat Gan, *Hair* had inspired Ya'akov "Yankele" Rotblit's "A Song for Peace" (1969). Its defiant words urge Israelis, "Let the sun rise / The morning to shine / The purest of prayers / Won't bring them [the war's dead] back to us . . . Lift your eyes with hope / not through the gun's sights / Sing a song for love / and not for wars . . . Don't say a day will come / Bring on the day!"⁷⁸

From one perspective, the War of Attrition was certainly a turning point in the genealogy of antiwar sentiment and protest in Israel, manifested among other signs by Levin's revue, Rotblit's song, the high school seniors' letter to Meir, and radical ideas that could be found in the pages of a few high school and university newspapers and underground publications. Nevertheless, research conducted at the time demonstrated conservatism among Israeli university students, as exhibited in their attitude toward politics, the university, and their parents. More than half of the students across the political spectrum expressed support of student rebelliousness *abroad* but only a tiny minority was in favor of having similar nonconformism practiced at home. Moreover, student associations began serving as the launching pad for political careers in the right-wing Likud Party. A journalist visiting campuses in May 1972 mostly found insouciance about politics of any kind.⁷⁹

Yes, Israeli youngsters listened to rock and roll, grew their hair longer, were more sexually active, and even experimented with drugs. However, there was a tendency back then as well as in later commentary about the Israeli 1960s to conflate countercultural accouterments with radicalism.⁸⁰ Proliferation of 1960s iconography of discontent—Che's dreamy image on that ubiquitous poster—did not readily translate into political action, and, like other forms of consumption, might even have been conducive to counterbalancing and normalizing the state of war. Tokens of the 1960s spirit, such as the Israeli rendition of John Lennon and Yoko Ono's "Give Peace a Chance," with dozens of local artists, could be folded into mainstream rhetoric, which paid plenty of lip service to *peace*. Just moments before singing began and as the tape was already rolling, the event's organizer, film director Uri Zohar, clarified that the participants recognize that the "situation" in Israel is different from Canada and Britain where the antiwar song was first performed. "We are not dumb," he said.⁸¹ And with all the controversy it stirred, Rotblit's "A Song for Peace" was performed by a military singing troupe, Lahakat Hanahal. The Israeli musical *Kfotz* (Jump) that premiered only a few months following *Hair* had a more biting and locally relevant political message. It featured rebellious youth, drugs, sexual promiscuity, antiwar, antimaterialism, antiparents, and anticonventions messages. Alas, unlike the imported musical, it utterly failed in the box office.[82]

In the movie *Late Summer Blues* (1987), whose plot takes place in the summer of 1970, high school seniors harbor strong doubts about the war and their impending military service. Still, at the last moment, the chief rebel among them decides to enlist. Could it be that the hesitations and quandaries of that generation never went too deep beyond the appropriation of radical aesthetics? Or was it the case that the termination of the War of Attrition in the summer of 1970 pulled the rug under whatever opposition movement could have evolved outside the incredibly small New Left circles? Studying the age group born in Israel between 1948 and 1955, sociologist Hanna Yablonka connects their reluctance to engage in radical politics with the intense personal and ideological investment that their parents—many of them Holocaust survivors—and the state had in their upbringing as the first cohort born into the Jewish national emancipation.[83]

Yet, the politically radical path—protest, demonstrations, riots, refusal—largely not taken beyond the Panthers' challenge, was still bubbling under the surface. It would emerge stronger after the 1973 war, when protest forced the resignation of Meir and Dayan and, more so, during the turn of the 1980s, with the peace process with Egypt and the Peace Now movement that did not actually espouse radical politics. As important, and for the long run arguably more consequential, were signs of dissent on the religious-nationalist Right, culminating with the post-war rise of the settlers' movement Gush Emunim.

Conclusion

From the golden age of the musical to the age of Aquarius—Israel seemingly followed lock step the transformation of Broadway and the West End. As a genre, the musical was well integrated into Israeli consumerist culture and remains so today.[84] Curiously, while these productions, some rather lavish, were staged with foreign assistance—directors, choreographers, musicians, set designers, as well as stage equipment—they also generated national feelings. In the case of Godik's shows it was a sense of achievement and pride. With *Hair* the mainstream sentiment was "this is *not* about us." The performance that sought to cancel the stage/audience partition paradoxically enhanced a sense of difference, a contrast that announced the condition of supposed incommensurability.

The links between *West Side Story* and *Kazablan* betray a deeper imitative thread in the transference of cultural forms. It tapped into the American tradition of employing the commercial musical as a venue for liberal social commentary even before *Hair*, as evident in Broadway classics, from *Showboat* to *South Pacific*, and later, in Stephen Sondheim's musicals. While responding to authentic social rifts, both the theatrical and cinematic versions of *Kazablan* were also designed as export products, in other words, they were already conceived to correspond with cultural codes and traditions abroad.

TEN

The American Figure in the Israeli Mind

Filmed in Israel, *Cast a Giant Shadow* (1965) presents a fictionalized account of the life and death of Mickey Marcus, an American army colonel who in 1947 volunteered to help build the nascent military forces of the yet-to-be-declared State of Israel. As the IDF's first general, he soon assumed the command of the Jerusalem front. Tragically, in June 1948, upon returning to this headquarters in the middle of the night, Marcus was misrecognized and fatally shot by an Israeli sentry who did not speak English. The big budget star-cluttered Hollywood film whose cast includes Kirk Douglas, John Wayne, Frank Sinatra, and Angie Dickenson—lionizes Marcus, demonstrating the growing visibility of Jewish and Zionist themes in American popular culture, especially following the cinematic adaptation of Leon Uris's *Exodus* (1960).[1]

The American characters, Jews and non-Jews, that populated Israeli culture at the turn of the 1970s were significantly less heroic. We have encountered a few of them already, donors in the film *Sallah Shabati* and tourists buying trinkets in the *shuk* in *Kazablan*. The following discussion focuses on the portrayal of American figures in both popular and high culture. It first explores three popular works: the Godik-produced musical titled, in English, *I Like Mike* (1968), on ambitious parents' thwarted efforts to have their daughter marry a rich American visitor; director Uri Zohar's film of the same year, *Kol mamzer melech* (*Every Bastard a King*), depicting Israeli society on the eve and the aftermath of the Six-Day War; and Amos Kollek's 1971 novel published first in English, *Don't Ask Me If I Love*, a transparent attempt to produce an American-style paperback.

Serving as venues for appropriating American cultural forms—this was certainly the case with the musical and the novel—the three works negotiate the contradictory pulls that dominated the growing Israeli-American intimacy. The roles they grant American characters are ambiguous, betraying an ongoing anxiety about the potential loss of autonomy posed by a foreign presence. Perceived threats to Zionist ideology or the Israeli way of life, especially Israeli masculinity, inspired different resolutions. In *I Like Mike* two of the main protagonists find a way to fulfill their American dream and still adhere to the principles of Zionism. In *Every Bastard a King* and *Don't Ask Me If I Love* a resolution involves the death of the American character. Sex and gender are recurrent themes. American women reappear as objects of desire and men define themselves against the masculinity of American types.

Gender is also paramount in two avant-garde plays with which the chapter concludes, Nissim Aloni's *American Princess* (1963) and Hanoch Levin's *The Whore from Ohio* (1978). They were written slightly outside the book's time frame, and yet they provide a perspective which is essential to our discussion. Both the eponymous "princess" and "whore" are phantasmagorial creatures who never materialize on stage. They portray in reified form mythological American traits, demonstratively powerful and profoundly menacing, whether the exploitative might of American mass culture or the impossibility and inherent cruelty of the American dream.

On Socrates and *Schmates*

Written by Aaron Meged, *I Like Mike* was first staged in 1954 as a satire on the bourgeois parents' dream of having an affluent American Jew as a son-in-law. The title is obviously a riff on the 1950s political slogan "I Like Ike." In 1961, the play was adapted into a tremendously popular comic film. Six years later, Godik enlisted Yoel Zilberg, who was Otto Preminger's assistant director for *Exodus*, lyricist Haim Heffer, and musician Dov (Dubi) Seltzer to reimagine the original play for retelling the story of the Six-Day War's home front in song and dance. Godik brought back from New York *Kazablan*'s choreographer Crandall Diehl.

Thus, on the eve of hostilities, during the tense few weeks known as the "waiting period," Yaffa and Binyamin Arieli (actors Avraham Mor and Lia Dolitzkaya) receive a telegram that Mike, the son of a friend, Joe Abrahams, who had made it big in the United States, is about to arrive in Israel. "We are going soon to America," Yaffa informs her neighbor. "What is the occasion?" the neighbor asks. "Our Tamara is getting married with an American millionaire." "Since when?" the neighbor insists. "Since ten minutes ago," Yaffa is confident.[2] Her horoscope instructed her to expect a visit from abroad that would alter her family's life.

At the airport the much-anticipated guest is nowhere to be found. But at a corner on a suitcase cart sits a curly-haired young man, wearing a sheepskin jacket, a chain belt, and a necklace made of chrysanthemums. To everybody's surprise this turns out to be Mike (Lior Yeiny), who immediately launches into an upbeat song that inventories the basic needs of life. Initially, these necessities are modest—a loaf of bread, a jug of wine, and most of all love, love, love all the time. But with each stanza, Mike adds another comfort, a roof, a bed to sleep in—preferably at the Hilton—a car that protects one's feet from getting tired—a Cadillac would do—and a rich father who occasionally lends you some money.[3]

Beneath the hippie facade the predictably bourgeois Arielis recognize a rich American kid who would make a fine match for their older daughter Tamara (Dalia Friedland). They fantasize about comfortable retirement and becoming the object of great jealousy for landing such an affluent son-in-law. Tamara already has a boyfriend, Micha (Motti Barkan). However, the long-haired, miniskirt-sporting Tamara is a model and an aspiring film actress who loves the good life, and Micha, in contrast, is immersed in the ascetic existence of a university philosophy student. Tamara threatens him in a song titled "Its Either Me or Spinoza," in which she insightfully reminds him that as brilliant as he was Socrates only wore *schmates*. Under her parents' pressure Tamara toys with the idea of Mike as a future partner and the prospects of an American career, or, at a minimum, she uses Mike to prod Micha to become somewhat more ambitious. Meanwhile, Micha gives Tamara's flirta-

FIGURE 10.1 Surprise at the airport! In the musical *I Like Mike* (1968), the parents who dream about marrying their daughter to a rich American are alarmed to discover next to the El Al counter at Lod Airport that their prospective son-in-law Mike is a hippie. Left to right, Lior Yeiny, Avraham More, and Lia Dolitzkaya (Photographer Ya'akov Agor / Courtesy of the Israeli Center for the Documentation of the Performing Arts, Tel Aviv University)

tious young sister Tzipi (Shula Chen) an English lesson during which they sing, "We love English. English, we love you."

The second act finds the protagonists in the immediate aftermath of the war. The war, joked the critics, takes place during the intermission. Everything has changed. Micha turns out to be a heroic paratrooper who leads the first army column to reach the Jordan River. He is no less than "the commander of the entire West Bank." Tamara and Micha are in each other arms again. Mike volunteers to pick pears at a kibbutz.

I Like Mike pokes fun at some postwar practices, for instance, the Israelis who throng to West Bank's open markets in search of bargains. In Ramallah's *shuk* the Arielis run into Mike, donning an Israeli *tembel* hat and buying presents for his "daddy" and his shrink. Nevertheless, the musical expresses the wish that the war would transform Israeli society from defeatism, mindless indulgence, and ethnic and political divisions to sincerity, high values, and revitalized Zionism. The playbill describes *I Like Mike*'s rebirth as one of the unexpected consequences of the war. Director Zilberg opines, "After the war many things have changed. Our borders changed. Our atmosphere changed. Even the youth, as it turned out, was discovered under new light."[4]

The musical raises concerns about the future of the soldiers who fought in the war. Today we are "in fashion," they sing, but tomorrow will we be forgotten? Will people stop when we hitchhike? Hinting at the prewar recession, they ask whether they will end up unemployed. However, the show concludes with a sentimental and self-congratulatory display of Israeli patriotism manifested in a song, "A Toast for This People," that celebrates how in June 1967 the rather fractured Israeli society (an echo of *Kazablan*) stepped up to the plate. including the "children of Yemen, children of Algeria, children of the Yekim [German Jews], children of Akiva [the Religious Zionist youth movement], and children of the discotheques."

As it expresses Israeli self-satisfaction, the musical also documents the Tel Aviv consumerist lifestyle. The set displays a stunning array of neon signs, traffic lights, and streets advertisements. The stage is brimming with miniskirts, brightly colored outfits, and other late 1960s paraphernalia. Costume designer Lydia Pincus-Gani selected clothing that reportedly represented next year's fashion and she arranged the stage according to "color groups." Characters are busy with discotheques and movies and the national football betting (*toto*). The opening scene takes place in a Dizengoff Street coffee shop, where Yaffa Arieli is begrudging the neighbors for their new dishwasher. The show's playbill employs the "I Like Mike" title to market El Al flights, Matzkin fashion, Tadiran TV sets, CBS records of Godik's shows, and Mars Furniture—"I Like Mars."

The potential dissonance between Israeli war-born chauvinism and indulgence in 1960s-inflected, American-inspired consumerism finds its resolution in the character of Mike. In the 1961 film version, the cowboy-hat wearing Mike (Seymour Gitin) and the Israeli Micha (Haim Topol), in that version, a kibbutznik, are doppelgängers, two resourceful alpha males who know how to get the women they desire. In the 1968 musical, Mike and Micha are diametrically opposed. Whereas Micha the soldier/philosopher embodies manly seriousness, Mike is a caricature of both the hippie and the everyday American cousin. He is affable but a bit of a buffoon—a loud, freeloading, party animal whose version of progressive politics and flower-power cannot be taken at face value. The musical's frivolity and insincerity are pro-jected on him. Thus, the coupling of American consumerism and Israeli patriotism is predicated on belittling the American protagonist and disarming the threat that the counterculture might present.

The happy conclusion is similarly configured. In the end, it is not Mike but Micha and Tamara who are about to leave the country for the United States. The musical provides the ultimate Zionist remedy for Tamara's all-consuming yearning for America. She is traveling there under a safe pretext because Micha was offered a position as an official emissary of the State of Israel, a *shaliah*. Mike, in contrast, announces that in Israel he discovered how "wonderful" it was to bring the wilderness into bloom and declares his wish to establish a kibbutz of beatniks and hippies.

Similar geolibidinal dynamics are maintained in the popular *bourekas* romp, *Charlie Vahetzi* (*Charlie and a Half*, 1974). The rich parents wish their daughter would marry the nerdish, pudgy, effeminate American Robert Dimenstein (comedian Tuvia Tzafir), who in his most ludicrous moment is wearing Bermuda shorts and holding his beloved cello. (Apparently, the *Israel on $5 and $10 a Day* guidebook strongly recommended that tourists refrain from wearing Bermuda shorts in Israel lest they become a target of ridicule.)[5] But the would-be groom loses the glamorous blond to Charlie, a big-hearted small-time crook played by Yehuda Barkan. At the conclusion of the film, Charlie's young sidekick Miko (the "Half") a poor, resourceful orphan is moving with his older sister to America. This time around there is no Zionist cover story for leaving the country. Charlie in fact expresses the hope that America would have a civilizing effect on Miko and that the street urchin would straighten up.

Avraham Heffner's film *But Where is Daniel Wax* (1972), one of the primary examples of the Israeli artsy, "new sensitivity" genre,[6] also normalizes the Israeli Diaspora in the United States. At the film's conclusion the main protagonist Benny Schpitz (Lior Yeiny), an Israeli singer who had embarked on a thriving career in America, is waving to his friends from an ascending escalator at Lod Airport on his way back *home* to the United States. Neither he nor the film apologizes. At the turn of the 1970s, official Israel also began tempering its approach and rhetoric concerning Israelis living abroad, known pejoratively as *yordim*, "descenders." Efforts were initiated either to lure them back with a range of privileges or to have them participate in Israeli economic life. Treasury Minister Pinchas Sapir told a group of former Israelis gathering at the Beverly Hills Hilton that he understood there was probably a reason why they were living abroad.[7]

Israeli cinema produced another hippie by the name of Mike. The English-language 1972 film *American Hippie in Israel* (in Hebrew *Hatrempist*, or The hitchhiker) is filled with nudity, sex, pot smoking, and antiwar and antiestablishment pronouncements. This Mike (Asher Tzarfati) is a troubled Vietnam veteran who arrives in Israel with his rabbit-skin jacket and bowler hat. Wherever he goes he is haunted by two mysterious gun-toting mime-like men in black who then kill dozens of hippies that follow Mike in the streets of Tel Aviv. Mike escapes with three free-spirited Israelis (two women and one man). He is now heading south to establish a commune of freedom on a deserted tiny island south of Eilat.

However, once the foursome become stranded on the island without food and water—their boat disappeared, and the surrounding water is shark infested—their primal violence surfaces. The men divide the island between them and abuse the women. Finally, they all destroy each other. Sometimes billed as the worst film ever made in Israel, *The American Hippie* could not find a distributor in 1972, but some forty years later it became a cult film with scores of devotees.[8]

"Everyone Thinks He Is a General"

Written by actor/director Uri Zohar and journalist Eli Tavor, the film *Every Bastard a King* is a decidedly grittier depiction of the war.[9] Much like *I Like Mike*, it begins in May 1967 with an American visitor, in this case a famous journalist, Roy Hemmings, who arrives in the Middle East accompanied by his wife Eileen to report on the brewing conflict. The mustachioed Hemmings (Austrian American actor William Berger, known for his roles in Spaghetti Westerns) is an Ernest Hemingway archetype, a boozing and womanizing writer who is a busy chronicling global conflicts. Yoram, his talkative driver played by Yehoram Gaon, is the resourceful and fiercely independent salt-of-the-earth Israeli.

Yoram introduces Hemmings to his more polished friend Rafi Cohen, a character based on the peace activist Avraham "Abie" Nathan. Like the historical Nathan, Rafi (Oded Kotler) is a restaurateur, a pilot, and a committed peace activist. The film reenacts Nathan's famous 1966 unauthorized flight in the name of peace to Port Said, Egypt. Nathan took off in a small single-engine propeller biplane he named Shalom 1. He was then unceremoniously deported and sent back to Israel. Eager not just to report on current events but also to help the region, Hemmings agrees to support Rafi's latest peace initiatives and even delivers a gift of money.

However, Hemmings soon loses control over Rafi, his protégé, Yoram his driver, and even Eileen (the Italian actress Pier Angeli), who turns out to be neither his wife nor an American but a former Israeli who hides her identity. She is as restless as Rafi and Yoram, with whom she finds herself in bed. Hemmings's greatest failure, however, is that his keen wish to understand Israelis is repeatedly foiled. They prove enigmatic, hard to decipher, offering cryptic and sometimes incomprehensible answers to his questions. Unmoved by clear ideology or principle, they instead act viscerally, often guided solely by their guts. The risk-loving pilot Rafi rebuffs Hemmings's ambition to understand his "inner motivation," telling him curtly that he has no mother, no father, and no psychology. "If you want to understand me," he blurts out, "fly."

Finally, the weary and increasingly cynical Hemmings observes the war he thought would never come—because, as he put it, in this garbage heap of a world there is no flag worth fighting for—from his hotel room. History also left the peace seeker Rafi behind. The film seems to raise doubts about his personal drive. Is he really after peace or is it publicity and an adrenaline rush that he is seeking? With the onset of the war the movie veers into a thirty-minute docudrama depicting the story of the soldier Yossi Lapper, a historical figure who was awarded a medal of valor for fighting alone in a stranded tank for eight hours during the battle of Khan Younis. Now a lieutenant in a paratrooper unit Yoram gets to Lapper's tank under fire and drags him out. The tour guide who before the war wanted to work little and live well because, as he contended, the big projects such as Zionism or the kibbutz were ostensibly over, turns out to be a war hero.[10]

The war transforms Hemmings as well. In a symbolically heavy concluding scene, he unwittingly steps into a minefield to help two little kids retrieve their lost goat. He is warned to keep still, but rather than wait for rescuers, he decides to follow Rafi's and Yoram's daredevil spirit. The moment he moves, a mine blows up under his feet and kills him. The film begins with Hemmings's coffin being fork-lifted into the belly of an El Al airplane. Hemmings might have failed his mission, but he left behind, on his tape recorder, one major insight that serves as the film's organizing theme.

> Israel is not a country. It is not even, as someone suggested, a state of mind. It is simply a disorderly systematic collection of paradoxes that somehow seems to make sense. Don't ask me to explain why. Whatever you may say about Israel or the Israelis the opposite is equally true. Every man woman and child here seemed to be mobilized for war and yet every time they want to say hello, goodbye, how's your grandmother, or what's up they say *shalom*, which means peace and in some crazy way they make you believe they mean it. There is no aristocracy of rank or wealth. There is not even a sense of rank in their army, not because they are so democratic but because everyone thinks he is a general.

Every Bastard a King appears to celebrate the individuality and agency of ordinary Israelis but it also problematizes Israelis' inflated sense of self. Zohar, however, offered a somewhat different interpretation of his film. He saw Yoram and Rafi as the Janus face of the same Israeli attitude. No one is born a king or a bastard, he explained, every person takes responsibility. Hemmings, in contrast, stands for the "international intelligentsia"—alienated and cynical, suspicious of idealism and sacrifice. Zohar gave as an example none other than the French philosopher Jean-Paul Sartre, who toured the Middle East before the war and then wrote about peace but did nothing else to promote it.[11] He defined Hemmings as "a little Sartre, American, smart, who has an opinion about everything, and here he comes across two who are willing in every morning to [risk their lives]. One because he is crazy and believes he will bring peace, the other because he must fight for his bare existence and at the end of the day it's the same."[12]

Hemmings ultimately stands for American power and its ambition to intervene in local conflicts. His coffin is draped in the American flag as though he were a diplomat or a soldier. At the same time, his character also symbolizes American weakness or even impotence. An aging has-been whose prime is likely behind him, he can change nothing. He barely understands the situation. One *unlucky* bastard, he dies.

Early Israeli films occasionally featured American characters either as a marketing device for potential audiences abroad or to affirm a Zionist message through an admiring foreigner. *Every Bastard a King* manifests even more strongly a cultural proclivity of gazing at Israel through imaginary foreign eyes. Zohar organized the entire film around Hemmings's bewilderment or supposed insight about Israeli society even as the film disparages him and the power he represents. The film peddles a certain image of Israeli society that is ultimately aggrandizing even while the heroism it celebrates is attuned to 1960s-inflected fascination with unruliness and social outsiders. The egalitarianism it purports to portray no longer rests on ideology and collectivism but is an affective disposition shared by Israelis as individuals. The film was well received by audiences and critics alike, crowned as one of the best Israeli films up to that point. It also won prizes for its director and cinematographer at the Chicago and San Francisco film festivals. In Denmark, however, it had to be renamed *We Are All Kings* in order not to offend the royal family.[13]

Don't Ask

Amos Kollek wrote *Don't Ask Me If I Love* when he was only twenty-two-years old. The novel exemplifies the distance that Israeli culture traversed in just a few years after the Six-Day War. Kollek's is a triangular story. Assaf Ryke, a son of a politically powerful and incredibly rich Israeli banker and businessman, his childhood friend Ram who is also a commissioned officer in Assaf's paratrooper unit (we have here a third narrative involving a paratrooper), and Joy, a willowy American blond who becomes Assaf's love interest. Assaf does not hide the fact that he is attracted to Joy because of her stereotypically non-Jewish looks.

Kollek recently revealed that he named the protagonist Assaf after Moshe Dayan's son, actor/director Assi Dayan. But in many respects, Assaf stands for Kollek himself, a son of the celebrated Jerusalem mayor Teddy Kollek. Assaf lives in his parents' Rehavia neighborhood mansion. He drives a white Triumph sports car he received for his eighteenth birthday, which he likes to push to the limit, listening to the engine roar and the tires scream, speeding and running red lights. Assaf drinks gallons of Coca-Cola as a sexy voice over the radio tells him, "You're better off with Coca-Cola . . . Ice Cold."[14] He is constantly in search for women to bed and other cures for his endemic restlessness. As Kollek had done, Assaf spent a year in the United States. The elder Ryke believes that being in America is a necessary part of one's education. "You have to see projects on a scale found only in America in order to really understand how this world is run." He promises, "It will broaden your horizons."[15]

The War of Attrition supplies the geopolitical background—soldiers' funerals, personal sacrifice, the morbid sense of an Israeli "lost generation," and the resultant pessimism, black humor, even self-destruction. Assaf almost gets killed as a reservist in the Jordan Valley chasing PLO infiltrators. Ultimately, he represents a new social archetype, not the daring and self-sacrificing individuality of *Every Bastard a King* but the arrogant individualism of an ambitious young man hungry for money and fame. Seeking to become a famous writer and filmmaker, he harbors astonishingly little respect for anything else, whether Jewish tradition, social conventions, or the state.

In a fashion that foreshadows the popularity of Ayn Rand in mid-70s Israel, he declares, "The safest idea is to be yourself. Do what you want and the hell with the rest. I am me. I am the only one who is me."[16] But this seemingly narcissistic quest for material gain is served as a Sixties-style rebellion against his parents' generation and life in a garrison state. At his father's urging, he attends a ruling party event where he delivers an outrageous speech that argues for returning the West Bank and Sinai in exchange for peace. He provokes, "The younger generation in this country does not believe in the eternal Jewish fate of suffering. They don't want just to fight all the time, they want to live, too."[17]

Ram is killed in a Jordan Valley pursuit of PLO militants. Joy, whom Assaf marries after a convoluted affair, dies when a terrorist bomb sets off in a Jerusalem supermarket. However, by the conclusion of the novel, we discover its conceit. Assaf, who is writing a script about a love affair between an Israeli man and an American woman, meets a Hollywood producer who counsels him to keep the female character—so American audiences could identify with her—but then to kill her just before the end. "You just have to increase the number of scenes with her and shorten the story after her death."[18] He further advises Assaf to follow the blunt, nonsentimental style of movies such as *Easy Rider* and *Midnight Cowboy* and accept that the antihero is a fresh and more attractive device for a story line about Israel.

Kollek wrote and first published *Don't Ask Me If I Love* in English. In the script that Assaf writes, the protagonist maintains, "Number one rule: write in English, even if you can't spell butter. A best-selling author in Hebrew hardly makes a living and is forever unknown outside his country, unless he gets hijacked or wins a beauty contest, which doesn't often happen."[19] But Kollek's supposed exercise of metafiction, of telling the story of the making of his novel, allows him to distance himself from such an assertion. The passage was supposedly written only as an exercise in crafting a clever monologue, part of the prospective novel's protagonist's seduction techniques. The reader is left questioning whether the novel with all its autobiographical trappings and the boldness of Assaf's political stance was nothing more than a cynical attempt to author a formulaic bestseller for the American market, whether by glorifying or satirizing the main character's ambitions.

Whereas the novel provides ample evidence for the American cultural invasion, it is pervaded with anti-American sentiments. Assaf warns that America is seeking to remake the world with a religious-like zeal, "attaching labels of meaning to each of its items, instead of prices."[20] The growing Israeli dependence on the United States angers him. If Israel were more independent and did not have to crawl to the Americans for everything the Arabs would not stand a chance. Proclaiming that Washington would eventually sell out Israel, he profoundly mistrusts the Nixon administration and its intentions in the Middle East. Assaf treats with contempt an American Jew he meets at a Jerusalem party, screaming at him, "Yankee Go Home!" He didn't want Joy to convert to Judaism. With ostensibly an eye to the American reader he also goes on a sight-seeing tour in Jerusalem, bringing Joy, Ram, and the reader to sites such as the Western Wall, which he typically detests, "All those goddam people, standing by some goddam wall, crying for a goddam building that maybe stood here a goddam thousand years ago, when we don't even get those dozen goddam Phantoms."[21]

Some of the critical sentiments are expressed by Joy. On Ram's death she remarks sarcastically, "Maybe it's better than being killed by the National Guard."[22] But Assaf does not have a very favorable view of the American Left either. Joy is portrayed as having gone through a politically progressive phase. She also experimented with drugs and promiscuity. "I had what you might call a 'self-actualization mania.' . . . I had to do everything and understand everything."[23] However, she eventually recoiled at the supposed extremism of radical politics in the United States.[24] As if this was not enough, the novel has her visit Harlem, where she was gang-raped by three Black men.

Israeli critics couldn't forgive Kollek for breaking a taboo and writing

FIGURE 10.2   The Israeli experience ensconced in a curvaceous Coke-like bottle. Cover illustration for the novel *Don't Ask Me If I Love* (1971). Author Amos Kollek was the model for the illustration of the protagonist Assaf Rike on top. (Designer Rod Lord / Weidenfeld & Nicolson)

in English. They dismissed the novel, but it was warmly endorsed by authors Leon Uris and James Michener, both casting Kollek as an important and original voice of his generation. For a back cover blurb, Uris writes, "Kollek . . . presents the most concise and illuminating insight into young people of any writer I have read in his generation." Michener agrees, "The American reader will derive from this book a vital insight into what the typical young Israeli is thinking these days, and some of the thoughts may be startling."[25] However, a *Kirkus* review speculated that that readers would be surprised by the familiarity of the protagonist's grievances. "In fact Assaf sounds like any American you might know."[26] In 1979, the book became a motion picture shot with Kollek in the role of Assaf.

Assaf is a synthetic amalgamation of James Dean and the mythological Uri, the protagonist of Moshe Shamir's iconic 1947 novel/play, *He Walked through the Fields*, which in 1967 became a film starring Assi Dayan. It might be ironic that a book that is so intentionally and openly derivative could also be innovative, but arguably there is some merit to such a claim. The novel might be contrived, a banal appropriation, but its depiction—and embodiment—of cynicism and crude materialism at the core of a new Israeli identity could, in retrospect, be seen as both original and insightful, perhaps even prescient. The novel was quite successful in the American book market.

Geolibidinal Encounters

As *I Like Mike* and *Every Bastard a King*, *Don't Ask Me If I Love* betrays a wish for greater intimacy, tangible or symbolic, with American customs, people, and things—together with complicated efforts to keep America at bay. Yet, as Israelis moved more closely into the American orbit, they were also busy guarding their sense of distinction. For that purpose, *America* is often split into contending elements, some the product of projections and even violent wish fulfillment. Mike is ridiculed and then rejected. Hemmings and Joy are killed. The other hippie Mike is also dead; his demise belies his vociferous antiviolence message. All four works involve sexual relationships between Israelis and Americans or the potential of such encounters.

The Israeli male's voracious sexual drive is a recurrent theme in turn-of-the-1970s Israeli cinema, evident, for example, in Uri Zohar's three films known as the Tel Aviv Trilogy, *Metzitzim* or *Peeping Toms* (1972), *Big Eyes* (1974), and *Save the Lifeguard* (1977). It was evident in other movies he directed during the period as well, especially the *Rooster* (1971), about an army reservist (Topol) who receives a furlough to get a divorce and then sleeps his way from the Suez to Haifa, where he also beds his estranged wife. Another film, *Hitromemut* or *Take Off* (1970) revolves around wife swapping.

One recurrent motif in Israeli films is the female American visitor as an object of sexual desire. In *Save the Lifeguard*, the lifeguard's assistant, a Sancho Panza character (Gabi Amrani), ironically nicknamed "the handsome," puts on an American flag-themed full body bathing suit. An Uncle Sam image adorns one of the walls in his apartment. With a hopelessly broken English he relentlessly pursues female American tourists, including a middle-aged woman and a younger individual pretending to be an American tourist.

Another example is the 1973 film *Hatzad hasheni* (The other side; titled in English, *Take Two*). A young American photographer, Sunny (Shari Smith) falls for a dune-buggy-driving film and commercial director Doron (Ori Levi). Doron represents the new pleasure-seeking lifestyle. Hopping from one bed to another, he is hard to pin down. But when he realizes that he loves Sunny, it might be too late. The nudity-filled film speaks English for at least half of its length. One critic noticed that whereas director Baruch Diener's earlier film, *They Were Ten* (1960) depicts the idealism and struggles of the early Zionist pioneers, in *Take Two* it is the young wide-eyed American rather than the gruff, cynical middle-aged Israeli that stands for idealism and the desire for a better world.[27]

The Israeli man / American woman pairing is rarely inverted. Shalom Hanoch's popular song (singer, Dafna Armoni) "Ella" (1984) is a political song that warns against naive overreliance on US power. Standing for Israel, the eponymous Ella is an infatuated young girl while the man she is madly in love with is the "king of the neighborhood" with a new and shiny motorcycle. This is her first love and one day when he will not want her anymore, poor Ella would find herself thrown out on the road heartbroken, so predicts Hanoch. Nevertheless, most listeners were likely unaware of Hanoch's political message, hidden underneath the failed love story. In general, overt expressions of anti-American sentiments were uncommon in Israeli popular culture. More typical was another 1984 song (music and lyrics, Uzi Hitman; singer, Zohar Argov) about an Israeli who against his initial plans decides not to settle in the United States but to return home. Its title is, "The Land of Israel Is My America."

The Princess and the Courtesan

The most piercing assaults on American cultural hegemony were also the most stylized, abstracted, and indirect. A reworking of Greek mythology in the guise of avant-garde police drama, Nissim Aloni's *American Princess* (1963) focuses on a deposed king of a fictional European nation, now living in an imaginary Latin American country and going by the name Felix von Schwank—and his son, Ferdinand, or Freddie. Shining his crown every day, the father dreams of returning to power. Meanwhile, he makes a living teaching French. His relationship with his son is complex, to say the least, and is shaped by their respective memories of Freddie's mother, who died giving birth. Unbeknown to the father, both he and his son frequent the same prostitute on different days of the week. Layer after layer, therefore, the plot retraces the contours of the Oedipal triangle.

A mysterious American lady, Dolly Kokomakis, contacts the king, sends him a large tape recorder, and puts him on a monthly retainer of a thousand pesos, so he would chronicle his life. The king's memory is by now rather cloudy, but this is beside the point. As it turns out, Dolly plans to shoot a movie based on his life. He refuses to sign up for "the right to turn me into a king preserved in celluloid reels, pudding-royale for the palate of [female] social workers." He would not deliver his monarchy as a spectacle, thundering, "I am not a museum!"[28] But Freddie, who does not harbor any illusion about the monarchy, agrees to participate in the film. A director of failed biopics about monarchs—he once transformed Napoleon's life story into a musical comedy—shows up. Of course, there is little resemblance between the film script and the king's life, on which it is supposedly based.

The king is to be substituted by a movie actor. Plastic surgery prepares him perfectly for each role. He declares, "A major question recently is what a man is. . . . Let me respond, colleagues, a profound answer: yes, plastic surgery (applause) every day a new operation, colleagues! Every morning a new face! Every evening a fresh ego, a fresh personal biography, a rainbow character."[29] Freddie toils hard to convince his father to join the production, promising him that with public relations and newspaper interviews, Dolly will return him back to his old glory, to the palace. But the king is adamant. However, Dolly the American princess, who like other characters besides the father and son, never appears on stage, insists, and at the last moment, the king relents and goes on stage. Following the script, Freddie shoots his father with a revolver without realizing that the plastic surgery-addicted actor was replaced by the real king and that his pistol is loaded with a real bullet. The drama begins with police interrogation of this patricide/regicide case.

American Princess traces the clash between Old World and New World, heroic culture and democratic entertainment, theater and mass-produced movies. It ultimately critiques modernity and its incarnation in the insatiable, devouring force that is the American cultural industry. The father/son conflict, a profound dynamic of family life, is rescripted and banalized. What is alive, fragile, and still full of hope, despite epic failures and disappointments, is distorted, exploited, smothered. Dolly, as the play implies, is in effect Persephone, the mythological queen of the underworld.

American culture might be committed to egalitarian myth-breaking but democratization yields conformity and mediocrity and new hierarchies as insinuated in the idea of an American princess.[30] On the now-democratic country he once ruled, Bogomania, the king laments, "gray, gray, gray . . . the clothes are gray, the buildings are gray, the heart is gray . . . all are hypochondriacs, all the democrats! Neurotic! Suicidal! Every day an airplane falls out of the sky!"[31] The confusion between life and its representation affords an early glimpse into the coming postmodernity.[32] Otherwise, Aloni's father and son drama is configured as a universal fable. None of the characters answers to a Jewish or Hebrew name. There is no direct allusion to Israeli society, except for one obvious wink in which Israel—referred to as Palestine—is described in passing as, "A small country in emancipating Africa. Very fanatical. A lot of folklore."[33]

Fifteen year later, the playwright Hanoch Levin authored an equally bleak drama, *The Whore from Ohio* (1978), at the center of which resides another father, son, and prostitute triangle.[34] It is set again in nondescript corner of the world. The father—a beggar—seeks sex without pay. The prostitute wants his money, for which she pretends to give him love. The son is the soberest and the most cynical of the three, but eventually he joins his father's craving for the whore from Ohio. She is not a specific individual but an extreme, and extremely inverted iteration of the American dream. She is longingly described by the father in the following passage:

> I heard of one brothel in Ohio, it is twice and a half larger than our entire country. The whores don't sit in small rooms with a sink; every whore has a huge villa, surrounded by a flower garden, four cars, a yacht, an airplane, two young gynecologists are close by twenty-four hours a day, and a battalion of Negroes. The whore from Ohio is so rich that she does not take any money, and since she does not take any money, she does not need you. She therefore does not allow you to get inside; no, the whore from Ohio rides on a thoroughbred horse in her private forest, behind her rides the gynecologist on duty with a bag, and four Negro valets carrying equipment, while you, the client, are standing outside by the gate, looking at the mailbox rubbing yourself. Then, an enormous Negro guard shows up, grabs you by the collar and throws you out of there like a rag. This is my dream: a whore in Ohio and die![35]

Ohio's whore is therefore not really a prostitute as much as a grand promise that is inherently unattainable. The characters' daydreams and night dreams are heavily occupied with fragments of other, similarly impossible apparitions that invoke American opulence. With all its misogynistic and racist accents, Levin's play presents what Lauren Berlant would label "cruel optimism," an unachievable fantasy of the good life.[36] The miserable prostitute muses that she can meet an American tourist, clean up, and find herself inside a marble swimming pool in Los Angeles. "It won't happen, but the possibility is there."[37] The father fantasizes that his son is a movie star that disguises himself as a beggar just to study for a role. He has three houses in Hollywood and is married to the actress Virginia Mayo. The son dreams that his father is an industrialist with steel, sugar, and cotton plants, airplanes, and four hotels in Ohio.

While in Aloni's play the leveling power of cultural democracy extinguishes in the name of entertainment, beauty and hope, the American dream of the *Whore of Ohio* is not about gray equality but an almost unimaginable disparity of power and affluence that is still attached to an absurd hope that renders the lives of the socially marginal profoundly grotesque.

Levin's later work would often revolve around dreams and delirious apparitions of travels to and from foreign lands. In the *Rubber Merchants* (1978) the character Jane and her state, Texas, occupy the fantasies of the two male protagonists. In *Suitcase Packers* (1983), the main figures constantly travel back and forth as the play depicts another failure of the American dream. In the satirical cabaret, *The Patriot* (1982), the protagonist wishes to immigrate to America and gets a visa after he is asked to spit in his mother's face as a proof that he would not bring her with him. He is ultimately barred from traveling to United States but is sent to the Albanian front, where he dies. Aloni also returned to the Oedipal triangle, immigrants, and exiles in his play *Eddie King* (1975). It takes place in New York City and follows the rise and fall of a poor immigrant who becomes a "king" in the demimonde of gangsters.

Conclusion

Universalizing his drama, Aloni was one of the first Israeli authors who sought to be a citizen of the world.[38] But while his and Levin's plays could be construed as generalizable observations about modernity, human psychology, or the lingering power of ancient myths—they also interrogate the homeland/exile, Promised Land/Diaspora, inside/outside dyads that define the Israeli experience. Whereas the American who fashions herself a princess and the Ohioan prostitute who is completely unreachable reside off stage, they dominate the aspirations and fears of those in clear view and participate in their world-making chimeras.[39] Moreover, both Aloni and Levin came from poor neighborhoods in the south of Tel Aviv, and beneath the universalist veneer, those locales on the social margins of Israeli society are present in their drama.

Critic Omri Yavin sees in Levin's and similar plays a subversive inversion of the desire for Zion. "If once we were there [in the Diaspora] and we longed for the Land of Israel, and even eroticized the country . . . suddenly, everything turned upside down and all people in Tel Aviv want is the whore from Ohio . . . or the one from Texas."[40] Unlike how *I Like Mike* and *Don't Ask Me*

If I Love and other works we encountered at the beginning of this chapter document the craving for American things, the American way of life, and America itself, the *American Princess* and the *Whore from Ohio* neither seek satisfaction nor contemplate resolution.

American characters portrayed in these plays might substantiate the impression of toxic anti-American sentiments, but the playwrights' main purpose is arguably to question the motivation behind, the desirability, and the ultimate success of the aspiration to negate the Old World Zionism supposedly left behind. Absent in their respective work is the glorification of the self-assured modern sabra. Levin's characters pepper their talk with words and expressions translated from Yiddish, and he purposefully selected nonsabra actors for their performance.[41] This is not another iteration of the *return* motif we visited in chapter 8. The point is not that the Diaspora returns; it never left. It is still very much part of the culture that otherwise denies it and, at the same time, fails to metamorphose into an imaginary Western ideal it so much yearns for.[42]

Conclusion

The October 1973 war reversed national priorities, rendering untenable the notion that the existential questions facing Israel were a thing of the past. It snuffed out, albeit only temporarily, Israeli overconfidence as well as the atmosphere of exuberance that characterized Tel Aviv–centered culture. Several fads and a few performances were also causalities of the war. For a few years the social disparity in Israel was pushed back on the national agenda. The war attested to the growing Israeli geopolitical reliance on the United States, and yet it was analogized to the American failure in Vietnam for how it eroded confidence in political elites, government, and state institutions. The Vietnam analogy would return with the Lebanon War of the early 1980s and the consequent sense that Israel was stuck in a quagmire. Ultimately, the engagement with American culture, politics, and technology and the social processes explored throughout the book vigorously continued.

Two decades later, Americanization emerged once again as topic of intense public debate. Rather than Coca-Cola, it was McDonald's golden arches, introduced to Israel in 1993, that stood for the deluge of American ideas, practices, and things. The burgers-churning fast-food chain was joined by a slew of other brand names, including Pizza Hut, Toys "R" Us, and

Office Depot. Israelis became accustomed to shopping in air-conditioned malls and having food and other products delivered to their doorsteps. Instead of the single public TV station and a few public radio outlets of yore, they were now watching several TV channels on their cable box and listening to commercial radio stations on their car radios. English edged more persistently and deeper into their daily lives, especially with the advent of the Internet. New high-rises punctured the Tel Aviv skyline. In the following decade Israel would have its own baseball league. Major political parties adopted American-style primaries as the process for selecting their parliamentary candidate lists.[1] American consultants are now a common feature of electoral campaigns. And all sides of the political arena today continue to appropriate American idioms, whether it is the Trumpist "fake news" or the slogan "Arab Lives Matter!" inspired by "Black Lives Matter!"

But wrestling with Americanization and the globalizing process in general was rendered urgent and immediate in the 1990s not by foreign cultural additives as much as by the parallel collapse of old institutions that hitherto signified what still distinguished Israel from the rest of the Western world, especially the deterioration of the power of unionized labor and the demise of unique experiments of communal life. Privatization was the key concept of 1990s Israel, manifested in the accelerated selling of government-owned companies and public land, the almost complete elimination of the Histadrut's industrial and financial arm, Hevrat Ha'ovdim, and the divvying up of property in kibbutzim. Proliferating consumerist opportunities and the culture at large became more conducive to individualism of choice, identity, and sensibility. Income stratification increased exponentially.

A stunningly successful high-tech industry gave birth to yet another new pioneering class of computer scientists, engineers, and digital-age entrepreneurs. The country was crowned "Start-Up Nation," home of burgeoning information technology enterprises.[2] With great zeal, the state fully embraced modern capitalism. Government liberalized its fiscal policies, reduced taxes, and receded from many of its previous economic and social responsibilities. Israel did not merely follow but in effect was modeling the neoliberal swerve. This process began with the economic crisis of the mid-1980s and the remedial program known as "The Stabilization Plan," which set the foundation for things to come. It was supported by the two major parties at the time, Likud on the Right and Labor as the heir of the old socialist Left.

By the 1990s, one individual, Benjamin Netanyahu, would come to personify Americanization and neoliberalism in its fullest incarnation. Many of his critics and political foes have regarded him as a foreign implant. Historian Tom Segev writes, "Netanyahu came of age in the United States; Washington, DC, is the capital of his inner world."[3] Nevertheless, Netanyahu's proficiency in American ways has not interfered whatsoever with his capacity to foster and politically benefit from patriotic sentiments. The agility with which he was able to shuttle culturally and politically between Washington and Jerusalem, at least until President Donald J. Trump left the White House, epitomized how the orbital relations encourage a local leader to be also a proud citizen of the American empire. Historian Charles Maier defines empire as "a form of political organization in which the social elements that rule in the dominant state . . . create a network of allied elites in regions abroad."[4] Even informal empires rely on alliances between elites in the metropole and the periphery.

The metropole/periphery ties are inherently unequal and yet reciprocal, and occasionally allow Israel to take the lead. Reflecting on Netanyahu's 2022 extreme right-wing coalition, journalist Thomas Friedman warns that Israel has become a harbinger of troubling political trends in Western democracies, an "Off Broadway to our Broadway."[5] Since the turn of the 1970s, to give another example, the Pentagon has embraced Israeli tactics and advice, most recently in the context of the so-called war against terror. In the cultural field, Israel has exported to the United States American-style products, including a range of popular TV shows from the action-filled *Fauda* to the drama of ultra-Orthodox life in *Shtisel*. Some American TV series—like the globe-trotting thriller *Homeland* or the psychotherapy-focused *In Treatment*—were based on Israeli shows. Moreover, like Rabin, Netanyahu has not hesitated to intervene in American politics; in fact, much more than his predecessor, he became strongly associated with the Republican Party.

At the turn of the 1970s the American gravitational pull was manifested in providing the building blocks for the rise of consumer society and was felt also through Great Society–era liberalism and its discontents, counterculturalism, feminism, and other forms of identity politics, including religious ultranationalism. From the American perspective it was then (but not much longer) feasible to couple a pro-Zionist stance with progressive politics. When politician and social activist Bella Abzug visited Israel in the summer of 1971, she declared herself "Leftist, feminist, anti-militarist, member of the Democratic Party and a fan of Israel."[6]

In Israel, Marcia Freedman's belief in the exemplary power of American pluralism, individual rights, and freedom of political contestation demonstrated how the United States could be championed as a paradigm for reforming public life in a society in which the old Left was stagnate, parochial, and haunted by scandals, and the New Left remained miniscule, fractious, and isolated. As late as the 1990s, Israelis could see the United States in this light. As against a choir of voices sounding alarm bells about the dreaded Americanization, author Amos Elon claimed in 1998 that Americanization inculcates positive values like inclusiveness, secularism, and the rule of law. "Luckily Americanization is a phenomenon in Israeli society since it saves us from becoming a fascist or a theocratic state."[7] Both American liberalism's inner strength and its power to save Israelis from the perils Elon underscored are now in doubt.

In recent decades, Israel and the United States have grown more alike and more different. Certainly, a few of the transformations explored throughout the book took deep root in Israeli society; technologism is one example, consumerism is another. However, the ethnic motif in music and popular culture assumed a different tenor after the 1970s. Yiddish has been fully recognized for its contributions to Jewish culture and history, although it is not spoken outside *haredi* circles. Yiddishism ultimately has enjoyed less traction in the Israeli argot than among Jews and non-Jews in New York City.

Netanyahu's Israel and America share both populist politics and a highly polarized electorate. The alt-Right of both countries relies heavily on religious fundamentalism. There have been efforts to further align American and Israeli conservatism, for instance, through the initiatives of the Kohelet Policy Forum, a think tank that through policy research and legislation proposals promotes a nationalist, prosettlement ideology together with a free-market, antiregulation agenda. It is lavishly funded by American donors.[8] Kohelet had a major role in formulating the judicial reform, known by its critics as the "judicial coup," that generated an unprecedented wave of public protest in early 2023. But Kohelet's motto, "National sovereignty—Individual liberty" does not cohere comfortably with Israeli right-wing politics. Despite the weight of American immigrants within it, Modern Orthodox settler nationalism emerged from a very different confluence of historical forces and ideologies than American Evangelical conservatism and "individual liberty" is not one of its core tenets.[9] For ultra-Orthodox parties, in particular, the continuation of state-funded social welfare is essential.

Identity politics that emerged in Israel in conjunction with the Global Sixties ultimately assumed a different trajectory. True, the Israeli Left adopted postcolonialism and inclusive norms that pertain to race, gender, sexuality, and other categories of difference. But Mizrahi identity politics largely veered rightward. The Mizrahi, ultra-Orthodox Shas Party constitutes one variant. Otherwise, a good deal of the still quite perceptible Mizrahi sense of grievance finds its political expression in Mizrahi voters' attachment to the decidedly Ashkenazi figure of Benjamin Netanyahu.

What brought Israel and the United States closer at times also accentuated what set them apart, as explored in the first two chapters of *Coca-Cola, Black Panthers, and Phantom Jets*. Thus, Israelis embraced Barbie dolls, Coca-Cola, blue jeans, and the supermarket, but consumption raised radically different political questions in the Israeli and American public spheres and triggered dissimilar state responses. Teasing out similarities and differences between the two countries, we should also bear in mind that that the comparative impulse itself is symptomatic of the orbital dynamics and their attendant ideological strings that encourage bundling Israel and the United States together. The comparative imagination is part of the subject matter of this book rather than what it seeks to present as a concluding argument. Generally, such comparisons run the risks of essentializing what is considered under the label *America*, isolating individual strains from other permutations of the transnational exchange, and ignoring change over time.

In contrast, *Israel in the American Orbit* advocates for the historicization of the Israeli-American encounter, paying attention to the details of historical contingencies, the practices and performances involved, as well as to the experience of individuals and communities, and the tactile or material dimensions of the transnational transfer. It underscores the diversity of meeting points and plurality of responses—from unthinking mimicry to strong resistance and everything in between—together with processes that worked on different, more circuitous, and often dialectical axes, such as the variegated Israeli reactions to the rise of Black Power in the United States. It is the range and unevenness of these responses rather than a single glocalizing or creolizing mechanism that guarantees that these two societies are and would continue to be distinct.

In 1977, the graphic artist David Tartakover, who throughout his career worked tirelessly to curate and preserve Israeli design artistry, produced a poster that simply announces in bold letters, "Israel is not America." Tartakover intimated that while everybody wanted America, he preferred to declare, "No!"[10] Decades later, when asked what in his view constitutes the essence of Israeliness he pointed to this work, and later explained that what he misses the most in modern Israel are clearly delineated borders.[11]

Tartakover's implicit conjoining of the borders separating Israel from the occupied territories and neighboring countries, on the one hand, and the often-trespassed metaphorical border that stands between Israel and the United States, on the other, is the point with which this book concludes. Ultimately, *Israel in the American Orbit* has documented the shifting boundaries under orbital dynamics—separating and bringing together the United States, its Jewish community, and Israel—and the manner they were imagined, crossed, collapsed, or guarded in a country whose borders and identity were in flux back then and ever since.

Notes

Preface
1. Original Hebrew titles, passages, lyrics, and nomenclature were translated to English by the author. Chapter 4 is a revised version of the previously published, "Your Part in the Phantom: American Technology, National Identity, and the War of Attrition," *Israel Studies* 24, no. 1 (Spring 2019): 174–99. Chapter 5 draws from three previously published articles, "Blackness in Translation: The Israeli Black Panthers, 1971," in *Blackness in Israel: Rethinking Racial Boundaries*, ed. Uri Dorchin and Gabriella Djerrahian (London: Routledge, 2020), 91–112; "The Politics of the Radical Analogy: The Case of the Israeli Black Panthers," in *Black Power beyond Borders*, ed. Nico Slate (New York: Palgrave, 2012), 81–106; and "What's in a Name? The Black Panthers in Israel," *The Sixties: A Journal of History, Politics and Culture* 1, no. 1 (June 2008): 9–26.

Introduction
1. Ruth Bondi, "Portnoy's Wife's Complaints," *Davar: Dvar Hashavu'a*, August 20, 1971, 8.
2. Amnon Rubinstein, "What We Have in 1970 We Didn't in 1948," *Haaretz*, September 30, 1970.
3. Hillel Halkin, "Americans in Israel," *Commentary*, May 1, 1972, 54.
4. *Al Hamishmar*, April 16, 1973.
5. *Ma'ariv*, July 7, 1970; Amos Elon, "Golda: A Portrait," *Haaretz: Musaf*, July 24, 1970, 38.
6. There are scores of books on Israel and the United States, focusing mostly on as-

pects of diplomatic relations, the Arab-Israeli conflict, the pro-Israel lobby, the peace process, and policymaking in general. See, for example, Tal, *The Making of an Alliance*; Aridan, *Advocating for Israel*; Ariel, *An Unusual Relationship*; Ben-Zvi, *The United States and Israel*; Mart, *Eyes on Israel*; Mearsheimer and Walt, *The Israel Lobby*; Olson, *America's Road to Jerusalem*; Merkley, *American Presidents, Religion, and Israel*; Spector, *Evangelicals and Israel*; Shaw and Goodman, *Hollywood and Israel*.

7. Helman, *Consumer Culture and Leisure in the Young State of Israel*, chaps. 4–5. The most vociferous voices against Americanization came from Maki, the Israeli communist party; see, for example, the communist daily *Kol Ha'am*, July 15, 1951, *Kol Ha'am*, January 1, 1952. For the pre-independence American presence see, for example, Brown, *The Israeli-American Connection*.

8. Gabbay, *Political Economy*, 246–48.

9. Goldin and Margo, "The Great Compression"; Picketty and Saez, "Income Inequality."

10. David Segal and Isabel Kershner, "Who Is Behind the Judicial Overhaul Now Dividing Israel? Two Americans," *New York Times*, March 20, 2023; Aaron Heller, "Israel's Crisis Has a Distinctly American Flavor," *New York Times*, March 27, 2023.

11. On American culture and iconography as lingua franca, see Kroes, "American Empire and Cultural Imperialism," 475.

12. "Watergate Israeli Style," *Ha'olam Hazeh*, May 16, 1973, 14–15; Dan Margalit, "Top Secret," *Haaretz: Musaf*, July 16, 1971, 5–7; *Lamerhav*, March 24, 1971.

13. "Members of Knesset's Dovecote," *Ha'olam Hazeh*, April 15, 1970, 15.

14. Robertson, "'Glocalization'"; Bauman, "On Glocalization"; Victor Roudometof defines glocalization as "globalization refracted through the local." Roudometof, *Glocalization*, 146.

15. See, for example, Wagnleitner, *Coca-Colanization and the Cold War*; Kuisel, *Seducing the French*; Kuisel, *The French Way*; Rydell, *Buffalo Bill in Bologna*; Zeitlin and Herrigel, *Americanization and Its Limits*; Conrad, *How The World Was Won*; Vučetić, *Coca-Cola Socialism*; Stephan, *Americanization and Anti-Americanism*; Malchow, *Special Relations*; Tota, *The Seduction of Brazil*; Bell and Bell, *Americanization and Australia*; Oldenziel and Zachman, *Cold War Kitchen*; Contreras, *In the Shadow of the Giant*; Abravanel, *Americanizing Britain*; Kroes, *If You've Seen One, You've Seen the Mall*; Wagnleitner and May, "Here, There and Everywhere."

16. Gelber, *Attrition: The Forgotten War*.

17. Quandt, *Decade of Decisions*, chap. 4.

18. In recent decades, the Israeli ambivalence toward American Jews received a few treatments. See, for example, Golan, *With Friends Like You*.

19. H.C.J. 58/68, *Shalit v. the Minister of the Interior*. Supreme Court of Israel 23(2) P.D. 477 (1969), 501-2. Also, see Lahav, *Judgment in Jerusalem*, 204-5.

20. *Israel Studies* journal dedicated its volume 5, issue 1 (Spring 2000) to the topic of Americanization. On the long history of turning Israel toward capitalism, see Krampf, *The Israeli Path to Neoliberalism*; Ben-Porat, *How Israel Became a Capitalist Society*. On the American impact on Israeli social sciences, see Uri Ram's *Israeli Sociology*. Mono-

graphs on the perception of Israel from the American vantage point include Kaplan, *Our American Israel*; Mitelpunkt, *Israel in the American Mind*.

21. *Lamerhav*, January 11, 1963; *Davar*, January 11, 1963.

22. Gilbert, LeGrand, and Salvatore, *Close Encounters of Empire*, represents the best of the genre. Also, see Zolov, *Refried Elvis*.

23. Pratt, "Arts of the Contact Zone," 34.

24. Melani McAlister makes an inspiring use of the concept of the "encounter," but her approach is limited to American engagements with representations of the Middle East. See McAlister, *Epic Encounters*.

25. A similar point was made by Amnon Rubinstein and Hillel Halkin in the articles mentioned at the beginning of the introduction (footnotes 2 and 3). For instance, Israelis exhibited enthusiasm about the Cold War when Americans had enough of it.

26. *Coca-Cola, Black Panthers, and Phantom Jets* provides a comprehensive but not exhaustive documentation of the Israeli-American exchange. Cultural fields that are not addressed here but have already attracted scholarly attention elsewhere include rock and roll music, art, architecture, and environmentalism. On art, see Ofrat, *New York–Tel Aviv*; on environmentalism, Tal, *Pollution in a Promised Land*, chap. 5; Orenstein, Tal, and Miller, *Between Ruin and Restoration*; on music, Regev and Seroussi, *Popular Music and National Culture*; Rappaport, *Israeli Rock*; on architecture, Klein, *The Beginning of Tel-Aviv's Americanization*.

27. Gurevitch, *On Israeli and Jewish Space*; Zubida and Lipshitz, *Stop—No Border*; Rachlevsky, *No Limit*.

28. Interview with Limor; interview with Segal; interview with Harpaz.

29. Aaron Bachar, "Ya Allah! This Is Like America," *Bamahane*, July 25, 1968, 14–15.

30. *Davar*, June 16, 1953.

31. *Davar*, November 25, 1971.

Chapter 1: Consumer Modernity and the *Everyday*

1. *Davar: Dvar Hashavu'a*, April 5, 1968, 11.

2. Levi Eshkol, Transcript of Voice of Israel Broadcast to the Nation, Jerusalem, February 21, 1966, in Lammfromm and Tsoref, *Levi Eshkol*, 502.

3. Gilly Izikowitz, "What Was the Meaning of the Orgy that Took Place Here before the War?," *Haaretz: Gallery*, September 4, 2013.

4. "Consumerism" is sometimes used as a pejorative term employed to denounce "a continuous and unremitting search for new, fashionable but superfluous things, which social critics have branded as causing personal discontent and public disengagement in advanced capitalism." Sassatelli, *Consumer Culture*, 2. In contrast, "consumerism" can denote consumer-protection activism or consumption as a tool for political movements. In recent decades consumerism has also been associated with techniques of self-making. On consumption and knowledge, see "Introduction: Commodities and the Politics of Value," in Appadurai, *The Social Life of Things*, 41–56. On twentieth-century American and European consumption, see Cross, *All Consuming Century*; Strasser, McGovern, and Judt, *Getting and Spending*. On theories of consumption, see Lury, *Consumer Cul-*

ture; Miles, *Consumerism as a Way of Life*; Featherstone, *Consumer Culture and Postmodernism*; Peterson, *Consumption and Everyday Life*; Daunton and Hilton, *The Politics of Consumption*.

5. *Davar*, August 29, 1958; *Haaretz*, August 29, 1958. Sheinblat, "The Importation of the American Supermarket Model to Israel."

6. On exclusive clubs, see *Haaretz: Musaf*, August 27, 1971, 16–18, 29. On fine dining, *Haaretz: Musaf*, October 15, 1971, 12–13, 28.

7. *Ma'ariv*, January 1, 1969.

8. *Davar: Dvar Hashavu'a*, June 12, 1970, 10.

9. *Davar: Dvar Hashavu'a*, May 16, 1969, 30.

10. *Davar: Dvar Hashavu'a*, October 10, 1969, 25.

11. Ross, *Fast Cars, Clean Bodies*, 4.

12. For histories of Israeli capitalism, see Ben-Porat, *How Israel Became a Capitalist Society*; Krampf, *The National Origins of the Market Economy*.

13. Georg Lukács, Herbert Marcuse, and Jean Baudrillard critiqued the permeation of commodities into social life and the general process of commodification or reification by which social relations themselves become things. Guy Debord writes, "The commodity emerged in its full-fledged form as a force aspiring to the complete colonization of social life." Debord, *The Society of the Spectacle*, 29.

14. Yablonka, *Children by the Book*, 278.

15. Krampf, *The National Origins of the Market Economy*, 105.

16. Daniel Bloch, "How Did Jeshurun Grow Fat?," *Davar: Dvar Hashavu'a*, November 29, 1974, 25.

17. Eshkol, Voice of Israel Broadcast, February 21, 1966, 502–3.

18. Neoliberals today reject the pie metaphor, for it implies that society rather than individuals own wealth or that wealth should be divisible.

19. *Davar*, February 5, 1970.

20. Bernstein, "Black Panthers," 247.

21. Shalev, *Labour and the Political Economy in Israel*, 215.

22. Kanovsky, *The Economic Impact of the Six-Day War*, 71; *New York Times*, April 8, 1968.

23. *Ma'ariv*, April 2, 1968; Kanovsky, *The Economic Impact of the Six-Day War*, 71.

24. *Ma'ariv*, March 21, 1968.

25. *Ma'ariv*, March 29, 1968.

26. Kanovsky, *The Economic Impact of the Six-Day War*, 128–29.

27. Sapir, *Hayesh Hagadol*, 492–93, 554.

28. *Ma'ariv*, March 17, 1972.

29. Central Bureau of Statistics, *Statistical Abstract of Israel* no. 4 (1973), 158–59; *Statistical Abstract of Israel* no. 28 (1977), 689.

30. *Statistical Abstract of Israel* (1973), 681.

31. Mann, *The Leader and the Media*, chap. 15.

32. *Ma'ariv*, March 31, 1967.

33. *Davar*, November 14, 1967.

34. *Ma'ariv*, June 17, 1968.
35. *Ma'ariv*, May 24, 1968.
36. *Davar*, August 18, 1969.
37. *Ma'ariv*, November 6, 1968; *Haaretz: Musaf*, May 24, 1968, 8–9.
38. *Davar*, June 26, 1969.
39. *Davar*, June 14, 1968.
40. *Davar*, July 2, 1969.
41. *Ma'ariv*, June 17, 1968.
42. *Ma'ariv*, November 13, 1969.
43. *Ma'ariv*, April 29, 1974; a sociological study determined that in its first two decades Israeli TV restrained individualism, hedonism, and pluralism and enhanced a sense of collective belonging. Katz, *Leisure Patterns in Israel*, 400.
44. *Ma'ariv*, August 4, 1972.
45. Gan, "Social Transformations in the Kibbutz Movement," 347.
46. *Ma'ariv: Yamim Veleylot*, February 25, 1972, 58.
47. *Ma'ariv*, September 16, 1970.
48. *Ma'ariv*, June 28, 1970.
49. *Ma'ariv*, December 18, 1968.
50. *Ma'ariv*, June 10, 1968.
51. *Ma'ariv*, June 24, 1968.
52. *Davar*, March 2, 1964.
53. *Yedioth Ahronoth: 7 Yamim*, July 15, 1966, 6–7.
54. *Ma'ariv*, January 7, 1972.
55. *Ma'ariv*, July 31, 1970.
56. *Davar: Dvar Hashavu'a*, June 12, 1970, 22.
57. *Ma'ariv*, January 3 1972; on sex and advertisement, see Tamar Meroz, "An Ad Named Desire," *Haaretz: Musaf*, January 9, 1970, 12–13.
58. *Ma'ariv: Yamim Veleylot*, January 15, 1971, 52.
59. *Ma'ariv: Yamim Veleylot*, June 20, 1969, 43.
60. *Ma'ariv*, December 29, 1970.
61. *Ma'ariv*, February 25, 1972.
62. *Ma'ariv: Yamim Veleylot*, February 25, 1972, 66.
63. Ibid., 61.
64. *Davar: Dvar Hashavu'a*, September 29, 1972, 2.
65. *Ma'ariv*, March 29, 1966; *Davar*, April 10, 1966.
66. Yuval Elizur, "This Is How I Overcame the Arab Boycott and Brought Coca-Cola to Israel," *Haaretz*, June 11, 2015.
67. *New York Times*, April 8, 1966; *Davar*, April 12, 1966.
68. *Davar*, April 14, 1966; *Yedioth Ahronoth*, April 13, 1966.
69. *New York Times*, April 8, 13, 1966.
70. The case was settled out of court. Tempo agreed to name its cola drink in English Tempo Kola rather than Tempo Cola. *New York Times*, April 14, 1966; *Ma'ariv*, May 4, 1967.

71. *New York Times*, April 13, 1966; *Ma'ariv*, April 13, 14, 1966; *Davar*, April 15, 1966.
72. *Ma'ariv*, April 17, 1966.
73. Ibid.; *Davar*, April 17, 1966.
74. *New York Times*, April 16, 1966.
75. *Ma'ariv*, September 24, 1967; *Yedioth Ahronoth*, March 29, 1967.
76. *Ma'ariv*, September 16, 1970.
77. *Ma'ariv*, April 1, 1968.
78. *Ma'ariv: Yamim Veleylot*, September 27, 1974, 31; *Davar: Dvar Hashavu'a*, June 1, 1973, 40; *Davar: Dvar Hashavu'a*, February 25, 1972, 40.
79. For example, *Ma'ariv: Yamim Veleylot*, January 10, 1969, 40.
80. *Ma'ariv*, May 5, 1968; *Yedioth Ahronoth*, May 6, 1968.
81. *Yedioth Ahronoth*, July 8, 1971.
82. *Ma'ariv*, February 10, 1971.
83. *Ha'olam Hazeh*, July 23, 1969, 3.
84. *Davar*, July 16, 1970; *Ma'ariv*, January 2, 1972.
85. *Ma'ariv*, May 5, 1968.
86. *Yedioth Ahronoth*, May 23, 1968.
87. Roth-Cohen and Limor, "From Craft to Industry," 72.
88. *Statistical Abstract of Israel* (1973), 286–87.
89. *Globes*, May 3, 1998, http://www.globes.co.il/news/article.aspx?did=117895; Roth-Cohen and Limor, "From Craft to Industry," 58–86.
90. *Haaretz: Musaf*, January 22, 1971, 8–10.
91. Nurit Halif, "Trumpeldor's Brother and the Keychains," *Haaretz: Musaf*, April 28, 1967, 6–7.
92. Lefebvre, *Everyday Life*, 108.
93. See, for instance, *Haaretz: Musaf*, December 15, 1967, 24–25.
94. *Davar*, September 29, 1972.
95. *Ma'ariv*, May 29, 1968.
96. *Ma'ariv*, March 29, 1971.
97. *Ma'ariv*, September 15, 1967. The Consumer Council approached the police commissioner claiming that sweepstakes violated the law that prohibits gambling.
98. *Davar*, November 19, 1969.
99. *Davar*, June 4, 1969.
100. *Davar*, December 26, 1966.
101. *Davar*, July 2, 1969.
102. *Ma'ariv*, July 10, 1969.
103. *Ma'ariv*, July 31, 1970.
104. *Ha'olam Hazeh*, September 3, 1969, 45.
105. *Davar*, October 24, 1965.
106. The title *Lahiton* is a neologism based on the newly minted (1960) Hebrew word for a blockbuster, *lahit*—derived from the root that denotes "sizzling hot," but also gestures toward the English word "hit"—and *iton*, a newspaper. Eilon Gilad, "How Did

Rivkah Micha'eli Turn 'Schlager' into 'Lahit,'" *Haaretz*, July 5, 2013, http://www.haaretz.co.il/.premium-1.2062225.

107. Eli Eshed, "*Lahiton*: The Story of a Magazine," *Makor Rishon*, May 19, 2008.

108. *Ma'ariv*, August 2, 1968.

109. *Davar*, July 26, 1968.

110. Nahum Barnea, "This Station Is 'Tasty,' 'Wonderful,' and 'So Thirst Quenching,'" *Davar: Dvar Hashavu'a*, September 19, 1969, 18.

111. *Davar*, January 23, 1970, 27.

112. *Ma'ariv*: *Yamim Veleylot*, July 31, 1970, 5, 33.

113. Ben-Amotz, *I Don't Give a Damn*, 161–62.

114. Ibid., 130–33.

115. Kimmerling, *The Invention and Decline of Israeliness*, chap. 6.

116. Grossman, "A Picture as a Souvenir"; Orna Eilon, "Eye Patch without Restraint," *Haaretz: Musaf*, May 2, 1969, 25.

117. *Slate*, June 11, 2013, http://www.slate.com/articles/arts/tv_club/features/2013/mad_men_season_6/week_10/mad_men_episode_guide_week_10_favors.html.

118. *Ma'ariv*, May 20, 1969. Marlboro ads in the Israeli press mostly featured urban scenes.

119. Nahum Barnea, "The Soldier as a Consumer, Part B: Bread with Everything," *Davar: Dvar Hashavu'a*, April 11, 1969, 8–9, 23.

120. Ro'ey Mendel, "Why Was the War of Attrition Forgotten?," *Ynet*, March 6, 2009, https://www.ynet.co.il/articles/0,7340,L-3680889,00.html.

121. The interview with *L'Express* appeared in *Ma'ariv*, May 19, 1969.

122. Dayan, *Vietnam Diary*, 68. On Dayan's Vietnam "lesson" and the late 1960s economic policy in the occupied territories, see Gazit, *The Carrot and the Stick*, 27–30, 213–34; Dayan, *New Map: Different Relationships*, 128–29.

123. Economic Peace Center, https://www.peacecom.org/en/; also, see Feldman, "Economic Peace."

124. *Ma'ariv*, April 13, 1973.

125. Nathan Alterman, "The Third Israel," *Ma'ariv*, May 9, 1969; Ehud Zmora and Idit Zartal, "Interview with Sapir," *Davar: Dvar Hashavu'a*, February 9, 1973, 7.

126. *Davar*, February 2, 1973.

127. Greenberg, "Pinchas Sapir and the 'Occupied Territories,'" 281–84.

128. "Independence Day Interview with Golda Meir," *Lamerhav*, April 22, 1969.

129. Eban, *Personal Witness*, 464.

130. Hanoch Levin: Homepage, https://www.hanochlevin.com/texts/1653.

Chapter 2: Keeping Up with the Cohens

1. Ruth Bondi, "Valley of the Dolls," *Davar: Dvar Hashavu'a*, December 15, 1972, 3; on Barbie's first arrival in Israel, Nurit Halif, "Barbie in Israel," *Haaretz: Musaf*, January 13, 1967, 23. The American dream for Israeli boys were action heroes: Popeye, Tarzan, and Tex. Tamar Meroz, "Popeye King of Israel," *Haaretz: Musaf*, August 6, 1971, 16–17, 34.

2. See, for example, a series of articles by Roman Priester in *Haaretz*'s weekly magazine, "The New Rich: Society of Plenty in Israel," January 15, 1971, 5–7; "A Deluge of Temptations," January 22, 1971, 8–10; "The Ambitious," January 29, 1971, 12–13.

3. Lammfromm and Tsoref, *Levi Eshkol*, 501–2.

4. On consumer activism see, for instance, Trentmann, *The Making of the Consumer*. On citizenship and consumption, see Cohen, *A Consumer's Republic*. On the use of patriotism and national symbols in commercial ads in early 1950s Israel, see Helman, *Consumer Culture and Leisure in the Young State of Israel*, 42–58.

5. Segev, *1967*, 45–46.

6. Benjamin Aktzin, "Fool's Paradise," *Ma'ariv*, January 30, 1970.

7. Ibid.; Also, Benjamin Aktzin, "Government Must Save," *Davar*, September 26, 1971.

8. Aryeh Eliav, "A Proposal for the Labor Party's Platform," *Davar*, June 29, 1973.

9. *Yedioth Ahronoth*, August 13, 1971.

10. *Ma'ariv*, July 19, 1970.

11. Y. Taria, "The Austerity Ideal and the Road to Hell," *Davar*, July 6, 1970.

12. Idit Zartal, "Price Hikes," *Davar: Dvar Hashavu'a*, January 5, 1973, 6.

13. *Ma'ariv*, October 4, 1973.

14. Levi Yitzhak Hayerushalmi, "'Follow Me' Also on the Economic Front," *Ma'ariv*, July 8, 1970.

15. *Herut*, September 5, 1965.

16. *Davar*, September 19, 1971.

17. Ibid.; Yoel Marcus, "The Sweet Life with the Expense Account," *Haaretz: Musaf*, March 12, 1971, 10–11.

18. Marcuse, *One-Dimensional Man*; Galbraith, *The Affluent Society*; Baudrillard, *The Consumer Society*; Horowitz, *The Anxieties of Affluence*.

19. Veblen, *The Theory of the Leisure Class*.

20. *Ma'ariv*, March 23, 1972.

21. *Ma'ariv*, July 3, 1970.

22. Ruth Bondi, "All Israel Are Linked To Each Other," *Davar: Dvar Hashavu'a*, December 22, 1972, 35.

23. Ibid.

24. On the "sucker" theme in Israeli culture and identity, see Roniger and Feiga, "The Frayer [Sucker] Culture and Israeli Identity."

25. Eli Eyal, "Poverty and Deprivation—In Money, Services, and Status," *Ma'ariv*, August 4, 1972.

26. Ibid.

27. *Davar*, October 17, 1969.

28. Ruth Bondi, "Five Minutes before the Deluge," *Davar: Dvar Hashavu'a*, December 12, 1969, 8–9, 34.

29. Aktzin, "Fool's Paradise," 18; Shmuel Schnitzer, "End of Season Sale," *Ma'ariv*, August 15, 1969.

30. *Davar*, July 6, 1970.

31. *Davar*, May 31, 1972.
32. *Davar*, September 19, 1971; *Davar*, May 31, 1972.
33. On consumer activism in the United States, see Glickman, *Buying Power*. On consumer associations and professionals in the United States and Europe, see Chatriot, *Expert Consumer*.
34. Prime Minister's Office: Israel Consumer Council (ICC). Israel State Archives (ISA), 7328/5-א.
35. Foreign Ministry: International Organization of Consumer Unions (IOCU). ISA, 2897/3-עץ.
36. Ministry of Trade and Industry: ICC. ISA, 46651/19-לב.
37. Mayer, *The Consumer Movement*, 25–33.
38. Israel Consumer Council—Main Office. ISA, 6220/19-לב.
39. *Ma'ariv*, January 16, 1967.
40. *Haaretz*, n.d., in ICC. ISA, 46651/14-לב. In response to *Haaretz*, January 30, 1967.
41. *Yedioth Ahronoth*, January 9, 1967; *Haaretz*, January 9, 1967; *Lamerhav*, January 12, 1967. ICC. ISA, 46651/14-לב.
42. *Jerusalem Post*, February 19, 1967.
43. *Hayom*, December 26, 1966; *Haaretz*, January 17, 1967; *Yedioth Ahronoth*, December 25, 1966.
44. "Report on the ICC Activities for 1967," The Office of the Minister Shulamit Aloni, January 2, 1968. ISA, 7250/11-ג.
45. Ministry of Trade and Industry: ICC. ISA, 46651/18-לב.
46. "Who Is Afraid of Shulamit Aloni," *Ha'olam Hazeh*, September 10, 1969, 13. Another contender for the title "The Israeli Ralph Nader" was journalist Baruch Nadel, see *Yedioth Ahronoth*, September 20, 1970.
47. *Haaretz: Musaf*, December 12, 1969, 36.
48. Kruk, "A New Profession in Israel—Product Design."
49. *Al Hamishmar*, January 29, 1967; *Lamerhav*, January 26, 1967.
50. Histadrut. Organization for Consumer Protection. "Consumer Bulletin," no. 2 (March 1967).
51. Ministry of Trade and Industry: ICC. ISA, 46651/17-לב.
52. Shraga Hargil, "Do You Know What You Have Purchased," *Att*, April 1967, 70–71.
53. *Davar*, December 12, 1968.
54. "Yosef Burg to M. Arnon, Cabinet Secretary," August 27, 1969. Prime Minister Office: ICC. ISA, 7328/5-א.
55. *Ma'ariv*, June 14, 1970.
56. *Ma'ariv*, February 16, 1970.
57. *Ma'ariv*, January 29, 1973.
58. *Ma'ariv*, January 30, 1973; *Davar*, January 30, 1973.
59. "Cleaning Week" campaigns in major cities began in the 1950s. The Central Zionist Archives, http://www.zionistarchives.org.il/Pages/SpringCleaning.aspx.
60. The Association for Better Housing. ISA, 5640/8-לב.

61. *Davar*, June 19, 1964.
62. *Herut*, July 1, 1964.
63. Ibid.
64. *Ma'ariv*, August 9, 1964.
65. *Herut*, July 1, 1964
66. *Davar*, June 19, 1964; *Davar*, December 27, 1965. On Orientalist representations of Mizrahi immigrants' domestic life, see Chacham, *Home within Home*, chap. 6.
67. *Ma'ariv*, December 21, 1964; *Herut*, December 29, 1964; *Ma'ariv Lano'ar*, April 18, 1967, 4–5.
68. *Haboker*, June 15, 1965.
69. *Ma'ariv*, June 8, 1965.
70. *Lamerhav*, February 10, 1965.
71. *Herut*, April 1, May 18, 1965.
72. *Herut*, October 28, 1964.
73. For example, journalist Abraham Rotem's column "Tel Aviv in Black and White," *Ma'ariv*, April 22, 1970; also see Roman Priester, "Quality of Life in 25-Year-Old Israel," *Haaretz: Musaf*, March 2, 1973, 9–11, 37. On pollution see, for example, Ami Shamir, "The Pollution Deluge and the Dam of Words," *Haaretz: Musaf*, June 23, 1972, 8–9; Uzi Benziman, "Ecology and Politics," *Haaretz: Musaf*, October 5, 1973, 7–9, October 12, 14–15, 29; Michael Shachar, "Pollution," *Bamahane*, February 9, 1971, 6–7.
74. Ya'akov Ha'elyon, "Dirty, Dirty, It Feels Like Crying," *Ma'ariv*, April 15, 1970.
75. *Davar*, June 28, 1971.
76. *Davar*, April 9, 1973.
77. *Davar*, December 25, 1970; also, see, Tuvia Carmel, "A City Suffocating with Love," *Haaretz: Musaf*, January 5, 1973, 7–9; Yair Kottler, "Manhattan in Jerusalem," *Haaretz: Musaf*, March 2, 1973, 12–14; Kottler, "Flying Towers," *Haaretz: Musaf*, March 9, 1973, 12–14.
78. *Ma'ariv*, January 15, 1971.
79. *Ma'ariv*, March 10, 1965.
80. *Ma'ariv*, November 4, 1970.
81. *Ma'ariv*, January 28, 1969.
82. *Ma'ariv*, November 16, 1960.
83. *Davar*, October 29, 1969, 3. In Rishon Letzion the JC demonstrated in front of city hall in opposition to building a sewage plant in nearby Gan Raveh. *Ma'ariv*, June 5, 1968.
84. *Ma'ariv*, November 23, 1961.
85. *Ma'ariv*, December 28, 1961.
86. *Ma'ariv*, November 6, 1963.
87. *Ma'ariv*, December 23, 1965.
88. *Ma'ariv*, July 11, 1960.
89. De Grazia, *Irresistible Empire*, 7.
90. *Davar*, September 7, 1972.
91. *Davar: Dvar Hashavu'a*, June 12, 1970, 25.

92. *Haaretz: Musaf*, May 7, 1971, 20; July 16, 1971, 21.

93. *Hedva veShlomik*, directed by Shmuel Imberman, script by Orna Spector and Yonathan Geffen (1971, Globus-United, Israel, 2005), DVD.

94. Offri Ilany, "The Cult of 'Hedva and Shlomik': 71% Rating," *Haaretz*, July 27, 2009, https://www.haaretz.co.il/gallery/television/2009-07-27/ty-article/0000017f -f857-d2d5-a9ff-f8df14d20001.

95. *Davar*, July 16, 1971.

96. Mann and Gon-Gross, *Galei Tzahal*, 67–79.

97. Doron Rosenblum, "Merchants' Culture," *Davar: Dvar Hashavu'a*, July 9, 1971, 13.

98. Gardiner, *Critiques of Everyday Life*, 94.

99. Uri Keisari, "Idols, Their Servants, and Their Smashers," *Ma'ariv: Yamim Veleylot*, February 25, 1972, 14–15.

100. *Davar*, March 14, 19, 1982.

101. Baruch, *Media*.

Chapter 3: Electioneering and the Feedback Loop

1. Interview with Brune.

2. *Ma'ariv*, March 13, 1973.

3. *Davar*, June 26, 1973.

4. Eleonora Lev, "Profile of the Month: Chich," *Att*, February 1974, 28–31.

5. *Yedioth Ahronoth*, August 28, 1973.

6. *Davar*, August 3, 12, 1973.

7. Bella Almog, "Stars at Home," *Yedioth Ahronoth: 7 Yamim*, August 17, 1973, 16–18; Doron Rosenblum, "Tea and Politics," *Haaretz: Musaf*, August 10, 1973, 7–8, 41.

8. Brune was able to force the party to run his own campaign but was not allowed to select candidates for the Likud's list.

9. *Ha'olam Hazeh*, July 11, 1973, 3, 37; *Davar*, August 12, 1973.

10. *Yedioth Ahronoth*, September 21, 1973.

11. *Yedioth Ahronoth*, January 27, 1974; *Davar*, December 24, 27, 1973.

12. *Davar*, December 28, 1973.

13. *Davar*, August 10; *Davar*, December 28, 1973.

14. *Yedioth Ahronoth*, January 27, 1974.

15. *Davar*, December 20, 1973.

16. *Yedioth Ahronoth*, May 12, 1974; Roman Priester, "A Finger on the Pulse," *Haaretz: Musaf*, August 17, 1973, 7–9.

17. *Ma'ariv*, February 6, 1974.

18. *Davar*, June 21, 1973; *Davar*, July 1, 1973.

19. Silvie Keshet, "They Call Me Chich," *Yedioth Ahronoth*, June 1, 1973.

20. *Ma'ariv*, February 12, 1974.

21. Doron Rosenblum, "A Day in the Life of Shlomo Lahat (Chich)," *Haaretz: Musaf*, February 15, 1974, 25.

22. *Ma'ariv*, February 8, 1974.

23. *Yedioth Ahronoth*, March 13, 1974.

24. *Ma'ariv*, February 8, 1974. By late February, Lahat met 2,400 employees. *Ma'ariv*, February 28, 1974.

25. Dov Goldstein, "Cup of Coffee with Shlomo (Chich) Lahat," *Ma'ariv: Yamim Veleylot*, January 11, 1974, 6–7.

26. *Ibid.*, 6.

27. *Ma'ariv*, August 10, 1973.

28. Frenkel, "The Politics of Translation," 284, 292. On the introduction of American management techniques and ideologies to Israel, see Frenkel, "The Invisible History of the Visible Hand." On the American effort to indoctrinate Israeli economic thinking in the 1950s, see Molcho, "Capitalism and the 'American Way' in Israel." On continuities between British colonial and American management instruction see, Frenkel and Shenhav, "From Americanization to Colonization."

29. *Davar*, October 8, 1964.

30. *Davar*, November 14, 1963.

31. *Davar*, November 29, 1965. The first lab was convened in 1962 at the Education Department of the Hebrew University. *Davar*, November 26, 1969.

32. Ibid.

33. Abraham Peleg, "Shortcut to Human Relations," *Ma'ariv: Yamim Veleylot*, December 11, 1970, 6.

34. Israel Segal, "Human Relations in a Lab," *Haaretz: Musaf*, November 13, 1970, 17.

35. Ibid., 32.

36. French and Golomb, "A Report."

37. Worley, "Robert Tannenbaum."

38. Tannenbaum, "Consulting and Being in Israel," 29; Shalev, "Documentation and Assessment of a Community Renewal Project."

39. *Davar*, January 17, 1971. Psychologist Lawrence Kohlberg's visit to Kibbutz Sasa in 1969 proved essential to his research on moral development. Power, Higgins, and Kohlberg, *Lawrence Kohlberg's Approach to Moral Education*, 37–48.

40. *Ma'ariv*, October 17, 1969.

41. *Ma'ariv*, September 8, 1970.

42. *Haaretz: Musaf*, October 18, 1968, 8–9, 38.

43. *Haaretz: Musaf*, January 5, 1973, 23.

44. *Davar*, October 6, 1972.

45. Paula Hirth, "Who Does What to Whom and Why?," *Haaretz: Musaf*, December 17, 1971, 16.

46. Ibid.; Nili Tal, "Yossi and Tzipora, Aliza and Uri," *Haaretz: Musaf*, July 23, 1971, 24–25.

47. Irit Shamgar, "How to Get Enthusiastic in 14 Lessons and 4,500 Liras?," *Ma'ariv*, January 19, 1979; *Davar*, August 1, 1979; *Yedioth Ahronoth*, January 25, 1973.

48. *Ma'ariv: Yamim Veleylot*, March 3, 1967, 27; *Davar*, July 1, 1968; Tamar Meroz, "May You Be Thinner," *Haaretz: Musaf*, June 13, 1969, 14–15, 20; *Davar*, July 2, 1973.

49. Converse, *Survey Research in the United States*; Herbst, *Numbered Voices*; Hillygus, "The Evolution of Election Polling"; Lilleker and Scullion, *Voters or Consumers*.

50. Roman Priester, "The Riddle of Public Opinion," *Haaretz: Musaf*, August 9, 1968, 6
51. *Ma'ariv*, June 25, 1970.
52. *Davar*, October 20, 1965; Arie Avneri, "How to Be Successful in Business with Trying," *Bamahane*, September 25, 1969, 10–11.
53. Elon, *The Israelis*, 311.
54. Priester, "A Finger on the Pulse."
55. *Ma'ariv*, November 3, 1965; *Lamerhav*, November 12, 1965.
56. *Davar*, September 13, 1973.
57. Arbel, "The American Soldier in Jerusalem," 98, 125.
58. Weimann, *Public Opinion Research in Israel*, 120; Gratch, *Twenty-Five Years of Social Research in Israel*; Stone and Troen, "Early Social Survey Research in and on Israel."
59. Weimann, *Public Opinion Research in Israel*, 47.
60. Arbel, "'The American Soldier' in Jerusalem," chap. 2; Arbel, "Fear in Hebrew."
61. Weimann, *Public Opinion Research in Israel*, 65.
62. Anderson, *Imagined Communities*.
63. Weimann, *Public Opinion Research in Israel*, 132.
64. Ibid., 282.
65. Ibid., 183, 188.
66. Ibid., 161.
67. Ibid., 71.
68. *Hatzofeh*, May 18, 1952.
69. On "morale" as a technology of control, see Ussishkin, *Morale: A Modern British History*.
70. *Haaretz*, February 18, 1973.
71. Lev, "Chich," 28–31.
72. Dov Goldstein, "Cup of Coffee with Yitzhak Rabin," *Ma'ariv: Yamim Veleylot*, April 13, 1973, 9.
73. Ibid.
74. Nixon also permitted Israel to continue its nuclear program largely uninterrupted, a topic of major concern for the two previous American administrations.
75. Dan Pattir, "Yitzhak Rabin's Direct Line," *Davar: Dvar Hashavu'a*, March 16, 1973, 5–7.
76. Interview with Eran.
77. Rabin, *Memoirs*, 221–22.
78. Bitan, *Political Diary*, 274.
79. Nixon and his national security advisor Henry Kissinger strongly opposed the amendment that in their view threatened to jeopardize their policy of détente and asked Israel to distance itself from this initiative.
80. *New York Times*, October 15, 1973. Interview with Eran.
81. Kochavi, *Nixon and Israel*, 2. Meir sent Nixon a telegram congratulating him for his speech on Vietnam. State of Israel Government Press Office. Press Bulletin, November 18, 1969. *Ma'ariv* Archive.
82. Kochavi, *Nixon and Israel*, 24.

83. Rabin, *Full-Time Wife*, 168.

84. Rabin, *Memoirs*, 130; "Rabin to Moshe Bitan," April 9, 1968. Bitan, *Political Diary*, 67; also, see Shlomo Argov's (Rabin's no. 2 in the embassy) assessment that Rabin developed a sweeping rejection of anything that transpired with the United States during Johnson's administration. "Shlomo Argov to Moshe Bitan," March 18, 1969. Ibid., 186.

85. Rabin, *Memoirs*, 131–32.

86. Ibid., 133.

87. Interview with Pattir; interview with Eran.

88. *Washington Post*, June 11, 1972. For Rabin's denial, see *Washington Post*, June 12, 1972; also, see *Ma'ariv*, June 12, 13, 15, 18, 20, 1972; *Al Hamishmar*, June 15, 18, 1972; *Davar*, June 12, 16, 18, 1972.

89. *Washington Post*, June 15, 1972.

90. Amnon Rubinstein, "Queen of the Jews," *Haaretz*, March 6, 1973.

91. Rabin, *Memoirs*, 223–27; Fischbach, *The Movement and the Middle East*.

92. Interview with Pattir.

93. Rabin, *Memoir*, 168; Bitan, *Political Diary*, 292.

94. Rabinovich, *Yitzhak Rabin*, 92.

95. Interview with Eran.

96. Eli Ashkenazi, "More than a Socialist or a Capitalist: The Right Man in the Right Time," *Walla!*, October 31, 2020, https://news.walla.co.il/item/3395554; Offer Aderet, "Beilin: I Don't Know What Was Rabin's Vision," *Haaretz*, October 23, 2015, https://www.haaretz.co.il/news/education/2015-10-23/ty-article/.premium/0000017f-f909-d47e-a37f-f93d94470000.

97. *Haaretz*, May 9, 1974.

98. Ansky, *The Selling of the Likud*; Ram, *The Globalization of Israel*, chap. 4; Aronoff, "The 'Americanization' of Israeli Politics."

Chapter 4: Technology Transfer: The Phantom Jet

1. Weizman, *On Eagles' Wings*, 255–56. The episode took place in July 1958. *IAF Magazine* 77, November 1968, 13.

2. In the late 1940s, American (mostly Jewish) volunteers were crucial in the establishment of the IAF, but after the war most of them returned to the United States.

3. *Yedioth Ahronoth*, September 7, 1969.

4. Amir Oren, "The Best Airplane in the World," *Bamahane*, May 16, 1970, 44.

5. [Patrick] Oliphant "Phantoms and Bargains," *Time*, January 17, 1972, 27.

6. *Haaretz*, February 18, 1972.

7. Amos Kenan, "The Ghosts Arrived," *Yedioth Ahronoth: Musaf Shabbat*, December 3, 1971, 17.

8. *Yedioth Ahronoth*, June 30, 1971.

9. *IAF Magazine* 70/171, September 1989, 25.

10. *Davar*, May 5, September 2, 1969; Kanovsky, *The Economic Impact of the Six-Day War*, 600.

11. *Ma'ariv*, August 26, 1969.

12. *Yedioth Ahronoth*, August 2, 1970.

13. The two children's letter is featured in *IAF Magazine* 80, December 1969, 44; on other children's initiatives for the Phantom drive, see *Haaretz: Musaf*, July 25, 1969, 14.

14. *Ma'ariv*, November 19, August 3, 1969.

15. *Davar*, January 1, 1969.

16. D[oron] Rosenblum, "Anatomy of a Phantom Squadron—1971," *IAF Magazine* 85, August 1971, 46.

17. Ben-Zvi, *Johnson and the Politics of Arms Sales to Israel*, 33–36.

18. Bronfeld, "From Skyhawk to Phantom."

19. "Special Issue: Twenty Year Anniversary for the Phantom," *IAF Magazine* 70/171, September 1989.

20. Interview with Colonel (ret.) Geva; interview with Colonel (ret.) Segal.

21. Ibid.

22. Interview with Limor.

23. Interview with Brigadier General (ret.) Eini.

24. Shapira, *Alone in the Sky*, 297; interview with Brigadier General (ret.) Shavit.

25. Shmuel Hetz, "Kurnass Crews Report no. 3," May 2, 1969. Air Dept. Equipment Dept. 5. 122–470. IDF Archives.

26. Lieblich, *My Ehud*, 155; interview with Colonel (ret.) Harpaz.

27. Interview with Lieutenant Colonel (ret.) Sarig.

28. Hetz, "Kurnass Crews Report no. 3." Navigators traveled to Davis-Monthan AFB in Tucson, Arizona, to study the airplane's combat systems.

29. Interview with Lieutenant Colonel (ret.) Yair.

30. Lieblich, *My Ehud*, 144, 146, 180.

31. Shapira, *Alone in the Sky*, 271.

32. Michel, "The Revolt of the Majors," 196–97; Sion, "Mutuality in the Dissemination of Military Innovations."

33. Interview with Brigadier General (ret.) Yaron.

34. Interview with Major General (ret.) Ivry.

35. Shapira, *Alone in the Sky*, 228; Ronen (Pekker), *Hawk in the Sky*, 89; Spector, *Loud and Clear*, 135, 208, 214–16.

36. *IAF Magazine* 82, July 1970, 8.

37. Ibid.

38. Shapira, *Hawk in the Sky*, 298.

39. Interview with Harpaz; also, see Danny Shalom, *Phantoms over Cairo*, 1:392.

40. Ronen, *Hawk in the Sky*, 309.

41. Shiff, *Wings over Suez*, 162.

42. Interview with Harpaz. In 1958, the Navy selected McDonnell's F-4H Phantom II over its competition, Vought's F8U-3Crusader III, despite the latter's superior speed and maneuverability, because the Navy preferred a two-seat, two-engine aircraft. Bugos, *Engineering the F-4 Phantom II*, 98. For the IDF definition of the "guy in the back seat," see "Colonel Aaron Yoely to Wing 4 Commander," August 24, 1969. Wing 4 Headquarters. 43–597/1971, Kurnass File, IDF Archives.

43. For structural explanations, see interviews with Ivry, Shavit, and Yaron.
44. *Ma'ariv*: *Yamim Veleylot*, September 12, 1969, 2.
45. Oval 726–1, May 19, 1972, *White House Tapes*. Richard Nixon Presidential Library and Museum, Yorba Linda, California, https://www.nixonlibrary.gov/media/33342.
46. Interview with Yair.
47. Uri Dan, "The Phantom Became a Reality," *Ma'ariv*: *Yamim Veleylot*, September 12, 1969, 2.
48. Interview with Colonel (ret.) Kaplan.
49. Interview with Segal.
50. Interview with Harpaz; "Rami Harpaz to Wing 4 Commander," Kurnass's Operational Requirements: Squadron's Proposals for Alterations, October 5, 1969, 597/1971 File 4. IDF Archives.
51. Spector, *Loud and Clear*, 173–74, 191.
52. Interview with Segal.
53. *Ma'ariv*, July 19, 1972.
54. Shalom, *Phantoms over Cairo*, 1:147.
55. Ibid., 150. Firms included IAI, Elta, Tadiran, and Elisra/Elbit.
56. Steinberg, "Technology, Weapons, and Industrial Development," 390, 392–93.
57. Bugos, *Engineering the F-4 Phantom II*, 191.
58. Ibid., 212.
59. Ibid., 3.
60. Interview with Yair.
61. Furman, *Alef-Alef*, 294–95. Spector, *Loud and Clear*, 230.
62. Interview with Harpaz.
63. Lieblich, *My Ehud*, 158.
64. Ibid. In the early years of Israel the idea of "professionalism" was associated with British colonial rule and was viewed with suspicion. Frenkel, "The Politics of Translation," 287.
65. Interview with Yair.
66. Interview with Colonel (ret.) Gordon; Bugos, *Engineering the F-4 Phantom II*, 107
67. Interviews with Segal and Geva.
68. *Yedioth Ahronoth*, May 10, 1970.
69. Interview with Harpaz; "Brochure to Commemorate the Reunion of the Phantom Delegation and Its American Instructors" (Privately published, 2009).
70. Bugos, *Engineering the F-4 Phantom II*, 7, 55–62, 205–10.
71. Interview with Segal.
72. Interview with Limor.
73. Spector, *Loud and Clear*, 278.
74. Interview with Lieutenant Colonel (ret.) Pridor; Harel, *We Have Great Power*, 183.
75. Interview with Pridor.
76. Harel, *We Have Great Power*, 252.

77. Ibid., 235. On the Israeli involvement with Rand, see *Bamahane*, January 13, 1970, 20–21; "Interview with Yehezkel Dror," *Bamahane*, February 23, 1972, 24–25.

78. Interview with Pridor.

79. Z[e'ev] Shiff, "America," *IAF Magazine* 83, November 70, 41; "Wing 4: Kurnass Absorption: Internal Instructions," Aug. 1969." Kurnass Aircraft, 62–598/1971, IAF, IDF Archives; Sapir, *Hayesh Hagadol*, 500.

80. Interview with Harpaz.

81. Shalom, *Phantoms over Cairo*, 1:472, 497.

82. Lieutenant Colonel M. Ronen, "Kurnass: Preliminary Maintenance Instructions," September 5, 1969. Kurnass File Matzad 5, 7/15-9/24, 1969, 123–470, 1978, IDF Archives.

83. Shalom, *Phantoms over Cairo*, 1:482.

84. Adamsky, *Operation Kavkaz*, 61–80.

85. Ginor and Remez, *The Soviet-Israeli War*.

86. Shiff, *Wings over Suez*, 190–91. Adamsky takes a more cautious view of the impact of technology on strategic decisions. Adamsky, *Operation Kavkaz*, 66–67.

87. Shalom, *Phantoms over Cairo*, 1:539. Additional Soviet arsenal included shoulder-fired Strela missiles and Shilka anti-aircraft guns.

88. Moshe Dayan predicted a coming "electronic summer" in March 1970. *Lamerhav*, March 22, 1970.

89. Interviews with Shavit and Spector.

90. Spector, *Loud and Clear*, 197; Interviews with Shavit and Ivry.

91. Halpern and Lapidot, *G Suit*, 67; interview with Eini.

92. Shalom, *Phantoms over Cairo*, 2:967.

93. Interview with Brigadier General (ret.) Bareket.

94. Interview with Ivry.

95. Spector, *Loud and Clear*, 195.

96. Interview with Major General (ret.) Ben-Nun.

97. Iftach Spector, "Kurnass, Versatility, and the Employment of Air Power at the Conclusion of the War of Attrition" (unpublished paper, 2005). [Hebrew]

98. Spector, "The Phantom's Fall," 34–39.

99. Yonay, *No Margin for Error*, 327; also, see Peled, *Days of Reckoning*, 357; Gordon, *Thirty Hours in October*, 424.

100. Interview with Ivry.

101. *Haaretz*, December 1, 2004; *Yedioth Ahronoth*, October 28, 2003.

102. Weizman, *On Eagles' Wings*, 270.

103. Weizman, *Hollow Land*, 239–44.

Chapter 5: Panthers in Black and White

1. By the summer of 1973 there were plans to add Black actors to the show, but the October war shortened its run. *Ha'olam Hazeh*, June 13, 1973, 21; interview with Almagor.

2. Conventional Jewish taxonomy foregrounds religious practices and distinguishes

European or "Ashkenazi" communities from descendants of Eastern communities (also translatable as "congregations" or "ethnicities") often linked to medieval Spain, hence "Sephardic." By the 1990s, the term "Eastern" (Mizrahi) had acquired a new political valence associated with an emerging progressive identity politics. See Shohat, "The Invention of the Mizrahim."

3. For the globalist approach, see, for example, Katsiaficas, *The Imagination of the New Left*.

4. Slate, introduction to *Black Power beyond Borders*, 5; also, see Mikey Melendez, *We Took the Streets*; Maeda, "Red Panthers, Red Guards, and Chinamen."

5. Established in 1962, Matzpen (or the Israeli Socialist Organization) was a staunchly anti-Zionist group. In 1970, it split three ways. See the documentary film *Matzpen: Anti-Zionist Israelis* (directed by Eran Torbiner; cinematography, Ra'anan Nachmias, 2003), DVD; Yuval-Davis, *Matzpen*; Lutz, "Matzpen." Other small New Left organizations—Siah and, later, Moked—also had links with the Black Panthers. On the Cellar, see *Bamahane*, March 3, 1971; A. Shlush, "The Black Panthers: Report to the Chief Police Commissioner," March 10, 1971. Jerusalem Police: The Black Panthers Files, A. Israel State Archives (ISA), Record Group (RG) 79:412/9.

6. Aaron Bachar, "Conversations in the 'Yellow Teahouse' Gave Birth to the 'Black Panthers,'" *Yedioth Ahronoth*, March 5, 1971; interview with Haim Hanegbi; Vigodar, "Matzpen Movement," 203.

7. *Yedioth Ahronoth*, January 20, 1971.

8. *Al Hamishmar*, January 13, 1971; *Ma'ariv*, January 20, 1971.

9. *Ma'ariv*, January 21, 1971.

10. "Dai" [Enough] [leaflet], Israeli Left Archive (ILA), International Institute of Social History, https://search.iisg.amsterdam/Record/COLL00308/ArchiveContent List.

11. Abraham Turjeman, "Intelligence Report: The Black Panthers," February 23, 1971, Jerusalem Police: The Black Panthers Files, B. ISA, RG 79:412/10.

12. *Haaretz*, March 3, 1971.

13. *Ma'ariv*, March 4, 1971; Bernstein, "The Black Panthers of Israel," 160.

14. Ibid., 159.

15. Lev and Shenhav, "The Construction of the Enemy Within."

16. *Haaretz*, February 1, 1971.

17. *Al Hamishmar*, May 11, 1971

18. *Ma'ariv*, March 7, 11, 1971. A few weeks after their first demonstrations the Panthers had 2,000 registered members and branches in Jerusalem, Tel Aviv, Ashdod, Dimona, Be'er Sheva, Givat Olga, and Kiryat Shmona. Sprinzak, *Politics of De-Legitimation*, 21.

19. On youth in Israel see, for example, Ami Shamir, "Youth without Barricades," *Haaretz: Musaf*, March 24, 1972, 7–9; Yair Kottler, "High Schoolers," *Haaretz: Musaf*, June 30, 1972, 16–17, 25. Zionism partook in the cult of youth but by the 1960s Israeli youth already disappointed the country's elders in their reluctance to participate in na-

tional causes and were dismissed as the "espresso generation." Elmaliach and Kidron, "Between Culture and Politics."

20. Aberjil immediately apologized. Turjeman, "Intelligence Report."

21. *Jerusalem Post*, May 19, 1971. On police brutality, see *Kol Ha'am*, June 3, 1971.

22. *Ma'ariv*, May 20, 1971.

23. Meir explained her quip in a letter she sent to the Histadrut and the Labor Party. *Ma'ariv*, November 7, 1971; Silvi Keshet, "The Panther Hunters," *Yedioth Ahronoth*, May 28, 1971.

24. The Knesset, "Protocol of the Knesset's Committee on Interior Affairs," August 24, 1971. ISA, RG 60:197/7. Other anti-Golda slogans in Panthers' demonstration included "Golda teach us English," "When will Golda dance in Buzaglo's [typical Moroccan name] wedding." Sprinzak, *Politics of De-Legitimation*, 18.

25. The instructions are included in the police publication *Dapei Hasbara*, no. 3, May 1971.

26. Althusser, "Ideology and Ideological State Apparatuses"; also, see Butler, *The Psychic Life of Power*, 106–11, 128–29.

27. *Ma'ariv*, November 4, 1972.

28. "Summary of the Meeting of the Minister of Police with 'Black Panthers' Representatives," May 28, 1971. ISA. On anti-Left sentiments among the Panthers, see *Ma'ariv*, May 5, 1971; also, see the movement's publication *Hapanter Hashahor* (The Black Panther), August 11, 1972, ILA.

29. Bernstein, "Black Panthers," 247.

30. Ibid., 205.

31. Baruch Nadel, "Screwed for Life," *Yedioth Ahronoth: 7 Yamim*, March 12, 1971, 11.

32. Hadash is a descendant of the Israeli Communist Party. By recruiting Biton, it sought, unsuccessfully, to make inroads into the poor Mizrahi population. Shas is the Worldwide Sephardic Association of Torah Keepers.

33. The report claimed that poverty rates in Israel are not substantially different than in the United States. Roter and Shamai, "Patterns of Poverty in Israel," 25.

34. On the new social programs, see Uzi Benziman, "Israel Is Getting Acquainted with the Panthers," *Haaretz*, September 19, 1971; Hofnong, *Protest and Butter*; Gal, *Social Security in Israel*; Doron and Kramer, *The Welfare State in Israel*; Michal Koreh demonstrates that social security taxation increased substantially a year *before* the Panthers' eruption in response not to social pressure but to fiscal considerations such as market stability and the balance of payments. Koreh, "The Golden Age of the Welfare State in Israel."

35. *Yedioth Ahronoth*, November 7, 1971.

36. "The Association for Civil Rights in Israel: The First Fifty Years," https://www.jubilee.acri.org.il/item/item1-1. The Panthers also inspired the Young Couples Movement that sent families to squat in apartments built for Russian immigrants.

37. *Tel Aviv Magazine*, October 7, 2005; also see *Ha'olam Hazeh*, March 3, 1971, 23. Bernstein points out that, at first, "Black Panthers" was a term of reference. The group

said they intended to be like the American Panthers, but community workers and journalists were quick to adopt the moniker. Bernstein, "Black Panthers," 157.

38. *Haaretz*, March 11, 17, 1971.

39. "Israel's Other War," *Time*, June 21, 1971, 30.

40. *Hapanter Hashahor*, November 9, 1972, ILA.

41. See, for instance, Epstein, "Open Letter to the Black Panther Party." On African Americans' identification with the Palestinian cause, see Fischbach, *Black Power and Palestine*.

42. Seymour Martin Lipset, "Antisemitism from Right to Left," *Haaretz: Musaf*, January 15, 1971, 12–13, 40. On the *David Frost Show* (April 1970), Carmichael named Adolf Hitler as the white man he admired the most.

43. *Lamerhav*, March 3, 1971.

44. *Yedioth Ahronoth*, March 5, 1971; *Lamerhav*, May 5, 1971.

45. *Ha'olam Hazeh*, March 3, 1971, 22–23.

46. *Ma'ariv*, May 26, 1971. For another plea for a name change, see *Ma'ariv*, May 29, 1971.

47. *Ma'ariv*, March 5, 1971.

48. *Ma'ariv*, June 1, 1971.

49. *Ma'ariv*, July 18, 1971.

50. *Davar*, May 28, 1971.

51. *Ma'ariv*, April 23, 1962; *Lamerhav*, September 16, 1960; *Davar*, September 16, 1960.

52. *Haaretz*, January 18, 1965; *Haboker*, January 18, 22, 1965; *Ma'ariv Lano'ar*, January 26, 1965, 16.

53. *Ha'olam Hazeh*, July 29, 1964. On Zionism as a project of Westernization, see Khazzoom, *Shifting Ethnic Boundaries and Inequality in Israel*.

54. *Yedioth Ahronoth*, June 1, 1971.

55. See Avineri, "University Protest Movements and Their Implications for the Jewish Communities"; Ze'ev Laqueur, "Slim Chances of Dialogue between Israelis and the American New Left," *Ma'ariv*, October 16, 1970; Raphael Rotstein, "The Dybbuk of the Jewish New Left in the U.S.," *Haaretz: Musaf*, June 12, 1970, 5–7, 34; Roni Eshel, "The Problem: How to Tame the Panthers," *Ma'ariv*, November 23, 1970; Eliezer Livneh, "Following the Black Panther," *Davar*, January 16, 1970.

56. Avineri, "Israel: Two Nations?," in Curtis and Chertoff, *Israel*, 181.

57. *New York Times Magazine*, September 12, 1971.

58. Philip Ben, "The 'Panthers'' Riots Damage Israel's Reputation in the U.S.," *Ma'ariv*, May 24, 1971.

59. *Ma'ariv*, June 1, 1971.

60. Ibid.

61. Myrdal, *An American Dilemma*.

62. Seymour Martin Lipset, "The Israeli Dilemma," in Curtis and Chertoff, *Israel*, 349–60.

63. Judith Miller, "Israel's Black Panthers," *The Progressive*, March 1972, 36–40.

64. Leibovitz, *Aliya*, 133.

65. On Naomi Kies, see Kaye/Kantrowitz and Klepfisz, *The Tribe of Dina*, 198–99; Y. Ben-Aaron, "Dr. Kies's Complaint," May 11, 1971. ISA, RG 79:412/9; Bernstein, "Black Panthers," 171–72.

66. Ibid., 208.

67. *Ma'ariv*, July 18, 1971; *Al Hamishmar*, July 30, 1971; Bernstein, "Black Panthers," 106–7; interview with Shemesh.

68. *Ma'ariv*, May 20, 1971. Social cleavages in Israel also drew the attention of CIA analysts. See Central Intelligence Agency. Directorate of Intelligence. "Intelligence Memorandum: Israel: Problems behind the Battle Lines," May 10, 1972, no. 0864/72.

69. "Soviet Union: Limited Leniency," *Time*, January 11, 1971, 19.

70. *Al Hamishmar*, January 13, 1971. In 1969, soon after the Ba'ath Party assumed power, nine Iraqi Jews were executed as Zionist spies.

71. *Ma'ariv*, May 26, 1971. By May 1971, three different Panther groups attempted to register formally as nonprofit organizations.

72. *Davar*, November 4, 1971. Interview with Charlie Biton; Abraham Turjeman, "The Black Panthers' Travel to Italy," September 30, 1971. ISA, RG 79:412/10.

73. *Dvar Hapanterim Hashhorim* (The Black Panthers' bulletin), June 1971, 6, ILA.

74. Lev and Shenhav, "Don't Say Worker—But Panther!," 144.

75. Flyer for the August 3, 1971, White and Blue Panthers Demonstration, ILA.

76. *Ha'olam Hazeh*, September 17 (3–7), October 8 (3–5), and October 29 (3–5), 1953.

77. Frankel, "The Politics of the Radical Analogy."

78. Interview with Shemesh. Charlie Biton named his daughter Angela in tribute to Davis. Interview with Biton.

79. Martin, "From Negro to Black to African American."

80. Daniel Dagan, "Begin Asked the 'Panthers' to Change Their Name," *Ma'ariv*, May 26, 1971. The moniker "Black Jewish Lions" was taken by a rival group in Tel Aviv. *Ma'ariv*, May 27, 1971.

81. Hanoch Bartov, "Who Is Marginal Here?," *Ma'ariv*, March 8, 1971; also see Uri Keisari, "Hellenists of a New Kind," *Haaretz*, March 12, 1971.

82. Knesset Debates, Seventh Knesset, Second Session, vol. 61, 2734.

83. Bernstein, "Black Panthers," 179.

84. *Dvar Hapanterim Hashhorim*, June 1971, ILA. The Panthers never added "Israel" to their formal title.

85. Bernstein, "Black Panthers," 171.

86. See, for instance, Rogin, *Blackface, White Noise*.

87. Roni Armon, "Interview with Reuven Aberjil," in *The Black Panthers Today: Reuven Aberjil Speaks* [compact disc]. Israel, Salon Mazal, n.d.

88. *Haaretz*, March 7, 1971.

89. Bernstein, "Black Panthers," 201. On early Israeli television coverage of impoverished communities, see Chetrit, *The Mizrahi Struggle in Israel*, 129.

90. "Demonstration in Favor of Changing the Name of Zion Square" (flier), ILA.

91. Bernstein, "Black Panthers," 193. *Ma'ariv*, January 20, 1971; Avneri, *The Social Welfare Pioneer*, 336.

92. Bernstein, "Black Panthers," appendix, 390.
93. Lev and Shenhav, "The Construction of the Enemy Within," 147.
94. Flier for the August 3, 1971, White and Blue Panthers Demonstration, ILA.
95. Geula Cohen, "We Do Not Support Violence," *Ma'ariv: Yamim Veleylot*, July 2, 1971, 23–24.
96. Kahane arrived on September 12, 1971, but opened the first chapter of the JDL in Jerusalem earlier in the year. *Haaretz*, March 19, 1971.
97. Dolgin, *Jewish Identity and the JDL*, 37–38, 115; Sandquist, *Strangers in the Land*, 358.
98. Dolgin, *Jewish Identity*, 160.
99. Quoted in Magid, *Meir Kahane*, 83.
100. Sprinzak, *The Ascendance of Israel's Radical Right*, 55; Beckerman, *When They Come for Us*, 230. On the COINTELPRO scheme, see Alcalay, "Memory/Imagination/Resistance," 853–55.
101. Sprinzak, *The Ascendance of Israel's Radical Right*, 241.
102. Ibid., 238.
103. The police forced a rapprochement between the two groups as a condition for the release of the detainees. Interview with Shemesh.
104. Interview with Almagor; also see, Hilo Glazer, "Bring the Day: 40 Years to the Musical *Don't Call Me Black!*," *Makor Rishon* (NRG), https://www.makorrishon.co.il/nrg/online/47/ART2/389/899.html.
105. *Al Hamishmar*, September 13, 1972.
106. *Haaretz*, June 30, 1971.
107. *Al Hamishmar*, July 27, 1972. See also, *Yedioth Ahronoth*, August 29, 1972.
108. The Mizrahi Democratic Rainbow—New Discourse. http://www.ha-keshet.org.il/.

Chapter 6: American Gangster in the Promised Land

1. Interview with Alroy. Lansky also began a long-term affair with a young Israeli, see Maya Guez, "He Was a Known Gangster, I Was a Young Waitress: This Was My Love Affair with the Mob," *Haaretz*, July 24, 2019, https://www.haaretz.co.il/magazine/2019-07-24/ty-article-magazine/.premium/0000017f-ed9b-d4cd-af7f-edfb07ef0000.
2. *Yedioth Ahronoth*, November 7, 8, 1972; *Ma'ariv*, November 8, 1972.
3. The most painstakingly researched Lansky biography is Lacey, *Little Man*.
4. *Ma'ariv*, October 1, 1971.
5. William Schulz, "The Shocking Success of 'Public Enemy No. 1,'" *Reader's Digest*, May 1970, 54.
6. The article by Nicolas Gage in *The Atlantic Monthly* (July 1970) was translated to Hebrew and published in *Yedioth Ahronoth*, https://www.theatlantic.com/magazine/archive/1970/07/the-little-big-man-who-laughs-at-the-law/661732/.
7. Kislev's first series of thirteen articles was published between April 15 and June 4, 1971, and the second of nine articles between August 18 and September 29, 1972. It prompted an official report by Attorney General Meir Shamgar, who conceded a rise in

crime but denied the existence of Mafia-like organized crime in Israel. *Davar*, September 19, 1971. In 1978, another body, the Shimron Commission, was appointed to investigate organized crime.

8. *Yedioth Ahronoth: Musaf Shabbat*, October 23, 1970, 6–7, 20.
9. *Ma'ariv*, March 14, 1972.
10. Interview with Bach.
11. Ibid.
12. *Yedioth Ahronoth*, March 23, 1972.
13. *Ma'ariv*, March 24, 1972.
14. *Haaretz*, September 13, 1972; *Ma'ariv*, September 12, 1972; Kline, "The Lansky Case."
15. *Ma'ariv*, July 2, 4, 5, 1971.
16. Interview with Alroy. On Jewish gangsters, including Lansky, as protectors and benefactors of their communities, see Rockaway, "Hoodlum Hero."
17. *Ma'ariv*, July 2, 1971.
18. Ibid.
19. *Ma'ariv*, July 5, 1971.
20. *Ma'ariv*, October 5, 1971.
21. *Al Hamishmar*, July 9, 1971; *Davar*, July 9, 1971; *Yedioth Ahronoth*, September 1, 1971.
22. *Yedioth Ahronoth*, November 1, 1971.
23. *Yedioth Ahronoth*, September 19, 1971.
24. *Yedioth Ahronoth*, June 8, 11, 1971. Another alleged associate of Lansky's Jewish Mafia, Joe "Doc" Stacher, arrived in Israel a few years earlier and was already a citizen. *Ha'olam Hazeh*, March 9, 1977, 28–29, 32.
25. *Yedioth Ahronoth*, June 17, 1971.
26. *Ha'olam Hazeh*, June 9, 1971, 17.
27. *Al Hamishmar*, July 12, 1971.
28. Burg's recollection of his conversation with Meir is quoted in Lacey, *Little Man*, 334.
29. Interview with Alroy.
30. Bach concedes that a major consideration was that the good name of the State of Israel abroad could be sullied. Interview with Bach; *Yedioth Ahronoth*, December 13, 1971.
31. *Ma'ariv*, November 15, 1971.
32. *Ma'ariv*, June 21, 1971.
33. *Haaretz*, September 8, 1971.
34. Ibid.; *Ha'olam Hazeh*, June 16, 1970, 20; July 13, 1971, 13–14; April 14, 1973, 21; *Yedioth Ahronoth*, September 2, 1971.
35. Yoel Marcus, "The Schnorr Industry," *Haaretz: Musaf*, May 28, 1971, 5–7; Nathan Alterman, "The Generals and the *Magbit*," *Ma'ariv*, December 8, 1967; Yehiel Limor, "A New School in Israel—For Schnorrers," *Ma'ariv*, November 20, 1972.
36. *The Jewish Floridian*, July 7, 1967, 7.
37. Interview with Sarig.

38. Shalit was a navy major who petitioned the High Court to have his children whose mother was not Jewish registered by the Interior Ministry as Jews under the nationality clause. In a 5-4 decision, the court granted his request.

39. *Jerusalem Post*, September 24, 1972; *Yedioth Ahronoth*, September 25, 1972.

40. *New York Times*, October 9, 1971.

41. *Ma'ariv*, July 9, 1971.

42. *Yedioth Ahronoth*, September 15, 1971.

43. *Miami News*, September 19, 1972, in Lacey, *Little Man*, 404–5.

44. *New York Times*, November 9, 1972; also, see letter to the editor, *Yedioth Ahronoth*, November 20, 1972.

45. Uri Avnery, "Kahane: The Path of a Jewish Fuhrer," *Ha'olam Hazeh*, October 4, 1972, 13–15.

46. *Yedioth Ahronoth*, September 28, 1970.

47. *New York Daily News*, February 25, 1971.

48. See for instance, "Israel Embassy, Washington, DC to Foreign Ministry," January 11, 1971. Foreign Ministry: United States/Jewish Defense League, J.D.L. Israel State Archives (ISA), 4550/9-חצ. On Kahane's attempt to communicate with Israeli diplomats, see "Zvi Caspi to Rehavam Amir," May 28, 1970. Ibid.

49. Minutes of Cabinet meeting on anti-Soviet terror, June 8, 1970, January 17, 1971. ISA, 4550/9-חצ. For a dire warning from Israeli diplomats about the damage incurred by Kahane and the JDL see, for example, "Rehavam Amir, General Consul in New York City, to S[hmuel] Divon," January 20, 1971. ISA, 4550/9-חצ.

50. "M[ichael] Elizur to Eitan Ben Zur," September 1, 1971. ISA, 4550/9-חצ. The embassy request was made on June 24, 1971.

51. "Ya'akov Shimshon Shapira, Minister of Justice, to [Abba Eban] Foreign Minister," August 1, 1971. ISA, 4550/9-חצ.

52. "Meir Rosenne, Foreign Ministry Legal Counsel, to Foreign Ministry Director General [Gideon Raphael]," July 7, 1971. ISA, 4550/9-חצ.

53. Sprinzak, *The Ascendance of Israel's Radical Right*, 233–45. Sprinzak underscores fascism as a mode of political behavior rather than ideology, but Kahane's ideology was not terribly different from other political movements that fall under the rubric of fascism, except for its deep religiosity. I disagree with Shaul Magid's contention that Kahane's antiliberal mindset "had no organic roots in Israel." Magid, *Meir Kahane*, 6, 194.

54. On Kahane's "catastrophic messianism" see Sprinzak, *The Ascendance of Israel's Radical Right*, 220–23. Magid labels Kahane's view of the Jewish fate "Judeo-pessimism." Magid, *Meir Kahane*, 87.

55. Paul Gould, "Riddle of the Rabbi," *Jerusalem Post*, April 30, 1971.

56. "M[ichel] Elitzur to E[itan] Ben Zur," September 1, 1971. ISA, 4550/9-חצ. Kahane's father was a close associate of Ze'ev Jabotinsky, the founder and leader of right-wing Revisionist Zionism.

57. *Ma'ariv*, July 5, 1971.

58. *Jerusalem Post*, October 8, 1972; *Davar*, November 18, 1974. Other co-conspirators suspected that Kahane informed the police about the scheme.

59. *Jerusalem Post*, September 28, 1971.
60. Kahane, *Rabbi Meir Kahane*, 347.
61. *Ma'ariv*, June 30, 1973.
62. *Jerusalem Post*, March 11, 1973.
63. Kahane, *Rabbi Meir Kahane*, 317–20.
64. *Haaretz*, January 31, February 5, 13, 1973.
65. *Ma'ariv*, May 10, 1972.
66. See, for example, Nahum Barnea, "No More, Rabbi Kahane!," *Davar*, September 29, 1972.
67. See "Minutes of the Knesset Committee on the Interior, Feb. 13, 1973," Seventh Knesset, Committee on the Interior: Actions of the Jewish Defense League. ISA, 494/5-ב.
68. Kottler, *Heil Kahane*, 143–44.
69. "Attorney General Meir Shamgar to the Prime Minister Office," April 2, 1973. ISA, 17078/19-לב. The court was adjourned in May 1973 and the trial was never resumed. Kahane, *Rabbi Meir Kahane*, 331.
70. Amos Shapira, "'Defense' League Is Dangerous to the Country," *Ott: Labor Party Weekly* (Tel Aviv), December 16, 1971, 16–17.
71. *Davar*, January 5, 1972.
72. Eli Eyal, "Who Will Fight Terror?," *Ma'ariv: Yamim Veleylot*, September 29, 1972, 3–4.
73. *Haaretz*, September 29, 1972.
74. Kottler, *Heil Kahane*, 148.
75. Ibid., 161–68.
76. *Jerusalem Post*, October 14, 1971,
77. The group's nomenclature has been rather fluid. In Hebrew, they were first identified as Kushim Ivriim—Negro Hebrews or Black Hebrews, and more recently as the Hebrews of Dimona or African Hebrew Israelites. At the turn of the 1970s they called themselves the Original Hebrew Israelite Nation of Jerusalem, and were often identified in the English-language press including the *Jerusalem Post* as Black Hebrew Israelites. https://africanhebrewisraelitesofjerusalem.com/. Also, see Jackson, *Thin Description*; Singer, "Symbolic Identity Formation"; Markowitz, "Already Black . . . and Proud and Righteous"; Markowitz, "Israel as Africa."
78. *New York Times*, December 23, 1969. The group's leader Hizkiyahu Blackwell declared, "We've waited about 400 years for this." *Haaretz*, December 24, 1969; Ilan Nachshon, "I Feel Like a Jew—and No Force in the World Will Change That," *Yedioth Ahronoth*, December 23, 1969.
79. *Jerusalem Post*, October 15, 1971.
80. Interview with Cathrielah Baht Israel.
81. Interview with Peninah Baht Israel. On the initial good relations, see *Ma'ariv*, May 22, 1970.
82. *Lamerhav*, March 13, 1970.
83. *Yedioth Ahronoth*, October 8, December 16, 1971.

84. *Yedioth Ahronoth*, January 21, 1972; *New York Times*, January 21, 1972.
85. *Haaretz*, October 8, 1971; *Jerusalem Post*, December 23, 1974.
86. Glass, "Report," 35; *Yedioth Ahronoth*, November 16, 1971.
87. ADL Bulletin 29, February 2, 1972, 1. Foreign Ministry: Black Hebrews, A. ISA, 8061/3-חצ; *Jerusalem Post*, March 23, 1972; Yoella Har-Shefi, "The Black Gospel," *Yedioth Ahronoth*: 7 *Yamim*, February 18, 1972, 17–19, 51; by the 1990s the Hebrew Israelites have adopted right-wing positions, supporting, for instance, the continued occupation of the West Bank on religious grounds. Michaeli, "Another Exodus," 82.
88. *Haaretz*, July 30, 1972. For thank-you notes from military units' commanders to the Black Israelites, see Foreign Ministry: Black Hebrews. ISA, 5737/14-חצ.
89. Ronen Medzini and Yonat Atlas, "The Hebrews Community: Hope following Peres's Visit," *Ynet*, August 23, 2008, https://www.ynet.co.il/articles/0,7340,L-35860 25,00.html.
90. *Los Angeles Times*, January 10, 2015.
91. Roy Chicky Arad, "Why Don't the Hebrews from Dimona Get Citizenship?," *Haaretz*, April 20, 2017, https://www.haaretz.co.il/magazine/tozeret/2017-04-20/ty-article/.premium/0000017f-e4d5-d7b2-a77f-e7d72e850000; Orly Vilnai, "Facing a Wall," *Haaretz*, January 12, 2021, https://www.haaretz.co.il/opinions/orly/2021-01-12/ty-article/.premium/0000017f-dbe2-d856-a37f-ffe2c71a0000; Almog Ben Zikri, "Court Suspended Deportation Process for Tens of Members of the Hebrews Community in Dimona," *Haaretz*, October 12, 2021, https://www.haaretz.co.il/news/education/2021-10-12/ty-article/.premium/0000017f-ef6b-d8a1-a5ff-ffebb7f70000. Israeli organizations that oppose illegal immigration, for example, the Israeli Immigration Policy Center, continue to associate the Israelites with lawlessness.
92. *Ma'ariv*, December 24, 1971.
93. *Haaretz*, December 17, 1971.
94. Shulamit Korn, "Dimona: A Black Misunderstanding," *Jerusalem Post: Weekend Magazine*, October 15, 1971, 6; *Toronto Star*, February 22, 1972, ISA, 8061/3-חצ; also, see "Mordechai Shalev to Shlomo Argov," March 8, 1970. Foreign Ministry: Immigration and Absorption. ISA, 4485/3-חצ.
95. *New York Post*, December 15, 1970; *Philadelphia Inquirer*, October 12, 1971. The Black and White Jews were led by an African American, Rudolph (Yehuda) Windsor, author of *From Babylon to Timbuktu: A History of the Ancient Black Races Including the Black Hebrews* (New York: Exposition Press, 1969). He traveled to Israel and met with both government officials and the Israelites. Foreign Ministry: Immigration and Absorption: Black Jews, B. ISA, 4485/4-חצ.
96. Henry Schwarzschild, "Israel: Importing American Jewish Racism," *Sh'ma: A Journal of Jewish Responsibility*, no. 18 (1971): 144.
97. Robert Coleman, "A Black Jew Speaks," *The Jewish Observer*, November 1970, 11–13; also, see *Detroit Jewish News*, December 25, 1970; "Zvi Kaspi, New York Consulate, to Consular Dept. Foreign Ministry," December 16, 1970. ISA, 4485/4-חצ.
98. Minister Shlomo Argov, December 25, 1969. Foreign Ministry: Black "Jews."

ISA, 3825/10-חצ; Philip Benn, "A New Problem: Who Is a Black Jew in the U.S." *Ma'ariv*, June 19, 1973.

99. Mordechai Shalev, "Black Jews," May 1970. ISA, 4485/3-חצ.

100. "Telegram from Yosef Burg, Minister of the Interior, to the Israeli Embassy in Washington, DC," n.d. Foreign Ministry Files: Liberia-Judaism. ISA, 4593/41-חצ. The Foreign Ministry suspected conspiracy. "Mordechai Shalev to Legal Counsel T[heodore] Miron," December 25, 1969. ISA, 3825/10-חצ. Early on, officials speculated that a Jewish organization interested in improving Black/Jewish relations was underwriting the move from Liberia to Israel. Two years later, an Israeli diplomat in Chicago heard from a figure in the Black community that Ben Ammi had ties with China and that his group included anti-Israeli elements sent to Israel for the purpose of espionage. "Arieh Haskel, Public Diplomacy Consul to Public Diplomacy Director in Washington DC," March 1, 1972. Foreign Ministry: Black Jews. ISA, 5193/24-חצ.

101. *Ma'ariv*, October 21, 1971.

102. Ibid. Also see letters to Meir from individuals in the United States and Israel opining about whether the Israelites should be deported or allowed to stay. Prime Minister Golda Meir's Office: Black Hebrews. ISA, 6483/17-ג.

103. See, for instance, "Moshe Yeger to Mordechai Shalev," March 5, 1970. ISA, 4593/41-חצ.

104. *Yedioth Ahronoth*, October 7, 8, 1971.

105. *New York Times*, August 31, 1971.

106. "Avraham Cohen, Ambassador to Liberia, to the Foreign Ministry," October 22, 1971. ISA, 8061/3-חצ. The Egyptian Socialist Party declared that Egypt was willing to open its gates to the Black Hebrews who would be deported from Israel. Glass, "Report," 11.

107. Carmi, *Immigration and the Law of Return*, 23.

108. Following the mass immigration from the former Soviet Union in the 1990s, hundreds of thousands of non-Jews became Israeli citizens under the Law of Return. Lustick, "Israel as a Non-Arab State"; Weiss, "The Golem and Its Creator."

109. *Yedioth Ahronoth*, December 8, 1972; *Jerusalem Post*, January 9, 1973.

110. "Elizur to Legal Counsel [Meir Rosenne]," December 24, 1972. Foreign Ministry: US/Jewish Community: Black Hebrews. ISA, 5297/1-חצ; "Meeting on the Black Hebrews," November 8, 1977. Foreign Ministry: Israel-U.S. ISA, 6825/1-חצ; "Minister of the Interior Yosef Burg to Attorney General Meir Shamgar," February 22, 1974. ISA, 5737/14-חצ.

111. "Zvi Brosh to the Director of the North American Department," December 19, 1972. ISA, 5297/1-חצ.

112. Yiftachel, *Ethnocracy*.

113. According to a report in the *Jerusalem Post*, January 19, 1978, actor Louis Gossett Jr. claimed to have been interrogated at Lod Airport six times, on one occasion under the threat of a gun. See Glass, "Report," 43.

114. *New York Times*, October 9, 1971.

115. Interview with Huebner; Huebner, *A Life Story*, 170–72, 179–80.

116. Prince Gavriel claims that prejudice in Israel was never as bad as the racism he had experienced during his childhood in Chicago. Interview with Prince Gavriel.

117. *Jerusalem Post*, May 29, 1998.

118. Roger Hercz, "Israel Probes Roots of American Settler Extremism," *United Press International*, February 28, 1994, BC cycle. A similar proposal was raised following Rabin's assassination. *Associated Press International*, November 11, 1995.

119. Inspired by Robert Rockaway's book, *But He Was Good to His Mother* (New York: Gefen, 2000), the one-man play *Lansky*, written by Richard Krevolin and Joseph Bologna, was first staged Off Broadway in early 2009. Also, see the 2021 film *Lansky*, starring Harvey Keitel, directed by Eytan Rockaway, written by Robert Rockaway and Eytan Rockaway.

120. *Jerusalem Post*, February 28, 1999.

Chapter 7: Emissaries of Liberalism in Crisis

1. Israel Central Bureau of Statistics, *Annual Report* 24 (1973), 117.

2. Avruch, *American Immigrants in Israel*, 37; Berman, "Why North Americans Migrate to Israel," 143n1.

3. Since the 1960s Israel has been a magnet for hundreds of thousands (350,000 between 1967 and the beginning of the twenty-first century) Jewish and non-Jewish kibbutz volunteers. They included future politicians (Bernie Sanders), artists (Annie Leibovitz), actors (Bob Hoskins, Sigourney Weaver), and comedians (Jerry Seinfeld, Sasha Baron Cohen). *Ma'ariv*, August 7, 2005.

4. Orian, *The Ethnic Problem in the Israeli Theater*, 111–36; Yanai, "Intermezzo with Nola Chilton."

5. *Bamahane*, August 29, 1973, 19.

6. The Hebrew expression was translated from the German in which *die hunde*—treasure—became *der hund*—the dog; also, see *Ma'ariv Lano'ar*, February 27, 1979, 18; *Ma'ariv*, February 2, 1979; *Ma'ariv: Shavu'a Tov*, June 22, 1984, 6.

7. Lahav, *Judgment in Jerusalem*, xiv. On the American turn in Israeli legal education, see Lahav, "American Moment[s]"; Sandberg, "Cultural Colonialism."

8. Avruch, *American Immigrants in Israel*, 91; Gitelman, *Becoming Israelis*, 69; also, see Jubas, "The Adjustment Process of Americans and Canadians in Israel."

9. Avruch, *American Immigrants in Israel*, 203.

10. Jay Shapiro, *From Both Sides Now: An American-Israeli Odyssey* (Tel Aviv: Dvir Katzman, 1983), 24–25; quoted in Waxman, *American Aliya*, 140.

11. Avruch, *American Immigrants in Israel*, 171.

12. Gitelman, *Becoming Israelis*, 169.

13. Rabin, *Memoirs*, 228.

14. Gitelman, *Becoming Israelis*, 226.

15. Ibid., 209.

16. *Ma'ariv*, February 22, 1980.

17. Hirschhorn, *City on a Hilltop*, 23.

18. Ibid., 15, 231–33.

19. Waxman, *American Aliya*, 161.
20. Hirschhorn, *City on a Hilltop*, 20.
21. *New York Times*, August 7, 1995, quoted in Hirschhorn, *City on a Hilltop*, 137.
22. Sugrue, *Origins of the Urban Crisis*.
23. Critchlow, *Phyllis Schlafly and Grassroots Conservatism*.
24. Gitelman, *Becoming Israelis*, 209.
25. See, for instance, Smith, "Americanization and UK Higher Education."
26. Ram, *The Return of Martin Buber*, chap. 5; Ram, *Israeli Sociology*, chap. 5.
27. Ruth Bondi, "Ten Little Americans," *Davar: Dvar Hashavu'a*, September 27, 1968, 9.
28. See, for instance, Hollinger, *Science, Jews, and Secular Culture*.
29. Ryan, *Blaming the Victim*.
30. Horwitz, "Social Work and Civil Disobedience."
31. Hebrew University, "The Story of the Baerwald School for Social Work and Social Welfare," Filter Film Production, YouTube video, https://www.youtube.com/watch?v=qXo4zqih4X0.
32. *Lamerhav*, January 9, 1967.
33. Lotte Salzberger and Y[ona] M. Rosenfeld, "Israel Society Is Lacking a Comprehensive Social Policy," *Davar*, May 23, 1966; also, see Doron, "Poverty in Israel."
34. Lotte Salzberger and Y[ona] M. Rosenfeld, "Ideology and Social Deprivation," *Davar*, May 24, 1966; "For an Organized and Active Public Opinion," *Davar*, May 30, 1966. For a critique of Salzberger and Rosenfeld's argument by the director of the National Insurance Institute, see Giora Lotan, "Achievements and Failures in Social Policy," *Davar*, July 4, 1966.
35. Yehuda Gotholf, "What Is Common and Different between Israeli and World Workers," *Davar*, April 30, 1967.
36. *Ma'ariv*, January 18, 1970.
37. On community action and grassroots organization, see, for example, Nadasen, *Welfare Warriors*; Kornbluh, *The Battle for Welfare Rights*; Carroll, *Mobilizing New York*.
38. Yosef Tzuriel, "Welfare Recipients Must Organize to Present Their Demands," *Ma'ariv*, January 26, 1971.
39. Ibid.; Yosef Tzuriel, "Welfare Services' Main Deficiency: Support as a Charity Not Right," *Ma'ariv*, January 18, 1970.
40. Lerner, "Affirmative Action in Israel"; Jaffe, *Unequal by Chance*, 65; Jaffe, "Manpower Supply and Admissions Policy."
41. Reichner and Jaffe, *Social Pioneer*, 51.
42. *Ma'ariv*, January 26, 1971.
43. Reichner and Jaffe, *Social Pioneer*, 60.
44. Kaufman, "Panthers in the Establishment," 371–72; Amiel, "Community Organizing," 104, 107–8; Torczyner, "The Political Context of Social Change"; Fisher, *Let the People Decide*.
45. Kaufman, "Panthers in the Establishment," 377.
46. Ibid., 378; Amiel, "Community Organizing," 105–6.
47. Ibid., 105.

48. Ibid., 109.

49. Avneri, *The Social Welfare Pioneer*, 336.

50. Reichner and Jaffe, *Social Pioneer*, 64–65.

51. *Davar*, March 10, 1972. Efforts to exhaust welfare funds were also part of an American welfare rights strategy, although in the United States the rationale was to instigate a crisis that would hasten a fundamental political change. See Piven and Cloward, "The Weight of the Poor," originally published in the *Nation* in 1966.

52. Nahum Barnea, "Poor Services," *Davar: Dvar Hashavu'a*, November 12, 1971, 9, 28. On Jaffe and American social workers in Jerusalem, see Amiel, "Community Organizing," 108.

53. *Davar: Dvar Hashavu'a*, November 12, 1971, 28.

54. *Ma'ariv*, February 2, 1972; *Davar*, June 28, 1972.

55. Doron Rosenblum, "Social Worker as a Bazaar Haggler," *Davar: Dvar Hashavu'a*, July 7, 1972, 28.

56. Reichner and Jaffe, *Social Pioneer*, 171.

57. King, *Project Renewal*, 101.

58. Amiel, "Community Organizing," 108.

59. Resnik, "Discourse Structuration in Israel"; The *reforma* and *integratzia* would inspire perennial scholarly debates over their motivation and results. See, for instance, Swirski, *Education in Israel*; Resh and Kfir, "Educational Integration in Israel"; Resh and Dar, "The Rise and Fall of School Integration in Israel."

60. *Ma'ariv*, May 26, 1977; also, see Coleman, "School Integration in Two Societies."

61. *Davar*, February 7, 1974.

62. *Att*, April 1974, 32.

63. Norit Bretzky, "Marcia the 'Liberator' Settles in the Knesset," *Ma'ariv: Yamim Veleylot*, February 1, 1974, 10–11, 31; *Davar*, February 7, December 30, 1974.

64. Freedman, *Memoir*, 55; also, see *Yedioth Ahronoth*, June 21, 1973. For a largely literary view of the American influence on Israeli feminism, see Feldman, "From *The Madwoman in the Attic* to *The Women's Room*."

65. *Yedioth Ahronoth*, September 23, 1973.

66. Oriana Fallaci, "Golda Meir: On Being a Woman," *Ms.*, April 1973, 74–104; also, see Triger, "Golda Meir's Reluctant Feminism." On the Fallaci interview, see Lahav, *The Only Woman in the Room*, 223–27. On Meir's relationship to modern feminism, ibid., 105–10, 254–55, 258–59.

67. *Ma'ariv*, July 7, 1974.

68. Sima Kadmon, "Woman's Room," *Ma'ariv: Sofshavu'a*, July 17, 1987, 12.

69. Safran, *Don't Wanna Be Nice Girls*, 78.

70. Freedman, *Memoir*, 49.

71. Talma Yagol, "His Helper—Against Him," *Yedioth Ahronoth: 7 Yamim*, May 12, 1972, 18.

72. Safran, *Don't Wanna Be Nice Girls*, 81.

73. Yagol, "His Helper—Against Him," 17.

74. Freedman, *Memoir*, 90.
75. *Davar*, June 28, 1976.
76. Freedman, *Memoir*, 95.
77. *Davar*, September. 10, 1976.
78. *Davar*, July 15, 1976; *Haaretz*, May 9, 2000.
79. *Ma'ariv*, July 15, 1976.
80. *Haaretz*, May 9, 2000.
81. Freedman, *Memoir*, 121.
82. *Ma'ariv*, June 5, 1975.
83. Safran, *Don't Wanna Be Nice Girls*, 69. For an example of women's hostility to feminism, see Ruth Schreiver, "The Battle Moves to the Domestic Arena," *Yedioth Ahronoth*, July 4, 1974.
84. Freedman, *Memoir*, 14–15.
85. *Ma'ariv*, July 17, 1987.
86. *Ma'ariv*, April 22, 1976.
87. Safran, *Don't Wanna Be Nice Girls*, 140.
88. *Jerusalem Post*, November 11, 1974.
89. Ibid.
90. *Davar*, December 30, 1974.
91. *Ma'ariv*, April 1, 2019, https://www.maariv.co.il/news/israel/Article-692335.
92. *Yedioth Ahronoth*, November 9, 1966.
93. *Yedioth Ahronoth*, October 20, 1966
94. Galily and Bar-Eli, "From Tal Brody to European Champions," 402; *Yedioth Ahronoth*, October 18, 1967; *Yedioth Ahronoth*, November 13, 1966.
95. *Yedioth Ahronoth*, May 18, 1969; *Yedioth Ahronoth*, August 20, 1970.
96. *Yedioth Ahronoth*, April 13, 1967.
97. Galily and Bar-Eli, "From Tal Brody to European Champions," 406. On Brody as a role model, see *Haaretz: Musaf*, February 23, 1968, 7.
98. *Yedioth Ahronoth*, September 1, 1980.
99. *Ma'ariv*, February 17, 2017, https://sport1.maariv.co.il/%D7%9B%D7%AA%D7%91%D7%94/198454.
100. Galily and Sheard, "Cultural Imperialism and Sport," 64.
101. *Yedioth Ahronoth*, October 18, 1967.
102. Galily and Bar-Eli, "From Tal Brody to European Champions," 408.
103. *Ma'ariv: Shavu'a Sport*, November 27, 1986, 3–5.
104. Ibid.
105. *Ma'ariv*, January 4, 1977.
106. Galily and Sheard, "Cultural Imperialism and Sport," 56; Mordechai Rosenblum, "The Americans," *Ma'ariv*, December 1, 1976.
107. Maccabi Tel Aviv would also win the European Cup in its different iterations in 1981, 2001, 2004, 2005, and 2014.
108. Galily and Bar-Eli, "From Tal Brody to European Champions," 414.
109. *Ma'ariv*, February 18, 1977. On the victory see, "Channel 2 News: The Yellow

Victory of 1977," YouTube video, https://www.youtube.com/watch?v=hWyYpVF-d8A&list=PLKrTdtsW7HEgqGNzh4rXq5-GusSOCjTUz.

110. Galily and Bar-Eli, "From Tal Brody to European Champions," 416.

111. *Ma'ariv*, October 23, 1981.

112. *Ma'ariv: Shavu'a Sport*, November 12, 1986, 3–5; On the basketball team as a commune, *Bamahane*, June 5, 1973, 14.

113. Smadar Shir, "Let's Play Basketball," *Ma'ariv: Sofshavu'a*, December 12, 1980, 37–38.

114. *Yedioth Ahronoth*, November 3, 1976.

115. Laskier, "Israeli Activism American Style."

116. *Ma'ariv*, March 19, 1969.

117. Yaniv Zach, "Channel 1 Is 35 Years Old," *Ma'ariv: Musaf Pesah*, April 16, 2003, 8, 12.

Chapter 8: Back to Anatevka

1. In the early 1950s, Prime Minister Ben-Gurion adopted an aggressive antidiasporic stance. Weissbrod, "From Labour Zionism to New Zionism," 789.

2. This popular ethnicized subculture was paralleled by the production of high-end fashion, ceramics, fabrics, carpets, and glasswork that blended ethnic, largely Middle Eastern, and modern motifs. Manufactured most famously by Maskit Company, these artifacts constituted an export-oriented Israeli style deemed authentic. El Or and Regev, "The Making of an Israeli Style," 316–20.

3. Solomon, *Wonder of Wonders*, 50.

4. *Yedioth Ahronoth: 7 Yamim*, December 4, 1965, 11.

5. Dan Almagor, "The Reincarnations of Tevye the Dairyman in *Fiddler on the Roof*." Cameri Theater, Tel Aviv. Playbill, 2009. The Israeli Center for the Documentation of the Performing Arts; interview with Almagor.

6. Solomon, *Wonder of Wonders*, 248.

7. *New York Times*, June 9, 1965.

8. *Haaretz*, June 8, 1965.

9. *Lamerhav*, June 11, 1965.

10. *Yedioth Ahronoth*, June 10, 1965.

11. *Al Hamishmar*, June 18, 1965.

12. *Davar*, November 26, 1965.

13. Jacobson, *Roots Too*, 7.

14. *Yedioth Ahronoth*, November 2, 1969.

15. Ali Mohar, "Shalom Aleichem, Shalom Aleichem," *Davar: Dvar Hashavu'a*, February 23, 1973, 20–21; Shimon Manueli, "Ah, the *Shammes* Got *Finef*," *Bamahane*, December 17, 1968, 12–13; Shalom Rosenfeld, "American Fashion: Researching Ameryiddish," *Ma'ariv*, February 7, 1969.

16. Calvin Trillin, "Lester Drentluss, A Jewish Boy from Baltimore, Attempts to Make It through the Summer of 1967," *The Atlantic*, January 1968, 43. For the Hebrew

translation of Trillin's piece, see *Ma'ariv*, April 5, 1968. On Leo Rosten's book *The Joys of Yiddish* (1968) see *Yedioth Ahronoth*, October 29, 1971.

17. *Yedioth Ahronoth*, April 3, November 22, 1967.
18. *Davar*, May 22, 1969.
19. *Davar*, May 20, 1969; *Yedioth Ahronoth*, February 15, 1968.
20. *Yedioth Ahronoth*, May 21, 1967.
21. *Ma'ariv*, May 29, 1967; *Yedioth Ahronoth*, February 15, 1968. It was recently revealed that on several occasions while performing in Europe Topol assisted the Israeli Mossad. *Haaretz*, April 12, 2023, https://www.haaretz.co.il/magazine/2023-04-12/ty-article-magazine/.highlight/00000187-6a67-dde0-afb7-7e7766fd0000.
22. *Yedioth Ahronoth*, June 9, 1967.
23. *Davar*, December 16, 1971.
24. *Yedioth Ahronoth*, September 15, 1968; *Yedioth Ahronoth*, December 12, 1967; *Ma'ariv*: *Yamim Veleylot*, December 8, 1967, 5.
25. *Davar*, December 5, 1967.
26. *Yedioth Ahronoth*, November 19, 1967.
27. *Yedioth Ahronoth*, February 12, 1968; *Ma'ariv*, January 28, 1971; *Yedioth Ahronoth*, June 26, 1969; *Ma'ariv*, November 27, 1968.
28. *Davar: Dvar Hashavu'a*, January 23, 1970, 10–11.
29. Ibid.
30. *Ma'ariv*, July 17, 1970.
31. *Davar*, February 1, 1972.
32. *Yedioth Ahronoth*: *7 Yamim*, December 4, 1970, 21.
33. *Ma'ariv*, July 2, 1969
34. *Ma'ariv*, September 24, 1967.
35. *Ma'ariv*, July 13, 1970.
36. *Al Hamishmar*, June 25, 1965.
37. On the history of the term *kuni lemel*, see *Davar*, October 14, 1966. *Shnei Kuni Lemel*, directed by Israel Becker, story by Abraham Goldfaden and Israel Becker (1966; Sisu Home Entertainment, 2005), DVD.
38. *The Komediant*, directed by Arnon Goldfinger, script by Oshra Schwartz (Lama Productions, 1999), DVD.
39. Shohat, *Israeli Cinema*, 142–43.
40. Bunim, *Here Is Bunim*, 76–85.
41. *Davar*, July 8, 1966.
42. Yerushalmi. *The Director's Stage*, 233.
43. *Ma'ariv*, July 11, 1966.
44. *Davar*, November 19, 1969.
45. *The Komediant*.
46. *Davar*, September 20, 1970.
47. *Ma'ariv*, November 6, 1966.
48. *Ma'ariv*, January 28, 1971.

49. Interview with Nitzan.
50. *New York Times*, November 23, 1971.
51. While *Kuni Lemel* was derived from a post-Enlightenment genre that satirized Hasidut, *Ish hasid haya* represents another secular perception born in the late nineteenth century and marked by idealization. See, Dan, "The End of Frumkinian Hasidism."
52. Orian, "The Search for Jewish Identity in the Israeli Theater," 105.
53. *Ma'ariv: Yamim Veleylot*, October 30, 1964, 6.
54. *Yedioth Ahronoth: 7 Leylot*, January 12, 2018, 9.
55. On *Spoon River Hill*, see Michael Ohad, "Everybody Is Sleeping on the Hill," *Haaretz: Musaf*, March 8, 1968, 14–15; Mendel Kohansky, "Spoon River Epitaph," *The Jerusalem Post: Weekend Magazine*, March 22, 1968, 12.
56. Interview with Yizraeli.
57. *Haaretz*, September 17, 1968; interview with Yizraeli.
58. Michael Ohad, "But This Village Was Truly Tiny," *Haaretz: Musaf*, October 11, 1968, 13.
59. *New York Times*, November 11, 1971. On the selection of individual tales and the history of the revue, see Almagor, "Ish Hasid."
60. *Haaretz*, October 11, 1968.
61. Moshe Natan, "Painted Flowers in a Wedding That Ended," *Bamahane*, October 22, 1968, 23.
62. *Al Hamishmar*, October 25, 1968.
63. *Ma'ariv*, October 31, 1968.
64. *Davar*, October 25, 1968; *Yedioth Ahronoth*, October 22, 1968.
65. *Haaretz*, October 18, 1968.
66. Ruth Bondi, "HaBa'al Shem Tov's Second Epiphany," *Davar: Dvar Hashavu'a*, October 11, 1968, 24.
67. *Yedioth Ahronoth: Leylot Hashavu'a*, January 8, 1970, 5.
68. *Davar*, May 26, 1970.
69. *Yedioth Ahronoth: Leylot Hashavu'a*, November 18, 1971, 3.
70. *New York Times*, November 11, 1971.
71. *Yedioth Ahronoth: 7 Yamim*, November 12, 1971, 15.
72. *Variety*, December 1, 1971; *New York Times*, November 23, 1971.
73. *The Christian Science Monitor*, November 26, 1971.
74. Lee Mishkin, "New Israeli Musical Unveiled at Edison," *The Morning Telegraph*, November 24, 1971; *The Record*, November 23, 1971, 19.
75. *Yedioth Ahronoth*, November 18, 1971.
76. *Davar*, August 20, 1970.
77. *Davar*, August 27, 1970.
78. *Yedioth Ahronoth: Leylot Hashavu'a*, September 10, 1970, 5.
79. *Ma'ariv*, September 3, 1968.
80. *Ma'ariv*, September 6, 1963.

81. Steinhardt, "American Neo-Hasids."
82. Kligman, "On the Creators and Consumers of Orthodox Popular Music."
83. Ophir, *Rabbi Shlomo Carlebach*, 43.
84. Ibid., 63.
85. Ibid., 78–79.
86. *Yedioth Ahronoth*, August 31, 1966.
87. Ophir, *Rabbi Shlomo Carlebach*, 86.
88. Ibid., 85.
89. Coopersmith, *Holy Beggars*, 247.
90. Israel Segal, "A High Voice without Off-Key Notes," *Haaretz: Musaf*, October 23, 1970, 12–13.
91. *Ma'ariv*, September 17, 1968.
92. On Carlebach's vision, Shaul Magid, "Carlebach's Broken Mirror," *Tablet Magazine*, November 1, 2012, https://www.tabletmag.com/sections/arts-letters/articles/carlebach-broken-mirror.
93. Ariel, "Hasidism in the Age of Aquarius," 147; Ariel, "Can Adam and Eve Reconcile?"; on the House of Love and Prayer, see Coopersmith, *Holy Beggars*.
94. Ophir, *Rabbi Shlomo Carlebach*, 96–104.
95. Blustein, "Shlomo Carlebach's Shadow Side"; Robin Cembalest, "Fetherman File," *Forward*, March 20, 1998.
96. *Ma'ariv*, July 23, 1971; *Yedioth Ahronoth*, July 21, 1967.
97. *Tikkun*, Sept/Oct 1997, 53–56. Ophir, *Rabbi Shlomo Carlebach*, 130.
98. Ibid., 151, 171; Magid, "Carlebach's Broken Mirror."
99. See, for instance, *Yedioth Ahronoth: Leylot Hashavu'a*, July 29, 1971, 5.
100. *Yedioth Ahronoth*, August 2, 1970. Critics often made the distinction between the "authentic" Carlebach and commercialized Hasidic pop. *Yedioth Ahronoth: Leylot Hashavu'a*, September 17, 1970, 5.
101. *Yedioth Ahronoth*, June 29, 1972.
102. *Yedioth Ahronoth: Leylot Hashavu'a*, October 2, 1969, 5.
103. *Yedioth Ahronoth: 24 Sha'ot*, August 15, 1972, 21.
104. YouTube video, https://www.youtube.com/watch?v=tpMAQyBHLnQ.
105. *Yedioth Ahronoth: 7 Yamim*, November 12, 1971, 15.
106. *Davar*, February 8, 1973, 5; Also, see *Yedioth Ahronoth: Leylot Hashavu'a*, June 18, 1970, 6.
107. *Haaretz: Musaf*, August 29, 1975, 16–17.
108. *Yedioth Ahronoth*, October 26, 1970.
109. *Yedioth Ahronoth*, October 11, 1974. On TV religious programs as an effort at bridging observant and nonobservant Jews, see *Yedioth Ahronoth*, December 1, 1974.
110. *Ma'ariv*, September 23, 1971.
111. *Ma'ariv*, September 19, 28, October 1, 1971.
112. *Kikar Hashabbat*, December 28, 2016, https://www.kikar.co.il/abroad/217582.html; Aviad, *Return to Judaism*, 17.

113. Ibid., x–xi.

114. *Yedioth Ahronoth*, March 11, 12, 1971; *Davar*, March 12, 1971; *Ma'ariv*, March 11, 1971.

115. *Yedioth Ahronoth*, January 12, 1973; *Davar*, March 28, 1971; Uzi Benziman, "An Empire Called Chabad," *Haaretz: Musaf*, January 7, 1972, 5–7, 21; Tamar Meroz, "Inside Chabad Village," *Haaretz: Musaf*, April 12, 1974, 15–17; Yerushalmi, *At a Moment of Truth*, 65–102.

116. For a survey of cults, New Age groups, and psychological marathons in Israel, see Zohar, *Happiness Knows No End*.

117. *Yedioth Ahronoth: 7 Yamim*, May 10, 1974, 15. Also see, Ofra Elyagon, "The Israeli Victims of the Maharishi Guru," *Ma'ariv*, March 29, 1974; Tamar Meroz, "People Who Are Searching for Themselves," *Haaretz: Musaf*, October 10, 1969, 16–18.

118. *Hatzofeh*, September 27, 1968. Nitzan partnered with another child of a religious family—Nira Rabinowitz—in performing and recording Yiddish songs. *Yedioth Ahronoth: Leylot Hashavu'a*, March 6, 1969, 13; *Yedioth Ahronoth: Leylot Hashavu'a*, August 27, 1970, 4.

119. *Yedioth Ahronoth*, April 10, June 14, 1972.

120. Immanuel Bar-Kadma, "Heffer—For a Solo Performance and for a Whole Show," *Yedioth Ahronoth: 7 Yamim*, June 4, 1971, 21.

121. Shandler, *Adventures in Yiddishland*, 22–30, 193–203.

122. *Yedioth Ahronoth*, July 28, 1971.

123. *Yedioth Ahronoth: 7 Yamim*, April 24, 1970, 15; *Yedioth Ahronoth*, July 31, 1973.

124. *Davar*, November 13, 1968.

125. Mirit Shem Orr, "Orchard with a Scent of Bourekas," *Davar: Dvar Hashavu'a*, September 4, 1970, 12, 29; *The Jerusalem Post*, September 18, 1970. On Bimot Theater and folklore, see *Lamerhav*, October 30, 1970; *Haaretz*, September 1, 1970.

126. Solomon, *Wonder of Wonders*, 146.

127. *Yedioth Ahronoth: 7 Yamim*, March 19, 1971, 4–5.

128. Don-Yehiya and Liebman, "The Dilemma of Traditional Culture in a Modern State," 476; also, see Liebman, "Towards the Study of Popular Religion in Israel"; Liebman and Don-Yehia, *Civil Religion in Israel*.

129. *Yedioth Ahronoth: 7 Yamim*, September 22, 1972, 29. Also, see Silvi Keshet, "The Religious Revolution," *Haaretz: Musaf*, June 21, 1968, 10, 32; Bondi, "HaBa'al Shem Tov's Second Epiphany."

Chapter 9: America on Stage

1. Tamar Meroz, "The Hairy Fair," *Haaretz: Musaf*, May 22, 1970, 16–17, 28.

2. *Lahiton*, August 18, 1972, 6.

3. *Jerusalem Post*, February 14, 1964.

4. *Al Hamishmar*, February 14, 1964.

5. *Yedioth Ahronoth: 7 Yamim*, January 31, 1964, 11.

6. *Waiting for Godik*, directed and written by Ari Davidowitz, produced by Amir Harel and Ayelet Kit (Lama Production, 2007); interview with Almagor.

7. *Ma'ariv*, February 17, 1964.
8. *Yedioth Ahronoth: 7 Yamim*, June 22, 1966, 9.
9. Godik's initials GG or *gag* mean "roof" in Hebrew. Today, the Alhambra houses a Scientology center.
10. On the changing meaning of the pioneering ethos, see Gutwein, "'Bourgeois *Chalutziut*.'"
11. Giora Godik Theater. *My Fair Lady*, playbill, 1964. The Israeli Center for the Documentation of the Performing Arts.
12. *Waiting for Godik*.
13. *My Fair Lady*, playbill.
14. *Yedioth Ahronoth: 7 Yamim*, January 27, 1967, 6.
15. *Haboker*, February 19, 1965.
16. Foulkes, *A Place for Us*, 163.
17. *Haboker*, February 14, 1961.
18. *Ma'ariv*, February 10, 1961
19. *Ma'ariv*, February 17, 1961.
20. *Haaretz*, February 24, 1961.
21. Foulkes, *A Place for Us*, 167–68.
22. Aranne is quoted in Greenberg, *Zalman Aranne*, 307. *Kazablan*, book by Yigal Mossinson and Yoel Silberg; music by Dov Seltzer; lyrics by Haim Heffer, Amos Ettinger, and Dan Almagor; sets by Arie Navon; producer Giora Godik.
23. On the original play *Kazablan*, see Orian, *The Ethnic Problem in the Israeli Theater*, 77–92.
24. *Lamerhav*, December 30, 1966.
25. *Davar*, December 30, 1966.
26. *Davar: Dvar Hashavu'a*, June 29, 1973, 10; also, see Nili Tal, "Sippur parvarim," *Haaretz: Musaf*, June 19, 1973, 32–33.
27. For a behind-the-scenes account of *Kazablan*'s production, see *Yedioth Ahronoth*, April 24, 2016, https://www.yediot.co.il/articles/0,7340,L-4795727,00.html.
28. Davidowitz, *Waiting for Godik*.
29. For an early critique of the *bourekas* genre, see Yehuda Judd Ne'eman, "Level Zero in Cinema," *Cinema* 5 (1975): 20–23 [Hebrew]; also, see Shohat, *Israeli Cinema*, chap. 3.
30. *Hair, the American Tribal Rock Musical*, book and lyrics, Gerome Ragni and James Rado; music, Galt MacDermot; translated and adopted by Ehud Manor; directed by Patrick Garland; musical director, Steve Gillette; choreography and staging, Oliver Tobias.
31. *Haaretz*, February 13, 1970; *Davar*, February 19, 1970.
32. Manor, *I Have No Other Country*, 178–79.
33. Immanuel Bar-Kadma, "The 'Hair' That Gave Rise to a New Era," *Yedioth Ahronoth: 7 Yamim*, May 29, 1970, 15.
34. Meroz, "Hairy Fair," 28.
35. *Davar*, September 10, 1970.

36. Meroz, "Hairy Fair," 17.
37. Ibid.
38. Ibid.
39. *Ha'olam Hazeh*, May 20, 1970, 20–21.
40. Sarit Ishai Levi, "The Way We Were," *Hadashot: Musaf*, June 7, 1991, 41.
41. *Ha'olam Hazeh*, June 9, 1970, cover, 18–20.
42. *Yedioth Ahronoth*, June 17, 1970.
43. *Davar*, June 11, 1970.
44. *Ma'ariv*, March 14, 1971.
45. Michael Ohad, "Twentieth-Century Hair," *Haaretz: Musaf*, September 18, 1970, 15.
46. Ibid., 29.
47. *Ma'ariv*, May 28, 1970.
48. Mirit Shem-Or, "Our Hair," *Davar: Dvar Hashavu'a*, May 29, 1970, 30.
49. *Davar*, October 23, 1970.
50. "King of the Bath Came to Israel," *Ha'olam Hazeh*, June 9, 1970, 20.
51. *Davar*, January 4, 1971.
52. *Davar: Dvar Hashavu'a*, May 29, 1970, 9; Mendel Kohansky, "The Scene in Hebrew," *Jerusalem Post: Weekend Magazine*, June 12, 1970, 16.
53. Ohad, "Twentieth-Century Hair," 29; *Al Hamishmar*, September 11, 1970; George Harris, an actor from Grenada, who would have a successful career on the London stage, fled the country after reportedly beating up a female actress, Margalit Ankory. *Ha'olam Hazeh*, August 12, 1970, 20.
54. *Davar: Dvar Hashavu'a*, May 29, 1970, 8. After the initial three months and the conclusion of their contracts, many of the foreign actors left and were replaced. *Yedioth Ahronoth*, August 10, 1970; *Haaretz*, August 20, 1970.
55. *Ma'ariv*, July 5, 1970.
56. Ohad, "Twentieth-Century Hair," 29.
57. *Al Hamishmar*, September 11, 1970.
58. *Davar: Dvar Hashavu'a*, May 29, 1970, 8–9; also, see *Al Hamishmar*, June 12, 1970; *Ma'ariv*, June 22, 1970.
59. *Hatzofeh*, n.d. Hair file. The Israeli Center for the Documentation of the Performing Arts.
60. *Davar*, June 8, 1970.
61. *Yedioth Ahronoth*, June 14, 1970.
62. "Who Is Afraid of Homosexuals," *Ha'olam Hazeh*, January 14, 1970, 27.
63. *Haaretz*, April 28, 1970.
64. *Haaretz*, June 11, 1970.
65. *Hatzofeh*, n.d.
66. *Yedioth Ahronoth*, June 14, 1970.
67. *Yedioth Ahronoth*, June 16, 1970.
68. *Davar*, June 12, 1970.
69. *Ha'olam Hazeh*, June 9, 1970, 18–20.
70. *Yedioth Ahronoth*, June 16, 1970.

71. IsraelChannel, "Hair in Hebrew, Live in Israel 1970, rehearsals & performances," YouTube video, https://youtube.com/watch?v=x5icuLLqezc.

72. Ohad, "Twentieth-Century Hair," 29.

73. Ibid.

74. *Ma'ariv*, May 28, 1970.

75. *Davar*, June 29, 1970.

76. *Davar: Dvar Hashavu'a*, May 29, 1970, 30.

77. Ohad, "Twentieth-Century Hair," 29.

78. Yair Rosenblum webpage, https://yairrosenblum.co.il/song/%D7%A9%D7%99%D7%A8-%D7%9C%D7%A9%D7%9C%D7%95%D7%9D/.

79. Elmaliach and Kidron, "Between Culture and Politics," 88; on the radical publication *NASHUS*, acronym for "youth seeking change," see Ran Dagoni, "Death to the Establishment—Immediately!," *Lamerhav*, January 8, 1971; also, see Ami Shamir, "The Students' Thundering Apathy," *Haaretz: Musaf*, May 18, 1972, 7–9; Shapira and Etzioni-Halevy, *Who Is the Israeli Student?*, chap. 1. In 1970, Michael Kleiner, a future Likud member of Knesset, was elected as the chair of the Tel Aviv University Student Association.

80. For the culturalist approach, see Taub, "The American Sixties in Israel"; Dubnov, "The Missing Beat Generation." For a different reading of 1960s Israel, see Elmaliach and Kidron, "Between Culture and Politics."

81. Eshel Studios, "Israeli Artists: Give Peace a Chance," YouTube video, https://blog.nli.org.il/sipur-give-peace-a-chance/.

82. Helga Dudman, "*Kfotz*, Son of *Hair*," *Jerusalem Post*, November 20, 1970; Michael Ohad, "Do You Have a High School Senior Son?," *Haaretz: Musaf*, November 13, 1970, 14–5, 38. On *Hair*'s and *Kfotz*'s roles in the emergence of Israeli rock, see Schab and Shalev, "The Rock Musical and the Beginning of Rock Music in Israel in the Early 70s."

83. Yablonka, *Children by the Book*, chaps. 13–14.

84. *Haaretz*, October 16, 2022.

Chapter 10: The American Figure in the Israeli Mind

1. *Cast a Giant Shadow*, directed by Melville Shavelson, written by Melville Shavelson and Ted Berkman, cinematography by Aldo Tonti (1966; KL Studio Classics, 2014); Shavelson, *How to Make a Jewish Movie*.

2. Giora Godik Theater. *I Like Mike*, "Annotated Director's Script," 1968, 18. The Israeli Center for the Documentation of the Performing Arts.

3. Michael Ohad, "Meged Is Waiting for Godik," *Haaretz: Musaf*, February 9, 1968, 14–5, 26. Matchmaking across the Atlantic proved seductive for Broadway as well. In 1961 the musical *Milk and Honey* (book, Don Appel; music and lyrics, Jerry Harman) featured a group of Jewish widows, members of Hadassah, who arrive in Israel hoping, beyond sightseeing, to catch husbands as well; also, see *Ma'ariv: Yamim Veleylot*, February 5, 1965, 14.

4. Giora Godik Theater. *I Like Mike*, playbill, 1968. The Israeli Center for the Documentation of the Performing Arts.

5. *Bamahane*, October 29, 1968, 16.

6. Schweitzer, *The New Sensitivity*.

7. *Haaretz: Musaf*, January 19, 1970, 14–15.

8. Alexandra Oliver, "Is This the Worst Israeli Film Ever Made?," *Partisan*, April 13, 2015, http://www.partisanmagazine.com/reviews/2015/3/31/the-appalled-eye-1; Gil Shefler, "Finding New Life as a Cult Classic," *Forward*, January 26, 2011, https://forward.com/culture/film-tv/134946/finding-new-life-as-a-cult-classic/. Another countercultural turn-of-the-1970s Israeli film, Yaki Yosha's *Shalom: Prayer for the Road* (1973) employed themes prevalent in American cinema to critically examine Israeli society; see Schweitzer, *The New Sensitivity*, chap. 6.

9. *Kol mamzer melech*, directed by Uri Zohar, script by Eli Tavor and Uri Zohar, cinematography by David Gurfinkel (1968; NMC United King, 2012), DVD. Preminger, *Reflections on Cinema and Ethos*, 73–80.

10. Tamar Avidar, "Everybody—A Hero," *Ma'ariv: Yamim Veleylot*, July 5, 1968, 20–21; Michael Ohad, "Jesus, the Playboy, and the Man in the Burning Tank," *Haaretz: Musaf*, February 23, 1968, 22–23, 27.

11. *Yedioth Ahronoth: 7 Yamim*, July 5, 1968, 11; *Davar: Dvar Hashavu'a*, April 5, 1968, 20–21.

12. *Davar: Dvar Hashavu'a*, April 5, 1968, 21. In early 1967, Jean-Paul Sartre visited Egypt, Israel, and Gaza, but on the eve of the June war he bitterly disappointed intellectuals in the Arab world who had been drawn to his work by signing a petition on behalf of Israel, as did many other left-leaning figures in France for fear of a "second Holocaust." See Di-Capua, *No Exit*. According to Tavor, working on the film began before the war and focused initially on the Abbie Nathan story. Tavor, "Bastards Born in the War," *Ha'olam Hazeh*, July 10, 1968, 35.

13. *Al Hamishmar*, July 19, 1958; *Davar: Dvar Hashavu'a*, July 12, 1968, 20; *Yedioth Ahronoth*, June 22, November 19, December 8, 1968.

14. Kollek, *Don't Ask Me If I Love*, 142.

15. Ibid., 9.

16. Ibid., 26.

17. Ibid., 197.

18. Ibid., 269.

19. Ibid., 94–95.

20. Ibid., 129.

21. Ibid., 167–68.

22. Ibid., 105.

23. Ibid., 129.

24. Ibid., 129.

25. Ibid., back cover.

26. *Kirkus*, May 27, 1971, https://www.kirkusreviews.com/book-reviews/amos-kollek/dont-ask-me-if-i-love/#review.

27. *Haaretz: Musaf*, February 23, 1973, 56–57.

28. Aloni, *American Princess*, 29.

29. Ibid., 94–95.
30. On the oxymoronic idea of an American princess see, Oz, *Fields and Language*, 190.
31. Aloni, *American Princess*, 32.
32. Ben-Mordechai, "Myth, Reality, Parody."
33. Aloni, *American Princess*, 27.
34. On the affinity of the two plays see, Yavin, *Between Pjojy and Shchouchy*, 225n2.
35. Levin, *The Whore from Ohio*.
36. Berlant, *Cruel Optimism*.
37. Levin, *The Whore from Ohio*.
38. Bar Yosef, *Kri'ot u-shrikot*, 98.
39. On the active role of off stage in Aloni's work see Levi, *Israeli Theater*, 135. On homeland/Diaspora in Aloni's plays, see Ben Mordechai, "The Homeland is the True Diaspora," 570.
40. Esti Segal, "An Eye for a Finger," *2nd Opinion*, July 10, 2010, http://web.archive.org/web/20160303230448/http://2nd-ops.com/editors/?p=5184; Yavin, *Between Pjojy and Shchouchy*, 221–22.
41. Shaked, *About Stories and Plays*, 247–48; Laor, *Hanoch Levin*, 35.
42. Ibid., 32.

Conclusion

1. Parties united around a single personality—such as Yair Lapid's centrist Yesh Atid (There is a future), have not adopted any democratic process for that purpose.
2. Senor and Singer, *Start-up Nation*.
3. Segev, *Elvis in Jerusalem*, 65.
4. Maier, *Among Empires*, 7.
5. Thomas L. Friedman, "The Israel We Knew Is Gone," *The New York Times*, November 4, 2022. Also, see Thomas L. Friedman, "Order vs. Disorder, Part 2," *The New York Times*, July 15, 2014.
6. *Davar*, August 11, 1971.
7. *Haaretz: Musaf*, February 13, 1998, 38, quoted in Azaryahu, "McIsrael," 53.
8. Kohelet Policy Forum, https://en.kohelet.org.il; *Haaretz*, March 11, 2021, https://www.haaretz.co.il/news/politi/2021-03-11/ty-article-magazine/.highlight/0000017f-e82e-dea7-adff-f9ffb21d0000; *Haaretz*, March 30, 2023, https://www.haaretz.co.il/opinions/2023-03-30/ty-article-opinion/.premium/00000187-2da5-db91-adcf-3fb79c570000.
9. On the ideology of the religious Right in Israel, see, for instance, Ravitzky, *Messianism, Zionism and Jewish Religious Radicalism*.
10. *Globes*, May 19, 2015, https://www.globes.co.il/news/docview.aspx?did=1001037675.
11. *Ynet*, December 19, 2011, https://www.ynet.co.il/articles/0,7340,L-4163582,00.html.

Bibliography

Archives and Libraries
Israel State Archives
Sha'ar Zion-Beit Ariela Library
IDF and Defense Establishment Archives
The Israeli Center for the Documentation of the Performing Arts, Tel Aviv University
The Anda Zimand Film Archive, Tel Aviv University
The National Library of Israel
Ma'ariv Archive

Israeli Periodicals

NEWSPAPERS
Al Hamishmar; Davar; Globes; Haaretz; Haboker; Hatzofeh; Hayom; Herut; Jerusalem Post; Kol Ha'am; Lamerhav; Ma'ariv; Makor Rishon; Yedioth Ahronoth.

MAGAZINES
Att; Bamahane; Ha'olam Hazeh; Israel Air Force Magazine; La'isha; Tel Aviv Magazine; Lahiton; Ma'ariv Lano'ar.

NEWSPAPER WEEKLY SUPPLEMENTS
Al Hamishmar: Hotam; Davar: Dvar Hashavu'a; Haaretz: Musaf; Hadashot: Musaf; Jerusalem Post: Weekend Magazine; Ma'ariv: Yamim Veleylot, Sofshavu'a, Shavu'a Sport, Shavu'a Tov; Yedioth Ahronoth: 7 Yamim, Leylot Hashavu'a.

INTERNET NEWS OUTLETS
Haaretz; Globes; Kikar Hashabat; Ma'ariv Online; Walla!; Ynet.

North American Publications
The Atlantic; Christian Science Monitor; The Forward; The Jewish Floridian; The Jewish Observer; Kirkus; Los Angeles Times; The Morning Telegraph (NYC); The Progressive; The Record; Miami News; Ms.; New York Daily News; New York Times; Partisan; Philadelphia Inquirer; Reader's Digest; Tikkun; Toronto Star; Variety; Washington Post.

Interviews
Ya'akov Agmon, July 19, 2016, Tel Aviv.
Dan Almagor, August 2, 2009, Afeka.
Yoram Alroy, March 26, 2009, Ramat Gan.
Gavriel Bach, March 30, 2009, Jerusalem.
Cathrielah Baht Israel, July 24, 2016, Dimona.
Peninah Baht Israel, July 24, 2016, Dimona.
Yeshayahu "Shaike" Bareket, January 27, 2015, Ramat Hasharon.
Avihu Ben-Nun, December 6, 2015. Rishon Letzion.
Charlie Biton, January 8, 2008, Mevaseret Tzion.
Natan Brune, January 14, 2018, Tel Aviv.
Menachem Eini, November 20, 2015, Tel Aviv.
Amos Eran, July 13, 2016, Herzliya.
Prince Gavriel (HaGadol), July 24, 2016, Dimona.
Shmuel Gordon, January 28, 2015, Abu Ghosh.
Israel "Solo" Geva, January 19, 2015, Ramat Aviv.
Haim Hanegbi, January 15, 2007, Ramat Aviv.
Rami Harpaz, January 21, 2015, Kibbutz Hazore'a.
Yehudith Huebner, March 30, 2009, Jerusalem.
David Ivry, January 27, 2015, Tel Aviv.
Nadav Kaplan, December 8, 2015, Avihayil.
Nissan Limor, January 16, 2013, Tel Aviv.
Shlomo Nitzan, July 20, 2017, Tel Aviv.
Dan Pattir, November 30, 2015, Ramat Aviv.
Adir Pridor, November 29, 2015, Herzliya.
Yossi Sarig, January 20, 2015, Ganei Tikva.
Nathan Segal, January 27, 2015, Petah Tikva.
Aharon "Yalo" Shavit, June 1, 2014, Tel Aviv.
Kokhavi Shemesh, January 14, 2007, Rishon Letzion.
Iftach Spector, January 25, 2015, Ramot Hashavim.
David Yair, June 1, 2014, Ramat Hasharon.
Haim Yaron, January 22, 2015, Bnei Dror.
Yossi Yizraeli, January 31, 2017, Ramat Aviv.

Books and Articles

Abravanel, Genevieve. *Americanizing Britain: The Rise of Modernism in the Age of the Entertainment Empire*. Oxford: Oxford University Press, 2012.

Ackerman, Walter. "The Americanization of Israeli Education." *Israel Studies* 5, no. 1 (Spring 2000): 228–43.

Adamsky, Dima. *Operation Kavkaz: Soviet Intervention and Israeli Intelligence Failure in the War of Attrition*. Tel Aviv: Ma'arachot, 2006. [Hebrew]

Alcalay, Amiel. "Memory/Imagination/Resistance." *South Atlantic Quarterly* 102, no. 4 (2003): 851–59.

Almagor, Dan. "Ish Hasid—and The Treasure under the Bridge." *Bama Drama Quarterly* 29, no. 139–40 (1996): 115–28. [Hebrew]

Almog, Oz. *The Sabra—A Profile*. Tel Aviv: Am Oved, 2004. [Hebrew]

Aloni, Nissim. *The American Princess*. Tel Aviv: Yedioth Ahronoth/Hemed, 2002. [Hebrew]

Althusser, Louis. "Ideology and Ideological State Apparatuses (Notes towards an Investigation)." In *Lenin and Philosophy and Other Essays*, 121–76. New York: NYU Press, 2001.

Amiel, Avner. "Community Organizing and Neighborhood Planning in Jerusalem." In *Israeli Planners and Designers: Profiles of Community Builders*. Edited by John Forester, Raphaël Fischler, and Deborah Shmueli, 101–14. Albany: State University of New York Press, 2001.

Anderson, Benedict. *Imagined Communities: Reflections on the Origin and Spread of Nationalism*. London: Verso, 1983.

Ansky, Alex. *The Selling of the Likud*. Tel Aviv: Zmora, 1978. [Hebrew]

Appadurai, Arjun, ed. *The Social Life of Things: Commodities in Social Perspective*. Cambridge: Cambridge University Press, 1986.

Arbel, Tal. "'The American Soldier' in Jerusalem: How Social Science and Social Scientists Travel." PhD diss., Harvard University, 2016.

Arbel, Tal. "Fear in Hebrew: Militarized Behaviorism and the Cultural Politics of Science in Translation." *Historical Studies in the Natural Sciences* 49, no. 5 (Nov. 2019): 471–503.

Aridan, Natan. *Advocating for Israel: Diplomats and Lobbyists from Truman to Nixon*. Lanham, MD: Lexington, 2017.

Ariel, Yaakov. "Hasidism in the Age of Aquarius: The House of Love and Prayer in San Francisco, 1967–1977." *Religion and American Culture* 13, no. 2 (Summer 2003): 139–65.

Ariel, Yaakov. "Can Adam and Eve Reconcile? Gender and Sexuality in a New Jewish Religious Movement." *Nova Religio: The Journal of Alternative and Emergent Religions* 9, no. 4 (May 2006): 53–78.

Ariel, Yaakov. *An Unusual Relationship: Evangelical Christians and Jews*. New York: New York University Press, 2013.

Aronoff, Myron J. "The 'Americanization' of Israeli Politics: Political and Cultural Change." *Israel Studies* 5, no. 1 (Spring 2000): 92–126.

Aviad, Janet. *Return to Judaism: Religious Renewal in Israel*. Chicago: University of Chicago Press, 1985.

Avineri, Shlomo. "University Protest Movements and Their Implications for the Jewish Communities." *Study Circle on Diaspora Jewry*. Jerusalem: The Hebrew University, 1970. [Hebrew]

Avneri, Arie. *The Social Welfare Pioneer: Dr. Israel Katz, Leader of the Welfare Revolution in Israel*. Tel Aviv: Ma'ariv, 2013. [Hebrew]

Avruch, Kevin. *American Immigrants in Israel: Social Identities and Change*. Chicago: University of Chicago Press, 1981.

Azaryahu, Maoz. "McIsrael? On the 'Americanization of Israel.'" *Israel Studies* 5, no. 1 (Spring 2001): 41–64.

Bar-Yosef, Hamutal. *Kri'ot u-shrikot: Essays*. Jerusalem: Carmel, 2005. [Hebrew]

Barthes, Roland. *Mythologies*. Translated by Annette Lavers. New York: Hill and Wang, 1972.

Baruch, Adam. *Media: Anthology, 1972–2008*. Edited by Shira Aviad, Rino Tzror, and Moran Shuv. Or Yehuda: Dvir, 2010. [Hebrew]

Baudrillard, Jean. *The Consumer Society: Myths and Structures*. Translated by Christ Turner. Thousand Oaks, CA: Sage, 1998.

Bauman, Zygmunt. "On Glocalization: Or Globalization for Some, Localization for Some Others." *Thesis Eleven* 54, no. 1 (1998): 37–49.

Beckerman, Gal. *When They'll Come for Us, We'll Be Gone: The Epic Struggle to Save Soviet Jewry*. New York: HarperCollins, 2011.

Bell, Philip, and Roger Bell, eds. *Americanization and Australia*. Sydney: University of New South Wales Press, 1998.

Ben-Amotz, Dahn. *I Don't Give a Damn*. Tel Aviv: Bitan, 1973. [Hebrew]

Ben-Mordechai, Yitzhak. "Myth, Reality, Parody: On the Structure and Meaning of Nissim Aloni's 'The American Princess.'" *Jerusalem Studies in Hebrew Literature* 18 (2001): 293–308. [Hebrew]

Ben-Mordechai, Yitzhak. "The Homeland Is the True Diaspora—On Nissim Aloni's World." *Iyunim bitkumat Israel: Studies in Zionism, the Yishuv and the State of Israel* 12 (2002): 567–90. [Hebrew]

Ben-Porat, Amir. *How Israel Became a Capitalist Society*. Haifa: Pardes, 2011. [Hebrew]

Ben-Zvi, Abraham. *The United States and Israel: The Limits of the Special Relationship*. New York: Columbia University Press, 1993.

Ben-Zvi, Abraham. *Lyndon B. Johnson and the Politics of Arms Sales to Israel*. London: Routledge, 2004.

Berlant, Lauren. *Cruel Optimism*. Durham, NC: Duke University Press, 2011.

Berman, Gerald. "Why North Americans Migrate to Israel." *The Jewish Journal of Sociology* 21, no. 2 (1979): 135–44.

Bernstein, Deborah. "The Black Panthers of Israel, 1971–1972: Contradictions and Protest in the Process of Nation-Building." PhD diss., University of Sussex, 1976.

Bitan, Moshe. *Political Diary, 1967–1970*. Tel Aviv: Olam Hadash, 2014. [Hebrew]

Blander, Dana. "Nation-Building from the Perspective of Public Opinion." *Israeli Sociology* 6, no. 1 (2004): 9–37. [Hebrew]
Blustein, Sarah. "Shlomo Carlebach's Shadow Side." *Lilith* 23, no. 1 (Spring 1998): 10–17.
Breins, Paul. *Tough Jews: Political Fantasies and the Moral Dilemma of American Jewry.* New York: Basic Books, 1990.
Bronfeld, Saul. "From Skyhawk to Phantom: The Beginning of an Aerial Friendship." *The Fisher Institute for Air and Space Strategic Studies* (January 2011). [Hebrew].
Brown, Michael. "The American Element in the Rise of Golda Meir, 1906–1929." *Jewish History* 6, nos. 1–2 (1992): 35–50.
Brown, Michael. *The Israeli-American Connection: Its Roots in the Yishuv, 1915–1945.* Detroit: Wayne State University Press, 1996.
Bugos, Glenn E. *Engineering the F-4 Phantom II: Parts into Systems.* Annapolis, MD: Naval Institute Press, 1996.
Bunim, Shmuel. *Here Is Bunim.* Tel Aviv: Dvir, 1994. [Hebrew]
Butler, Judith. *The Psychic Life of Power: Theories in Subjection.* Stanford, CA: Stanford University Press, 1997.
Carroll, Tamar W. *Mobilizing New York: AIDS, Antipoverty and Feminist Activism.* Chapel Hill: University of North Carolina Press, 2015.
Chacham, Michal. *Home within Home: Domestic Discourse and the Invention of Modern "Ashkenaziness."* Tel Aviv: Gama, 2020. [Hebrew]
Chatriot, Alain, Marie-Emmanuelle Chessel, and Matthew Hilton, eds. *The Expert Consumer: Associations and Professionals in Consumer Society.* Aldershot: Ashgate, 2006.
Chetrit, Sami Shalom. *The Mizrahi Struggle in Israel, 1948–2003.* Tel Aviv: Am Oved, 2004. [Hebrew]
Cohen, Lizabeth. *A Consumer's Republic: The Politics of Mass Consumption in Postwar America.* New York: Vintage Books, 2003.
Coleman, James. *Equality of Educational Opportunity.* Washington, DC: Department of Health, Education, and Welfare, 1966.
Coleman, James. "School Integration in Two Societies." *Megamot* 23, no. 3/4 (1977): 261–64. [Hebrew]
Conrad, Peter. *How the World Was Won: The Americanization of Everywhere.* London: Thames & Hudson, 2014.
Contreras, Joseph. *In the Shadow of the Giant: The Americanization of Modern Mexico.* New Brunswick, NJ: Rutgers University Press, 2009.
Converse, Jean M. *Survey Research in the United States: Roots and Emergence, 1890–1960.* Berkeley: University of California Press, 1987.
Coopersmith, Aryae. *Holy Beggars: A Journey from Haight Street to Jerusalem.* El Granada, CA: One World Lights, 2011.
Critchlow, Donald T. *Phyllis Schlafly and Grassroots Conservatism: A Woman's Crusade.* Princeton, NJ: Princeton University Press, 2008.

Cross, Gary. *An All-Consuming Century: Why Commercialism Won in Modern America.* New York: Columbia University Press, 2000.
Curtis, Michael, and Mordecai S. Chertoff, eds. *Israel: Social Structure and Change.* New Brunswick, NJ: Transaction Books, 1973.
Dan, Joseph. "The End of Frumkinian Hasidism." *Jerusalem Studies in Jewish Thought* 15 (1999): 61–274. [Hebrew]
Daunton, Martin, and Matthew Hilton, eds. *The Politics of Consumption: Material Culture and Politics in Europe and America.* Oxford: Berg, 2001.
Dayan, Moshe. *Vietnam Diary.* Tel Aviv: Dvir, 1966. [Hebrew]
Dayan, Moshe. *New Map—Different Relationships.* Tel Aviv: Ma'ariv/Shikmona, 1969. [Hebrew]
Debord, Guy. *The Society of the Spectacle.* Translated by Donald Nicholson-Smith. Brooklyn: Zone, 1994.
De Grazia, Victoria. *Irresistible Empire: America's Advance through Twentieth-Century Europe.* Cambridge, MA: Harvard University Press, 2006.
Di-Capua, Yoav. *No Exit: Arab Existentialism, Jean-Paul Sartre and Decolonization.* Chicago: University of Chicago Press, 2018.
Dolgin, Janet L. *Jewish Identity and the JDL.* Princeton, NJ: Princeton University Press, 1977.
Don-Yehiya, Eliezer, and Yeshayahu Liebman. "The Dilemma of Traditional Culture in a Modern State: Transformations and Developments in 'Civic Religion' in Israel." *Megamot* 28, no. 4 (Aug. 1984): 461–85. [Hebrew]
Doron, Abraham, and Ralph Kramer. *The Welfare State in Israel: The Evolution of Social Security Policy and Practice.* Boulder, CO: Westview, 1991.
Doron, Avraham. "Poverty in Israel." *Ammot: Bimonthly for Social Affairs and Literature* 2, no. 4 (Feb.–March 1964): 7–13. [Hebrew]
Dubnov, Arie M. "The Missing Beat Generation: Coming of Age and Nostalgism in Arik Einstein's Music." *Jewish Social Studies: History, Culture, Society* 21, no. 1 (Fall 2015): 49–88.
Eban, Abba. *Personal Witness: Israel through My Eyes.* New York: G. P. Putnam's Sons, 1992.
Eisenstadt, Mimi, and David Bar-Gal. "The Conception and Birth of the Baerwald School of Social Work at the Hebrew University, 1953–58." *Society and Welfare* 30, no. 1 (March 2010): 9–27. [Hebrew]
Elmaliach, Tal, and Anat Kidron. "Between Culture and Politics: Young Protest in Israel." "Israel 1967–1977: Continuity and Turning." Thematic series, *Iyunim bitkumat Israel: Studies in Zionism, the Yishuv and the State of Israel* 11 (2017): 78–101. [Hebrew]
Elon, Amos. *The Israelis: Founders and Sons.* New York: Holt, Rinehart & Winston, 1971.
El Or, Tamar, and Motti Regev. "The Making of an Israeli Style, 1967–73." "Israel 1967–1977: Continuity and Turning." Thematic series, *Iyunim bitkumat Israel: Studies in Zionism, the Yishuv and the State of Israel* 11 (2017): 308–33. [Hebrew]

Engel, Gerard. "North American Jewish Settlers in Israel." *The American Jewish Yearbook* 71 (1970): 161–87.
Epstein, Itzhak. "Open Letter to the Black Panther Party." *Jewish Radicalism: A Selected Anthology*. Edited by Jack Nusan Porter and Peter Dreier, 64–71. New York: Grove Press, 1973.
Featherstone, Mike. *Consumer Culture and Postmodernism*. London: Sage, 2007.
Feldman, Nitzan. "Economic Peace: Theory and Reality." *Strategic Assessment: A Multidisciplinary Journal on National Security* 12, no. 3 (November 2009): 17–24.
Feldman, Yael S. "From *The Madwoman in the Attic* to *The Women's Room*: The American Roots of Israeli Feminism." *Israel Studies* 5, no. 1 (Spring 2001): 266–86.
Fiedler, Lutz. "Matzpen: A Different Israeli History." In *The Routledge Handbook of the Global Sixties: Between Protest and Nation-Building*. Edited by Chen Jian et al., 457–68. London: Routledge, 2018.
First, Anat, and Eli Avraham. "Jerusalemite Longing for New York: The Manifestation of American Imagery in Israeli Advertisement." *Megamot* 42, no. 4 (Sept. 2003): 652–70. [Hebrew]
Fischbach, Michael R. *Black Power and Palestine: Transnational Countries of Color*. Stanford, CA: Stanford University Press, 2019.
Fischbach, Michael R. *The Movement and the Middle East: How the Arab-Israeli Conflict Divided the American Left*. Stanford, CA: Stanford University Press, 2020.
Fisher, Robert. *Let the People Decide: Neighborhood Organizing in America*. Woodbridge, CT: Twayne, 1994.
Foner, Philip S., ed. *The Black Panthers Speak*. Philadelphia: J. B. Lippincott, 1970.
Foulkes, Julia L. *A Place for Us: West Side Story and New York*. Chicago: University of Chicago Press, 2016.
Frankel, Oz. "What's in a Name? The Black Panthers in Israel." *The Sixties: A Journal of History, Politics and Culture* 1, no. 1 (June 2008): 9–26.
Frankel, Oz. "The Politics of the Radical Analogy: The Case of the Israeli Black Panthers." In *Black Power beyond Borders*. Edited by Nico Slate, 81–106. New York: Palgrave, 2012.
Frankel, Oz. "Your Part in the Phantom: American Technology, National Identity, and the War of Attrition." *Israel Studies* 24, no. 1 (Spring 2019): 174–99.
Frankel, Oz. "Blackness in Translation: The Israeli Black Panthers, 1971." In *Blackness in Israel: Rethinking Racial Boundaries*. Edited by Uri Dorchin and Gabriella Djerrahian, 91–112. New York: Routledge, 2021.
Freedman, Marcia. *Exile in the Promised Land: A Memoir*. Ithaca, NY: Firebrand Books, 1990.
French, John R. P., Jr., and Naphtali Golomb. "A Report to the American Council for the Behavioral Sciences in the Kibbutz Management and Social Research Center." Institute for Social Research, University of Michigan, Ann Arbor. July 1968.
Frenkel, Michal. "The Invisible History of the Visible Hand: The Institutionalization of Israel's Field of Management." PhD diss., Tel Aviv University, 2000. [Hebrew]
Frenkel, Michal, and Yehuda Shenhav. "From Americanization to Colonization: The

Diffusion of Productivity Models Revisited." *Organization Studies* 24, no. 9 (2003): 1537–61.

Frenkel, Michal. "The Politics of Translation: How State-Level Political Relations Affect the Cross-National Travel of Management Ideas." *Organization* 12, no. 2 (2005): 275–301.

Frust, Shifra. "The Popular Music Festivals as a Mirror of Changes in the Israeli Society." MA thesis, Bar-Ilan University, 1999. [Hebrew]

Furman, Giora. *Alef-Alef: Was It Real or Not*. Tel Aviv: Miskal, 2004. [Hebrew]

Gabbay, Yoram. *Political Economy: The Gap between Perception and Reality*. Tel Aviv: Hakibbutz Hameuchad, 2009. [Hebrew]

Gal, John. *Social Security in Israel*. Jerusalem: Magnes, 2004. [Hebrew]

Galily, Yair, and Michael Bar-Eli. "From Tal Brody to European Champions: Early Americanization and the 'Golden Age' of Israeli Basketball, 1965–1979." *Journal of Sport History* 32, no. 3 (Fall 2005): 401–22.

Galily, Yair, and Ken Sheard. "Cultural Imperialism and Sport: The Americanization of Israeli Basketball." *Culture, Sport, Society* 5, no. 2 (Summer 2002): 55–78.

Gan, Alon. "Social Transformations in the Kibbutz Movement in the 1960s." *Iyunim bitkumat Israel: Studies in Zionism, the Yishuv and the State of Israel* 16 (2006): 343–72. [Hebrew]

Gardiner, Michael E. *Critiques of Everyday Life*. London: Routledge, 2000.

Gazit, Shlomo. *The Carrot and the Stick: Israel's Policy in Judea and Samaria, 1967–68*. Washington, DC: B'nai B'rith Books, 1995.

Gelber, Yoav. *Attrition: The Forgotten War*. Haman Industrial Park: Dvir, 2017. [Hebrew]

Gilboa, Noa K. "'Nugni-Nugni Guitara' [Play-Play Guitar!]: The *Kaveret* Band and Israeli Identity, 1967–1976." *Israelis* 7 (2015): 138–81. [Hebrew]

Ginor, Isabella, and Gideon Remez. *The Soviet-Israeli War, 1967–1973: The USSR's Military Intervention in the Egyptian-Israeli Conflict*. Oxford: Oxford University Press, 2017.

Gitelman, Zvi. *Becoming Israelis: Political Resocialization of Soviet and American Immigrants*. New York: Praeger, 1982.

Glendon, Mary Ann. *Rights Talk: The Impoverishment of Political Discourse*. New York: Free Press, 1991.

Glickman, Lawrence B. *Buying Power: A History of Consumer Activism in America*. Chicago: University of Chicago Press, 2009.

Golan, Matti. *With Friends Like You: What Israelis Really Think about American Jews*. Translated by Hillel Halkin. New York: Free Press, 1992.

Goldin, Claudia, and Robert Margo, "The Great Compression: The Wage Structure in the United States in Mid-Century." *Quarterly Journal of Economics* 107, no. 1 (Feb. 1992): 1–34.

Gordon, Shmuel. *Thirty Hours in October*. Tel Aviv: Ma'ariv, 2008. [Hebrew]

Gratch, Haya, ed. *Twenty-Five Years of Social Research in Israel: A Review of the Work of the Israel Institute of Applied Social Research, 1947–1971*. Jerusalem: Jerusalem Academic Press, 1973.

Greenberg, Cheryl Lynn. *Troubling the Waters: Black-Jewish Relations in the American Century*. Princeton, NJ: Princeton University Press, 2010.

Greenberg, Yitzhak. "Pinhas Sapir and the Issue of the 'Occupied Territories': From Perceptiveness to Passivity." *Iyunim bitkumat Israel: Studies in Zionism, the Yishuv and the State of Israel* 15 (2005): 275–300. [Hebrew]

Greenberg, Yitzhak. *Zalman Aranne: Politician and Intellectual*. Tel Aviv: Hakibbutz Hameuchad, 2018. [Hebrew]

Grossman, Haim. "A Picture as a Souvenir: Moshe Dayan—Portrait of an Israeli Hero through the Prism of Applied Art." *Israel: Studies in Zionism and the State of Israel, History, Society, Culture* 13 (2008): 181–208. [Hebrew]

Gurevitch, Zali. *On Israeli and Jewish Space*. Tel Aviv: Am Oved, 2007. [Hebrew]

Gutwein, Danny. "'Bourgeois *Halutziut*': Popular Culture and the Ethos of Israel's 'Established Middle Class'—the Lyrics of Naomi Shemer, 1956–1967." *Israel: Studies in Zionism and the State of Israel, History, Society, Culture* 20 (Spring 2012): 21–80. [Hebrew]

HaGadol, Prince Gavriel, and Odehyah Baht Israel. *The Impregnable People: An Exodus of African Americans Back to Africa*. Washington, DC: Communicators Press, 1992.

Halkin, Hillel. "Americans in Israel." *Commentary* 53 (May 1972): 54–63.

Halpern, Merav, and Aaron Lapidot. *G Suit: Pages from the Logbook of the Israeli Air Force*. Tel Aviv: Ministry of Defense, 1987. [Hebrew]

Harel, Ezrah Menashe. *We Have Great Power*. Privately Published, 2010. [Hebrew]

Hazleton, Lesley. *Israeli Women: The Reality behind the Myth*. New York: Simon and Schuster, 1977.

Hed, Ronit. "Looking Back with Anger." *New Israel Fund: Written Seedling* [Shatil shebachtav] no. 11 (June 2002): 3–7. [Hebrew]

Helman, Anat. *Consumer Culture and Leisure in the Young State of Israel*. Jerusalem: The Zalman Shazar Center, 2020. [Hebrew]

Herbst, Susan. *Numbered Voices: How Opinion Polling Has Shaped American Politics*. Chicago: Chicago University Press, 1993.

Hillygus, D. Sunshine. "The Evolution of Election Polling in the United States." *Public Opinion Quarterly* 75, no. 5 (2011): 962–81.

Hirschhorn, Sara Yael. *City on a Hilltop: American Jews and the Israeli Settler Movement*. Cambridge, MA: Harvard University Press, 2017.

Hofnong, Menachem. *Protest and Butter: The Black Panthers' Demonstrations and Allocations for Social Needs*. Jerusalem: Nevo, 2006. [Hebrew]

Hollinger, David A. *Science, Jews, and Secular Culture: Studies in Mid-Twentieth-Century American Intellectual History*. Princeton, NJ: Princeton University Press, 1996.

Horowitz, Daniel. *The Anxieties of Affluence: Critiques of American Consumer Culture, 1939–1979*. Amherst: University of Massachusetts Press, 2005.

Horwitz, Menachem. "Social Work and Civil Disobedience." *Welfare Ministry: Social Issues Bimonthly* 17 (Nov. 1973): 8–11. [Hebrew]

Huebner, Yehudith. *A Life Story*. Jerusalem: Shashar, 2001. [Hebrew]

Jackson, John L., Jr. *Thin Description: Ethnography and the African Hebrew Israelites of Jerusalem.* Cambridge, MA: Harvard University Press, 2013.

Jacobson, Matthew Frye. *Roots Too: White Ethnic Revival in Post-Civil Right America.* Cambridge, MA: Harvard University Press, 2009.

Jaffe, Eliezer D. "The Social Work Establishment and Social Change in Israel." Welfare Ministry. *Social Issue Bimonthly* 13 (Sept. 1969): 11–15. [Hebrew]

Jaffe, Eliezer D. "Manpower Supply and Admissions Policy in Israeli Social Work Education." *Journal of Jewish Communal Service* 53, no. 3 (1977): 242–49.

Jaffe, Eliezer D. *Unequal by Chance: Opportunity-Deprived, Disadvantaged Students in Higher Education in Israel.* Jerusalem: Geffen, 1988.

Joseph, Gilbert M., Catherine C. LeGrand, and Ricardo Salvatore, eds. *Close Encounters of Empire: Writing the Cultural History of U.S.-Latin American Relations.* Durham, NC: Duke University Press, 1998.

Jubas, Harry. "The Adjustment Process of Americans and Canadians in Israel and Their Integration into Israel Society." PhD diss., Michigan State University, 1974.

Kahane, Libby. *Rabbi Meir Kahane: His Life and Thought.* Vol. 1, 1923–1975. Jerusalem: Institute for Publication of the Writing of Rabbi Meir Kahane, 2008.

Kanovsky, Eliyahu. *The Economic Impact of the Six-Day War: Israel, the Occupied Territories, Egypt, Jordan.* New York: Praeger, 1970.

Kaplan, Amy. *Our American Israel.* Cambridge, MA: Harvard University Press, 2018.

Kaplan, Steven. "Black and White, Blue and White and Beyond the Pale: Ethiopian Jews and the Discourse of Colour in Israel." *Jewish Culture and History* 5, no. 1 (2002): 51–68.

Katsiaficas, George. *The Imagination of the New Left: A Global Analysis.* Boston, MA: South End Press, 1987.

Katz, Elihu, and Michael Gurevitch. *The Culture of Leisure in Israel: Patterns of Spending Time and Consuming Culture.* Tel Aviv: Am Oved, 1973. [Hebrew]

Katz, Elihu et al. *Leisure Patterns in Israel: Changes in Cultural Activity, 1970–1990.* Tel Aviv: Open University, 2000. [Hebrew]

Kaufman, Menachem. "From Philanthropy to Commitment: The Six-Day War and the United Jewish Appeal." *Journal of Israeli History* 15, no. 2 (1994): 161–91.

Kaufman, Rony. "Panthers in the Establishment: Involvement of Jerusalem Municipality Social Workers in Public Struggles and Social Protest Movements, 1965–1985." In *Justice Instead of Charity: Chapters in the Development of Social Work in Israel.* Edited by John Gal and Roni Holler, 366–93. Sdeh Boker: The Ben-Gurion Research Institute for the Study of Israel and Zionism, 2019. [Hebrew]

Kaye/Kantrowitz, Melanie, and Irena Klepfisz, eds. *The Tribe of Dina: A Jewish Women's Anthology.* Montpelier, VT: Sinister Wisdom Books, 1986.

Khazzoom, Aziza. *Shifting Ethnic Boundaries and Inequality in Israel; Or, How the Polish Peddler Became a German Intellectual.* Stanford, CA: Stanford University Press, 2008.

Kimmerling, Baruch. *The Invention and Decline of Israeliness: State, Society, and the Military.* Berkeley: University of California Press, 2001.

King, Paul, Orli Hacohen, Hillel Frisch, and Daniel J. Elazar. *Project Renewal in Israel:*

Urban Revitalization through Partnership. Lanham, MD: University Press of America, 1987.

Klagsbrun, Francine. *Lioness: Golda Meir and the Nation of Israel*. New York: Schocken, 2017.

Klein, Yossi (Joseph). *The Beginning of Tel-Aviv's Americanization*. Jerusalem: Carmel, 2011. [Hebrew]

Kligman, Mark. "On the Creators and Consumers of Orthodox Popular Music in Brooklyn." *YIVO Annual of Jewish Social Science* 23 (1996): 259–93.

Klimke, Martin. *The Other Alliance: Student Protest in West Germany and the United States in the Global Sixties*. Princeton, NJ: Princeton University Press, 2010.

Kline, Claude. "The Lansky Case." *Israel Law Review* 8 (1973): 286–95.

Kochavi, Noam. *Nixon and Israel: Forging a Conservative Partnership*. Albany: State University of New York Press, 2009.

Koreh, Michal. "The Golden Age of the Welfare State in Israel." "Israel 1967–1977: Continuity and Turning." Thematic series, *Iyunim bitkumat Israel: Studies in Zionism, the Yishuv and the State of Israel* 11 (2017): 159–84.

Kornbluh, Felicia. *The Battle for Welfare Rights: Politics and Poverty in Modern America*. Philadelphia: University of Pennsylvania Press, 2007.

Kottler, Yair. *Heil Kahane*. Tel Aviv: Modan, 1985. [Hebrew]

Kramer, Paul A. "Power and Connection: Imperial Histories of the United States in the World." *American Historical Review* 116, no. 5 (Dec. 2011): 1348–91.

Krampf, Arie. *The National Origins of the Market Economy: Economic Developmentalism during the Formation of the Israeli Capitalism*. Jerusalem: Magnes, 2015. [Hebrew]

Krampf, Arie. *The Israeli Path to Neoliberalism: The State, Continuity and Change*. London: Routledge, 2018.

Krampf, Arie, Uri Ansenberg, and Barak Zur. "Bringing Politics Back In: Embedded Neoliberalism in Israel during Rabin's Second Government." *Israel Studies Review* 37, no. 2 (June 2022): 1–35.

Kroes, Rob. *If You've Seen One, You've Seen the Mall: European and American Mass Culture*. Urbana: University of Illinois Press, 1996.

Kroes, Rob. "American Empire and Cultural Imperialism: a View from the Receiving End." *Diplomatic History* 23, no. 3 (Summer 1999): 463–77.

Kruk, Hadas. "A New Profession in Israel—Product Design: The Institutional Initiatives to Promote the Profession, 1956–1975." MA thesis, Tel Aviv University, 2003. [Hebrew]

Kuisel, Richard F. *Seducing the French: The Dilemma of Americanization*. Berkeley: University of California Press, 1993.

Kuisel, Richard F. *The French Way: How France Embraced and Rejected American Values and Power*. Princeton, NJ: Princeton University Press, 2011.

Lacey, Robert. *Little Man: Meyer Lansky and the Gangster Life*. New York: Little, Brown, 1991.

Lahav, Pnina. *Judgment in Jerusalem: Chief Justice Simon Agranat and the Zionist Century*. Berkeley: University of California Press, 1990.

Lahav, Pnina. "American Moment[s]: When, How, and Why Did Israeli Law Faculties Come to Resemble Elite U.S. Law Schools?" "Histories of Legal Transplantations." *Theoretical Inquiries in Law* 10, no. 2 (July 2009): 653–97.

Lahav, Pnina. *The Only Woman in the Room: Golda Meir and Her Path to Power*. Princeton, NJ: Princeton University Press, 2023.

Lammfromm, Arnon, and Hagai Tsoref, eds. *Commemorative Series: The Presidents and Prime Ministers of Israel: Levi Eshkol: The Third Prime Minister, Selected Documents (1895–1969)*. Jerusalem: Israel State Archives, 2002. [Hebrew]

Laskier, Michael M. "Israeli Activism American Style: Civil Liberties, Environmental, and Peace Organizations as Pressure Groups for Social Change, 1970s–1990s." *Israel Studies* 5, no. 1 (Spring 2000): 128–52.

Lefebvre, Henri. *Everyday Life in the Modern World*. Translated by Sacha Rabinovitch. New Brunswick, NJ: Transaction Books, 1984.

Lehman-Wilzig, Sam. *Public Protest in Israel, 1949–1992*. Ramat Gan: Bar-Ilan University Press, 1992. [Hebrew]

Leibovitz, Liel. *Aliya: Three Generations of American-Jewish Immigration to Israel*. New York: St. Martin Press, 2005.

Lerner, Natan. "Affirmative Action in Israel." In *International Perspective on Affirmative Action: A Bellagio Conference*, 110–53. New York: The Rockefeller Foundation, 1984.

Lev, Tali. "'We Will Erase the Past of Those Who Have Past,' The Full Protocol of the Black Panthers Meeting with the Prime Minister of Israel, April 1971." *Theory and Criticism* 32 (Spring 2008): 197–226. [Hebrew]

Lev, Tali, and Yehuda Shenhav. "'Don't Say Worker—But Panther!': The Black Panthers and the Politics of Identity in the Early 1970s." *Theory and Criticism* 35 (Autumn 2009): 141–64. [Hebrew]

Lev, Tali, and Yehuda Shenhav. "The Social Construction of the Enemy Within: The Black Panthers as a Target of Moral Panic." *Israeli Sociology* 12, no. 1 (Spring 2010): 135–57. [Hebrew]

Levi, Shimon. *Israeli Theater: Spaces, Times and Plots*. Tel Aviv: Resling, 2016. [Hebrew]

Levin, Hanoch. *The Whore from Ohio*. (1978). Hanoch Levin: Official Site: https://www.hanochlevin.com/texts/1408.

Lieblich, Amalia. *My Ehud*. Tel Aviv: Air Force Association, 2008. [Hebrew]

Liebman, Charles. "Toward the Study of Popular Religion in Israel." *Megamot* 23, no. 2 (April 1977): 95–109. [Hebrew]

Liebman, Charles, and Eliezer Don-Yehiya. *Civil Religion in Israel: Traditional Judaism and Political Culture in the Jewish State*. Berkeley: University of California Press, 1983.

Lilleker, Darren, and Richard Scullion, eds. *Voters or Consumers: Imagining the Contemporary Electorate*. Newcastle: Cambridge Scholars Publishing, 2008.

Lury, Celia. *Consumer Culture*. New Brunswick, NJ: Rutgers University Press, 2011.

Lustick, Ian S. "Israel as a Non-Arab State: The Political Implications of Mass Immigration of Non-Jews." *Middle East Journal* 53, no. 3 (Summer 1999): 417–33.

Maeda, Daryl J. "Red Panthers, Red Guards, and Chinamen: Constructing Asian

American Identity through Performing Blackness, 1969–1972." *American Quarterly* 57, no. 4 (Dec. 2005): 1079–1103.

Magid, Shaul. *Meir Kahane: The Public Life and Political Thought of an American Jewish Radical*. Princeton, NJ: Princeton University Press, 2021.

Maier, Charles S. *Among Empires: American Ascendancy and Its Predecessors*. Cambridge, MA: Harvard University Press, 2006.

Malchow, Howard. *Special Relations: The Americanization of Britain?* Stanford, CA: Stanford University Press, 2011.

Mann, Rafi. *The Leader and the Media: David Ben-Gurion and the Struggle over Israel's Public Sphere, 1948–1963*. Tel Aviv: Am Oved, 2012. [Hebrew]

Mann, Raphael, and Tsippy Gon-Gross. *Galei Tzahal Round the Clock*. Tel Aviv: Ministry of Defense, 1991. [Hebrew]

Manor, Ehud. *I Have No Other Country: Songs as a Biography*. Edited by Dubi Lentz. Tel Aviv: Hakibbutz Hameuchad, 2003. [Hebrew]

Marcuse, Herbert. *One-Dimensional Man: Studies in the Ideology of Advanced Industrial Society*. Boston: Beacon Press, 1964.

Markowitz, Fran. "Israel as Africa, Africa as Israel: 'Divine Geography' in the Personal Narratives and Community Identity of the Black Hebrew Israelites." *Anthropological Quarterly* 69, no. 4 (Oct. 1996): 193–205.

Markowitz, Fran. "Already Black . . . and Proud and Righteous: The African Hebrew Israelite Community in the State of Israel." In *Blackness in Israel: Rethinking Racial Boundaries*. Edited by Uri Dorchin and Gabriella Djerrahian, 198–213. New York: Routledge, 2021.

Mart, Michelle. *Eyes on Israel: How America Came to View Israel as an Ally*. Albany: State University of New York Press, 2006.

Martin, Ben L. "From Negro to Black to African American: The Power of Names and Naming." *Political Science Quarterly* 106, no. 1 (Spring 1991): 83–107.

Mayer, Robert N. *The Consumer Movement: Guardians of the Marketplace*. Boston: Twayne, 1989.

McAlister, Melani. *Epic Encounters: Culture, Media, and U.S. Interests in the Middle East since 1945*. Berkeley: University of California Press, 2005.

Mearsheimer, John L., and Stephen M. Walt. *The Israel Lobby and U.S. Foreign Policy*. New York: Farrar, Straus and Giroux, 2007.

Melendez, Mikey. *We Took the Streets: Fighting for Latino Rights with the Young Lords*. New York: St. Martin's Press, 2003.

Merkley, Paul C. *American Presidents, Religion and Israel: The Heirs of Cyrus*. Westport, CT: Praeger, 2004.

Messick, Hank. *Lansky*. New York: G. P. Putnam's Sons, 1971.

Michaeli, Ethan. "Another Exodus: The Hebrew Israelites from Chicago to Dimona." In *Black Zion: African American Religious Encounters with Judaism*. Edited by Yvonne Chireau and Nathaniel Deutsch, 73–90. Oxford: Oxford University Press, 2000.

Michel, Marshal L., III. "The Revolt of the Majors: How the Air Force Changed after Vietnam." PhD diss., Auburn University, 2006.

Miles, Steven. *Consumerism: As a Way of Life*. London: Sage, 1998.
Mitelpunkt, Shaul. *Israel in the American Mind: The Cultural Politics of US-Israeli Relations, 1958–1988*. Cambridge: Cambridge University Press, 2018.
Molcho, Avner. "Capitalism and the 'American Way' in Israel: Productivity, Management and the Capitalist Ethos in American Technical Aid in the 1950s." In *Society and Economy in Israel: Historical and Contemporary Perspectives*. Edited by Avi Bareli, Daniel Gutwein, and Tuvia Friling, 263–94. Sdeh Boker: Ben-Gurion Institute for the Study of Israel and Zionism, 2005. [Hebrew]
Munk, Yael. "*Salach Shabati*: The Precursor of a Subversive Popular Cinema in Israel." *Pe'amim: Studies in Oriental Jewry* 135 (Spring 2013): 145–62. [Hebrew]
Myrdal, Gunnar. *An American Dilemma: The Negro Problem and Modern Democracy*. New York: Harper and Brothers, 1944.
Nadasen, Premilla. *Welfare Warriors: The Welfare Rights Movement in the United States*. New York: Routledge, 2005.
Nir, Dov. *Landscapes of France: Essays and Travels*. Tel Aviv: Masada, 1960. [Hebrew]
Offer, Shira. "The Ethiopian Community in Israel: Segregation and the Creation of a Racial Cleavage." *Ethnic and Racial Studies* 30, no. 3 (2007): 461–80.
Ofrat, Gideon. *New York–Tel Aviv: The American Connection of Israeli Art*. Tel Aviv: Ofer Levin Foundation for Israeli Art, 2016. [Hebrew]
Oldenziel, Ruth, and Karin Zachmann, eds. *Cold War Kitchen: Americanization, Technology, and European Users*. Cambridge, MA: MIT Press, 2008.
Olson, Jason M. *America's Road to Jerusalem: The Impact of the Six-Day War on Protestant Politics*. Lanham, MD: Lexington, 2018.
Ophir (Offenbacher), Natan. *Rabbi Shlomo Carlebach: Life, Mission, and Legacy*. Rishon Letzion: Miskal Israel, 2017. [Hebrew]
Orenstein, Daniel E., Alon Tal, and Char Miller, eds. *Between Ruin and Restoration: An Environmental History of Israel*. Pittsburgh, PA: Pittsburgh University Press, 2013.
Orian, Dan. "The Search for Jewish Identity in the Israeli Theater (*Ish hasid haya*, 1968)." *Bama Drama Quarterly* 139–40 (1996): 99–114. [Hebrew]
Orian, Dan. *The Ethnic Problem in the Israeli Theater*. Tel Aviv: Open University, 2004. [Hebrew]
Oz, Avraham. *Fields and Language: Hebrew Drama and the Zionist Narrative*. Tel Aviv: Resling, 2014. [Hebrew]
Peled, Benjamin. *Days of Reckoning*. Ben-Shemen: Modan, 2004. [Hebrew]
Peterson, Mark. *Consumption and Everyday Life*. London: Routledge, 2017.
Picketty, Thomas, and Emmanuel Saez. "Income Inequality in the United States. 1913–1998." *Quarterly Journal of Economics* 118, no. 1 (Feb. 2003): 1–39.
Piven, Frances Fox, and Richard Cloward. "The Weight of the Poor: A Strategy to End Poverty (reprinted with a new introduction by Frances Fox Piven)." *New Political Science* 33, no. 3 (2011): 271–84.
Power, F. Clark, Ann Higgins, and Lawrence Kohlberg. *Lawrence Kohlberg's Approach to Moral Education*. New York: Columbia University Press, 1989.
Pratt, Mary Louise. "Arts of the Contact Zone." *Profession* (1991): 33–40.

Preminger, Aner. *Reflections on Cinema and Ethos*. Tel Aviv: Resling, 2017. [Hebrew]
Quandt, William B. *Decade of Decisions: American Policy toward the Arab-Israeli Conflict, 1967–1976*. Berkeley: University of California Press, 1977.
Rabin, Leah. *Full-Time Wife*. Tel Aviv: Edanim, 1988. [Hebrew]
Rabin, Yitzhak. *The Rabin Memoirs*. Boston: Little, Brown, 1979.
Rabinovich, Itamar. *Yitzhak Rabin: Soldier, Leader, Statesman*. New Haven, CT: Yale University Press, 2017.
Rachlevsky, Sefi. *No Limit*. Tel Aviv: Kineret, Zmora-Bitan, Or Yehuda: Dvir, 2008. [Hebrew]
Ram, Uri. *The Globalization of Israel: McWorld in Tel Aviv, Jihad in Jerusalem*. New York: Routledge, 2007.
Ram, Uri. *The Return of Martin Buber: National and Social Thought in Israel from Buber to the Neo-Buberians*. Tel Aviv: Resling, 2015. [Hebrew]
Ram, Uri. *Israeli Sociology: History of Ideas, 1882–2018*. Sdeh Boker: Ben-Gurion Institute for the Study of Israel and Zionism, 2020. [Hebrew]
Ratner, David. "Rap, Racism, and Visibility: Black Music as a Mediator of Young Israeli-Ethiopians' Experience of Being 'Black' in a 'White' Society." *African and Black Diaspora: An International Journal* 12, no. 1 (2019): 94–108.
Rappaport, Noam. *Israeli Rock, 1967–1973*. Tel Aviv: Marom, 2018. [Hebrew]
Ravitzky, Aviezer. *Messianism, Zionism and Jewish Religious Radicalism*. Chicago: Chicago University Press, 1996.
Regev, Motti, and Edwin Seroussi. *Popular Music and National Culture in Israel*. Berkeley: University of California Press, 2004.
Reichner, Elyashiv, and Eliezer D. Jaffe. *A Social Pioneer: The Life and Work of Prof. Eliezer D. Jaffe*. Translated by Toby Klein Greenwald. Privately published, 2022.
Resh, Nura, and Drora Kfir. "Educational Integration in Israel: Thirty Years of Hesitant Policy in View of Changing Ideology." *Megamot* 43, no. 1 (Feb. 2004): 33–63. [Hebrew].
Resh, Nura, and Yechezkel Dar. "The Rise and Fall of School Integration in Israel: Research and Policy Analysis." *British Education Research Journal* 38, no. 6 (Dec. 2012): 929–51.
Resnik, Julia. "Discourse Structuration in Israel, Democratization of Education, Democratization of Education and the Impact of the Global Education Network." *Journal of Education Policy* 22, no. 3 (May 2007): 215–40.
Robertson, Roland. "'Glocalization': Time-Space and Homogeneity-Heterogeneity." In *Global Modernities*. Edited by Mike Featherstone, Scott Lash, and Roland Robertson, 25–44. London: Sage, 1995.
Rockaway, Robert A. "Hoodlum Hero: The Jewish Gangster as Defender of His People, 1919–1949." *American Jewish History* 82, no. 1/4 (1994): 215–35.
Rogin, Michael. *Blackface, White Noise: Jewish Immigrants in the Hollywood Melting Pot*. Berkeley: University of California Press, 1998.
Ronen (Pekker), Ran. *Hawk in the Sky*. Tel Aviv: Yedioth Ahronoth, 2002. [Hebrew]
Roniger, Louise, and Michael Feiga. "The *Frayer* [Sucker] Culture and Israeli Identity." *Alpayim* 7 (1993): 118–37. [Hebrew]

Ross, Kristin. *Fast Cars, Clean Bodies: Decolonization and the Reordering of French Culture.* Cambridge, MA: MIT Press, 1996.

Rosten, Leo. *The Joys of Yiddish.* New York: McGraw Hill, 1968.

Roter, Raphael, and Nira Shamai. "Patterns of Poverty in Israel—First Findings." *Social Security* 1 (Feb. 1971): 17–28. [Hebrew]

Roth-Cohen, Asnat, and Yehiel Limor. "'From Craft to Industry': Factors, Processes and Turning Points in the Development of the Advertisement Industry in Israel." *Media Frames: Israeli Journal of Communication* 14 (Spring 2015): 58–86. [Hebrew]

Roudometof, Victor. *Glocalization: A Critical Introduction.* New York: Routledge, 2016.

Ryan, William. *Blaming the Victim.* New York: Pantheon, 1971.

Rydell, Robert W. *Buffalo Bill in Bologna: The Americanization of the World.* Chicago: University of Chicago Press, 2005.

Safran, Hanna. *Don't Wanna Be Nice Girls: The Struggle for Suffrage and the New Feminism in Israel.* Haifa: Pardes, 2006. [Hebrew]

Sandberg, Haim. "Cultural Colonialism: The Americanization of Legal Education in Israel." *Hamishpat* 27 (Aug. 2009): 52–60. [Hebrew]

Sandquist, Eric. *Strangers in the Land: Blacks, Jews, Post-Holocaust America.* Cambridge, MA: Harvard University Press, 2005.

Sapir, Michal. *Hayesh Hagadol: A Biography of Pinchas Sapir.* Tel Aviv: Miskal, 2011. [Hebrew]

Sassatelli, Roberta. *Consumer Culture: History, Theory and Politics.* Thousand Oaks, CA: Sage, 2007.

Schab, Alon, and Eran Shalev. "The Rock Musical and the Beginning of Rock Music in Israel in the Early 70s." *Journal of Israeli History* 40, no. 1 (May 2023): 1–25.

Schweitzer, Ariel. *The New Sensitivity: Modern Israeli Cinema in the 1960s and 1970s.* Translated by Erga Heller. Tel Aviv: Bavel, 2013. [Hebrew]

Segev, Tom. *Elvis in Jerusalem: Post-Zionism and the Americanization of Israel.* Translated by Haim Watzman. New York: Metropolitan, 2002.

Segev, Tom. *1967: Israel, the War, and the Year that Transformed the Middle East.* Translated by Jessica Cohen. New York: Henry Holt, 2007.

Segev, Zohar. "American Zionists' Place in Israel after Statehood: From Involved Partners to Outside Supporters." *American Jewish History* 93, no. 3 (2007): 277–302.

Senor, Dan, and Saul Singer. *Start-Up Nation: The Story of Israel's Economic Miracle.* New York: Twelve, 2009.

Shaked, Gershon. *About Stories and Plays.* Jerusalem: Keter, 1992. [Hebrew]

Shalev, Michael. *Labour and the Political Economy in Israel.* Oxford: Oxford University Press, 1992.

Shalev, Moshe. "Documentation and Assessment of a Community Renewal Project: A Case of an Israeli Kibbutz." PhD diss., University of California, Los Angeles, 1976.

Shalom, Danny. *Phantoms over Cairo: Israeli Air Force in the War of Attrition.* Rishon Letzion: Ba'avir, 2007. [Hebrew]

Shandler, Jeffrey. *Adventures in Yiddishland: Postvernacular Language and Culture.* Berkeley: University of California Press, 2008.

Shapira, Daniel. *Alone in the Sky*. Tel Aviv: Ma'ariv-Hed Artzi, 1994. [Hebrew]
Shapira, Rina, and Eva Etzioni-Halevy. *Who Is the Israeli Student?* Tel Aviv: Am Oved, 1973. [Hebrew]
Shavelson, Melville. *How to Make a Jewish Movie*. London: W. H. Allen, 1971.
Shaw, Tony, and Giora Goodman. *Hollywood and Israel: A History*. New York: Columbia University Press, 2022.
Sheinblat, Hemi. "The Importation of the American Supermarket Model to Israel, 1957–67." *Iyunim: Multidisciplinary Studies in Israeli and Modern Jewish Society* 38 (Dec. 2022): 87–114. [Hebrew]
Shiff, Ze'ev. *Wings over Suez: The Story of the Israeli Air Corps during the War of Attrition*. Haifa: Shikmona, 1970. [Hebrew]
Shohat, Ella. *Israeli Cinema: East/West and the Politics of Representation*. Austin: University of Texas Press, 1987.
Shohat, Ella. "The Invention of the Mizrahim." *Journal of Palestine Studies* 29, no. 1 (Autumn 1999): 5–20.
Singer, Merrill. "Symbolic Identity Formation in an African American Religious Sect: The Black Hebrew Israelites." In *Black Zion: African American Religious Encounters with Judaism*. Edited by Yvonne Chireau and Nathaniel Deutsch, 55–72. Oxford: Oxford University Press, 2000.
Sion, Dan. "Mutuality in the Dissemination of Military Innovations: The USAF Tactical Command and the IAF, 1973–1991." *The Fisher Institute for Air and Space Strategic Studies* (Dec. 2014). [Hebrew]
Slate, Nico, ed. *Black Power beyond Borders: The Global Dimension of the Black Power Movement*. New York: Palgrave, 2012.
Smith, David, Lewis Baston, Jean Bocock, and Peter Scott. "Americanization and UK Higher Education: Towards a History of Transatlantic Influence on Policy and Practice." *Journal of Education Policy* 17, no. 4 (July–Aug. 2002): 443–61.
Solomon, Alisa. *Wonder of Wonders: A Cultural History of Fiddler on the Roof*. New York: Metropolitan Books, 2013.
Spector, Stephen. *Evangelicals and Israel: The Story of American Christian Zionism*. New York: Oxford University Press, 2009.
Spector, Iftach. *Loud and Clear*. Tel Aviv: Yedioth, 2007. [Hebrew]
Spector, Iftach. "The Phantom's Fall." *Ma'arachot* 422 (Dec. 2008): 34–39. [Hebrew]
Sprinzak, Ehud. *Early Manifestations of the Politics of De-Legitimation in Israel, 1967–1972*. Jerusalem: Levi Eshkol Institute, The Hebrew University, 1973. [Hebrew]
Sprinzak, Ehud. "The Emergence of the Israeli Radical Right." *Comparative Politics* 21, no. 2 (1989): 171–92.
Sprinzak, Ehud. *The Ascendance of Israel's Radical Right*. Oxford: Oxford University Press, 1991.
Staub, Michael E. *Torn at the Roots: The Crisis of Jewish Liberalism in Postwar America*. New York: Columbia University Press, 2002.
Steinberg, Gerald M. "Technology, Weapons, and Industrial Development: The Case of Israel." *Technology in Society* 7, no. 4 (1985): 387–98.

Steinhardt, Joanna. "American Neo-Hasids in the Land of Israel." *Nova Religio* 13, no. 4 (2010): 22–42.
Stephan, Alexander, ed. *Americanization and Anti-Americanism: The German Encounter with American Culture after 1945*. New York: Berghahn, 2004.
Stone, A. Russell, and Ilan S. Troen. "Early Social Research in and on Israel." In *Israel: The First Decade of Independence*. Edited by Ilan Troen and Noah Lucas, 375–99. Albany: State University of New York Press, 1995.
Strasser, Susan, Charles McGovern, and Matthias Judt, eds. *Getting and Spending: European and American Consumer Societies in the Twentieth Century*. Cambridge: Cambridge University Press, 1998.
Sugrue, Thomas J. *The Origins of the Urban Crisis: Race and Inequality in Postwar Detroit*. Princeton, NJ: Princeton University Press, 1996.
Swirski, Shlomo. *Education in Israel: Schooling for Inequality*. Tel Aviv: Breirot, 1990. [Hebrew]
Tal, Alon. *Pollution in a Promised Land: An Environmental History of Israel*. Berkeley: University of California Press, 2002.
Tal, David. *The Making of an Alliance: The Origins and Development of the US-Israel Relationship*. Cambridge: Cambridge University Press, 2022.
Talmon, Miri. *Israeli Graffiti: Nostalgia, Groups, and Collective Identity in Israeli Cinema*. Tel Aviv: Open University, 2001. [Hebrew]
Tannenbaum, Richard. "Consulting and Being in Israel: Two Sketches." *Journal of Humanistic Psychology* 12, no. 1 (Jan. 1973): 25–41.
Taub, Gadi. "The American Sixties in Israel: From Rebellion to Conformism." *Iyunim bitkumat Israel: Studies in Zionism, the Yishuv and the State of Israel* 13 (2003): 1–28. [Hebrew]
Torczyner, Jimmy. "The Political Context of Social Change: A Case Study of Innovation in Adversity in Jerusalem." *The Journal of Applied Behavioral Science* 8, no. 3 (May 1972): 287–317.
Tota, Antonio Pedro. *The Seduction of Brazil: The Americanization of Brazil during World War II*. Translated by Lorena B. Ellis. Austin: University of Texas Press, 2009.
Trentmann, Frank, ed. *The Making of the Consumer: Knowledge, Power and Identity in the Modern World*. Oxford: Berg, 2006.
Triger, Zvi. "Golda Meir's Reluctant Feminism: The Pre-State Years." *Israel Studies* 19, no. 3 (Fall 2014): 108–33.
Tyrrell, Ian. *Reforming the World: The Creation of America's Moral Empire*. Princeton, NJ: Princeton University Press, 2010.
Ussishkin, Daniel. *Morale: A Modern British History*. Oxford: Oxford University Press, 2017.
Veblen, Thorstein. *The Theory of the Leisure Class: An Economic Study of Institutions*. New York: Macmillan, 1899.
Vigodar, Shimshon. "Matzpen Movement." "Fifty to Forty-Eight: Critical Moments in the History of the State of Israel." Special issue, *Theory and Criticism* 12–13 (1999): 199–204. [Hebrew]

Vučetić, Radina. *Coca-Cola Socialism: Americanization of Yugoslav Culture in the Sixties*. Translated by John K. Cox. Budapest: Central European University Press, 2018.

Yablonka, Hanna. *Children by the Book: Biography of a Generation: The First Native Israeli Born 1948–1955*. Tel Aviv: Miskal, 2018. [Hebrew]

Wagnleitner, Reinhold, and Elaine May, eds. *"Here, There and Everywhere": The Foreign Politics of American Popular Culture*. Lebanon, NH: University Press of New England, 2000.

Wagnleitner, Reinhold. *Coca-Colanization and the Cold War: The Cultural Mission of the United States and Austria after the Second World War*. Chapel Hill: University of North Carolina Press, 2007.

Waxman, Chaim I. *American Aliya: Portrait of an Innovative Migration Movement*. Detroit: Wayne State University Press, 1989.

Weimann, Gabriel. *The Pioneering Story of Public Opinion Research in Israel: The Israel Institute for Applied Social Research, 1947–1997*. Tel Aviv: Tzivonim, 2015. [Hebrew]

Weiss, Yfaat. "The Golem and Its Creator: Or How the Jewish Nation-State Became Multiethnic." *Theory and Criticism* 19 (Autumn 2001): 45–69. [Hebrew]

Weissbrod, Lilly. "From Labour Zionism to New Zionism: Ideological Change in Israel." *Theory and Society* 10, no. 6 (Nov. 1981): 777–803.

Weizman, Eyal. *Hollow Land: Israel's Architecture of Occupation*. London: Verso, 2007.

Weizman, Ezer. *On Eagles' Wings*. Berkeley, CA: Penguin, 1979.

Worley, Christopher, Anthony G., Petrella, and Linda Thorne. "Robert Tannenbaum: An Examined Life." In *The Palgrave Handbook of Organizational Change Thinkers*. Edited by D. B. Szabla et al., 1655–71. London: Palgrave Macmillan, 2017.

Yanai, Zvi. "Intermezzo with Nola Chilton." *Mahshavot* 46 (July 1977): 13–19. [Hebrew]

Yavin, Omri. *Between Pjojy and Shchouchy and between Tel-Aviv and Ohio: Space and Place in Hanoch Levin's Plays*. Jerusalem: Magnes, 2009. [Hebrew]

Yerushalmi, Dorit. *The Director's Stage: On Directors in the Israeli Theater*. Or Yehuda: Zmora-Bitan, Dvir, 2013. [Hebrew]

Yerushalmi, Shalom, Yossi Elitov, and Arye Ehrlich. *At the Moment of Truth: The Lubavitcher Rebbe and the Political-Security Dialogue with Decision-Makers in Israel*. Haman Industrial Park: Kineret, Zmora-Bitan, Dvir, 2017. [Hebrew]

Yiftachel, Oren. *Ethnocracy: Land and Identity Politics in Israel/Palestine*. Philadelphia: University of Pennsylvania Press, 2006.

Yonay, Ehud. *No Margin for Error: The Making of the Israeli Air Force*. New York: Pantheon, 1993.

Yuval-Davis, Nira. *Matzpen: The Socialist Organization in Israel*. Jerusalem: The Hebrew University, 1977. [Hebrew]

Zameret, Zvi, and Hanna Yablonka, eds. *The Third Decade, 1968–1978*. Jerusalem: Yad Ben-Zvi, 2008. [Hebrew]

Zeitlin, Jonathan, and Gary Herrigel, eds. *Americanization and Its Limits: Reworking US Technology and Management in Post-War Europe and Japan*. Oxford: Oxford University Press, 2000.

Zohar, Gaby. *Happiness Knows No End: On the Mystical Cults, New Age Groups, and Psychological Marathons in Israel*. Tel Aviv: Sa'ar, 1992. [Hebrew]

Zolov, Eric. *Refried Elvis: The Rise of the Mexican Counterculture*. Berkeley: University of California Press, 1999.

Zubida, Hani, and Raanan Lipshitz, eds. *Stop—No Border in Front of You! About Borders and the Lack of Them in Israel 2017*. Rishon Letzion: Miskal, 2017. [Hebrew]

Index

Aberjil, Reuven, 146, 151, 156, 162
Abzug, Bella, 296
advertisement: for American products, 23, 24; and consumer advocacy, 72, 75; in electioneering, 91, 93, 94, 100; for grooming, 40–41; industry, 44, 22, 45–46, 61; nudity in, 1, 40; for the Phantom drive, 55, 115; in playbills, 263, 276; and polling, 100; propriety terms in, 34–35, 40; sex in, 40–41. *See also* Barthes, Ronald; Coca-Cola; Dahaf Agency; English; gender; marketing
affirmative action (Israel), 203–4
African Americans: and American Jews, x–xi, 142; and antisemitism, 10, 151–52, 153, 154, 318n42; as basketball players, 196, 215; and Black Power, 2, 6, 10, 16, 141, 142, 152, 153, 154, 156, 164, 171, 185, 298; and the civil rights movement, 10, 42, 71, 118, 153, 156, 166, 218, 237; and the Coleman Report, 207–8;

Ethiopian Jews and, 168; as *Hair* performers, 10, 261, 264; historical struggle of, 16, 140, 167, 237; and identity politics, 165; and Israelis in the US, x, 110, 118; Israeli attitude toward, 153–54; Israeli Black Panthers' identification with, 153; Israeli culture's portrayal of, 140, 153–54, 166, 167, 237; profiling of, 191. *See also* analogies and comparisons; Black Hebrew Israelites; Black Panther Party; Black Panthers (Israel); Kahane, Meir; King, Martin Luther, Jr.; National Welfare Rights Organization; racism
African Hebrew Israelite Nation of Jerusalem. *See* Black Hebrew Israelites
Agmon, Ya'akov (Bimot Theater), 51, 222, 233, 237, 247, 248, 266
Agranat, Shimon, 6, 174, 177, 195
Agudat Yisrael Party, 34

Ahdut Ha'avoda Party, 100
Aktzin, Binyamin, 63–64, 69
Alberstein, Chava, 247
Aleichem, Sholom, 22, 225, 226, 228, 231
Alhambra Hall (Jaffa), 253, 258, 259, 261
Alinsky, Saul, 205
Almagor, Dan, 140, 153, 166, 224–25, 226, 236–37, 238, 239, 252
Almogy, Yosef, 78
Alon, Yigal, 263–64
Aloni, Miri, 244
Aloni, Nissim, 17, 273, 287–88, 289–90.
Aloni, Shulamit, 72–74, 76, 210, 213
Alroy, Yoram, 172, 175
Alternan, Nathan, 32–33, 51
Althusser, Louis, 148
American dream, the, 17, 273, 289–90, 305n1
American kitchen, 39
American Hippie in Israel, 278, 285
American immigrants. *See* immigrants, American
American Jews: and African Americans, 152, 153–54; ambivalence toward, 11, 106, 177, 300n18; in the cultural industry, 8, 256; and Richard Nixon, 107; in the social sciences, 201; support of Israel, 11, 42–43, 109, 177. *See also* Black Panthers (Israel): reaction of American Jews to; *hazara bitshuva*; immigrants, American; *and specific individuals*
Americanization, 12, 15, 215, 226, 293–96, 300n20, 301n26: of basketball, 196; criticism of, 1, 3, 86, 136, 137, 215–16, 226, 300n15; limitations of and alternatives to the concept, 7–8, 13; and military industry, 98, 113; of politics, 105, 110; and "secondary Americanization," 7; and social welfare services, 206. *See also* Israeli Air Force; feminism; immigrants, American; musicals

American Princess, The, 13, 273, 287–88, 291
Amidar Company, 77, 78
Amkor Company, 35, 39, 46
analogies and comparisons, 7, 14, 39, 297: African Americans/Mizrahim, 10, 16, 152, 153, 156, 158, 159, 161, 167, 168, 206; African Americans/women, 210; African Americans/Palestinians, 156; of "backlash" politics, 153; hawks and doves, 7; Israel/US, 7; organized crime, 7, 172–73, 320–21n7; and *West Side Story*, 256; and Vietnam, 293
Anti-Defamation League (ADL), 42, 177
antisemitism, xi, 10, 11, 107, 118, 151–52, 154, 164, 175, 179, 185, 197, 224, 237
Arab boycott, 28, 25, 42–43
Aronson, Shlomo, 218–19
Arrane, Zalman, 256–57
Association for Better Housing (ABH), 62, 77–80
Association for Civil Rights in Israel, 150
Association of Black and White Jews (Philadelphia), 188, 324n95
Ashkenazim (Ashkenazi), 10, 26, 143, 158, 160, 248, 297: and "Ashkenazicization," 158; and east European cultural revival, 10, 16, 222; epithet for, 260; Golda Meir as epitome of, 196, 223; and the Labor Party, 150; non-Ashkenazim's perception of, 140, 143, 161, 206; and oriental culture, 164; prioritized in housing design, 80; portrayal in popular culture, 231, 249, 257, 258, 259, 260; in schools, 207–208; Western identity of, 10. *See also* analogies and comparisons; elites; Hasidic folklore; Yiddish; Yiddishism
Avineri, Shlomo, 154–55
Avner, Amiel, 196, 204–5, 206–7
Avnery, Uri, 176
Ayalon, Dalia, 99

Bach, Gavriel, 173–74
Baht-Israel, Cathrielah, 186
Baht-Israel, Peninah, 186
Baldwin, James, 153–54
Bale, John, 195
Barbie doll, 60, 297, 305n1
Bardugu, Avi, 151
Bar-Kadma, Immanuel, 252, 335n120, 335n33
Barkan, Yehuda, 231, 234, 277
Barnea, Nahum, 70, 206, 305n110, 305n119;
Bar-Nir, Dov, 226
Bar Shavit, Shlomo, 259–60
Barthes, Roland, 41
Bartov, Hanoch, 160
Baruch, Adam, 86–87
Bashan, Yigal, 54, 243
basketball, 12, 16: Americanization of, 214–16; American recruits, 196, 214–15; Black players, 10, 215; as a middle-class sport, 217; professionalization of, 215; and the social value of sports, 217–18; Tal Brody's impact on, 195, 196, 214. *See also* Brody, Tal; Dayan, Moshe; Maccabi Tel Aviv
Baudrillard, Jean, 41, 67, 302n13
Bavli, Hanna, 117
Becker, Israel, 231–32, 234
Begin, Menachem, 86, 102, 150, 159, 184, 206, 249
Beilin, Yossi, 259
Ben, Philip, 155
Ben Aharon, Yitzhak, 13, 53, 70, 76–77
Ben-Amotz, Dahn, 51, 53–54, 144, 248
Ben-Gurion, David, 29, 24, 86, 222, 330n1
Ben-Gvir, Itamar, 192–93
Ben-Israel, Benn Ammi (Ben Carter), 185–188, 190–192, 194, 325n100
Ben-Itto, Hadassah, 184
Ben-Natan, Asher, 229
Ben-Nun, Avihu, 117, 120, 127, 128, 133, 135, 136, 137

Ben Simhon, Shaul, 146
Berkowitz, Isaac Dov, 226
Bernstein, Leonard, 256
Biton, Charlie, 148, 149, 150, 157, 317n32, 319n78
Black Hebrew Israelites (African Hebrew Israelite Nation of Jerusalem), 10, 11, 16, 18, 170: and Black nationalism, 185, 187; in Dimona, 185–86; and fears of invasion, 190; government's response to, 171, 185, 188–191, 192; history of, 185; in Liberia, 185; and Meir Kahane, 165, 184–85; and permanent residency, 187; public protests of, 187, 190. *See also* Baht-Israel, Cathrielah; Baht-Israel, Peninah; Ben-Israel, Benn Ammi; Burg, Yosef, Huebner, Yehudith
Black Panthers (Israel), 1, 2, 11, 16, 18, 166, 270: advent of, 10, 140–142, 317n18; American Jewish reaction to, 154–56; and Blackness, 158–59; and Black Panther Party, 141, 157; breaking taboos, 157, 160; and campaign for Russian Jews, 143, 157; and cultural representations, 163–64; demands, 30, 143–44; 146, 149, 156, 162; and feminists, 210; fracture of, 149–50, 157; and Golda Meir, 141, 144; 146–47; 151, 152, 162, 164, 317n24; ideology, 148–50, 162; and immigrants' benefits, 197; in *Kazablan* (film), 259; moniker of, 151–52, 317–18n37; and New Left, 141, 142, 143, 144, 145, 149, 150, 157, 162; and *pantherism*, 64, 142, 152, 160; and the police, 143, 144, 146, 147, 148, 149, 150, 154, 156, 158, 162; political surveillance of, 147; in public memory, 168; and street theater, 161, 162–63; publications, 163; reactions to, 145, 151, 157, 192; as "screwed over," 158, 161, 162; and the social gap, 61, 68, 142–43, 149; social workers' support of, 196, 204–5, 206; welfare policies inspired by, 4,

Black Panthers (Israel) (*continued*)
150, 317n34; and Yiddish, 158, 163, 164, 249. See also analogies and comparisons; Black Panthers Party; Davis, Angela; Diaspora; "Global Sixties"; Kies, Naomi; Matzpen; Yiddish; *and individual members*
Blackey, Eileen, 201–2
Black Panthers Party (BPP), 16, 141, 151–52, 157
Blues for Mister Charlie, 153–4
Bondi, Ruth, 1, 60, 67, 238
Boshes, Hedda, 84, 238
Bourdieu, Pierre, 14, 27
bourekas film genre, 231, 235, 259, 260, 277, 335n29. See also *Kazablan*; *Lupu*
Boys in the Band, 266
Bracha, Dani, 216
Brandt, Willie, 229
Broadway, 6, 12, 17, 193, 259: Israeli shows on, 19, 239; Jewish presence on, 256; Jewish themed performances, 222–24, 337n3; and production quality, 251, 252. See also Godik, Giora; musicals
Brody, Tal, 16, 194–95, 196, 213–218
Brezhnev, Leonid 182
Brown, George 228
Brune, Nathan, 6, 90–91, 92, 93, 309n8
Buber, Martin, 200, 237
Bunim, Shmuel, 233
Burg, Yosef, 76, 169–70, 173, 174, 176–77, 178, 188, 189
Burstein, Pesach, 221, 222, 232–33
Burstein, Ya'akov, 155
Burstyn, Mike, 193, 232–35
Bustan Sepharadi, 222, 247–48
But Where Is Daniel Wax, 277

Carlebach, Shlomo, 11, 222, 223, 239–243, 246. See also Ashkenazim; ethnicism; Hasidut, Hasidic folklore
Carmichael, Stokely (Kwame Ture), 152, 318n42

Cast A Giant Shadow, 272
Chabad-Lubavitch, 240, 245, 246. See also Carlebach, Sholomo; Schneerson, Menachem Mendel; Schneersohn, Yosef Yitzhak; Shazar, Zalman
Chagall, Marc, 221, 224
Chasani, Michael, 152–53
Chen, Shula, 54, 275
Chilton, Nora, 195
cleanliness, 26–27, 67, 77 80, 81, 94, 197: and personal hygiene, 26, 28, 40, 41, 45, 59, 77; public drives for, 27, 58, 78; and social/racial hierarchies, 58. See also Association for Better Housing; consumerism; cooling and refrigeration technology; Council for a Beautiful Israel, Lahat, Shlomo; *Malkat ambatya*
Cleaver, Eldridge, 151, 152
Coca-Cola, 15, 21, 64, 103, 293, 297: Bnei Brak plant, 43; campaign to bring to Israel, 42–43; domestication of, 12, 25, 38, 44; in fiction, 281–82; marketing of, 38, 44, 45, 47, 49; reengineered bottle cap (*shasgor*), 12, 38; as symbol of American hegemony, 21, 42, 43. See also advertisement; Anti-Defamation League; Arab boycott; consumerism
Cohen, Shalom, 149, 158
Coleman, James ("Coleman Report"), 207–8
Coleman, Robert, 188
Colombo, Joe, 179
commercialism, 23, 46, 49, 62: and non-commercial media, 84–86, in theater, 253, 255, 271
commodification: and colonization, 25, 27; of politicians, 9, 100, of sports, 215; theory of, 302n13
consumerism (consumption), 4, 6, 9, 13, 15, 24–25, 29, 240, 294, 295, 296, 297: as activism, 4, 43, 62, 71, 73, 76, 79; and advocacy, 71–72, 73–77; and the

body, 40–41, 99; and celebrity culture, 22, 50–51; and citizenship, 15, 57, 61, 62, 72–73, 89; and civil society, 25, 82–84; and civilizing mission, 15, 27–28, 62, 77–78; and "consumer revolution" (US), 72; and counterculture, 269; critiques of, 41, 60–61, 63–64, 67–68; cultural, 17, 22, 251, 253, 270; definitions of, 22, 70–71, 301n4; dream life of, 48; and Europe, 24–25; excessive, 62, 64–67; and the family, 25, 26–27, 36, 37, 39, 67; and the figure of the consumer, 61, 87–88; and the Histadrut, 29, 76–77; and IDF soldiers, 56; and individualism, 25, 36, 45, 50–51, 56; justification of, 28, 53; and knowledge, 22, 34–35; and leisure, 23, 24, 25; and the occupied territories, 28–29, 56–58; and pleasure, 22, 23, 40, 53, 61; and politics, 89, 100; and religiosity, 247, 249; cultural representations of, 277; and rights, 61, 71, 72, 73; satire of, 49, 50, 85–86; and "sign-consumption," 46; and space/time, 26, 37–39; and the "standard of living," 22, 24, 29, 30, 31, 56, 57, 59, 60, 63, 64, 65, 68, 80, 103; and the state, 15, 27, 29, 39, 62, 63, 82, 87, 88; statistics of, 22, 33–34, 37, 39, 45; upscale, 22, 23, 29–30, 65; and US contradictory role in shaping, 5, 62, 87; venues for, 22–23; and war, 28, 52–54, 55, 56. *See also* advertisement; Aloni, Shulamit; Baudrillard, Jean; Better Housing Society; Coca-Cola; Council for a Beautiful Israel; economic policies; *everyday*; feedback loop; Galbraith, Kenneth; Gender; Histadrut; Israel Consumer Council; Marcuse, Herbert; Nader, Ralph; neocapitalism; "quality of life"; Sapir, Pinchas; Veblen, Thorenstein; WeightWatchers

"contact zone," 13, 90
cooling and refrigeration technology, 12, 22, 26, 37–39, 47, 54, 56, 64. *See also* Sunfrost Company
Costello, Frank, 169
Council for a Beautiful Israel, 44, 81–82
Counterculture, 6: derision of, 11, 277; and Eastern spirituality, 223; and Evangelicalism, 239; in Israeli cinema, 278, 338n8; and Israeli youth, 11; and Jewish revival, 11, 12, 17, 240, 242, 246; vs. political radicalism, 269. *See also American Hippie in Israel*; Carlebach, Shlomo; *Hair*; *I Like Mike*; *Ish hasid haya*
CSKA Moskva, 216–17

Dafna, Sasha, 230
Dahaf Agency, 44, 100, 111
Dale Carnegie, x, 6, 90, 99
Dallas, 86
Dan, Uri, 123, 174–75
Davis, Angela, 159, 319n78
Dayan, Assi, 281, 285
Dayan, Moshe, 50, 118, 281: on the Black Panthers (Israel); 118; as an icon, 54–55; and Meir Kahane, 183–84; and occupied territories, 56–58; patronage of Maccabi Tel Aviv, 217; resignation, 270; and strategic bombing, 133–34; visit to Vietnam, 57
Dayan, Yael, 160
Debord, Guy, 302n13
de Gaulle, Charles, ix
design: American support for, 75; and Bezalel Academy of Arts and Design, 195; of Coca-Cola's *shasgor*, 38; and curating design artistry, 298; of jewelry, 23; product, 75–76, 80, 330n2; and the Phantom jet, 115, 123, 124, 125, 126, 130, 139; posters, 47; theatrical sets, 271

Diaspora (diasporic), 41, 142, 171, 178, 237, 257: archetypes of, 234; Black, 158; domestic, 18, 142, 291; vs. the Holy Land, 290, of Israelis abroad, 18, 277; the misery of, 175, 225, 228; negation of, 8, 66, 177, 221, 228, 330n1; return of, 2, 18, 183, 238, 248–49; in the US, 8, 142, 228. *See also* American Jews; Black Panthers (Israel); Soviet Jews
Diaspora Yeshiva, 223, 245
Diehl, Crandall, 256, 259, 274
Diker, Regina, 99
Di Megile, 221, 233
Dixon, Robert, 120
Dizzingof Street (Tel Aviv), 23, 86, 262, 263, 276
Don't Ask Me If I Love, 273, 281–285, 290–91
Don't Call Me Black, 140, 153, 166, 167, 237
Dreikurs, Rudolf, 97–98
Duberman, Martin, 166, 236–37

Eastern religions, 4, 241, 242, 246–47
Easy Rider, 283
Eban, Abba, 58, 100, 239
economic policies: for controlling consumption, 15, 29–30, 60–61, 69–70; and exports, 19, 30, 31, 32, 75, 125, 271, 295; and pluralistic economy, 30–33; and recession, 4, 21, 22, 28, 31, 61, 69, 71, 72. *See also* consumerism; Horowitz, David; Eshkol, Levi; Gaffney, Arnon; Histadrut; Mandelbaum, Moshe; Sapir; Pinchas; Patainkin, Don
"economic peace," 57
education reform, 207–8
Eini, Menachem, 119, 131, 135
Einstein, Arik, 239
Eisenstadt, Shmuel Noah, 200
El Al Israel Airlines, 83, 230, 249, 275, 276
Elbaz, Ya'akov, 147
Eliav, Aryeh "Lova," 64, 213

Elite Company, 45, 215
elites, 18, 62: alienation from the everyman, 87; and American newcomers, 197; Ashkenazi, 10, 140, 141, 150, 165; and consumer behavior, 15; cultural priorities of, 63, 84; and elitism, 212; and empire, 295; eroded confidence in, 293; vs. European elites, 62; and McCarthyism, 18; and Meir Lansky, 176; and the West, 10; and whiteness, 10, 154
Elon, Amos, 19, 296
English, 105, 160, 195, 272, 286, 294, 303n70: in advertisements, 24, 35, 40, 41; in basketball, 215; in corporate nomenclature, 37–8; and *Don't Ask Me If I Love*, 283, 285; and exporting cinema and theater, 221, 222, 286; in feminist consciousness raising, 212; and *Fiddler on the Roof*, 225, 227; and Golda Meir, 195, 317n24; and *Hair*, 260, 261; in the Israeli Air Force, 117, 127, 133; instruction, x, 275; Israeli authors writing in, 19, 273, 283; and Mike Burstyn's performances, 222, 234, 235; opposition to usage of, 160, 213, 284–85; and social pretense, 86; Tal Brody's, 212, 217; terms adopted, 67, 77, 153, 160, 174; in titles of Israeli songs, publications, and shows, 50, 272, 304n106; and *West Side Story* in Israel, 251. *See also American Hippie in Israel*; Dayan, Yael; Kollek, Amos
environmentalism, 4, 80, 218, 301n26
Eran, Amos, 106–7
Esalen Institute (encounter groups), 90, 98–99
Eshkol, Levi, 21–22, 30, 31–32, 61, 105, 117, 177, 222, 223, 256
Ethiopian Jews (Beta Israel community), 168
ethnicism, 8, 17, 161, 222, 231, 248, 249, 255
Ettinger, Amos, 221

Evers, Medgar, 237
everyday, the, 13, 59, 73: the colonization of, 25–27; consumerist, 14, 25, 48, 215; military, 28, 52–54, 56; and boundaries, 27, and systems of domination, 27–29. *See also* Lefebvre, Henri; Situationist International
Evron, Boaz, 225, 265

F-4E Phantom II. *See* Phantom 4E II
Fallaci, Oriana, 208–9
Family Affairs, 84
Farley, James A., 43
Federal Bureau of Investigation (FBI), 165, 169, 170, 173, 174, 175, 179
feedback loop, 9, 59, 90: and democracy, 104; and human relations, 96; and market research, 100–101; 103, 104; and management, 98; and morale, 102, 103; and the ombudsman, 98; and politics, 15, 89–90, 101; and soldiers as consumers, 56, 59. *See also* consumerism; Guttman, Louis; Lahat, Shlomo
Feinberg, Abraham 43
feminism (Israel), 2, 4, 6, 16, 196, 296: as an American import, 14, 210, 212; birth of, 209–210; and breast cancer, 212; and consciousness raising, 212; divisions within, 210; and domestic abuse, 211–12; opposition to, 212; and reproductive rights, 210–11. *See also* Aloni, Shulamit; English; Freedman, Marcia; Ortal, Dorit; Safir, Marilyn; Resnik, Ruth
Fiddler on the Roof (film), 228, 230
Fiddler on the Roof (musical), 10, 17, 221, 222, 232, 236, 258: and American liberalism, 227; on Broadway, 223–224; critical response to, 225–26; global success, 227; Israeli production, 224–25; and Israeli *Tevyes* abroad, 227–30; and Jewish stereotypes, 248; official embrace of, 230; and Yiddish drama, 230, 231. *See also* Almagor, Dan; *Ish hasid haya*: as anti-*Fiddler*; Robbins, Jerome; Rodensky, Shmuel; Stein, Joseph; Topol, Haim
Ford, Gerald, 107
Fordism, 95
France, ix, 27, 28, 46, 56, 62, 157: and American culture, 6–7; and consumerism, 25, 27, 41; and decolonization, 27; military aircraft from, 15, 105, 112, 120–21, 123, 125, 126, 127, 128, 132, 134, 136, 138; and military industry, 125; and New Left in Israel, 210; relations with Israel, ix, 51, 125, 338n12. *See also* de Gaulle, Charles; Sartre, Jean-Paul
Freedman, Marcia, 4, 16, 195, 196, 198, 219: activism, 209–10, 213; arrest, 210–11; immigration, 209; as member of Knesset, 208, 210, 211–12, 213; return to the US, 213; and statistical research, 208; and the US as a model for reform, 212–13, 296. *See also* feminism
French (language), 44, 78, 127, 233, 287
Friedan, Betty, 208
Friedman, Thomas, 295, 339n5
fundraising: ambivalence about, 177–78; for the Phantom deal (*see under* Phantom 4E II: public drive); Israel Bonds, 49, 76, 91, 177; Israel Emergency Funds, 177

Gaffney, Arnon, 37
Gahal/Likud Party, 66, 81, 87, 102, 206, 295: and the Black Panthers (Israel), 150, 159; the Liberal Party in, 91, 92, 105; and Meir Kahane, 184; and neoliberalism, 294–95; and the 1977 elections, 111; and polling, 101; and students' politics, 269, 337n79; and Tel Aviv mayoral campaign (1973), 90–94. *See also* Begin, Menachem; Lahat, Shlomo; Netanyahu, Benjamin; Sharon, Ariel

368 Index

Galbraith, John Kenneth, 67, 306n18
Galei Tzahal (IDF Radio Station), 51, 85
Galili, Yisrael, 139
Gamzu, Haim, 225, 238, 256
Gaon, Yehoram, 153, 221, 247, 248, 253, 259, 278
Gardosh, Kriel "Dosh," 82
Garland, Patrick, 260, 261, 267
Garvey, Marcus (Back to Africa movement), 185, 187
gay liberation, 6, 266
Gazit, Amit, 263
Geffen, Yonathan, 49, 66
gender, 14, 60, 160, 208, 209: in avant-garde drama, 273, 287–90; and consumer protection, 76–77; and marketing, 41, 43; military jets and, 120–21; in popular culture, 273; stereotypes, 208; and war, 209. *See also* advertisement; feminism; *geolibidinal*; masculinity
geolibidinal, 14, 277, 285–287.
George Air Force Base (California), 117, 118, 119, 121, 126, 129
"Give Peace a Chance," 269
Glazer-Ta'asa, Miriam, 246
globalization, 7, 8, 11, 12–13, 14, 26, 294
glocalization, 7, 14, 212, 298, 300n14
"Global Sixties," 141, 268, 297
Godik, Giora, 6, 17, 256, 258, 259, 260, 261, 265, 272, 273–74, 276: corporate practices of, 254; early career, 251–52; and ethnic-themed shows, 255, 258; failures, 254–55; and the introduction of the Broadway musical, 251, 254, 271; and the impresario as a cultural hero, 248; love of America, 254; as a risk-taking entrepreneur, 17, 251, 253–54. *See also* Broadway; Kaniuk, Yoram; musicals; *and specific productions*
Golan, Menachem, 230–31, 259
Goldfaden, Abraham, 221, 231, 232

Goldstein, Baruch, 192, 198, 242–43
Goldstein, Moshe "Golly," 268
Goldman, Nahum, 266
Goldstein, Mordechai, 245, 246
Graham, Billy, 110
Griffith, Robert, 256
Guri, Haim, 28
Gush Emonim, 184, 270
Guttman, Louis, 102–104

Hacohen, Shmuel Avidor, 245
Hadash (The Democratic Front for Peace and Equality Party), 150, 317n32
Hadassah: Women's Zionist Organization of America, 44, 205, 337n3
Ha'elyon, Ya'akov, 81, 115
Hagal Hakal Radio Station, 45, 52
Haganah, 102, 174–75
Hair, 10, 17, 239, 251, 271: audience, 263, 264; Black performers in, 261, 264; classification of, 265–6; commercialization of, 250, 262–63; cultural effects, 140, 235, 239, 268–69, 270; and the hippie "tribe", 17, 261–2; and personal transformation, 263; production of, 250, 260–1; nudity in, 262, 264, 265; political relevance in Israel, 266–68; *and individual performers and crew members*
Halkin, Hillel, 1–2, 301n25
Halpern, Seymour, 42
Hankin, Ehud, 119, 120, 127
Hanoch, Shalom, 286
Harel, Ezrah Menashe, 130–31
Harpaz, Rami, 119, 121–122, 127, 128
Harriman, W. Averell, 116
Harris, Shaul, 206
Hasidic folklore, 10, 12, 16, 166, 222, 232, 235, 240: and the IDF's Rabbinical Choir, 243; and neo-Hasid movement, 240; and pop/rock music, 222, 239, 244; and popularization of religion, 245; song festival, 243; and national

culture, 249. *See also* Carlebach, Shlomo; *Fiddler on the Roof*; Hadidut; *Ish hasid haya*; Judaism; *Shnei Kuni Lemel*
Hasidut, 235, 236, 237, 238, 240, 241–42, 246, 249, 332n51. *See also* Chabad-Lubavicher
hazara bitshuva (return to the faith), 223, 240–41, 245–46. *See also* Carlebach, Shlomo; Chabad-Lubavitcher; Diaspora Yeshiva; Goldstein, Mordechai
Heffer, Haim, 22, 220, 221, 233, 247, 248, 259, 273
Hebrew University, 2, 196, 200, 201
Hedva veShlomik, 84–86
Heinemann, Gustav, 229
Herlitz, Esther, 64
Herman, Abraham, 42
Hertz, Anita, 261
Hertzberg, Arthur, 155
Hetz, Shmuel, 117, 118, 119, 120, 124, 131, 135, 136
"high school seniors' letter," the, 145, 266, 269
Hillel, Shlomo, 158, 183, 211–212
hippies, 17, 194, 222, 235, 237, 239, 241, 242, 246, 250, 261, 263, 264, 268, 274, 275, 276, 277, 278, 285. *See also American Hippie in Israel*; counterculture; *I Like Mike*
Hirsch, Moshe, 198
Histadrut, 67, 69, 92, 101, 110, 149, 154, 205, 248: and consumer advocacy, 71, 76–77; and consumption 29; and executive indulgence, 66, 67; Hevrat Ha'ovdim (Society of Workers), 30, 32, 294; and human relations, 95, 96; and the "package deal," 70; Pinchas Sapir's support of, 33; and religion, 245; and social workers' union, 203, 206; and strikes, 53. *See also* Ben Aharon, Yitzhak; Yadlin, Asher

Hock, Bernie, 209
Hod, Mordechai, 122, 125, 131, 133, 135, 136
Hollywood, 86, 118, 283, 289: and Americanization, 3; and French "new wave", 6; Jewish themes in, 227; press coverage of, 50; representation of Israel in, 19, 272
Holm, Hanya, 252
Holocaust, 29, 70, 154, 181, 222, 238, 242, 247, 256, 270, 338n12
homo economicus, 70, 129
Hope, Bob, 177–78
Horowitz, David, 31, 68, 69
House of Love and Prayer (San Francisco), 222, 242
How to Succeed in Business without Trying, 252, 255
Huebner, Yehudith, 192
human relations (HR), x, 4, 14, 90, 91, 95–98

I Don't Give a Damn, 53–54
I Dream of Jeannie, 84
I Like Mike, 17, 272, 273–78, 285, 290
immigrants, American, 16, 101, 194–96, 197, 206, 218–219; as agents of Americanization, 197–98, 212–13; and the crisis of liberalism, 199–200; motivation for immigration, 197–98, 215; and political extremism, 198; and the settlers' movement, 198–99, 297; and social activism, 156, 196, 204, 206, 213, 218. *See also* basketball; feminism; *hazara bitshuva; and individual immigrants*
International Organization of Consumer Unions (IOCU), 71
In White America, 166, 236–37
Ish hassid haya, 12, 166, 222, 223, 235–39, 245, 248, 332n51: as anti-*Fiddler*, 235; on Broadway, 239; and the counterculture, 222; critical response to, 238; popularizing Hasidic folklore, 243,

Ish hassid haya (continued)
247; as a "secular synagogue," 237. *See also* Almagor, Dan; Hacohen, Shmuel Avidor; Litani, Danny; Nitzan, Shlomo; Yizraeli, Yossi
Israel Aerospace Industries (IAI), 98, 125, 195
Israel Consumer Council (ICC), 15, 62: and consciousness raising, 73–76; and design, 75–76; and export, 75; and milk delivery 73; mission, 71–72; publications, 74, 76; shaming tactics of, 74–75; and sweepstakes, 48, 304n97; and television sets, 35, 76; and Western norms, 72, 74. *See also* Aloni, Shulamit; consumerism
Israel Defense Forces (IDF), 44, 105, 187, 251, 272: and Americanization, 5, 6, 105, 108; and celebrity culture, 50, 54; and the citizen-soldier, 28; entertainment troupes, 54, 244; Green Island raid, 52, habitus of, 105; "Jewish Awareness" campaigns, 245; morale, 102, 104; ombudsman, 98; positions for female soldiers, 208; Rabbinical Choir, 243, 244. *See also* feedback loop: soldiers as consumers; Galey Zahal; Israeli Air Force; Lahat, Shlomo; Marcus, Mickey; Rabin, Yitzhak Six-Day War; War of Attrition; Yom-Kippur War
Israeli Air Force (IAF): and American technicians, 132–33; and American technology, 112, 113, 124, 127–28, 132; debriefing practice, 124; French arsenal, 105, 112, 120, 125, 134; knowledge exchange with the US, 120; and the Lavi project, 126; operations research, 129–30; pilots' ethos, competitiveness 127; pilots' ethos, improvisation, 136; pilots' ethos, individualism, 122; pilots' ethos, inquisitiveness, 123–24; and professionalism, 128; representing Israel, 118, 177–78; reputation of, 120, 123; resistance to Americanization, 136, 137; social life, 118; technological entrepreneurialism, 124. *See also* English; Hod, Mordechai; Ivry, David; masculinity; Operation Moked; Operation Priha; Peled, Benjamin "Benny"; Phantom 4E II; Six-Day War; United States Air Force; War of Attrition; Yom Kippur War
Israeli Black Panthers. *See* Black Panthers (Israel)
Israeli economy. *See* economic policies
Israeli Institute for Product Design (Institute for Packaging and Design), 75–76
Ivry, David, 128, 136, 137

Jackson, Henry, 106–7, 194
Jaffe, Eliezer, 196, 203–4, 205, 206, 218, 219
Jagger, Chris, 261
Japanese Red Army, 192
Jesus Freaks, 239
Jewish Agency, 77, 155, 163
Jewish Defense League (JDL), 4, 6, 142, 164–65, 179–84, 188, 192, 320n96
Jewish Joint Distribution Committee (JDC), 201
Jews for Jesus, 223, 241
Johnson, Lyndon, 43, 72, 91, 106, 107, 116, 117, 201, 227
Judaism: Conservative, 188, 190; conversion to, 190, 215, 216, 283; and Eastern spirituality, 242; and El Al, 230; *haredi*/ultra-Orthodox, 7, 25, 64, 150, 198, 241, 243, 245, 247, 249, 264, 295, 296, 297; and "Jewish awareness" campaigns, 245; and national culture, 249; Orthodox, 198, 234, 235, 240, 245,

249, 297; popularization of, 238, 245; Reform, 190; and theatrical performances, 225, 226. *See also* African Americans: Black Jews; Black Hebrew Israelites; Carlebach, Shlomo; Chabad-Lubavitch; *hazara bitshuva*; Law of Return

Junior Chamber (JC), 82–84, 308n83

Kach Party, 164, 166, 181, 192–92. *See also* Ben-Gvir, Itamar; Goldstein, Mordechai; Jewish Defense League; Kahane, Meir

Kahane, Meir, 16, 170, 171, 194, 199, 322n53: apocalyptic views, 166, 242; and the Black Panther Party, 16, 142, 164–65; and Black Panthers (Israel), 166; and crisis of liberalism, 199; immigration, 142, 180, 320n96; on Meir Lansky, 176; and Mizrahi Jews, 165–66; racism of, 4, 10, 166, 180–83; public responses to, 183–84, 192; Shlomo Carlebach and, 242–43; and street theater, 165, 181–82; and Soviet Jews, 179, 181, 182; and terror, 179, 181–82. *See also* Black Hebrew Israelites: and Meir Kahane; Jewish Defense League; Kach

Kaniuk, Yoram, 254, 265, 267

Katmor, Jacques, 223

Karavan, Dani, 235, 236

Katz, Elihu ,103–4, 218–19,

Katz, Israel, 68, 150, 203, 205

Katz, Josie, 195

Kazablan (film), 259–60, 272

Kazablan (musical), 221, 251, 255, 256, 257–260, 271, 276

Keisari, Uri, 86, 252

Keller, Mel, 195

Kelman, Wolfe, 188

Kenan, Amos, 22, 53, 114, 144

Kennedy, John Fitzgerald, 30, 72, 91, 227

Kennedy, Robert, 107

Keshet, Sassi ,54

Kfotz, 270

kibbutzim, 99, 101, 115, 122, 124 202, 213, 215, 228, 230, 238, 262, 268: and behavioral science, 14, 96–97, 310n39; and consumption, 63; and modern appliances, 37; in popular culture, 84, 85, 86, 234, 275, 276, 277, 281; privatization of, 294; and religiosity, 240, 245; volunteers in, 6, 194, 326n3; during Zionism's pioneering era, 208

Kies, Naomi, 157, 198

King, Martin Luther, Jr., 10, 42, 106, 153, 188, 199

Kishon, Ephraim, 233, 234

Kislev, Ran, 173, 320n7

Kissinger, Henry, 107, 311n79

Klein, Ralph, 214, 216

Kohelet Policy Forum, 5, 296–97

Kohlberg, Lawrence, 310n39

Kollek, Amos, 17, 160, 273, 281–285

Kollek, Teddy, 82, 143, 144, 151, 160, 204, 205, 281

Kol mamzer melech (Every Bastard a King), 17, 273, 278–281, 282, 285

Koren, David, 230

Koren, Yitzhak, 183

Koppel, Moshe, 5

Kottler, Yair, 184

Ladino, 247, 248, 249

Lahakt Hanahal, 244, 269–70

Lahat, Shlomo "Chich", 5–6, 15, 89, 90–95, 100: childhood, 94; electioneering tactics, 90, 91–92, 100; ideology, 95; IDF general, 104, 105; mayor of Tel Aviv, 95, 110–11; and meet-and-greet events, 93; mocked for "American style" campaign, 93, 95. *See also* Brune, Natan; Gahal/Likud; "quality of life"; human relations

Lahav, Yohanan, 178

Lansky, Meyer, 11, 16, 18, 179, 188, 192, 194: escape to Israel 169–170; High Court of Justice and, 173–74, 177, 178; official response to, 176–77, 188, 190, 192; and organized crime, 171–73, 176; in popular culture, 170, 193; public debate about, 175–76; and public relations campaign, 174–175; return to the US, 178–79; support of Zionism, 174–75, 177. *See also* antisemitism; Bach, Gavriel; Diaspora; Federal Bureau of Investigation; Law of Return; moral panics
Laskov, Haim, 98
Late Summer Blues, 270
Law of Return, 16, 170, 172, 178, 185, 190, 191, 197
Leary, Timothy, 241
Lefebvre, Henri, 14, 25, 29, 46
Levantinization, 10, 81, 197
Levin, Hanoch, 17, 58–59, 273, 288–291. See also *Malkat ambatia*; *Whore from Ohio*
liberalism, 3–4, 219, 227, 295, 296; in crisis, 16, 196, 199; and illiberalism, 4, 199, 201; and market liberalization, 33; and rights, 16, 61, 71, 73, 150, 196, 199, 200, 204, 205, 206, 209, 210, 213, 296; and the social sciences, 200; and volunteerism, 196. *See also* neoliberalism
Liberia, 184, 185, 186, 189, 325n100
Liff, Samuel "Biff," 252
Lifschitz, Nechama, 247
Limor, Nissan, 118
Lipset, Seymour Martin, 155–56
Litani, Danny, 235, 236, 238
Lod Airport, x, 185, 186, 190, 191–92, 233, 275, 277, 325n113
Luciano, Lucky, 169
Lupu, 231, 234
Lux, Lilian, 232

Maccabee Beer, 44
Maccabi Tel Aviv (basketball), 12, 16, 214, 215: victory in the European Championship Cup (1977), 216–17. *See also* basketball; Brody, Tal; CSKA Moskva; Dayan, Moshe
Madden, John, 120
Magnus, Miri, 167
Malavsky, Shmuel 244
Malka, Eddi, 157, 164
Malkat ambatya (*Bathtub Queen*), 58–59, 266, 267, 268
Mandelbaum, Moshe, 33
Manger, Itzik, 221, 233, 247
Manor, Ehud, 167, 260
Mapai/Labor Party, 31, 33, 72, 83, 85, 103, 183, 210, 213: and Ashkenazi elite, 150; and bossism, 95; and class rhetoric, 161; and liberal economy, 32, 294–95; and Mizrahi leadership, 144; power struggles in, 70; and political polling, 100, 101; and the private sector, 31; and the "social gap," 64; Tel Aviv mayoral campaign (1973), 89, 92–94. *See also* Aloni, Shulamit; Ben Aharon, Yitzhak; Meir, Golda; Rabin, Yitzhak; Rabinowitz, Yahushua; Sapir, Pinchas; Sarid, Yossi
Marciano, Sa'adia, 30, 143, 149, 150, 151, 152, 155
Marcus, Mickey, 272
Marcus, Yoel, 22
Marcuse, Herbert, 4, 67, 302n13
marketing: keychains, 46, 48, 54, 98; raffles and lotteries, 46, 48, 49, 79, 263; sweepstakes, 25, 46, 48–49; as technique for public mobilization, 82, 115–16. *See also* advertisement; consumerism; gender
Marshall Plan, 25
Marx, Karl, 27, 68
masculinity (masculinist) 184, 228: cult of, 209; and *Fiddler on the Roof*, 228; and grooming, 41; Israeli vs. American, 273; in New Journalism, 87; and

pantherism, 160; and marketing, 14, 41; and pilots, 56, 122; and soldiers, 41. See also gender, *geolibidinal*
Matrix Management, 129, 130, 131
Matzpen (Israeli Socialist Organization), 143, 144, 145, 149, 157, 210, 316n5
Meged, Aaron, 84, 273
Meir, Golda: American childhood, 6, 95; on Black Hebrew Israelites, 187, 189–90; on excessive consumption, 67; on feminism, 208–9; on foreign fads, 2; and Israel's image abroad, 233; Jewish sentimentality of, 249; on Meir Kahane, 180, 181; on Meir Lansky, 177; on Palestinian labor, 58; as patron of cultural productions, 230, 238, 239, 256, 247; portrayal of, 59, 114, 264, 268; and Richard Nixon, 107, 109, 311n81; resignation, 270; and Soviet Jews, 157; and Yiddish, 223, 247; and Yitzhak Rabin, 110; and War of Attrition, 131, 133, 135, 136, 137, 139. See also Black Panthers: and Golda Meir; "high school seniors' letter"; Mapai/Labor Party; moral panics
Me Nobody Knows, The, 166–67
Michener, James, 1, 285
Mifal Hapais (National Lottery), 49, 115
Midnight Cowboy, 283
military-industrial complex (Israel), 2, 113, 125–26, 139. See also Israel Aerospace Industry
military-industrial complex (US), 15, 98, 128, 130. See also Phantom 4E II
Miller, Judith, 156
Mitchell, John, 173
Mizrahi, Shimon, 214
Mizrahim, 26, 157: alienation from elites and the state, 148, 150; and Black Power, 2, 10, 142; Ashkenazi culture's impact on, 222; Blackness and racialization of, 16, 158–59, 259; culture and tradition of, 164; epithets for, 159, 260;

and identity politics, 150; material exploitation of, 148–49; and Mizrahi Democratic Rainbow, 168; in the police force, 147; political parties' and movements' solicitation of, 144, 148, 150, 165–66; 317n32; in popular culture, 231, 235, 243–44, 248, 257, 259; poverty among, 140–41, 142, 145; representation in politics and institutions, 146, 149, 150; rightward turn, 31, 150, 297; in schools, 207–8; and *Sephardic* terminology, 315–16n2; as welfare recipients, 204, 206; and Western values in housing and consumption, 15, 27, 28, 62, 63, 78. See also Ashkenazim; analogies and comparisons; Black Panthers (Israel); *Bustan Sephardi*; elites; Kahane, Meir; Ladino; *Romansero Sephardi*; Yiddish
Moore, Roger, 50
Moorer, Thomas, 123
moral panics, 11, 13, 192: Black Hebrew Israelites, 188–89, 192; Black Panthers (Israel), 144, 192; Eastern religion and New Age, 246; Meir Lansky, 176, 188, 192. See also "high school seniors' letter"
Mossinson, Yigal, 256
musicals: 6, 17, 223–30, 252–268, 270–72, 273–78: and foreign performers and crews, 252, 255, 256, 260, 261–62, 271–72; 274, 315n1; and Habima Theater, 253; as social commentary, 271. See also Alhambra Hall; Godik, Giora; *and specific musicals*
My Fair Lady, 12, 224, 225, 251, 252, 254

Nader, Ralph, 4, 71, 74
Naor, Yosef, 135
National Religious Party, 176. See also Burg, Yosef; Chasani, Michael; Shapira, Haim-Moshe

Nasser, Gamal Abdul, 115, 133, 264, 266, 268
Nathan, Avraham "Abie," 278–79
Nathan, Moshe, 258–59
National Insurance Institute, 68, 203
National Organization of Women (US), 208
National Welfare Rights Organization (US), 203
Netanyahu, Benjamin, 5, 57, 109, 193, 295, 296, 297
Navon, Yitzhak, 247, 247, 248
neocapitalism, 29, 30
neoliberalism 3, 12, 25, 31, 111, 294, 295, 302n18
New Journalism, 87
New Left, 1, 4, 10, 270, 296: and Black Power, 152, 154; and feminism, 210; Jewish participation in, 10, 11; tactics of, 181; as a threat, 11, 110, 154. *See also* Matzpen; Shasi
Ninio, Avraham, 231
Niri, Aaron, 73
Nitzan, Shlomo, 235, 236, 237, 248, 334n118
Nixon, Richard, 33, 106, 107, 108, 109, 110, 114, 123, 130, 171, 283
Nusseibeh, Anwar, 178

occupation, the, 15, 17, 59, 63, 145: Black Hebrew Israelites' support of, 324n87; and consumerism, 25; and new markets for Israeli merchandise, 28; and the Palestinian standard of living, 56–58; and the settlers' movement, 7, 184, 198–199, 218, 242–43, 270, 297; and the "vertical fix", 139. *See also* Palestinians; Dayan, Moshe; *Malkat ambatya*
Ocean Hill/Brownsville teachers strike, 154, 164
Ofek, Oriel, 84
Operation Caucasus, 134

Operation Moked, 129, 130
Operation Priha, 133–34
orbital relations, 11, 125, 285, 295, 298: and boundary crossing, 17, 107, 112, 298, and the comparative imagination, 8, 299–98; and locational practice, 17–19; meaning of, 3
Ormsby-Gore, Alice, 261
Ortal, Dorit, 212
Ottenheimer, Albert, 256

Paglin, Amichai, 181
Palestine Liberation Organization (PLO), 145, 267
Palestinian Popular Front, 192
Palestinians, the, 19, 28, 104, 145, 161, 165, 198, 212: and Blackness, 155–156, 159; and economic policy in the occupied territories, 57–58; as laborers, 29, 57, 61, and Mizrahi Jews, 168; refugees, 178. *See also* Dayan, Moshe; "economic peace"; Kahane, Meir; occupation
Papo, Aaron, 184
Patinkin, Don, 31, 195
Pattir, Dan, 110
Paul Baerwald School of Social Work and Social Welfare, 196, 201–2, 203, 204
Peled, Benjamin "Benny," 131
Peled, Micky (Solan Productions), 243
Peres, Shimon, 187
Perlmutter, Simcha, 198
Perry, Aulcie (Elisha Ben Avraham), 215
Phantom 4E II, 6, 69: as an affective object, 116, 138; combat capacities of, 113, 126, 132, 313n42; in a children's book, 115; in commercial advertisement, 24; and "electronic warfare," 135–36; modification of, 12, 16, 123–25, 138; and McDonnell (McDonnell Douglas), 123, 125, 130, 131, 132; Mirage jet compared to, 120–21; as a multinational project, 125–26; and national

trust in, 114, 115; public drive for, 55, 115–116, 138; purchase of, 116–17; as the state-of-the-art, 114; training to operate, 117–120; and US/Israel relations, 115; and War of Attrition, 131–37. *See also* Ben-Nun, Avihu; Eini, Menachem; Harpaz, Rami; Hetz Shmuel; Hod, Mordechai; Israeli Air Force; Spector, Yiftach; technologism; United States Air Force; Yair, David
Pick, Tzvika 239, 244, 262, 268
Pincus-Gani, Lydia, 276
Podhurst, Bob, 215, 217
postcolonialism, 13, 161, 168, 259, 297
Pridor, Adir, 129–30
Prince, Hal, 224, 256
professionalism, 5, 127, 128, 138, 214, 215, 254, 314n64
Project Renewal, 206–7

"quality of life," 4, 81, 94

Rabin, Nehemia, 105
Rabin, Yitzhak, 6, 15, 111, 133, 198: ambassador to the US, 90; and America's decline, 105–6; and American Jews, 106, 109; IDF chief of staff, 105; and free market economy, 110; friendship with Richard Nixon, 108–9, 312n84; intervention in US elections, 109, 295; prime minister, 111, 217; and US-Israeli "special relations," 106–7. *See also* Eran, Amos; Kissinger, Henry; Meir, Golda; Nixon, Richard; Pattir, Dan
Rabinowitz, Yehoshua, 89, 92, 93–94, 101, 110, 111
race, 8, 9, 10, 58, 118, 168, 190, 229, 297: and the American experience, 10, 11, 118, 141, 142, 152, 153, 158–59, 171, 197, 199, 201, 207–8, 218, 219; and Blackness, 16, 141, 157, 158, 159, 161; and French consumerism, 27; and Israeli elites becoming whiter, 10, 154; and the politics of pigmentation, 158, 168; in popular culture, 140, 251,255, 259; and profiling, 191; and racial analogies, 10, 152, 153, 158, 159, 161, 168; and masquerade, 14, 142, 162, 167; and social science, 10, 16, 201, 207–8; terminology of, 159, 161; and whiteness, 156, 157, 158, 161, 190, 208, 210. *See also* African Americans; Baldwin, James; Black Hebrew Israelites; Black Panther Party; Black Panthers (Israel), *Blues to Mister Charlie*; Ethiopian Jews; *In White America*; Kahane, Meir; *Raisin in the Sun*
racism, 4, 9, 10, 141, 153, 166, 171, 181, 183, 184, 190, 192, 242, 326n116
Rafi Party (Israel Workers List), 32
Raisin in the Sun, 153
Ram, Uri, 12, 200
Raphael, Yitzhak, 163
Ratz (Citizen Rights Movement), 208, 213
Resnik, Ruth, 210
reviews: book, 19, 284–85; film, 281, 286; music, 50, 333n100; television, 84–86; theater, 225–26, 227, 238, 252, 256, 258–59, 265–67, 290. *See also* individual critics
Robbins, Jerome, 224, 225, 248, 256, 259
Rockefeller, Nelson, 194
Rodensky, Shmuel, 227 228–29, 230
Rogers, William, 136
Romansero Sephardi, 247
Rosenblum, Doron, 85, 244
Rosenblum, Yair, 53, 244
Rosenfeld, Shalom, 152
Rosenfeld, Yona, 202, 206
Rotblit, Ya'akov "Yankele," 269
Rubinstein, Amnon, 1, 109, 301n25
Rufeisen, Oswald (Brother Daniel), 190

sabra, 105, 124, 184, 213, 234, 238, 248, 262, 291
Safir, Marilyn, 209

Sallah Shabati, 233, 272
Salzberger, Lotte, 202
Sanderson, Danny, 195
Sapir, Pinchas, 31, 32, 33, 58, 68, 131, 177, 278
Sapir, Yosef, 81
Sarid, Yossi, 93, 102
Sartre, Jean-Paul, 280, 338n12
Save the Lifeguard, 286
Schachter-Shalomi, Zalman, 240
Schlafly, Phyllis, 199
Schneerson, Menachem Mendel (seventh Lubavitcher Rebbe), 223, 246
Schneersohn, Yosef Yitzhak, (sixth Lubavitcher Rebbe), 240
Schwarzenegger, Arnold, 50
Schwebel, Ivan, 195
Schwimmer, Adolph "Al," 195
Segev, Tom, 12, 295
Seker Economic Services, 100–101
Seltzer, Dov (Dubi), 221, 259, 273
service clubs, 25, 82. *See also* Junior Chamber
Shalev, Mordechai, 189
Shalit (who-is-a-Jew?) Affair, 178, 190, 322n38
Shamgar, Meir, 180
Shapira, Danny, 121
Shapira, Haim-Moshe, 185
Shapira, Ya'akov Shimshon, 176, 181
Sharon, Ariel, 105
Shasi (Israel Socialist Left), 210
Shas Party (Worldwide Sephardic Association of Torah Keepers), 150, 297
Shavit, Abraham "Buma," 83
Shazar, Rachel, 77
Shazar, Zalman, 238, 246
Sheftel, Yoram, 176
Sheli (Peace for Israel Party), 150
Shemer, Naomi, 50, 220
Shemesh, Kokhavi, 148, 159
Sherf, Ze'ev, 32, 163, 205
Shnei kuni lemel, 222, 231–32, 233

shnorr. See fundraising
Shoshan, Gabi, 262, 263
Siegel, Benjamin "Bugsy," 169, 175
Silberg, Moshe, 11
Sills, Paul (*Story Theater*), 235
Silver, Lou, 215, 216
Silverman, Bat Sheva, 99
Simone, Nina, 241
Situationist International, 25
Six-Day (June 1967) War, ix, 2, 3, 8, 11, 18, 28, 32, 42, 52, 56, 59, 61, 64, 103, 108, 112, 116, 119, 129, 138, 143, 154, 156, 177, 194, 195, 209, 215, 220, 228, 229, 259, 273, 274, 281. *See also* Operation Moked; operations research
Smith, Hanoch, 101–2
Soblen, Robert, 178
social work, 37, 200, 206: and Baerwald School of Social Work, 197, 201–2, 202–3; and Black Panthers (Israel), 148, 204–6; and social workers as activists, 203, 205, 207. *See also* affirmative action; Amiel Avner; Jaffe, Eliezer; National Welfare Rights Organization
sociology, 36, 97, 200, 218
Soldier Aid Association, 44, 49
Soviet/Russian Jews, 155 157, 163, 164, 180, 181, 184, 223, 240, 247.
Soviet Union (USSR) 100; and American diplomacy, 108, 114, 165, 180, 311n79; arms supply to Egypt and Syria, 51, 105, 116; and the Cold War, 18, 178; Jewish immigration policy, 107, 142, 155, 157, 163, 164, 179, 181, 182, 184, 216; military technology, 120, 123, 134, 135, 136, 315n87; and War of Attrition, 113, 132, 133–34, 136. *See also* Jewish Defense League; Kahane, Meir; Nixon, Richard; Soviet/Russian Jews
Spector, Yiftach, 136, 137
SS Shalom, 30, 249
Spoon River Hill, 237

Stein, Joseph, 224, 226
Students for Democratic Society (SDS), 109
Sunfrost Company, 37–38

Take Two (Hatzad hasheni), 286
Tamir, Shmuel, 66, 183
Tannenbaum, Robert, 97
Tartakover, David, 298
technologism, 138–39, 296
Tel Aviv University, 200
television, 3, 21, 50, 56, 86, 247: ads for TV sets, 24, 35, 45, 46; American shows, 62, 84, 86; and celebrity culture, 50, 51; introduction to Israel, 33–4; Israeli shows, 84–85, 86, 244; living room reconfigured for, 35–36; and politics, 102, 162, 184; and the public sphere, 100, 162; and single channel viewing, 26, 36; and sociability, 35–36; and technical knowledge, 34–5, 76. *See also* Boshes, Hedda; Katz, Elihu; *and individual programs*
Tempo Soft Drink Company, 42, 43, 45, 47, 48
terrorism, 8, 51, 56, 57, 68, 139, 164, 165, 179, 180, 181, 183, 184, 192, 282, 295
Tevye and His Seven Daughters, 221, 230–31
Tobias, Oliver, 260, 261
Topol, Haim, 227–28, 230, 233, 234, 276, 286, 331n21
tourism/tourists, 6, 19, 30, 169, 191, 194, 213, 234, 243, 259, 272, 277, 286, 289
Tzaban, Yair, 192
Tzarfati, Tzadi, 262, 263, 268

Unites States: arms supply, 112–13; 114, 116, 117; crime in, 5, 7, 153, 169, 170, 171, 173, 174, 177, 179, 197, 198; as empire, 11, 24, 84, 200, 295; and the "Great Society," 4, 33, 153, 201, 239, 295; as Israel's ally, 2, 10, 107; Israelis' grim view of, 5, 152–53; Israelis' knowledge about, 14, 18–19, 173; and Israel's nuclear program, 116, 311n74; social unrest in, 5, 152–53, 105–6; and Vietnam, 7, 57, 106, 107, 109, 227, 247, 278, 293, 311n8; and visitors from Israel, 117–19, 130–31, 152–53, 173, 177–78. *See also* African Americans; America Jews; Federal Bureau of Investigation; immigrants, American; Nixon, Richard
United States Air Force (USAF), 123, 124, 127: and economic management, 129; and electronic warfare, 135; formalities of, 118; Israeli Air Force's advice, 119; Israeli pilots' impressions of, 121–23; and social life, 118, 119; in Vietnam, 118, 119, 121, 123, 135. *See also* Dixon, Robert; George Air Base; Madden, John
University of Haifa, 209
urban renewal, 80–82, 258
Uris, Leon, 1, 272, 285

Vardimon, Orgad, 260
Veblen, Thorstein, 27, 67
volunteerism, 16, 196, 206, 218

Wadi Salib (Haifa) riots, 36, 145
War of Attrition, 8, 70, 104, 106, 133, 261, 166: and antiwar sentiment, 58, 266, 269–70; ceasefire, 136, 143; and consumerism, 28, 51; and front/home front split, 28, 53; in Israeli culture, 58, 262, 282; and the Israeli *everyday*, 56; nomenclature, 133; stalemate, 133. *See also* Dayan, Moshe; *Don't Ask Me If I Love*; *Hair*; Israel Defense Forces; Israeli Air Force; *Malkat ambatya*; Meir, Golda; Operation Caucasus; Operation Priha
Watergate Scandal, 7, 101, 173
WeightWatchers, 4, 99
Weldheim, Kurt, 187

welfare state, 4: and Black Panthers (Israel), 150, 163, 317n34, Israel as a, 202; and the "Poverty Report" (1971), 150; and social security, 150, 20; and the welfare ministry, 37, 203. *See also* Katz, Israel; Rosenfeld, Yona; Salzberger, Lotte; social work

West Side Story, 251, 252, 255–57, 258, 271

Wise, George, 200

Whore from Ohio, The, 17, 273, 288–89, 290–91

Women's International Zionist Organization (WIZO), 71, 194, 205, 211

Woodstock Religious and Mystical Festival, 7, 242

Yadlin, Asher, 32

Yair, David, 119, 123, 134

Yariv, Ziva, 176

Yarom, Uri, 112

Yeiny, Lior, 274, 275, 277

Yiddish, 16, 17, 158, 177, 221, 222–23, 225, 247, 248, 296; and authenticity, 248; and Black Panthers (Israel), 163, 164, 223, 249; and literature, 230, 231; and music, 244, 247, 334n118; as *post-vernacular*, 247; and Soviet Jews, 222, 247; and theater, 231–32; 232–33, 234, 291. *See also* Aleichem, Sholom; Burstein, Pesach; Burstyn, Mike, *Di Megila*, Lifschitz, Nechama; Lux, Lilian; Manger, Yitzik; Meir, Golda

Yiddishism (*Yiddishkeit*), 16, 54, 222, 223, 226, 227, 231, 248, 249, 296

Yizraeli, Yossi, 235, 237, 238, 244

Yom-Kippur (October 1973) War, 3, 93, 106, 131, 137, 139, 149, 154, 187, 198, 209, 247, 249, 293

Zero Defects Management, 98

Zilberg, Yoel, 273, 275

Zionism, 50, 254, 213: and antisemitism, 154; and anti-Zionism, 151, 157, 246, 316n5; Black nationalism and, 153, 185, 187, 191; and Black Panthers (Israel), 160, 161, 162, 170; and consumerism, 24; and the cult of youth, 316n19; and the Diaspora, 142, 248, 291; and *Fiddler on the Roof*, 225, 228, 230; fundraising techniques of, 115; in Hollywood, 272, and investments in Israel, 32; and *Ish hasid haya*, 237; and Israel as both Jewish and democratic, 184; and Meir Lansky, 175, 176; and the *modern*, 63; in its pioneering stage, 11, 253, 286; and the Palestinians, 19; and population dispersion, 65; as secondary motivation for immigration, 197; Six-Day War as confirmation of, 221, 228, 275, 279; and Yiddish, 222; and the Zionist Left, 64, 72, 150, 238, 296

Zohar, Uri, 17, 269, 273, 278, 280, 281, 285

Zurabin, Eliezer, 111